# walk4one
*Paving a Path to Unity*

A 15,636 kilometres walk around the world
for the unity of Christians

An autobiographical account by
## Samuel Clear

garratt
PUBLISHING

*For Mum*
…who stopped reading my weekly updates when the journey became too dangerous, resorting to asking family members, "Is he okay?" Thank you for never calling me home despite the dangers.

Published in Australia by
Garratt Publishing Pty Ltd, 32 Glenvale Crescent, Mulgrave, Victoria 3170
www.garrattpublishing.com.au

Copyright © Samuel Clear
First published in 2013
Second edition published in 2014
Paperback edition published in 2016
This edition published 2019

All rights reserved. Except as provided by the Australian copyright law, no part of this book may be reproduced in any way without permission in writing from the publisher.

Design and typesetting by Steve Alan Burnett, *amalgam essaybee*, amalgamsab.com
Images by © Samuel Clear and © Thinkstock

Scripture quotations are drawn from the New Revised Standard Version of the Bible, copyright © 1989 by the Division of Christian Education of the National Council of the Churches of Christ in the USA. Used by permission. All rights reserved.

The author and publisher gratefully acknowledge the permission granted to reproduce the copyright material in this book. Every effort has been made to trace copyright holders and to obtain their permission for the use of copyright material. The publisher apologises for any errors or omissions in the above list and would be grateful if notified of any corrections that should be incorporated in future reprints or editions of this book.

National Library of Australia (www.nla.gov.au) Cataloguing-in-Publication entry:
*Walk4one* / Samuel Clear
Subjects: *Christian union, Walking, Voyages around the world* 248.25

ISBN: 9781925073256 (paperback)

# Foreword

*What does seeking* the unity of the Christian Churches have to do with being Christian?

A fair question.

But perhaps an even fairer one is to ask, can we truly be Christian and not desire to work for the unity of the Churches? Can the Church proclaim God's call for unity and love among *all* peoples if she herself is not united?

Assuming that seeking such unity is, in fact, a necessary part of our being Christian, what would that unity look like? How would we know whether we are contributing towards its coming into being? Conversely, how would we know whether we might be delaying its coming into being?

These are some of the questions that Sam's account of his walk for unity—the *walk4one*—raises and explores. Does Sam answer them? Yes, he does ... in part. Even though he went to extraordinary lengths physically, mentally and spiritually in walking the world to spread the message for the need to promote Christian unity through prayer, dialogue, and shared work for the common good, it was—and remains—not just a task for one man alone.

It is for *all* Christians to share in. And it is in fact more than 'our task'. Strange as it may seem, Christian unity is really a *gift*—God's gift. Our work towards unity among the Christian Churches (and, ultimately, all people) is not to make it come about by our own efforts. Rather, it is to prepare our hearts and minds to receive unity as a gift from God, a grace, when and how God wills to give it—which is to say: when we are ready and able to receive it.

Just as we need to change our hearts and minds about God—that God really is merciful; that God really does forgive and heal us of our sins; that we do not need to earn God's love; indeed, that God loves us *unconditionally*—so too do we need to think rightly about God's desire for us to ... be ... one.

The night before Jesus died he prayed 'that they may all be one. As you, Father, are in me and I am in you, may they also be in us, so that the world may believe that you have sent me.' (John 17:21) Do we doubt that God desires Christians—indeed, all people—to be one in Christ? Or do we want to control something that should be a gift, a gift that is to be received gratefully and with joy?

I first learned of Sam's *walk4one* mission in January 2007, when I met Mary—Sam's mother—for the first time in Tasmania. I was struck by a few things. What an extraordinary undertaking Sam's walk was: it was a bold statement of faith in God's providence, and of belief in the truth of the call to Christian unity. But I was also struck by Mary's outlook. She also had to trust in God's providence, that God would accompany and go ahead of her son to assist him and bring him home safely in due course. Indeed, before Sam subsequently started sending weekly blogs, Mary said that she didn't want to know all the details of Sam's (mis)adventures when he wrote about them to his family and friends. Instead, she simply wanted to know each time that anyone heard from him whether he was okay. Just as well, really! Because there were times any mother would have gone out of her mind if she knew what was happening to her son…

A couple of weeks after meeting Mary I read a media report on Sam's progress and, later again, I started to read his blogs. They were engaging and inspiring, with a mixture of humour and pathos, adventure and reflection; and included some stunning photography—soulful portraits and breathtaking landscapes.

Later again, by the end of 2007, I thought that Sam's story should be recorded in a more permanent form— a book. People in years to come should be able to access Sam's *walk4one* story and be inspired to pray, dialogue and work for unity as a result of reading it and entering into its call to action and its hope.

So I emailed Sam. He liked the idea. In fact, he was so keen on it that he wanted to start work on the book straightaway and to have it published in time for his return to Australia and appearance at World Youth Day in Sydney in July 2008!

However, I suggested to Sam that he concentrate on the walk and the prayer and all its demands: its delights and surprises. The book could—and should—come later, after he had time to reflect and to decide which parts of the story would be best to include in a book. And that's what he did ... and did exceptionally well. In the end, the book took longer than the walk!

Sam's *walk4one* includes adventures and misadventures, events that are heartwarming and some heartbreaking, and each episode provides some really captivating reading. I won't preview the things that Sam has to say; I don't want to steal his thunder! Instead let me conclude with two quotes about the search for Christian unity. The first is from the Second Vatican Council's Decree on Ecumenism (1964):

> *The sacred mystery of the unity of the Church [lies] in Christ and through Christ, the Holy Spirit energising its various functions. It is a mystery that finds its highest exemplar and source in the unity of the Persons of the Trinity: the Father and the Son in the Holy Spirit, one God.*

The Church's unity is not to be found in a uniformity of our own devising, but in harmonious, life-receiving and life-giving diversity. And the second is from the Unity Statement of the 10th Assembly of the World Council of Churches (2013):

> *The unity of the Church, the unity of the human community and the unity of the whole creation belong together.*
> *They are inseparable.*

Christopher Brennan
Emmaus monastic community, Tasmania

# The Walk

**Prologue** *Australia* — 11
    Three years earlier: Melbourne, 2005 — 13

**Part 1** *South America* — 17
    Airports, Taxis & Prostitutes — 18
    Missions, Bus Drivers & that 47°C — 22
    Christmas Cheer, a Funeral Fiasco & Cow Candy — 35
    Food Poisoning, a Game Show Chemist & the Darkest Nights — 47
    The Broken Body, a Midnight Puma & the Barrel of a Gun — 65
    Stonings, Rats & the Witness of Unity — 98
    Colombian Assault, Glued Lips & Fireflies — 119

**Part 2** *Central and North America* — 131
    Surgery, a Drug-Induced Haze & a Pink Dinosaur — 132
    Scorpions, Highway Knives & a Thunderstorm Pursuit — 142
    Swindlers, Stalkers & Salmonella — 170
    Refugees, Earthquakes & the Kiss — 191
    A Racing Heart, a Dislodged Hip & Border Security — 211
    Bolting Snakes, Sex Crimes & a Tornadic Storm — 231
    Night Sprinklers, Agape & the Imposing Shirley Basin — 249
    Surgery, Thanksgiving & Homeland Security — 275
    Tendinitis, Orthodox Candles & Passport Mayhem — 297

**Part 3** *Russia and Europe* — 313
    Trans-Siberian Railway, Seized Knees & a Drunken Punch-Up — 314
    Heart Arrhythmia, the KGB & a Twilight Pursuit — 338
    Trumpets, Troubled Gear & New Boots — 361
    Hookers, Saints & Vatican City — 378
    Money, Monks & Cosmic Energy — 397
    Shower Screams, Spilt Blood & Crushing the Serpent's Head — 418
    Santiago de Compostela, A Health Scare & Cape Finesterre — 442

**Epilogue** *Australia* — 451

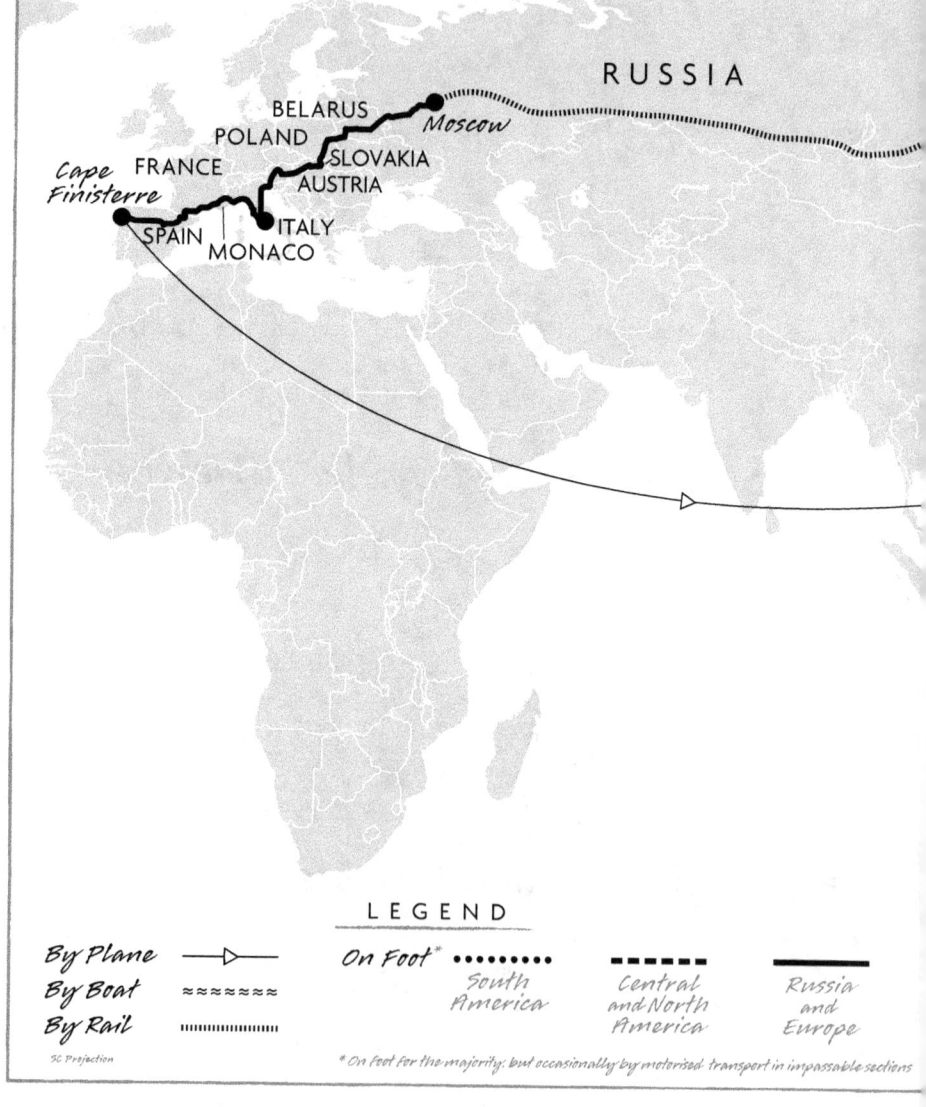

# Prologue

Australia

***Limping slightly***, one toe bleeding and the other foot recovering from a suspected stress fracture, I hobbled down the aisle of the Church of the Apostles in Launceston, Tasmania. I was home at last after a gruelling year and a half walk around the world. A winter jacket hid my gaunt 196 centimetre frame, leaving only my hollowed, weather-beaten face to bear witness to what had transpired in that year and a half. I was home, but was withdrawn and felt out of place. Everyone's apparent comfort and safety seemed ignorant, even foreign.

A few familiar faces turned and smiled, welcoming me home with whispered greetings. The church that had been home throughout my high school years was bigger than I remembered, but looked so plain compared to the churches of Latin America and Europe. Everything looked different, but the major change had occurred within me. Over the previous eighteen months I'd been held at gun point three times, mugged at knife point, bashed, abused, come face to face with dangerous animals, hospitalised, arrested and generally fought for my life more times than I cared to remember. It was no surprise that I'd changed, so much so that the once familiar now looked like fake copies: even the people.

Paying attention during Mass was difficult, distracted by nostalgic thoughts of how many times I'd wondered if I'd ever see home again. When Fr Richard began reading the Sunday Gospel though, my ears pricked up. I smiled. The Catholic Church uses a three-year reading cycle such that the majority of the bible is covered in that time. As he read I realised that it was exactly three years to the day since that whole missionary adventure had begun. The last time I had heard that particular passage I was compelled onto a path towards the complete unity of Christians and a 15,600 kilometres journey—on foot—across twenty countries.

# Three years earlier:
## Melbourne 2005

I picked up a book by Patrick Madrid to read before Sunday Mass. Amongst the compilation of testimonies of men and women who'd become Catholic, I found two testimonies of Evangelical preachers. I was intrigued to know how fundamentalist Evangelicals would end up calling themselves Catholic.

Their stories were remarkable, but what struck me was that their friends and family believed they'd disowned Christ, so reciprocated the gesture by disowning them. I was already aware of countless examples of Church disunity, plus my own struggles with non-Catholic Christians who'd taken fire at my beliefs without any desire for dialogue, but in this moment it was as if I had caught a glimpse of Christ's pain from the broken Church: his body. It was torn apart. I was standing at a car crash and I didn't even know first aid. All I could mutter was, "It's broken."

I quickly distanced myself, "There's nothing I can do. The brokenness is too big." I felt God place on my heart Luke 19:40, so I looked it up. It read, "I tell you, if these were silent, the stones would shout out." I shut my bible. The consequences of acting on this heartbreak were difficult to predict.

I headed to Mass, struggling to focus; in fact I made it through to the Gospel without paying attention at all. I tuned in when the priest read, "A man finds a treasure buried in a field and he goes away and sells everything he owns so to purchase the field." I tuned back out. I knew the passage well, but now it was personal. It cut deep and I was left struggling with a pull towards a seemingly impossible mission.

A few days later I expressed my confusion to God. "It's too big! What could I ever do to unite Christians? There's too much division, history and apathy. I'd love to help you but, sorry mate, you're on your own. I'm out."

Once I'd stopped justifying myself it felt like God said, "Sam, you're right, you can't fix it; but I can. It isn't too big for me. I need you to pray for unity."

As simple as that, I was at peace. I didn't have a degree in theology (I'd studied engineering and football) but prayer was something I could definitely do.

After dropping my Land Rover off for a service I walked the eleven kilometres from Mitcham to my work in Burwood, praying. "God," I asked, "if I was to invite others to pray for unity, is there a time in the day that I should ask them to do it?" *Four-O-One* popped into my head and I thought, "4:01. 4:01? God, that's stupid! What significance does 4:01 have?" Then it hit me. 4:01 was exactly what I'd been prompted to do—to *pray for one*—that is, to pray: *four, one*. After a quick apology, since it wasn't such a bad idea, I took on the daily 4:01 prayer for unity. I invited friends to set their alarms to do the same—not the engineering friends, the missionary ones—and some did, even taking the extra step of setting their alarm for 4:01 am as an extra sacrifice.

I was content with pm.

Frustration set in though when I attempted to extend the invitation to Christians from various denominations. I was repeatedly knocked back with tacked on advice like: "Unity already exists; you're just not a part of it. When you read your bible you'll become a Christian like us." The steady flow of refusals to even pray for Christian unity wore on me.

Towards the end of 2005, while sitting at the dining table, I flicked through a world atlas. I loved maps and ever since my relatively carefree childhood on Flinders Island with incredible room to roam I'd had a deep thirst for adventure, which almost always began with a highly scrutinised map. My mind drifted back to the division of the Church and, angry at the negative response to the invitation to pray for unity, I thought, "Why won't Christians even pray for unity in truth? How brilliant would it be to just sell up like St Francis did and head out on foot around the world to invite everyone to at least pray for unity?" I traced out a path from South America, through Central and North America, across Russia and down across Eastern Europe and Africa. Apart from the Bering Strait, it was all land. I imagined what it'd be like walking along the Pacific Ocean in Nicaragua or racing an incoming blizzard in Siberia. It was all nonsensical, but the thought of taking the invitation around the world never left me. Over the following year it slowly solidified.

Finding a safe path through Africa was a nightmare, so I looked towards the Atlantic Ocean in Spain as my end point. Aware that this 'action' was rather extreme I met with five people I considered further down their faith-walk than me, and I prayed: "Lord, if all five say yes, I'll do it." As it was, despite the glaring dangers, all five said yes and the fifth person, an elderly gentleman who'd founded Youth Mission Team Australia (my employer), responded with a succinct, "It's too ridiculous to be anything but from God. Go for your life Sammy. Send me a postcard."

The only advice offered from the 'wise five' came from Christopher Prowse, Auxiliary Bishop of Melbourne. He shook his finger at me and pleaded, "This is not to be an attempt at a world record for walking around the world. It's a mission about prayer, not walking. If you're in trouble, take a lift; just never lose sight of the prayer or the people. And take a train through the Siberian winter. You're not interested in evangelising polar bears."

I agreed with a smile.

For twelve months I meticulously compiled an itinerary. I was to begin in far eastern Brazil for 1,000 kilometres on foot, then cross the Amazon Basin in vehicles and boats, back on foot across Venezuela and Colombia, fly across the perilous Darian Gap into Panama, on foot all the way to Edmonton in Canada, fly across the Bering Strait to Vladivostok, take the train through Siberia and finish on foot from Moscow to Rome and on to Cape Finisterre in western Spain, from one side of the Atlantic to the other.

I trained hard: swimming, running, weights, playing basketball and walking forty kilometres every Saturday, week in, week out. The first forty-kilometre walk wrecked me, but over time my fitness improved and back-to-back days looked possible. Despite needing Portuguese for Brazil, I tried to learn Spanish, as the majority of the Americas spoke it. I didn't learn much. I saved what money I could and, as 2006 drew to a close, I sold my Land Rover and purchased all the gear I'd need. Everything fitted into one fifty-litre backpack. That was to be my life. As for sponsorship, I didn't seek any. Australians are great at giving money, but I wanted the invitation to be kept clear and simple: prayer.

The most important part of my preparation was spent on my knees. Mum insisted that it'd be safer to travel with a companion. I prayed for someone to join me, but it felt like God asked, "Why are you praying for someone else to join us? You are walking with me." It was difficult to convince people that heading off alone without a support crew would be okay, but I felt a quiet peace despite the enormity of the task.

I'd never even been overseas before.

I finished 2006 at the national YMT debrief in Wollongong, struggling to think of anything other than the journey ahead. I was a few days from setting off and the reality of what I was about to undertake sank in. The YMT founder made an appearance and in a private conversation asked me, "How are you feeling?" With all etiquette out the window I looked him in the eye and said, "I'm shit-scared."

He placed his hand on my shoulder and laughed, "I like your honesty."

Part 1

South America

*I was naïve*, over-confident in my fitness, couldn't speak the language and unsure as to how the mission should unfold. "Ignorance and enthusiasm shall overcome!" To know what the journey ahead would cost might have caused me to cower away. It had to come one moment at a time. The faster I could learn, the better. My greatest regret would take place in Brazil, where I opted for more vehicle travel than Bishop Prowse's instructions perhaps warranted, though recognising soft decisions became part of the mission. Outwardly it was a mission about prayer. Inwardly it was a lesson in trusting God.

## Airports, Taxis & Prostitutes
*12th–15th Dec 2006*

I hoped the 12th of December 2006 wouldn't be the last time I saw home. The twenty-two hour flight to Buenos Aires, Argentina, was long and uncomfortable. Airline seats aren't built for a guy 196 centimetres (6' 5") tall. I might as well have tried to take a nap in a kindergarten chair. The flight was late arriving, so I missed my connecting flight to São Paulo, Brazil, and was taxied to a hotel for the night.

The driver did everything but obey the road rules, racing down the highway at 140 km/h oblivious to the road markings and through a few red lights. I was in culture shock the whole way. Big 1960s trucks were everywhere, mostly on the side of the road with the driver dangling from the engine bay. And of all the motorbikes zipping past I only once saw a helmet. Even having previously owned an 1100cc Suzuki I was left dumbstruck.

After a dismal four-hour's sleep I headed back to the airport with a groggy driver who had no idea where to go. He tested my charade and drawing skills, but with an aggressive forward lean, and despite persistent drifting from lane to lane as he nodded off to sleep at 130 km/h, we made it in one piece.

Buenos Aires to São Paulo was a quick flight, leaving me with one day to rest before my final flight to João Pessoa. I was jet-lagged, didn't speak Portuguese, and fifteen minutes after arriving realised that my next flight was from the other side of the massive city. I jumped on a bus and then a train, but still had no idea where I was.

# South America

**LEGEND**

- By Plane →
- By Boat ≈≈≈≈≈≈
- On Foot* •••••••
- SC Projection
- ——— South America
- - - - - Central and North America

*On foot for the majority, but occasionally by motorized transport in impassable sections

walk4one *Paving a Path to Unity*

The view from trains seems to turn up the worst in a city. I'd never seen slums before. I'd never seen barefooted children playing on dirt tracks between shanty homes. I'd never seen so much pollution. The scenes flashing past smashed my preconceived expectations of walking through some of the most beautiful places on Earth. It was bleak.

I stepped off the train at a place called Se, into a confronting mass of yelling homeless men. I now know that they were money exchangers looking to do a deal with the foreigner, but they just scared me. I sought directions at an enormous cathedral towering over the Central Square, but left empty-handed and without being able to extend the invitation to pray for unity. I needed to learn Portuguese fast.

I felt very alone in a city of twenty-five million people. After only one minute I'd encountered beggars, homeless families asleep on the footpath, prostitutes, guards armed with automatic rifles and a group of seedy looking guys who didn't stop staring at me. It was too much. With a mixture of sadness, fear, embarrassment at my wealth and anger, I turned on my heals and skirted back to the relative safety of the cathedral, stopping at each beggar as I went. As I sat amongst the homeless men on the cathedral steps my nose began to bleed. I despised my decision to attempt the journey.

I shared my lunch with a few guys, shrugged my small backpack on and, with the help of a young well-dressed man named Tiago, I found out where I needed to go, jumped in a taxi and headed to a hotel near the second airport to sleep.

After breakfast I set off for the nearest church: São Judas. The reception was exceptional, but what stayed with me more than their welcome was the hour-long walk through leafy suburbia to get there. Every house was enclosed by razor wire, electric wire or broken glass cemented into wall tops, and every second corner had a prostitute waiting for her next customer. One woman wasn't wearing anything below the waist and she stood at a corner so the passers-by could see what was on offer. Men driving past approved with toots of the horn and broad smiles. She didn't respond to anything. She was lifeless, distant and used. Each street corner told a similar story and for most the happy ending must have seemed so far away.

I boarded my final flight to the eastern most point of the Americas late in the afternoon, touching down in João Pessoa at 2 am. I felt like I'd been walloped around the head with a baseball bat and when I stepped out onto the poorly lit tarmac the thick humidity nearly bowled me over. I wanted to get back on the plane and go home. It was still 30°C and the dense air made the simple act of breathing a workout.

I must have found a hotel because I woke up in one the next morning with a view over a tropical Atlantic beach with all-manner of tropical fruit street-vendors. I was scheduled to begin walking the next day, so took the chance to find the local bishop first. Nearly every single person on the street stopped and stared; tall white guy coming through! The humidity was draining. I dreaded the weeks ahead.

I considered popping in to a school called Lourdese to ask for directions, but couldn't be bothered so pushed on. As I walked past though I found myself staring at a statue pointing back at the school and I had a strong sense that I was supposed to go in. I begrudgingly turned around and headed into the front office and handed over the bishop's address. The secretary read it aloud and a parent sitting in the waiting room jumped up. He knew the place well and offered to drive me. He ushered me into his car and on up to the bishop's office we went. It was my first lesson in trusting God; follow His promptings.

The bishop's office received the 4:01 invitation with a smile and generously organised accommodation for me with a young energetic man from the Fochalare Community. After Mass and dinner I lay down for the final nervous sleep before attempting to travel the world—predominantly on foot—for the unity of the Church. After a journey of airports, taxis and prostitutes, João Pessoa also threw up something confronting. In a 500-year-old church near the cathedral sat a statue of Mary holding the infant Jesus. When the Dutch Reformists arrived many generations earlier they'd taken to the 'stone idol' with clubs, smashing it to pieces. The local Catholics then restored it piece-by-piece, using plaster where fragments had been lost permanently. If Christians were prepared to smash or painstakingly restore in the name of truth, how could they refuse the simple act of praying for it? It was a poignant marker for the beginning of the journey. There'd be a lot of smashing and rebuilding to come, mostly with me on the receiving end.

# Missions, Bus Drivers & that 47°C
## 16th–23rd Dec 2006

I was nervous; aware that if I failed in the tropical heat that day the next 5,000 kilometres to Mexico would be a near impossibility. My training in Melbourne produced a hottest day no more than 20°C. I wanted nothing more than to finish day one and be able to start the second.

With a man and a woman entangled in a bitter verbal fight nearby, I threaded rosary beads through the fence along Cape Branco, with the intention of doing the same at the other end in Spain, if I ever made it. The rosary was a great symbol of both prayer and theological division.

I hit the road at 10:30 am on a cloudless and hot 16th of December 2006, rounding the Cape, avoiding the arguing couple, to a spectacular view over the warm turquoise waters to the city of João Pessoa. Locals jumped in and out of the waves while I lugged a twelve-kilogram backpack – already sweating after only a minute.

After five minutes I was lost. A car pulled over and a girl asked in perfect English, "Where are you headed?" Her boyfriend had twice walked as a pilgrim on the Camino de Santiago in Spain and reckoned I must have been one too, though a long way from Spain. They insisted on playing their part in the mission by driving me to the outskirts of town. I didn't think much of it and saw it as a chance to straight away put the mission before walking, so I jumped in and we drove on discussing the need to pray for unity.

They headed onto the highway and rocketed past my first day's destination. I literally had to beg them to stop. I'd really

*First day on the road in Brazil*

hoped to do some walking; this wasn't the start I'd wanted. They dropped me at a secluded rural outpost and I prayed my way on foot across a barren landscape towards the nearest town: Caja. Every kilometre or so a stall selling tropical fruits added an unexpected comfort, particularly the fresh coconuts with straws poking out the top.

The temperature soared and when a large bus rumbled past the look on the driver's face was universal for 'you idiot'. I prayed my way to the small town of Caja and was immediately confronted by the poverty. I'd stepped back in time. The coastal affluence had disappeared and coarse mud-brick homes with doorless entrances dotted the roadside. A piece of propped up fibreboard kept the babies in and the dogs out. There wasn't a single blade of grass: nothing but dust, thorn bushes and withered remnants of the long-gone wet season.

I didn't blend in and one after another the conversations of those sitting outside their homes ground to a halt. Caja fell silent. Their eyes followed me down the road. Only the children playing soccer in the dusty stretches offered me any hint of a smile. I took the initiative, smiled at a group of adults and every single one of them immediately smiled back. Nine times out of ten the response was the same. All they wanted to know was that, despite my appearance, I was still human.

In the centre of Caja a young man sitting with friends gestured towards my walking poles, asking what they were for. I explained their use using mime and so began a twenty-minute charade conversation that snowballed as his friends joined in. The animated young man then invited me to stay the night. I was hesitant, unsure if people would take advantage of a rich westerner, but I did need a bed. I accepted and was shuffled down a flight of stairs into a cement semi-underground home.

After showering I was taken back out into the twilight to attend a Saturday night Assembly of God service. An Assembly of God church stood directly behind the house, but we were headed in the opposite direction. In Caja, a town of a thousand people, there had only been a Catholic church until the Assembly of God (AOG) was founded. Three preachers were raised up until they came to a theological sticking point that led to the formation of three individual AOG churches. One pastor kept the original building, one built a new one, and these guys I walked with simply met out in the open on a back street.

It was sad, and reinforced the need to pray for unity.

The burly preacher welcomed me to the street-lamp-lit service led from the back of a Chevrolet truck parked across a dirt road. A white sheet transformed it into a stage and the Chevrolet's suspension eased back and forth as the musicians piled on. A throng of people gathered en-masse across the street and received the invitation to pray for unity from the preacher as all eyes turned to inspect the towering white guy amongst them. I, in turn, received an invitation to stay and marry one of the young women whom they thrust in front of me. I just smiled, but we didn't share a common language so it was basically just awkward. It didn't seem to faze her though.

The service was spirited and although I didn't understand a single word I still enjoyed it. After the preacher welcomed, "the tall Catholic missionary", a woman sidled up alongside me pointing me to a bible verse. I looked it up in my small bible and it read, "You do not know why I have brought you here but you will in time." She smiled and left. The thought ran through my mind that perhaps she had an ulterior motive; that as a Catholic I'd benefit from attending the service, but I had to give her the benefit of doubt.

I slept the night back at the house in my hammock on the lower side veranda with the guys alongside in theirs. A fresh breeze was offset by a radio blasting at full volume all night. It was unbearable.

I groggily ate breakfast with the burly preacher, the Rev Samuel, but he stopped me, indicating that he was about to pray grace. Making doubly sure that I was watching he raised his eyes, lifted his arms and prayed, finishing with a nod in my direction with an expression of, "That's how you do it." I was incensed. If that wasn't bad enough he then noticed a rosary bracelet around my wrist. It was like a red rag to a bull. Offended, he preached at me until I reminded him that I didn't speak Portuguese. He paused and then slowly began a drawn out theological argument using our respective Portuguese and English bibles, and a lot of charades, accusing me of worshipping Mary and not accepting Jesus as the way. It took a long time to combine the teachings of the Catholic Church into mime and biblical passages, but to my surprise he accepted my explanation of the role of Mary, indicating that he'd never met a Catholic who was actually a Christian. It left me bewildered, because all I'd done was explain what the Catholic Church taught. The Reverend noted that Australian Catholics must be very different to the non-Christian Brazilian Catholics. It could've become ugly had we not simply focussed on our immediate common aim: breakfast.

A young English-speaking man arrived and asked on behalf of the reverend if I could do them a favour. "We need to build a new church. Can you contact your people in Australia and organise for $1 million to be sent here to help?" I nearly choked on my cereal. I wasn't whoever they thought I was, but I'd at least send out some emails for them.

The young men wanted to assist the mission, so drove me to a few churches before I was on my way … without an arranged wife. The next town was Riachão do Bacamarte and I intended to walk on, but as I crossed a bridge I spotted a church up on a hill to the south. It was a hot walk in the wrong direction, so I decided to skip it, but I felt God's tug: "You're here for the people, not the walk." I stopped on the edge of the bridge and looked over at the distant church, screwed my lips up and headed for it.

After a 30°C mid-morning climb up a steep hill I discovered that the church and the padre's house were locked. Two young girls ran up to the wrought-iron fence and yelled for the padre on my behalf. I didn't want to create a scene, but before I could stop them the youthful padre had appeared at the window and ran downstairs, welcoming me in with a huge smile and broken English. The two girls ran off laughing.

Padre Gome patiently listened to my explanation of the mission before offering me the spare bedroom. I wasn't intending to stay, but I accepted anyway. He whisked me off to Sunday lunch with some classic locals where the house was filled with cheer, particularly from the eighty-year-old grandfather who rarely shut up. I slipped off to the toilet at one point and the padre called for me. Without checking my Portuguese I yelled back, "I'm at work!" After a few giggles from the lounge room I realised my mistake.

The padre took three elderly women and me in his tiny hatchback to a remote community for midday Mass. I wasn't walking much or heading in the right direction, but the prayer invitation was spreading fast, even to remote villages in sweltering arid hill country surrounded by jagged peaks and sweeping valleys.

Over dinner the padre received a phone call. I could tell it was of a serious nature; he returned to the table sombre, raised his eyes and said, respectfully: "Your father is dead."

"What?" I replied. "My dad is dead?"

The padre thought for a second and corrected himself, "No, no, I mean, his father is dead. Sorry, my English isn't very good." A smile grew across his face as we ate and he began to laugh, "That was a bad mistake, yes?"

I confirmed his suspicion.

Sunday night Mass was attended by nearly the entire town decked out in their very best. I'd seen many of them that day and although they still stared at me they at least now smiled. I was a foot taller than everyone, except for the few who were two feet shorter. I sat at the back. Padre Gome invited me forward, but having heard my spiel already he simply introduced me and extended the invitation on my behalf. Everyone applauded, so I just stood there and smiled. They also applauded at the end of the homily and clapped their way through every song.

A fifty-strong group of raucous youths then took me on a walking night-tour of the town, introducing me to every person, building and tree we passed. I loved it there.

Over breakfast, the padre insisted that I travel by bus to Campina Grande, saying that the road was too dangerous to walk. I wasn't sure what 'too dangerous' meant, so I let him pay for my ticket and headed off to Campina Grande. I still want to walk that section. I didn't see anything from the bus that suggested it was dangerous.

The Campina Grande seminary welcomed me and the invitation continued to spread. I was intent on slogging it out on foot the next day, so with my backpack straps tight I headed off towards a small outpost community twenty-eight kilometres away, receiving the customary stop and stare from locals. I did my best to just smile and say hello, but received few replies.

I expected to be travelling through rainforest, but the view from one hilltop was of dry cactus-filled valleys between parched, barren mountains. On the steep valley wall I passed a memorial grotto with a cross on top and flowers at the base. It was perhaps a car accident memorial, but I'd never seen anything like it. I took a photo and walked on without giving it a second thought.

I arrived at the outpost before midday and was given a large meal free of charge. I felt good, so made the decision to just walk on praying to the large town of Soledade, another twenty-eight kilometres further on. It began to rain, which I preferred to the heat, and after praying a rosary the bus driver who'd given me the, "You idiot," look rumbled past again en route to João Pessoa. This time he just checked me out with perplexed wide eyes while I shielded myself from the ensuing water spray.

At a roadside restaurant, for a small fee, a young man offered me 'time' in the back of his panel van with the two young, attractive, lollipop-sucking, singlet and mini-skirt clad women accompanying him. I declined, "Thanks, but no thanks," I pushed on down the road praying for unity, and the upholding of human dignity.

Just shy of Soledade the sun set while massive thunderclouds billowed up on the horizon, glowing under the flicker of readily let loose lightning. After a huge day a young Baptist took on the prayer for unity while showing me to the Catholic church. A young man opened up and called for the padre, but as he did, a car pulled up behind us. He forgot all about me and ran out to the car, yelling back to the approaching padre. It was the bishop. He introduced himself and checked out my reference letters and itinerary, then gestured for me to pick up my bag and follow.

I jumped into the bishop's car with two seminarians and we took off west through the town and out along the open highway. I had no idea where I was being taken. The bishop and seminarians spoke passionately about the broken church all the way to a town called Juàzeirinho: my next day's destination. I was excited that the mission was being received well, but was really frustrated at not walking as much as I planned. I'd come to walk and pray, hadn't I?

The bishop introduced me to a tall, wiry padre: a glasses-wearing Dutchman with fluent English and a steely resolve. Padre Holandes organised for two young women to escort me to the local posada (small hostel) and join him for breakfast the next morning. I couldn't communicate well with the girls, but one of them managed to communicate that she liked me. She held my arm, pushed her leg against mine and rested her head against my arm. If we ever made eye contact the only thing she could do was smile. A lot. Once at the posada (a series of cement box rooms extending off a family's home) the over-familiar girl plonked herself down on the end of my bed and refused to leave. The other girl scolded her and they exchanged heated words until the respectable young lady grabbed her friend's arm and literally pulled her from the room. Goodnight.

Padre Holandes and I chatted at length over a huge breakfast. He said to me, "Don't walk today. Stay and meet the poorest of the town."

How could I refuse?

A few hours later, two ten-year-old girls collected me and I was ushered through the dusty back streets with each hand held. They were fascinated by my height, repeatedly tripping over as they looked back up at me instead of watching their path. It provided constant amusement for whoever hadn't tripped.

They guided me to a fortress-like mission within a three-metre high security fence. Padre Holandes and the local parish had founded it with the aim of providing support, education and friendship for street kids. The open air building with ample room for the kids to play on the cool concrete floor was enormous compared to the surrounding mud-brick homes. Students, dressed in blue and yellow t-shirts, welcomed me with wide eyes and cheeky smiles as I ducked through the doorway. They gathered in for an impromptu question and answer time as Padre Holandes cheerily translated. The main point of interest turned out to be my $350 adventure watch. They'd never seen anything like it. I handed it over and a few slipped it over their tiny wrists, beaming from ear to ear.

It was fun being there, but I felt a sadness I'd never felt before. In a relative sense, I was ridiculously wealthy.

A teacher suggested they take me on a tour of the facility and so, in an instant, a throng of kids were hanging off my arms, jostling for position as head tour guide. I pulled out my video camera, which nearly caused mass-hysteria, and turned the LCD screen around so they could see themselves. The poor kids in the middle were nearly crushed by those wanting to be in the shot. I handed the camera over to one young boy and off he went with ten directors in tow yelling instructions. I asked the padre, "What's to happen to them in the years to come?"

"We don't have the facilities to educate them for all their schooling," he said with obvious regret. "At about the age of twelve they will graduate. For most a life of labouring will then begin. They are always welcome back to visit and spend time with the younger ones though." Adulthood beckoned. I have no idea what their life was like on the outside but, from the scars on some of them and the aged look their small faces bore, I could only imagine that it wasn't pretty. At least in the mission they had friendship and safety.

After ten minutes worth of hugs, I took to the dusty, bumpy back roads with the padre in his Chevrolet ute. A homeless and seemingly family-less kid joined us, sitting up in the tray for the trek across the roughest dirt tracks imaginable. I was impressed with the padre's rally-style driving.

He drove me to a secluded settlement to meet a young English-speaking woman who'd recently become a Catholic. Her father was an Assembly of God preacher.

They had argued about faith and scripture for a long time, but without resolution; they'd now simply stopped talking about God. The padre had wanted us to meet for the encouragement. We chatted well into the night.

The next day I left money with the padre for the mission's upcoming Christmas lunch, thanked him for the invitation into his world and noted that I'd love to return one day. He smiled. "Anytime, Samuel. Anytime."

It was twenty-odd kilometres from Juàzeirinho to Junco do Seridó and the road stretched out along the base of dry barren hills. It was so hot. I was hardly pleased when the road took a sharp turn straight up into the baking hills, but I worked my walking poles hard and continued to pray, keeping my mouth shut to stop excess evaporation. As my first heel blister formed in the intense heat, the final hill-climb was beyond me. Just two kilometres from Junco, a passer-by offered me a lift and I took it.

I was disappointed to have given up so close to the end, feeling like I'd failed to offer a complete sacrifice. It would be a long journey if every day turned out like that. Either the conditions had to change or I had to toughen up.

A young English-speaking seminarian by the name of Eshmael took me in, while the kids of the town gathered to check out my size sixteen boots. Eshmael invited me to stay at his home and we rode there on the back of his small motorbike. He pointed out one after another, "This is my brother! And this is my brother too!" By the time he'd introduced thirty of the most diverse characters one family could ever produce, I realised he was mistaking the words 'brother' and 'friend'. I corrected his English, but he just smiled and rode on, introducing his brothers. The clan of Eshmael was substantial.

While dinner cooked, we visited the town's cemetery. His grandfather's funeral was the next day. It made me even more thankful for their generous hospitality. I stood back as they viewed the burial plot, but Eshmael called me over. Three graves sat side-by-side, those of his uncle and two cousins. He turned to me and said, "I killed them in a car accident." What do you say in reply to that? I couldn't get my head around the pain and confusion he and his family must have been experiencing. He retold the story of how his family was returning from Campina Grande in two cars and as they crossed the town boundary he decided to overtake his uncle on a blind corner, accelerating past just as a car came around the corner in front of them. Panicking, he had accelerated and swerved in front of his uncle, clipping the front of his car and sending it veering off the road into a violent roll down into the steep valley. All three people died. I'd seen the memorial a few days earlier and slowly my apathy was pushed out.

Eshmael's mother talked non-stop over dinner, not understanding that I didn't speak Portuguese. When she saw that I didn't understand what she'd said she'd grab my arm and repeat herself loudly.

"I'm Australian, not deaf."

She kept on talking and I just kept on smiling ignorantly. Eshmael jumped on the phone at the end of the night and handed me a contact for when I hit the town of Patos.

From Junco I hit the road before dawn, hoping to avoid the intense heat. I'd been told that the next town of Santa Luzia was only twenty kilometres away, so I anticipated a sprightly 10 am arrival. It was a tough climb over the hills, but it did end in a beautiful view back across the settlement as the sun peaked over the horizon beyond it.

The João Pessoa bus rumbled past again and the driver slowed slightly, talking to one of his passengers about my presence, before checking me out in the rear-vision mirror. I'd at least caught his attention.

The temperature rose sharply as the road disappeared through a jumble of mountains and valleys. The sun was hot, the road was hot, and the rocks on the side of the road seemed to radiate their own heat, making the steep canyons like giant ovens. I interceded for unity and prayed a rosary. The Friday sorrowful mysteries made walking through the unbearable wilderness heat just that little more palatable.

After twenty kilometres there was nothing but a dry riverbed snaking through a sharp, scorched valley. There was no Santa Luzia. My feet cooked and the backpack slid disgustingly over a lather of sweat as the kilometres rolled by. The temperature was tipping past 40°C. I reached for a drink from my water bladder, but it was empty. There was no sign of a town, just blurred cactus through shimmering heat.

Continuing on without water was like an adolescent game of 'dare'. The temptation to thumb a ride was enormous but, irritated at having fallen short the previous day, I put my head down and put one foot in front of the other.

Another hour melted by until a roadside restaurant on the edge of Santa Luzia shimmered into view. I knocked off the 29th kilometre in robotic fashion, making it on foot and alive, wanting nothing more than four or five lemonades. The town ground to a halt with expressionless stares but, thankfully, the Catholic church secretary invited me through for a much-needed shower. It was a beautiful gesture to a stranger. Only then did I find that the bandaid protecting my developing blister had melted through the sock. Tough day.

The padre encouraged the mission of prayer and paid for me to stay in the town's hotel. It was by far the nicest place I'd seen at that point, with a panoramic view and a pool. I slinked into the cool water and cruised up and down trying not to splash a sunbathing girl next to it. It was so nice to just soak.

"Samwell! Samwell!" The tranquillity was shattered as a second padre bounced into the hotel yelling for me. Embarrassed to be associated with the break of serenity, I jumped out of the pool just as the bikini girl slinked into it, staying underwater for a long time. I was invited to join him at a nearby village youth group and, although I was inclined to just go to bed, I agreed. He'd return to pick me up in two hours.

I wandered off to the highest point in town, where a Saint Sebastian shrine stood. It had one amazing view of the town and surrounding island-like mountains set to the orange glow of a beautiful sunset. The townsfolk who'd gathered for the sunset bombarded me with questions, but I was uncomfortable when they

Happy children play atop San Sebastián hill while, behind me, grown-ups consider mugging me...

focussed in on the value of my watch and camera. Light faded and the young men grew aggressive in their questioning while the few not talking just stared. It was time to go. Only now was it glaringly obvious that the shrine sat on a hill covered in shanty homes. They begged me to stay, but I was out of there and once out of direct view hastened to a jog through the maze of tin shed-homes.

Months later, a Costa Rican would view the video footage and tell me what some of the young men standing around me were saying. "Take him out. Get the camera! Just hit him! Take the camera!" I was glad to have moved when I did.

The padre and local English teacher, Almir, picked me up in the evening. Both men were full of personality and sharp wits. The youth group was equally as fun and they agreed to pray for unity at 4:01 each day. They then banded together to sing Christmas carols for me, until the mothers presented me with their own gift ... another stunning young woman to marry. Almir couldn't stop laughing, "She's so pretty! Stay!" I did my best to politely decline, citing that my journey wasn't over. They told me to hurry up and finish.

Still single, I was on the road by 5 am for the forty-two kilometres to Patos. It would be an unavoidably long day. I thought the pre-dawn start would help, but it didn't. I marched out across the plains towards the mountains and, just as the sun burst across the horizon, beads of sweat formed across my brow. My clothes stuck to me. The João Pessoa bus rumbled into view with its headlights flicking for nearly half a kilometre. As he rushed passed he enthusiastically waved me on and gave me the thumbs up while reaching for his two-way radio. I'd made a friend ... of sorts.

By 10:30 am it had tipped past 40°C. I was desperately seeking shade. The gushes of wind from passing trucks felt like they were coming from a fan-forced oven. At the halfway mark, a roadside restaurant provided the first relief from the blistering heat. Squinting through sweat-filled eyes, and with all the locals staring at me, I bought four bottles of lemonade, an ice cream and a salad. The woman serving behind the counter was in partial shock.

It was now 44°C and I had twenty-two kilometres still to walk. I considered staying the night, but decided it was prime time to do some hard yards for unity and make a statement. I was sweating as soon as I stepped outside and had only gone a few hundred metres before a guy, who was well beyond tipsy, tried diligently to invite me into the local strip joint and brothel. He became increasingly agitated each time I declined. He jogged after me, pointing to my $350 watch and then to his $5 one, indicating a swap. I laughed at him.

"No."

The poor bloke was actually taken aback. I gave him a wristband instead, which he was happy to accept.

My huge leather boots and twelve kilogram backpack made the wafting heat unbearable. By mid-afternoon it was 47°C; the road surface had tipped past 100°C. The rubber soles of my boots peeled off the bitumen and when a drop of water fell from my water mouthpiece and hit the road it evaporated in a sizzling flash. I was forced to sip water every few minutes to keep my temperature down. I drank more water than I'd planned and my speed decreased. Water ran out fast. The views of the monolith mountains were spectacular, but I couldn't have cared less.

I scrounged a cup of water from kids playing outside a farmhouse and walked on, thirty-two kilometres out of Santa Luzia, and another ten kilometres to go.

The final dark hour into Patos was hellish. My legs were like jelly, my arms were weary, and I repeatedly stumbled off the road. I stopped at one point, aimlessly staring into the darkness, contemplating lying down in the grass. I didn't want to take another step and I was concerned about doing serious damage to my body, if I hadn't already. I'd already stopped producing saliva.

The motivation to take another step, and then another, was found in Christ walking up Calvary. That gentle feeling of His presence in the moment was reassuring as I focussed on not stumbling in front of on-coming cars. I prayed for the strength to keep going and had an energy-burst enabling me to power on up a large hill from where I could see a beautiful sight; the lights of Patos. Fatigue set back in and the final three kilometres took nearly an hour, but relief was in sight.

Thirteen and a half hours after leaving Santa Luzia I staggered into a Patos service station, bought three litres of fluid and an ice cream, and sat against a cool petrol bowser as my body seized up. A young man threw me on the back of his scooter and whizzed me down the road to a hotel and without having eaten dinner, or even changing out of my clothes, I laid down on top of my bed, muttered, "Lord, thank you for this first week. Please unite all Christians as one," and fell asleep.

> *So do not worry about tomorrow, for tomorrow will bring worries of its own. Today's trouble is enough for today.*
> 
> Matthew 6:34

Total walked: *173 kilometres*

# Christmas Cheer, a Funeral Fiasco & Cow Candy
## 24th–31st Dec 2006

After twelve hours of sleep I woke in salt-encrusted clothes feeling like I'd been hit by a train. Eshmael had given me a contact in Patos by the name of Padre Paulo Jackson and he was relieved to see me because he'd been expecting me the previous night. The local radio station had been giving updates of my progress all day. Apparently, a certain bus driver had called the station, sparking conversation from other callers about what I was doing. I was satisfied with my decision to do the hard yards.

Padre Jackson gave me a room for two nights and took me out to visit the memorial of a local martyr. As we left we passed a woman begging and I felt a strong prompting to give her the money in my wallet. I'd withdrawn R$500 (A$330) and that was a lot more than I could spare. I couldn't bring myself to do it. I decided to at least give her something and opened my wallet up, but found nothing more than a R$50 (A$30) note. I'd forgotten that I'd set up a dummy wallet the day before in case I was robbed. R$450 were secure in my backpack with R$50 in my everyday accessible wallet. I'd missed the chance to trust God without reservation. I placed the note in her cup and jumped in the padre's car. The woman stared through the crowd at me, lifted her hand over her heart and bowed her head. It felt like God was saying, "I'll pay you back," but I was just frustrated at not having acted on faith.

Christmas Eve Mass was packed. Due to people's inability to see past me I hid away down the back, but when we stood up for the opening hymn heads turned. I towered over them. Two women in front of me only made it to my elbows. The kids in particular were transfixed on the circus attraction.

The Mass is the same the world over so my lack of Portuguese didn't stop me from participating. I just responded in English. It was a different story for the homily though and my mind wandered until I realised I'd understood two words from Padre Jackson: "Samwel" and "Ausdralia". From my leant-forward position I looked up to be met by a thousand eyes staring back at me. It was inevitable that one day I'd be caught not paying attention during Mass. The padre gestured for me to stand up. I tentatively obliged while he explained the mission, inviting them all to pray for unity. Their stares turned to smiles.

After shaking hands with a few hundred well-wishers, the place emptied and I was left standing alone on the night street. The padre was off to another Mass, so

I was on my own for Christmas Eve. The very last gentleman to hop in his car stepped back out, calling my name. In poor English Geraldo invited me to celebrate Christmas with him.

I had a fantastic evening celebrating with his loud extended family. His two teenage children drew me into the conversations and jokes were flying across the room. His beautiful daughter, Georgia, did most of the translating and if it became too loud she'd chat with me on the side, practising her English. When this family gathered, they went off! We ate, we laughed and we brought in Christmas with great cheer.

The padre and I spent Christmas day with the town's nuns and a few parish families out at a lakeside house for a barbeque, where he again spoke on my behalf.

I was back on the road on Boxing Day for a thirty kilometre walk to the town of Malta, singing and praying.

When I marched into town a local with no English asked: "Ausdralian?"

Surprised, I replied, "Yes, I am." He gestured for me to follow and, with the town staring on, he led me through the streets until a woman yelled out from a block away. He sent me on to her as she gestured for me to follow. We eventually arrived at a house where two teenage girls excitedly invited me in. I was so confused.

The girls grabbed a pile of envelopes and flicked through them frantically, holding one up with Portuguese across the bottom and English across the rest, "Welcome to Malta." I laughed and they flicked through again, holding up, "Are you hungry?" and then, "Would you like a shower?" Padre Jackson had phoned ahead, but the local English-speaking priest was heading out for the day, so he had written a series of cue cards for the girls to communicate with me. They were an absolute hoot and took great care of me. It was awkward though when one of them asked me, "Her looks? Her looks?" I presumed she was asking about the other girl. They found the corresponding cue card and held it up, "Her looks. Her looks!"

I struggled not to choke on my chicken. "No, no, it says, Relax. Relax."

The girl's friend, Patricia, took me to meet a young Baptist man. I extended the mission to him, but to my dismay he bluntly rejected it, taking aim at the Catholic Church, my flimsy faith, and that I couldn't speak Portuguese properly. "You don't speak much Portuguese. Why should I listen to you?" Biting my tongue, I meticulously laid out my faith, prayer life and standing with Christ. He slowly began to see the invitation to pray for unity as something other than me asking him to pray about becoming Catholic. We hit gold when he discovered that I had a similar taste in books and, although it took a while, our conversation wound up with: "I'd be happy to pray for the complete unity of the Church." It was a tough slog getting there.

Malta celebrated its birthday that night and the town was in a very festive mood. I joined in, dancing the traditional north-east Brazilian forro with Patricia, while the majority of the few-hundred-strong crowd turned to yell random instructions at me. I was soon on my 1–2–3–4 way. I wasn't, however, intent on taking it to the bizarre combination of Viennese Waltz and pole dancing that some of the teenagers engaged in …

After a dreary hammock sleep, I was escorted to a small town a few kilometres down the road to meet a number of the church-going locals. The locals all accepted the invitation to pray for unity, but their desire to show me every single religious artefact—coupled with the heat and mental labour of speaking a foreign language—wore on me. The town sat beautifully on the edge of a massive water reservoir with mountains in the distance, but the peacefulness of that lakeside village would be shattered in the near future. Tragic news would eventually reach me via email. None of us had any idea of the heartbreak to yet unfold.

I walked on praying through wafting heat to Pombal, which had a church and ice-creamery at its heart. The priest there, Padre Eunaldo, was also expecting me and, at evening Mass, he invited me forward after his homily to extend the mission to a receptive congregation.

I was slow rising in the morning and about to head off at 9 am when Padre Eunaldo asked me to stay. He wanted me to see their mission project. I struggled to weigh up 'the walking' versus 'the people', but chose to stay, trusting that God would somehow get me to Sousa that night. A seminarian by the name of Rodolfo arrived who, to my delight, spoke the most fluent English of anyone yet. He was self-taught. Any man with the determination to teach himself a language to the point of fluency would be a valuable addition in any church.

Padre Eunaldo, Rodolfo and I headed off to view the town's mission. Rodolfo explained as we drove: "Many families used to live in the town's rubbish dump, so we have tried to find them work. Little by little we have established permanent housing for them in the town too. We couldn't rightly proclaim the Gospel inside the church and ignore what was happening outside it."

"How many families lived there?" I asked.

"There were sixty families in the rubbish tip when we started. There are just twenty left. We have work for them, but no accommodation yet."

I was overwhelmed as we drove down a dusty track into the confusion of family shelters amongst massive islands of melting rotting rubbish, emitting a pungent smell. "How do they live in this?" I was lost for words.

No one was there at that time and Rodolfo translated for the padre as he explained: "We've built a recycling factory in Pombal to provide work for the people who don't have accommodation yet. They rummage through the tip early in the morning and late afternoon and then work with those materials at the factory during the hot day. The money they earn, they keep."

I thought it was important to film as we went, but I felt so pathetic standing there with my $1,000 camera. The padre asked if there were any Australian charities capable of helping them secure housing for the remaining twenty families. I assured him that I'd at least try. The second request for money in as many weeks was met with a lot more compassion than the first. This was a community seeking to unite itself, rather than for a fourth church building for those who were divided.

We drove back to the recycling factory in Pombal and the workers welcomed me with little more than a head nod. The small facility consisted of a metal press, cleaning appliances and a few sorting and wrapping machines. Church money well spent. The workers ranged in age from young children through to those who should have been enjoying retirement. Through the missions in Juàzeirinho and now Pombal I was inadvertently learning about unity in a very different light, not that I realised it at the time. It was the start of a steep learning curve.

By the time I set my sights on the nine-hour walk to Sousa it was already early afternoon. The padre grabbed Rodolfo and asked him translate. Rodolfo smiled, "The padre has a second proposal for you. He is saying Mass at 5 pm in Aparecida. It's just over halfway to Sousa. You can travel with us to Mass, invite the congregation to join in praying for unity and then walk the twenty kilometres

on to Sousa in the cool of the evening." Padre Eunaldo nodded, willing me on. His plan would spread the invitation further than if I walked all the way through that night, so we jumped in the car and drove on to Aparecida.

The padre and Rodolfo slipped out a door behind the altar to the sacristy, so I wandered aimlessly around the church checking it out. I nodded hello to the few people in there, but not one returned the greeting. They just continued talking softly. I didn't think much of it and when Rodolfo re-appeared he invited me out through a maze of corridors to a kitchen for a glass of water in front of a cool fan. I explained how the unspoken part of the mission to the non-English speakers was to pray at 4:01 every day. "It doesn't translate into Portuguese."

He laughed, "It's part of the mission—ask people to pray at that time anyway."

It was so nice in front of that fan that we lost track of time, so much so that we suddenly heard a packed congregation open up with the first hymn. We stumbled to our feet with nervous laughter, ran back through the corridors and reverently entered the church from behind the altar with our heads bowed. Rodolfo took up his place next to the padre and I slinked off to the side, taking up a vacant spot in the wings. A few hundred depressed-looking people had packed into the church.

When I looked back up at Padre Eunaldo my mouth literally fell open. I think my heart stopped too. Sitting at the front of the congregation was a weeping family and a coffin. I was fixated. "Uh-uh. No way. He has not invited me to speak at a funeral. He's made a mistake. He forgot there was a funeral and there's no way he's going to invite me to speak in front of a sobbing congregation." I felt queasy sitting in the sweltering church. I sank low into my seat. Each time we stood up I felt exposed, towering a few feet above everyone. I sweated through the homily, but to my relief the end came and went without me being called forward.

I relaxed and after Communion I knelt down, bowing my head in prayer. The padre stepped up to the microphone and said something I didn't understand, however two words came through crystal clear, "Samwell" and "Ausdraliano". I opened my eyes and saw him ushering me forward with a big smile, while the deceased's crying family stared at me. I cautiously rose to my feet, racing through a million and one options of what to say. I prayed as I stepped forward, "God, help me."

The one rule I took to the microphone was, "Don't try to be funny." Rodolfo walked up alongside to translate and as I looked out across the congregation every set of eyes was glued on me, except the deceased's granddaughter whose face was buried in her brother's shoulder. I took a glancing look at the coffin and wished I could hop in with him. Mumbling my introduction in Portuguese I reverted to English to explain the mission. I then turned to the family and offered my condolences and prayers for them. They mostly responded with a heartfelt nod and half a smile. I extended the invitation to pray for unity every day at 4:01 to the congregation, left it at that and eagerly took my seat back in the wings, to the sound of silence.

The coffin was carried out and the congregation followed in full voice, leaving me to contemplate mortality. With the sun setting I gathered my belongings, said goodbye to the padre and Rodolfo and set off hastily, nervous about someone taking offence to my participation in the funeral. Most people had responded well, but some had maintained a solid frown. I just wasn't sure if it had anything to do with me.

Happy to be out on the open road in near perfect twilight conditions, I prayed through the evening for the deceased gentleman, his family and for unity. The road to Sousa was a straight stretch with the only visible lights a distant town well off to the side. The moon and stars provided enough light to see all the way to the distant hills. I walked non-stop for nearly four hours, breaking the calm silence with a few songs for the final half an hour.

I found a hotel for the night before meeting the padre the next morning, who invited me to stay for lunch. It was up to my poor Portuguese to get us through all our conversation. For dessert he presented a container of homemade candy resembling solid Turkish Delight. I nibbled off the corner of a cube and quite liked the sweetness, much to everyone's delight. I put the question across, "What is it? What's it made from?" Wrong question.

The padre answered in Portuguese, "Sangue de vaca com açúcar." All I understood from that was 'com,' which meant 'with.' I shrugged my shoulders. He thought for a moment then looked up with a smile and went, "Moo!" That only confused me. I failed to see the connection. He ran his finger along a vein on the inside of his arm and repeated, "Moo!" then picked up the sugar bowl, "Açúcar." I understood. It was cow's blood with sugar. Fun for all the family. I was no longer hungry. I slipped the remaining piece into my pocket, but had to hide my laughter when the padre fetched a small container filled with the stuff as a gift. I just smiled and said thank you.

The heat and lack of sleep hurt, it was already after noon, and the next town of Cajazerias was a fair distance from Sousa. I contemplated staying for an unscheduled rest, but the Bishop of Cajazerias was apparently waiting for me. The padre was eager for me to continue but I wasn't even going to make it halfway before sunset. One of the young workers offered to ride me there on his motorbike, but I was beginning to realise how powerful the public witness of walking was, so I wanted to slug it out. I was struggling to keep up with the mission. It was outpacing me.

I relented. We zipped down the highway on his tiny motorbike at fifty km/h all the way to Cajazeiras and the bishop's front door. The secretary, Olinda, welcomed me in, but communication was difficult. She talked flat out in Portuguese and when I didn't understand she just talked louder. It didn't help.

The Spanish missionary bishop, José, welcomed me into his office and we stepped through the mission slowly with no common language. The Spanish I'd learnt prior to departure was useless. He was supportive and with thanks I reassured him that I'd be off in the morning to Juazeiro do Norte, but he rebuked me. I had to stay one day before continuing by bus. I was aware of Bishop Prowse's words back in Melbourne about the mission being about the people and not walking, but I reaffirmed that I was there to pray and walk. Bishop José stood firm and with authority told me I needed to stay and that it was too far to walk to Juazeiro do Norte. Olinda chimed in that it was also too dangerous. I did what was asked of me, but I was frustrated.

As a gesture of thanks for their hospitality I handed Olinda a small box of sangue de vaca com açúcar that I happened to be carrying. Her face lit up with joy. She was definitely going to enjoy it more than me.

The reason for the bishop's request was that three young men were being ordained. We arrived at the cathedral together and to my delight Rodolfo and Padre Eunaldo were present. Rodolfo and I sat down the back so that he could quietly translate for me. Bishop José asked me to stand at the end of the ordination and explained the invitation to pray for unity, imploring everyone to join in praying and working for a united Church.

A young man sitting near the front wore what looked like a traditional priests garb from a century ago. "Rodolfo, who's that?" The young man was initially a student with the three men being ordained, but was now an Anglican priest.

After Mass I introduced myself and we had a long chat about Church splits, theology and unity. I was taken by his willingness to be present at the ordination of his friends. It was anything but a token gesture. He shared his candid thoughts on unity and his love of the Church, happily agreeing to pray for unity.

The bishop had bought me a bus ticket to travel to Juazeiro do Norte at 3:30 am that night, so I didn't stay long. Rodolfo said farewell with a hug and I was back at the bishop's place to rest for a few hours. I still wanted to walk, but was up at 3 am to be greeted by the bishop and Olinda in the kitchen. I felt very cared for. He presented me with a gift: a letter to his good friend, the Bishop of Crato, requesting his hospitality for me.

A spectacular storm raged as we drove through the empty streets to the bus and said farewell. I didn't fit in the seat and couldn't sleep, but as the pitch-black countryside periodically lit up with lightning my mind drifted to how far the invitation had spread. It was difficult to look back at all the sections I hadn't walked. I wasn't a theologian or teacher, so there was no chance of having the opportunity to speak at length in each town. What I could do was make an undeniable statement about the scandal of disunity by putting myself in what others considered dangerous situations. Some of the journey so far had been dictated by fear, both my own and others, with little consideration for the mission.

For the first time my mind flicked back to home. I missed it. I missed being able to engage in normal conversation without introducing myself every hour.

The bus pulled into a wet Juazeiro do Norte at sunrise. I'd been told to check out the shrine to Padre Cicero, a man the locals were calling to be canonised, and with a point of the finger from a local I aimed accordingly, walking on through sweet misty rain.

After rescuing a rain-soaked kitten clinging to a tree branch I found a large church and entered to pray. I turned out to be ten minutes early for Sunday Mass. Perfect timing. Through the inquisitiveness of a few girls in the choir the prayer for unity was passed on quickly.

After Mass I stepped outside and could finally see the Padre Cicero statue, high on a hilltop seven kilometres away. It was a task to make my way up through a series of winding, twisting shantytowns towards it and I'm not sure the journey was worth it. I left dismayed. The locals claimed Padre Cicero was a saint and proceeded to build an enormous statue and basilica in his honour, well before the Church had approved it. As it turned out the case for his canonisation was rejected when the Vatican uncovered a shady part of his life that included strong links to a damaging gang in that area. The case wasn't closed as far as the locals were concerned, but it was a big investment into the unknown. The shrine was what the locals believed was important so it was where their attention was directed.

What ticked me off properly was the commercialisation there. Padre Cicero and Jesus statues were sold right along side Batman and Spiderman. The stores said everything about money and nothing about faith. There was also a museum with a chapel off to the side containing the Blessed Sacrament. The chapel was eerily empty, but the museum over-flowed with patrons having their photo taken with one of the Padre Cicero statues, kneeling before or holding onto them while praying. I moved back to the chapel for a while, sad at the confusing sight outside.

I visited the huge statue, where I watched people praying to Padre Cicero while placing their hands on the statue and looking skywards at the statue's head seven metres above. A few wrote prayers on its base and one couple wrapped a ribbon around it a number of times with their prayer typed on it repeatedly. I understood that it was important to express faith outwardly and to call on the intercession of the Saints, but I couldn't see anything suggesting Christianity (other than the Jesus dolls and the empty chapel). It left me with a very sour taste.

From the statue's height I could see out across farming land to the neighbouring city of Crato, so I set off towards it. The walk back down the hill through the shanty homes drew a lot of attention and locals walked out of their homes to jeer 'the American'. Two men taunted me, inviting me into their homes, "Eh! Eh Americano! Venha aqui! (Come here)," while making the Brazilian hand gesture for money. Another guy, raggedy and toothless, sat with his amigos in an open-air bar shouting angrily for me to stop and join them. His face was contorted with hatred and it only grew stronger as I walked on. There was no way I was stopping.

I crossed a bridge and stepped over a road kill that sent a shiver down my spine. The small-dinner-plate-sized tarantula epitomised unpleasantness.

I found a direct route to Crato along the dirt railway access road, but the bishop's residence appeared to be a well-kept secret. After visiting numerous churches I was finally pointed in the right direction and, tired, arrived at sunset. The bishop's young housekeeper was the only one home, but after reading Bishop José's letter she smiled and welcomed me in.

Bishop Dom Fernando Panico and his driver arrived soon after and extended their own greetings. No one spoke English so my Portuguese was again all we had until the driver had the bright idea to log onto Google-translate and communicate via the computer. It livened up the conversation significantly!

An open courtyard in the centre of the bishop's home allowed the cool night air to filter in, along with a mass of mosquitos. I played karate kid for fifteen minutes in my room, catching every single one of them before heading to sleep. It was the 31st of December 2006 and the small city of Crato was gearing up for New Year's Eve. I considered heading down for the fireworks, but when it started to rain again I was content to just fall asleep.

From Christmas to New Year's Eve, rubbish tips to funerals, it had been a full week, and if I was concerned about not having walked enough, I needn't have worried. The year ahead would be enormous. A very troubled 9,000 kilometres on foot lay ahead over the next twelve months alone … and a lot of prayer.

> *Very truly, I tell you, when you were younger, you used to fasten your own belt and to go wherever you wished. But when you grow old, you will stretch out your hands, and someone else will fasten a belt around you and take you where you do not wish to go.*
>
> John 21:18

Total walked: *252 kilometres*

# Food Poisoning, a Game Show Chemist & the Darkest Nights

*January 2007*

My routine was now essentially set. I'd rise early—often at 4 am—make the most of the cooler morning conditions and push out towards my next destination, praying as I went. It wasn't exactly smooth sailing though. I pretty much needed therapy by the end of the next week.

Bishop Dom Fernando invited me to spend New Year's Day with him as he fulfilled his duties, which was a fantastic opportunity to spread the invitation to pray for unity. We travelled into forest-clad hills surrounding Crato teeming with wildlife and alive with sound. I finally felt like I was in Brazil.

Bishop Dom Fernando welcomed me forward during an ordination and introduced the mission on my behalf, extending the prayer invitation; and again at our next stop: a Franciscan abbey in the jungle, for a New Year's Day lunch for the homeless. The humble monks there were definitely not a silent order.

In the afternoon we headed off towards our final Mass in Juazeiro do Norte at the Padre Cicero shrine. My eyes lit up. We slowed for the overcrowded, windy road up through the shanty homes and the locals affectionately waved the bishop through. When they caught sight of me in the back seat their expressions changed. I couldn't help but smile.

We drove past the statue, museum, and shops and down a dirt road to an open-air basilica that I hadn't even seen the previous day. It was mesmerising. The entire concrete structure spanned out from a central tower in an ever-increasing swirl. It was also only half finished and looked unfit for a large crowd to sit beneath; severely rusted steel reinforcement rods hung out ominously, and concrete-cancer was eating through some sections.

When Mass began, the few thousand people sang their hearts out under the few thousand tonnes of crumbling concrete columns swirling out above them. I was uneasy. My degree was in Mechanical Engineering, not Civil, but it still left me thinking, "Could we all sing a little softer? Please?"

The service was two hours long and I felt the pinch due to the heat and foreign language. I loved the life everyone brought to the celebration, but was again left despondent. Communion turned into a free-for-all. People pushed each other aside, reaching across one another to take the Eucharist, not receive it. I stood there in disbelief as everyone jostled for front spot. When I finally made it to one of the padres, he lifted the host and said in Portuguese, "The body of Christ."

As I said, "Amen," a woman reached over and took it out of his hands.

Another woman pushed straight past, ignoring the padre handing out Communion, and stood with arms wide open in front of a statue of Mary. I received Communion and walked back to my seat, looking back over my shoulder. I didn't understand. Why had she bypassed Christ in the Eucharist to pray in front of the statue? I love Mary and owe a great deal of my faith journey to her intercession and direction, but Mary is the ultimate signpost to Jesus: why would you bypass the destination? The only thing that filled me with a sense of peace there was the humble and prayerful man serving them from the office of bishop.

The bishop and I prayed together after breakfast before I left, but his hospitality hadn't ended. He lent across and handed me ten envelopes, each addressed to the parish of one of my designated stopping points for the next two weeks. I had no idea when he'd had the time to type the letters, but done it he had. I was indebted to him. And amongst the envelopes was the equivalent of A$100.

I headed off on foot through thick misty forest along a dead straight mountain plateau road towards Nova Olinda. I rested at a small cluster of homes in the middle of the day and bought a bag of fruit from two kids. I had no idea what it was. The fruit looked like a cross between a small orange and an apricot. I bit straight in and my face contorted at the tarty, sour taste. It was horrible! The two young boys stared at me blankly. I was about to toss the awful thing away when I peered in and, lo and behold, it was a sweet passionfruit.

No need to eat the skin …

Nova Olinda was remote and slow-paced, but Bishop Dom Fernando's letter ensured a quick invitation to stay the night at the priest's home, and a wonderful reception from a group of young adults eager to show me around.

I felt lethargic in the following morning's heat and the rainforest had disappeared completely. Dry, arid land abounded once more. I wasn't well and the lethargy deepened until my stomach rumbled and my bowel turned. I had gastro and was sent scampering for the bush.

It was a long time before I re-emerged.

Eventually, I walked on—worse for wear—and had to deal with a new problem: my past. Walking alone for long periods of time inevitably allowed for my entire life to be self-scrutinised, from theological questions to sporting moments and why certain things were the way they were. That afternoon I zeroed in on all the stupid, irresponsible, selfish decisions I'd ever made. It was tough to scrutinise my actions and the question of "… why? …" was the end result more often than not.

My sombre mood was broken when I stepped within a whisker of a 6' brown snake that shot out of the grass and up the embankment, sending me leaping road-wards. I despise snakes, but it had at least distracted me from my pity-party gastro lethargy.

The terrain dried out further every kilometre I pushed into the west. I again stepped over a snake, this time a red and black banded one. This one was dead. I was happy to make it to the open spaces of Aratama in the middle of the siesta, but struggled to find assistance. A young lady walked past on the opposite side of the deserted street, but when I asked for help she put her head down and walked on fast. I then noticed a woman standing in the doorway of her home staring at me so I motioned towards her, but she slinked inside, slammed the door and with a few rattles and clanks, locked it. I stood in the middle of the dusty street alone, and plodded on to find the church.

A young parish secretary and her family offered me accommodation, and when I mentioned the red and black banded snake their eyes lit up, "Was it red with black bands or black with red bands?" I shrugged my shoulders. They added, "One is harmless, but the other is deadly." All I took from that was not to go near red and black snakes—there's a 50% chance of death.

I was handed a towel and pointed to the communal shower up the back, but had no sooner set my gear down on the little bench inside the door-less cubicle when an old man turned up to make sure everything was okay. I told him I was fine. There was an awkward silence. He just stood there. I excused myself and told him I needed to shower. He stayed where he was, looking in. I asked politely for privacy, but he wouldn't budge, so I delayed showering by mucking around with my gear, one item at a time, checking them for quality in the hope that I'd bore him out of standing there. It worked. He wandered off and I quickly had a cold shower and washed the day away, finishing just before he re-appeared. "Dirty old man, leave me alone!"

I was seated for a huge dinner, but to my dismay they had no intention of joining me. Out of respect they sat without food until I'd finished. I tried to convince them to eat with me, but they refused, so I ate alone, with everyone staring. I'm renowned for being a slow eater and it normally doesn't bother me. This time it did.

With lethargy setting back in I said goodnight and headed to bed, but an hour later I was still awake, exhausted, and struggling. My body was reeling and by one in the morning I was horribly weak. My stomach felt like it was jammed halfway up my throat. I staggered through the darkened house, fumbling through the double locked screen-door out to the detached toilet. Groggy and faint, I curled up there for fifteen minutes, but with nothing eventuating I ventured back to bed, grabbing a bucket on the way.

Half an hour later I raced back outside. My stomach erupted into two and a half relentless hours of convulsions. I had the tell-tale signs of food poisoning and it drove me close to tears. The family cat kept me company and between retches I'd gaze skyward at the stars. It was 4 am when I crawled back into bed and prayed, "God, if I can't walk for unity, will you accept throwing up for it?"

By morning my head felt like it was about to split in half. I couldn't bring myself to eat the oil-soaked eggs they served up, opting for water only. I wandered up to the shower block to freshen up and wouldn't you know it, no sooner had I taken my t-shirt off and the dirty old man was back. I had some choice words to say to him this time before proceeding.

The family showed great concern for me and organised a lift to the next town: Potengi, nineteen kilometres away. Barely able to stay upright, they propped me up in a minivan and waved goodbye, reassuring me of their prayers. Fifteen minutes later I was in arid, desolate Potengi, wandering through to the church with Bishop Dom Fernando's letter, but the padre was absent. I met three young men and they happily showed me to a spare room, where I slept until 5 pm, awoke and ate, met the parishioners and then headed back to bed.

My room contained three beds, side by side, with a metre between each one. I'd slept on the far left but, when I returned, I discovered I was sharing a room with one of the three guys and he'd moved my gear off the middle bed onto the bed I'd slept in. I went to move it off my bed so I could sleep, but he insisted that I leave it there and sleep in the middle bed. It made no sense. He was adamant that I wasn't supposed to sleep on the far left bed and I was too tired to argue, so I took the fresh middle bed and the lights went out.

I prayed a silent prayer and closed my eyes. After a minute I rolled onto my side and my hand brushed past something. I straight away thought 'spider' and snatched my hand away and then flicked at it a few times, but it had already gone. Lying there on top of the sheets in that humid room, it slowly sank in that the 'spider' had felt like skin. My heart sank. He didn't just have his hand sitting on my bed did he? In my tired state I rationalised that his hand bridging the gap was just 'an accident'.

After a few minutes I felt the pressure of his hand being placed on the edge of the bed again. I was petrified. What does he want? Is he armed? I knocked it away, hoping he'd get the message, but the hand came straight back in that pitch-dark room, landing fair on my chest and sliding rapidly downwards. Immediately, I grabbed it and reefed it away with a wrenching twist, throwing his arm back across the gap, presumably still attached. He whimpered momentarily in the eerie darkness. I couldn't move. I felt violated and I just wanted to grab my gear and get out, but I was overcome with fear in that black room, with a man whose advances I'd just rejected with force. Adrenalin was pumping and my ears worked overtime, straining to hear any movement.

Half an hour passed and I was still wide-eyed. I prayed that he'd fall asleep and within ten minutes I heard his breathing change. He was asleep. I prayed fervently for another hour until I was just too tired to stay awake, even with the fear factor. I prayed, "Lord, into your hands I give my spirit," closed my eyes and slept.

I walked on early the next morning receiving the usual stares plus a few locked doors and peers out windows. The poverty was so much more desperate than the shantytowns I'd already seen. Litter was everywhere; old car tyres, rusting car bodies, deformed bicycles, pieces of timber, house tiles and general food packaging. A fire burned rubbish beside a house and the sound of cars, motorbikes and clanging blacksmith's hammers filled the air. The homes were mostly devoid of flooring, with nothing but bare earth. It was a sad sight, and I felt like I fitted in.

Thirty-three kilometres to Araripe, the thorny landscape with long grass along the edge of the road had me wary of snakes. I was sweating profusely. I used to play cricket and occasionally fielded in the slips. I hated the slips. Every time I took a catch I quietly resented it because I knew that if I just dropped a few the captain would move me. I told my coach that I hated fielding there and asked if I could field in front of the bat, but his reply was simple, "But you catch them, Sam! You have to want that edge to fly your way and you have to want to be the one in the team to catch it. Keep saying to yourself, 'Hit it to me,' as the bowler runs in, 'Hit it to me'." It took a long time to feel confident in slips and to learn to want the hard flying edge and the challenge of catching it. Snakes on the road to Araripe were no different. I wanted to find a snake before it found me. "Hit it to me." In a much shorter time than it took to master the fear of slip fielding, I was praying away while hunting the next snake with anticipation.

After a huge fruit-filled breakfast the next morning, I was off again, walking and praying up a massive hill alongside a number of men heading up to the local brickworks. Ahead of me was a man on a bicycle. His left leg was deformed and he struggled with all his might to pedal uphill with one leg. He could finally pedal no more and hopped off, limping slowly alongside. I couldn't bring myself to just walk past. I said good morning and gestured for him to jump back on while I pushed. He was confused, but after I smiled and repeated the gesture he smiled and hopped on. I pushed him on up the hill, but as he pedalled harder we picked up speed and I soon found myself running to keep pace. It was the uphill Brazilian bobsled! Sweat poured down my nose in the morning heat until we reached the top and he was able to turn off down a laneway with a thank you wave and a big smile. I was stuffed. Two kilometres down, thirty-odd dry, hot kilometres to go.

After yet another woman raced inside and bolted the door behind her—but without spotting any snakes— I entered Campos Sales at sunset to be palmed off by a man leaving the Baptist church. He just turned his back and walked off mid-introduction. However, a woman driving past saw it happen and stopped, asking if she could help me. When I told her what I was doing she swung around to the two kids in the back seat, told them to shove over and told me to get in. She wanted me to meet the entire seminary of Campos Sales.

I was welcomed in and invited to stay a day to rest, while introducing the mission at the 10 am Mass in town. The seminarians were amazing, and also comedic. "You've seen a lot of Brazil! See that up there? It's a Brazilian cloud!"

Thanks George.

I was glad I stayed a day. I was tired. My body was capable of recovering from the sickness, but I needed to be careful that fear didn't set in. I was now struggling to sleep, and that could become crippling. "Lord, may the days ahead be better; or at least grant me the patience to embrace them."

Up at 4:10 am and on the road fast in the cool pre-dawn, star-lit night, three stray dogs followed me down the road at close proximity, barking and snarling. After a few minutes I turned quickly, flinging my walking poles in the most threatening manner I could and they scattered with their tails between their legs. I resumed my peaceful walk as the night slid into dawn.

After nearly thirty kilometres at 40°C, I was happy to descend off a plateau around the edge of a mountain with a view of Fronteiras on sweeping farm plains below. The parish secretary called for her English-speaking niece, Amanda, who welcomed me into her family with a massive steak and rice meal, three bottles of Coke and two bottles of water. I needed it all.

Amanda's boyfriend invited me to join them for a drive up to the town's water reservoir for a swim. I was all in. Full-of-food, but in. The massive dam-wall spanned two high peaks behind Fronteiras with the body of water stretching along a valley, guarded on both sides by forested hills. A hundred metres out from the wall, in deep water, was a square metal-framed tower serving no apparent functional use, but with stairs winding around its perimeter and a small platform jutting out at every corner. It did make for a brilliant diving platform. The tower stood thirty-five metres tall and, although no one was taking the leap from the top, there was one guy taking the twenty metre challenge. Every time he stepped up he'd focus, clap his hands and leap.

We jumped in and joined the few locals heading straight for the tower. I just relaxed for a while and soaked, although I had an unexpected difficulty: I'd lost weight and my shorts no longer clung to my hips, so it was a bit of a slow one-handed swim to the tower. I was pointed up the rusty rickety staircase to the ten-metre platform as my right of passage. It was a cautious climb. I watched a few guys walk out along a steel platform and jump. It looked easy enough, but when I stepped up it suddenly looked higher. I couldn't help but smile when one local began sincerely encouraging me in fumbled English, "Courage. Courage." I took a deep breath and leapt, flailing through the air to accompanying applause, which was blocked out as I crashed underwater.

Once was enough. I swam, one-handed, from then on.

It was easier to extend the invitation to pray for unity that evening. The locals already knew me. However, my backpack water system had sprung a leak, causing me to walk with a damp backside, so before bed I wandered into the town's chemist to buy tape to patch it. I didn't know the Portuguese word for tape and everything in the chemist was behind a counter, so I couldn't just help myself. I was forced to explain my problem to the two women serving. Placing the water bladder on the counter I showed them what I needed and they had a quick discussion before producing a packet of plaster. I smiled and said, "No," and again explained my needs. They chatted again and this time lifted up a syringe. I laughed and shook my head, "No, no." Two customers walked in and decided to help, so I explained the problem once more while showing them the leaking bladder. The four conferred, came to agreement and then the two women fossicked around. One stood back up smiling, brandishing a pack of tampons. I nearly wet myself, "No, no!" The light-hearted debate between the women and ripples of laughter drew a crowd and when I declined their next proposal— a sling—the volume of suggestions shocked me. I turned to see twenty people crammed into the small shop, everyone offering their advice.

They quietened down as I again explained slowly—with a lot of mime—what I needed, but it set off a game-show-like bombardment of remedies that descended into stock-market-pit-like chaos. The poor women behind the counter looked at each other with resignation until one young bloke shut them all up and moved in alongside me, "Okay, Americano."

I corrected him, "Australiano."

His eyes lit up and he announced to everyone, "Australiano!" They cheered approvingly. I smiled and waved. He pointed to the water bladder and indicated for me to explain again what I needed. He didn't understand English but he listened attentively and appeared to translate and mime everything I'd said. The women turned to each other with a look of, "I don't know if we have that," but set about searching through the cupboards. One woman turned around holding a roll of tape. "Yes!" I exclaimed. The chemist erupted into cheers and rapturous applause, and the young man received pats on the back as we shook hands. I bought one roll of tape, but somehow everyone went home a winner.

I left Fronteiras well before sunrise, but the heat caught me fast and a group of buzzards pretty soon began circling. "Get lost you mangy vultures! I'm not done with yet." It was a very long haul to make it to Picos, and then on up through forested hills that seemed to go on forever. I stepped over a couple of dead snakes until I found a red and black banded one that was alive. I couldn't remember which one was deadly, so I just gave it a wide berth.

I stopped at a roadside restaurant for a break and, when I walked back out, all the buzzards were sitting in the tree outside! I had a few choice words to say, heaved my backpack on and walked off. They took flight behind me.

The town of Oiras was wedged between two hills with an overlooking Hollywood-like sign spelling out the town's name. It was home to two hospitable priests who accepted the bishop's letter and ushered me inside but, for some reason, I was introduced to the parish as Dr Clear. I'm not sure what I was a doctor of, but it stuck and everyone referred to me as the doctor from then on.

After fifty-seven kilometres of relentless sun, unbroken forest and circling buzzards, I found the quiet town of Nazaré do Piauí. The padre was chatting with locals and, after reading the bishop's letter, he smiled, extended his hand in friendship and welcomed me into his home. I had no idea what the letter said, but the response was always positive. I asked Padre Milton if it was okay for me to begin walking at 4:30 am so I could utilise the cool morning temperatures and he said, "Of course, that is fine." However, to my surprise, when I rolled out of bed at 4 am Padre Milton was sitting in the kitchen with breakfast ready. And when it came time to leave he walked me through the town to the open road, shook my hand and prayed for me in the pitch dark. I was moved by his generosity.

As I walked on in darkness I thought about Padre Milton's actions. I was at the mercy of others, but what he'd shown was that despite any concerns he may have had, or inconveniences I caused him, he put them aside to help. The apostle Peter tried to tell Jesus that they wouldn't let anything bad happen to Him and Jesus replied sternly, "Get behind me Satan." There's a natural tendency to protect people from harm but, when it comes to mission work, that's generally what you're placing yourself into: harm's way. Even while working in youth ministry in Australia my parents were concerned that I was harming my financial security. And they were right, I did harm my financial security, but I received something I'd choose over financial security any day. Walking down that darkened road through the forest I realised that many people had helped me by pushing the mission slightly to the side. Padre Milton had cared for the mission by stepping out to join, if only for a short distance.

The rising sun illuminated those mangy buzzards circling overhead again as I walked on through the most amazing forest I'd seen to that point, tall and thick for the forty-five kilometres approaching Floriano. Then I spotted what looked like a stick poking out from the undergrowth at eye level and waving in the breeze. Closer, I realised it wasn't a stick, and I slammed to a halt in surprise. It was a metre long, wiry thin, tan-coloured snake that jittered in the breeze, presumably waiting for an unsuspecting butterfly. It looked like the malnourished drug-abusing snake of the animal kingdom. I gave it a wide berth and refocussed … "Hit it to me."

The humidity spiked and, within a short period, a billowing thundercloud had formed above. Rain fell slowly before opening up into a torrent. It was fantastic. I was smiling from ear to ear and didn't even bother throwing my jacket on. I felt clean and cool. It was refreshing until: BOOM! Lightning cracked into the forest a short distance from me and there was no time between lightning and thunder. It scared the wits out of me. Without any time to contemplate my dilemma it happened again: BOOM! The darkness under that massive cloud vanished in a flash of white. As if the thunder had shaken the cloud to its core, the heavy rain increased beyond what I thought was possible. The air was so thick with rain that I could barely see a metre ahead. I now wished I'd put my jacket on. Lightning exploded around me. I had no option. I just walked on, one step at a time, praying fervently.

After no more than five minutes the downpour stopped, leaving me to splash my way up around the base of a mountain. I stopped at a large intersection to rest on a rock while removing my wet socks. A car pulled over with a man and three women in it. They simply wanted to know who I was, but when I told them what I was doing they didn't believe me. One of the girls started laughing and gave me a look of disbelief, "Really?" Right on cue, a second car pulled up and Padre Milton stepped out in his full priest garb carrying a packed lunch for me. He exclaimed in Portuguese: "Samuel! You have made it this far! Well done!" He turned to the man and three women. "He's walking around the world for unity. How brilliant is that?"

The four were speechless. One of the guys laughed and looked back at me with raised eyebrows. I just smiled and accepted the padre's lunch.

The buzzard entourage stayed with me all the way to beautiful Floriano on the edge of the Parnaiba River, where the Bishop of Crato's final letter again scored me a bed for a couple of nights and a generous acceptance of the mission. After walking 102 kilometres in two days, I needed a rest. I felt incredibly indebted to Bishop Dom Fernando Panico for his letters, whose gesture could be traced back even further to Eshmael, in Junco do Seridó, who'd placed a call through to Padre Jackson in Patos and set off a chain of organised hospitality.

A monumental ninety-seven kilometres lay between Floriano and São João dos Patos. I was up at 4:01 am, prayed for unity, and hit the road. I swiftly gained unwanted attention. Two large angry dogs on the dark riverbanks snarled and rushed in as close as they could without being hit by my walking poles. My heart pounded. It was difficult seeing them in the poor light and they moved fast. Their teeth flashed in my torchlight.

More dogs joined in until there was a pack on the hunt.

Night faded enough to improve visibility and, although I maintained my direction, it was slow and tiring keeping them at bay. They became increasingly confident, snapping at my heels. I picked up a rock, turned sharply and hurled it at the largest, most aggressive dog. As I launched it, my sleeve button hooked on the beaded rosary bracelet around my wrist and it snapped off. The rock flew straight at the big guy while the beads shot out in every direction at the other dogs, scattering them.

What an awesome weapon to have up my sleeve.

I headed out along a wilderness road with the scattered forest offering little shade and with no mobile phone; it was a risky day. Not long after passing the thirty kilometre mark, I heard the dreaded sound of air being sucked into the drinking tube. My water was gone. I'd managed a significant drink, so was good … for a while but, in the torrid afternoon heat, my time was short.

I dried out fast. There was hardly any traffic but I noticed a rise in rubbish so was hopeful that there was a roadhouse nearby. Five kilometres later I was walking painfully through tall palm forest on fertile plains staring down a sweltering road with no sign of civilisation. The elusive roadhouse never emerged. My body screamed for water. After forty-one kilometres I'd prayed nearly half the distance to São João dos Patos, but I'd also stopped sweating. I was dehydrated.

A public mini-van was good enough to stop for me, but with no seats left I had to sit on the floor, trying to stay conscious and wanting to escape my skin. That roadhouse did exist, a number of kilometres further on. Close, but not close enough. I rehydrated slowly in São João dos Patos before finding a posada, lying down in front of a fan and falling asleep for a long time.

The dehydration had hurt me, and the walk to the next town of Orozimbo, only five hours away, dragged on. Even so, I sang loudly to ward off the snakes lying near the road, which must have worked. The snakes stayed away. Having worn the skin right off my middle toe I hobbled inside a posada in Orozimbo and introduced myself, but the owner snapped at me in Portuguese and flicked her hand to get me out. I tentatively said in Portuguese, "I need a bed for one night," but she shooed me out the door scorning, "No beds are available for your people," and slammed the security door behind me. My people? I was livid. I glared at her through the screen before turning and walking on.

I sat on the edge of thick, overgrown wilderness sprawling to the west as the sun set, and wondered where I could lay my head. To my delight a man filling up his old truck at a nearby service station invited me to ride with him to the next town and there, without hesitation, an elderly Italian couple took me in. They also found medical supplies for my bleeding foot.

I stayed in Pastos Bons for a rest day before attempting any of the massive seventy-one kilometres to São Domingos. The forested hills gave way to a flat tableland filled with crops for as far as the eye could see. Soybeans and what appeared to be sugar beets were everywhere. It was spectacular, but the odd large tree standing by itself was a reminder of what had once been.

A cowboy rode towards me and asked, through gritted teeth, "You got any water?"

I pulled out an orange, "Would you like this?" Satisfaction was written all over his face as he accepted. But by the time I'd covered thirty kilometres, I was out of water myself and again grabbed a lift with a truck driver to São Domingos. I met some lively characters in the local store there, where a mass of kids shouted questions at me before walking me to the local church, introducing me to everyone as we went.

I was scheduled to begin the rampaging mad dash across the Amazon to Venezuela by any means possible from there, but I'd missed quite a few kilometres from João Pessoa and was two days ahead of schedule, so I decided to use them for walking.

Within an hour the next morning the flourishing forest once again merged into cropping land cutting a swather across the hill country. I approached a group of farmers preparing to spray a crop and one of them approached with a smile, "Samuel, the Australian!" I was stumped. He patted me on the shoulder, "I was in the store yesterday, but the kids were too loud and I couldn't introduce myself." He'd just hoped to see me that day. I was glad to have walked on. He passed on the invitation to pray for unity to the workers and after I explained my flimsy plan of trying to make São Raimando—ninety-five kilometres away—he happily offered a solution: "I live a few kilometres further on. Come and meet my family, have lunch with us and then continue walking for as far as you can from there."

I liked it.

We rode his motorbike to his home, ate well, prayed, and headed off in our separate directions with a handshake. I walked over thirty-five kilometres to an isolated stand of palms around an oasis of swamps where the water was barely visible due the abundance of vegetation. A hut sat alongside it and the owners, who eked out a subsistence living, offered me hammock-swinging space on the veranda for the night. It was a beautiful place to swing myself to sleep. It would have been even more so if I could sleep in hammocks.

The family had no spare food to offer, only bags of uncooked rice and beans so, with another forty-five kilometres to go to reach São Raimando, I grabbed a ride with a passing truck into the bustling town. I intended to walk on one more day, not that it was the smartest place to walk, but it was still doable.

The two local padres welcomed me enthusiastically, offering me a bed and lots of advice for the Amazon. They failed, however, to mention the pet iguana in the backyard, which made me dance like a man possessed when it shot out from the garden for a pat. Inside wasn't any safer. I forgot to duck through one doorway and slammed my forehead into the frame. It didn't move a millimetre. While holding back their grins, the padres were mildly sympathetic.

There was no way I could make the 120 kilometres to the rural city of Balsas, but I'd mistakenly entered it into my itinerary as being sixty-five kilometres away and was keen to try and make it. After navigating past a massive brown snake at sunrise I pushed on through a relentless day as the road narrowed and the grass grew thick and tall. By the time night fell there was obviously no sight of Balsas, not even from the huge hills I passed over. The thicket and forest along the narrow road scared me. I knew there were dangerous animals like anacondas, but I wasn't sure what else. With twilight fading I sank into darkness, walking on towards a setting crescent moon and Venus.

The traffic dropped to only a few cars an hour and strange noises emanated from the forest. While passing a swamp the noise of croaking frogs was overwhelming, until something let out a gurgling shrill that shut everything up. I kept my torch off, not wanting to bring attention to myself, and prayed on in complete darkness.

The kilometres wore on and with no sight of civilisation. I felt like I was walking into a dark abyss. When Venus and the crescent moon dipped beyond the horizon it was like dimming out the final light. It was black. There are moments from my journey that still send a shiver down my spine … but not this night. I prayed a pleading prayer of, "Lord, please light my way. Please help me," and only a few minutes later the first glimmer of light flickered off to my left, and then my right. I stopped. Pop … pop … pop … they were everywhere: fireflies. The grass lit up and within ten minutes the road looked like an airport runway with thousands of guiding lights. I prayed a prayer of thanks and the road suddenly lit up. The grass cast crazy shadows. I looked skyward in amazement: a shooting star blazed across the southern sky from east to west, lighting up the countryside in fluorescent green as it broke into smaller pieces. I'd never seen anything like it and as if that wasn't enough, on the northern horizon a massive storm cell flickered every few seconds from the lightning flashing within. It was that extra bit of light on a dark night.

I struggled physically after fifty kilometres, but the forest and thicket gave way to farms, so with much gratitude I farewelled the fireflies and gently removed the few that had hitched a ride on my shirt. The open farmland felt much safer.

With unspeakable relief I caught sight of a series of lights up ahead that looked like a roadhouse. I tried to run, but couldn't, so walked fast and—to my absolute joy—the roadhouse was still open. I drank, ate and chatted with the two lively workers and their one other customer offered me a ride to a hotel. I could've hugged him. I jumped into his tow truck and, with the windows down and Bob Marley playing through his stereo, we rumbled on to Balsas.

Reggae never sounded so good.

I stuck to my itinerary from Balsas, bussing it from town to town amidst spectacular jagged mountains along the edge of the Amazon Basin. I visited as many churches as possible and, for the most part, I was received well. One girl from an Assembly of God church wanted nothing to do with unity, only for me to read Romans so that I'd understand why the Catholic Church's teaching on justification was wrong. I knew the scripture she referred to so tried to explain how the Catholic Church does uphold Paul's teaching in context of all scripture, but she walked off mid-sentence, "You should just read it and pray about it." I hate that throwaway line.

I quickly grew tired of bus travel so I added another forty-two kilometres on foot out of Estreito towards Marabá. It was pretty inhospitable land out there, but I didn't care about the heat. The further I walked into the hot jungle, past welcoming tiny villages, the more I wished I hadn't set that area aside for public transport. I had a schedule to keep in order to make it home for World Youth Day though, and the extra one or two months to cross the Amazon was more of a personal goal than a mission-orientated one.

Two police officers and a travelling dentist combined to carry me the remaining 193 kilometres into benighted Marabá, all of them excited just to have someone to talk to. The dentist shouted me dinner in Marabá and imparted the one basic Amazon rule: "If someone pulls a gun on you, look at the ground. If you look at the ground they'll take what they want and run away, but if you look them in the eye they'll kill you." He pointed to a stain outside on the footpath, "See that blood there? It's from last week. The man was robbed and looked up as they ran off. The robber stopped running and shot him. Keep your head down."

Perhaps not walking across the Amazon was a good idea after all.

The Archbishop of Marabá welcomed me cautiously, ringing an English-speaking Indian missionary in a remote township to have the mission explained better to him. Padre Matthias translated it piece by piece and the archbishop's eyes lit up. He welcomed me for a second time, without reservation.

Padre Matthias drove all the way to Marabá in his tiny hatchback to pick me up, inviting me to stay for three days out at his remote missionary church on the edge of the Araguaia River. I loved it out there, but nothing stood out quite so much as the children swimming innocently in the river containing anacondas, piranhas and caiman (small crocodiles). I wasn't going to join them. The padre helped to no end in spreading the invitation to pray for unity, including over the radio and at a massive wedding.

We spoke at length about our tendency to become desensitised to Christ's sacrifice and, while wandering along the river, a provocative thought popped into my head. I wondered how I would respond if I walked into a church and instead of a crucifix I saw a statue of Jesus hanging from a noose. I think most people would be offended, even outraged, but, "Shouldn't that," I thought, "be my response every time I see a crucifix: offence at its necessity and a deeper appreciation of God's love?"

As the race across the Amazon approached, I was satisfied that the mission had been well received over the 835 kilometres on foot over six weeks, despite regretting the lost kilometres. Fighting-fit when I started, I'd still dropped eight kilograms. I'd learnt a lot, particularly about weakness. At Youth Mission Team Australia it was often said, when team members completed their year of voluntary mission work, that only then were they ready to do a year on YMT. My 'year', I hoped, would be Brazil. I hoped to learn fast and was eager to continue on, so long as God lit the way.

*Who made the great lights, for his steadfast love endures forever.*

Psalm 136:7

Total walked: *835 kilometres*

# The Broken Body, a Midnight Puma & the Barrel of a Gun

*February 2007*

The goal for the first two weeks of February was simple; traverse the Amazon Basin quickly using any means possible, walking only the streets of the few towns dotted along the Trans-Amazonian highway. I had to try and keep a lid on the nervous energy of having to cover the required distances between towns and not be left stranded in the middle of the Amazon.

After a short walk I scored two consecutive lifts on small motorbikes and, like Dumb and Dumber, we zipped along the dirt highway until lunchtime. I grabbed lunch at an army checkpoint, but was handed a plate of rice with strips of boiled sheep guts. No sauce. No pepper. Just boiled sheep guts on rice. The pressure was on to eat what was in front of me, so I said grace, picked up a fork-full of rice and tripe and shoved it in my mouth. The rice was consumed within a few seconds, but the rubbery tripe just wouldn't break down. It was so chewy that I nearly gagged. So I just swallowed the slippery, tasteless strip and set about disposing of the rest.

The family dog brushed past my leg. I peered down under the table and it gazed up with big brown eyes that seemed to say, "May I have some tripe, Sir?" Not wanting to offend the cooks, I scooped up rice with the fork while inconspicuously scooping up a piece of tripe with my fingers at the same time. The rice was delivered to my mouth, the fork then lowered to my lap and the piece of tripe dropped straight into the dog's waiting mouth.

With precision teamwork we finished off that entire meal.

After a little more walking through no-man's land, I was sitting up in a cattle truck next to three men. The driver insisted I have one drink with them and I have no idea what they poured me, but I'd suggest it was highly flammable. I in turn explained why I was walking and invited them to pray for unity. One nodded in agreement. The other two just laughed and drank up.

I asked the men what dangers I should be aware of out there and they launched into accounts of panther attacks. Great. Each man produced a large knife, explaining that panthers lie in wait and attack without warning. My eyes were wide open. "Have any of you been attacked?" The truck driver rolled up his sleeve and then pulled up his shirt. Long scars stretched across both. And with that, they wished me well.

There were a few hours of sunlight left as I pushed on along the narrowing orange-red sandy clay road with tall grass and clumps of forest closing in.

"Don't hit it to me!" I walked down the middle of the road praying my heart out.

The sun set well before I reached the town, but a humble fellow in a secluded hut at the bottom of a steep, slippery gully, invited me in to share dinner by candle light with his friends, and to sling my hammock on the veranda. Looking up at the moon resting above the Amazon, with frogs in full chorus, the isolation was inescapable. I'd never felt so far from home.

A petrol tanker hauled me the remaining 100 kilometres to Novo Repartimento the next morning, where I spotted a nun walking down the street. I caught up to her to ask for directions to the church, but she ignored me and kept walking. I repeated in Portuguese, "Excuse me. I'm a Catholic missionary from Australia. Do you know where the church is?" She put her head down and quickened her pace.

A good thing I didn't ask for food or money.

Altamira was a few hundred kilometres further into the Amazon and, while waiting for the bus, I sat under a tree in the town centre. A boy of about ten years of age came over, stood a small distance away and stared at me. When I said hello he responded with a massive smile and asked what all my gear was for. I tried to explain in Portuguese and he was shocked that I couldn't speak his language properly. Despite his age, Junior carried a shoe shining block with polish and cloths inside. He plonked it on the ground, sat on it and fired questions at me. When I pulled out my camera to show him some photos he nearly wet himself with joy. I didn't want to laugh, but his reactions were so innocent that I couldn't help it.

I asked about his job and the sort of life his family lived. It was pathetically basic and every wage helped. He admitted that they didn't always have food but sometimes things were great and they had two meals a day. I asked if I could pay him to polish my boots and he smiled, jumped off his polishing box and prompted me to put my boot up on it, but nearly had a laughing fit when he saw the size of them. He screamed at a friend to come and see. He was so daunted at how much work he had to do, so I reassured him, "I'll pay you double." It was a done deal and he worked hard, bringing them to a smooth shine.

I excused myself to walk across to a supermarket to gather food supplies, but Junior trailed me, hauling his work with him. I knew what I was after in the shop, but Junior still pointed out what was good and what was not. I asked him, "What would you like? Pick anything." He pulled his bottom lip in under his teeth and looked around before pointing to yoghurt. Good kid, my favourite too. I grabbed a tub each and we wandered back across the road to the tree to eat in silence. When the bus pulled in Junior said goodbye, smiled broadly and walked off lugging his work tools.

Along the 300 kilometres to Altamira we bogged down a number of times and had to get out to push. The slippery clay stuck to everything: the tyres, my polished boots and the clothes of the one guy who face-planted while pushing. We slipped and slid past stripped jungle, over-grown farmland and matted bush. It was wild and remote … just not the Amazon Rainforest.

The bus pulled up at the enormous, bridgeless, Xingu River well after sunset, and gently boarded a barge. Most passengers stayed curled up in their seats, but I stepped out to admire the scene. The only manmade light along the riverbanks was from the tiny barge office on each side, other than that the wide flat river lined with thick forest was in a dark blue haze under a shimmering moon. The deep chug of the diesel engine and the lapping of the Xingu's waters were the only sounds to be heard. It was beautiful.

We reached Altamira an hour later and I jumped off into an empty, poorly lit street. I was all alone. I had no idea in what direction to head, so I randomly chose right and walked on, eventually finding a rundown hotel.

At the Catholic church the next morning I met Diego, an English-speaking student of the Austrian-born bishop who was teaching him German. Diego assured me that he'd personally pass the invitation on to him. I noticed a poster on the wall of an older Caucasian woman, then a framed picture of her, before a young girl walked in wearing a t-shirt with her on the front. I turned to Diego, "Who is this lady?"

Dorothy Stang was an American nun working in Altamira alongside the bishop. She was a fervent defender of the poor, the marginalised and the abused, but also spoke out against illegal logging, poor work conditions, human rights abuses and land grabbing by ranchers and loggers. Stang stepped on many bad toes and for her efforts she was shot dead in a remote jungle village in February 2005.

Her death had become the exclamation mark of her life with international condemnation prompting the Brazilian government to take a more proactive role in preserving the Amazon rainforest and its people. Diego sighed, "It still isn't safe here though, particularly in the jungle." There remained substantial ill feeling between rival parties, but Sister Dorothy Stang remained a symbol of change and of stewardship for God's gifts.

I walked out along the main street past a few locked churches, with a number of locals directing me up a dead end road into thick jungle … deliberately? A young man came to my aid and redirected me. Walking was difficult in the sweltering heat, particularly sections that were re-stepped under the gaze of people who didn't want me there.

I landed a succession of short lifts, eventually getting crammed into a combi van with twelve others hidden behind bags or sitting on the floor. It was absurd! The incessant heat took it beyond a joke and with all the slipping, sliding, bumping and thumping I quickly felt ill. The loud over-revving engine just added to the uncomfortable space. We fell out of the van fifty kilometres later onto the sticky clay of Mineirinho as if being re-born. Fresh air! The invitation to pray for unity spread fast in the town with excitement.

My original concerns about walking along deserted clay roads through a stinking hot jungle teeming with all manner of dangerous animals had swayed me to not attempt it. It was indeed hot and sticky and the distances were long, but that was about it. The dangers associated with the jungle seemed distant and the only animals I'd seen in abundance were Hereford cows. I wanted nothing more than to just walk and pray, so I ditched the bus and left Mineirinho on foot for a few hours of mud-walking.

As lunch approached I scraped a few kilograms of clay off my boots and thumbed a ride from a log truck. It drew alongside me at near walking pace and the driver motioned for me to jump on as he continued up a steep hill. I scrambled on and found a place on the back of the open floor trailer, standing on the beams running across at metre intervals. In between them there was nothing but a straight drop to the road. We continued on up and down and side-to-side for forty kilometres, picking up speed in parts. It was like standing on a balance beam during an earthquake; I hung on to the safety beam behind the cab. And as if that wasn't intense enough, directly below me was the spinning driveshaft with only a few metres back to the hurtling trailer tyres.

One slip would be unforgiving.

I couldn't let the moment pass without capturing it on film ... only, the camera was in my backpack. I tightened my grip on the safety beam, checked through the cab's window that the road ahead was flat, took a settling breath and went for it, undoing the straps with my left hand and slipping my left arm out. I reached up to grab the safety rail, freeing the right hand, and brought it through with the intention of holding on to the strap and swinging the bag to my feet. However, halfway through ... Thump! Thump! ... the semi smashed through two potholes. The loose pack swung wide and the momentum crashed me into the safety beam; I held on with one hand like a cowboy on a bucking bronco. Just as I regained my balance, we hit another hole and it nearly sent me swinging around the other way. My teeth were gritted and my left arm strained to bursting point.

With the Amazon still flying past, I reefed the pack off, swung it down onto the beam and swapped hands, grabbing the camera. I slid my hand into its side strap just before … Thump! Thump! … we slammed through a few more potholes. I squeezed my knees into the bag while tightening my grip on the safety bar. It was at about that point that I thought maybe it hadn't been the best decision to grab the camera. I opened up the screen with my mouth and filmed some vertigo-inducing footage, describing what was happening, but it was difficult to hear anything over the roaring engine.

I eventually couldn't hold on any longer so, with another check of the road ahead, I turned and faced the back of the trailer with my heart racing. In one quick, fluent motion I let go of the railing, held onto my bag and let my backside slip down onto the beam I stood on while throwing my feet out across the gap to the next beam a metre away, firming up my position. Touchdown. Within seconds though … Thump! … I lost contact with the two beams and was airborne, clasping my backpack. Time stretched out as the road flew beneath me. With a painful thud, I landed back on the beam and threw my hands underneath it to stop it happening again.

After a few more potholes and careering through an overgrown bush sending twigs flying everywhere, I was relieved to eventually jump off.

All the churches in Uruará were locked, so I turned my attention to the road to Santarém. I hoped to travel along a little known 200 kilometre track cutting through the thick jungle to the banks of the Amazon River, but a few locals just shook their heads, saying there was no such road. I told them that the road would likely be known as just a track that headed into the jungle, but I had no idea how deep it penetrated.

I ended up on the north-western corner of Uruará looking down a back-road disappearing into the jungle's depths. Like a conquering prince, a young man named Tiargo trotted down the street on a stunning white horse. He stopped to say hello, so I asked if the track continued to Santarém. He thought for a moment, then slowly nodded his head, "Yes, it does. Many tracks out there though. Tracks for loggers. I've heard you can make it through." There was no way I was going to attempt a 200 kilometre crossing on foot through the jungle where unsigned tracks split, so I wandered back into town to ponder a plan.

I passed an Assembly of God church with a few people sitting out the back and they welcomed me with open arms, inviting me to share their barbequed food while the pastor rang an English-speaking member of the congregation. Manuel arrived soon after and through him I was invited to attend their evening service, before staying the night at his home.

The Assembly of God service was prayerful and, although I couldn't understand what was being said or sung, I understood its context. The pastor invited me to share the mission through Manuel's interpretation and everyone had a bible in hand so I referred to a few unity passages while extending the invitation. I thought everything had gone well, but it turned ugly. A number of the congregation were indignant that a Catholic had come into their church talking about unity and one young woman, who spoke fluent English, said: "I have a university education, I'm a lawyer, and I don't ever take things on face value. If you read your bible you'll find that the Catholic Church's teachings are not Christian!"

I screwed my lips up. "Well, I too have a university education and I too don't take things on face value. I am Catholic and believe the Catholic Church is fully Christian." It was the wrong thing to say. The invitation was lost and she angrily cut loose with, "Unity already exists within the Church! You Catholics just aren't a part of the Christian Church!" She ripped into me about the idolatry of statues and how we should only worship God, so I tried to explain that Catholics don't worship statues, but she wouldn't accept it and told me that I should stop my journey and just go home, adding, "Your mission is stupid."

The pastor stepped in with a smile, insisting that I stay in town for a while so he could teach me about the bible. I ignored his patronising comment, reaffirming that I was moving on. It was humbling. This was the exact reason why I was praying for unity.

Manuel patted me on the shoulder and invited me back to his house for dinner. He didn't say a word about the argument, but his wife couldn't hold back. Over dinner she became irate, at a loss as to why a statue-kissing, Mary-worshipping Catholic would have any interest in the Christian Church that worshipped Jesus alone. As much as I tried to explain that I was Christian and that I didn't worship Mary or statues or anything other than God she wouldn't accept it. I explained what the Catholic, Orthodox and Anglican Churches held the role of Mary to be within the Church, but that just agitated her more to the point of listing off what true Christians believe. Regardless of how many of her tests I passed, she continued to slam me for being a heretic. Manuel tried to change the subject, but she wouldn't let go, so he straight up told her to be quiet.

After dinner, Manuel and I wandered outside, apologising to each other. His home was incredible. Being a saw-miller he had plenty of resources to draw from, but in light of all the deforestation I'd seen and, with the story of Sr Dorothy Stang in mind, I politely asked what it was like being a saw-miller out there. Manuel sighed, "It is difficult because I come under fire for damaging the forest, but I believe my business is sustainable with good employment and good conditions for employees. We take good care of the jungle. We only log small areas, which are regenerated straight away. I am very happy with the new government regulations. The logging industry must always remain accountable." He thought for a moment and smiled, "I love the jungle. There's nothing like it and I hope it will always be there for everyone to enjoy. It's delicate." To my surprise he then commented on the murder of Dorothy Stang, "She was doing a good thing. She was standing up for the environment and for the people. There are dangerous people here and they are very greedy."

The orange Amazon clay had stained the bottom half of my trousers, so Manuel's wife kindly washed them. As she cleaned my burnt-orange shirt though I had to step in to tell her that every time I washed it orange die ran from it. She thought it was clay residue though and kept on washing. She wouldn't believe me and continued scrubbing away, ignoring my pleas to stop, "It isn't clay!" I just had to let her wash and wash.

Manuel confirmed that the road on the edge of town did cut through to Santarém on the Amazon River and an hour later proudly announced that he'd found a lift for me with one his workers. I was so happy.

The five-hour-long track through thick brooding jungle was stunning. Small logging plots with loggers working hard appeared amongst the vegetation occasionally before we disappeared back into thick jungle. Roads continually branched off and it wasn't at all obvious which track to take, but the driver knew exactly where we were. The jungle encroached so jealously on the road that it looked like it would soon reclaim the strip we drove along. We were a dot in an ocean of green.

The driver lost control on the slippery clay and did a full 180° spin … we continued down the road backwards. Despite the jungle growing right up to the track's edge, the pick-up didn't touch the surrounding vegetation. He apologised for the slip-up, but I just laughed, "That was brilliant!" It took a few minutes to turn the vehicle around with a cramped 7-point turn.

The forest ended abruptly as clear-felled strips of soybeans reached from horizon to horizon. Stripping a forest to replace it with a cash crop was pitiful and it made me hotter under the collar than anything I'd seen along the 843 kilometres from Marabá.

I wandered the streets of Santarém the next morning and caught my first glimpse of the mighty Amazon River. It was so much larger than I imagined. The opposite bank was barely visible and boats—from commercial fisherman to freightliners, passenger liners, yachts and tiny tinnies—filled the port. The area was so dependent on river travel that a floating Shell petrol station sat 100 metres offshore. The wonder of it didn't last long. A man walked past me, up to the water's edge in the middle of town, dropped his strides and opened his bowels into the river.

The ferry service to Manaus—nearly a thousand kilometres upstream—was still on its downstream run, and I was told it would be in at 2 am. I used the time to find a few churches, but no one was particularly interested in the mission, so I sat in an internet café to write my first blog. Two Australian friends had set up the walk4one website. I'd wanted to it to be pray4one, but they'd vetoed me. walk4one it was.

Later, I ran into two young Polish men and when they found out I was heading to Sunday Mass one of the guys lit up, "Oh, fantastic! I wanted to go today. I didn't even see a church though." His friend wasn't as excited, but hadn't been in a while so thought he probably should. The church was closed for repairs, so Mass was held in a large room above the parish offices. All the plastic chairs, most likely borrowed from the local pub, had the local beer's emblem plastered across the back. The three of us struggled to contain our laughter, "And tonight's Mass is brought to you by Cerpa Draught Beer."

On the ferry for a three-day trip on the Amazon to Manaus

I headed back in the late evening and sat at a small palm-roofed bar on the end of the wharf with a handful of English-speaking entertainment crew from an enormous docked cruise ship. The most outspoken guy was a Brit named Ashley, the ship's cabaret singer, and he had everyone singing along to tune after tune. If we didn't know the words it didn't matter, he just kept singing, while telling us how pathetic we were.

The ferry arrived behind schedule at 5 am, by which time I was exhausted. I bought my ticket and stepped on board to claim my hammock-swinging space. The departure time came and went while bags of rice were loaded. I could do nothing but wait. Stairs led up onto the roof, so I spent my time resting there with a view, watching the river life. When I returned to my hammock the ferry was full to capacity and everyone had slung a hammock, all 150 of them in a blaze of colour. The two hammocks either side of me were so close to mine that I was left with no way to get in. I just untied mine and searched for a new spot, which ended up being crammed underneath the noisy stairwell.

The ferry's engines finally revved up at 4 pm and we pushed off, crashing into the floating service station and crumpling its roof, before heading out across the river; Santarém, and an angry service station owner, slowly disappeared from view. The meeting of the muddy brown Amazon and clear Tapajós River set a distinct contrast down the middle of the river. We began on the Tapajós side, approached the precise line of muddy water and, with some sense of occasion, crossed the adivide. We were on the Amazon River.

Men cut through the vast wilderness paddling dugout canoes back to their swamp-dwelling stilt houses and the sunset splashed speckled colour across the landscape. The passengers introduced themselves slowly, uniting as a type of crammed family for the three-day trip. I was the only non-Brazilian, so was welcomed with curiosity, particularly as to why I was riding 'cattle class' with them.

Of all the perilous stuff I'd done so far, it was frustrating to sustain a bad injury while preparing to sleep. I placed one leg into the hammock and slid down, but this put all the sliding weight onto the left buttock and the top of my hamstring tore. It was like being set on fire and I curled up clutching my butt. Proper treatment wasn't available in the Amazon, and as I continued on in the weeks to come, scar tissue would form and cause intense pain for years to come. I also couldn't sleep on my back in a hammock: not easy.

I couldn't move much as we ploughed the waters west towards Manaus. When I jumped off in Manaus, a Muslim by the name of Mohammed walked me slowly to the city centre on his way home. He showed great interest in the mission for Christian unity, particularly the possibility of one day having unity for all who believed in God. He understood the need for unity amongst Christians, and for Muslims, commenting that various 'truths' had created much confusion. He wished me well and offered his prayers for the unity of Christians, Muslims and Jews. I was honoured to have met Mohammed.

In the sticky humidity of the historical city plaza was the Manaus Opera House. I spotted a tour group following their English-speaking guide, who turned out to be a cabaret singer named Ashley. We greeted each other with a big handshake and laughingly compared our respective journeys from Santarém. He invited me to join in his tour, so I followed along, relaxed and listened, and learnt all about the city in the heart of the Amazon.

I found a few churches where the invitation was well received and, at the final church—a huge Catholic one—the priest ushered me down to the presbytery to shower and rest. It was brilliant. One church worker named Paul helped spread the invitation to pray at 4:01.

I was on a bus in the evening for the long trip north through the night to Boa Vista. The 750-kilometre trip was uncomfortable with my knees jammed against the seat in front and the headrest finishing at my shoulders. Sleeping was but a dream.

I wasn't scheduled to start walking again until I'd crossed the Grand Savannah wilderness, 236 kilometres north of the Venezuelan border, but the conditions were great. I would have loved to have added a few extra weeks to take in more of the Amazon on foot, but that wasn't the mission plan. To make it back to Sydney in time for World Youth Day, which would provide a substantial platform to spread the invitation to pray for unity, was all-important. I did have a few days spare though, so from Boa Vista I headed off on foot towards Milagre, and the Venezuelan border.

In a conversation with a passing German tourist I was asked how old I was. I replied, "Twenty-seven," and the conversation moved on but, later, I suddenly interrupted him: "Hang on a second! What's the date today?"

He pondered for a moment, "It's the 10th of February."

I laughed, "I'm twenty-eight! Today's my birthday!" When there's no one to celebrate with, or wish you a happy birthday, I guess it's not that important.

I walked and prayed, thanking God for the journey across Brazil and interceding for the churches I'd passed. The torn hamstring had affected my sleep, but held up okay as I hobbled along. My injured body was a little like the injured Church. Over the twenty-eight years of my life to that point I'd broken fifteen bones, dislocated my shoulder several times with two subsequent shoulder reconstructions, had two ankle reconstructions, seven stitches in my finger, three in my eye-brow, skinned my foot, split my kidney in half (that one nearly killed me), had pneumonia twice, was asthmatic as a child, was bitten by a snake and—once upon a time—tore my left hamstring in a hammock. All those injuries hurt, some more than others, and most would have stopped me from walking to the shop, let alone 900 kilometres on foot across Brazil, yet despite those injuries I was still able to walk a lot further than your average postman. Each injury received treatment and was allowed time to heal, as frustrating as that often was. It required humility to slow down and allow healing to take place and it often hurt even more in attending to it. A classic case was putting a dislocated shoulder back in while everyone else stood around pointing at me in horror. The same was true for the church. For divided Christians it requires humility and patience to allow injuries to heal and more often than not it's the initial tending to that hurts most. The consequence of not tending to injuries though is far worse and unfortunately that's what we appear to have. If the doctor had discarded the part of my body that was injured because it no longer functioned as it should, I'd have one leg, no arms, a pretty warped torso and a toothless smile.

The Church—the Body of Christ—is even more disfigured.

After a number of hours of walking and then two consecutive lifts I was standing on the Venezuelan border, 1,678 kilometres from Santarém. A mischievous border guard tested my walking poles while I took in the view out across the incredible Venezuelan highlands of sweeping savannah surrounded by towering flat-topped mountains. It reminded me of Tasmania. The air was cool and there was no trace of the Amazon Basin. Brazil was such a diverse, incredibly challenging, but beautiful experience. I lamented not walking as much as I'd planned, but was satisfied with how far the mission had come. Brazil was the training ground. The real fight now began.

I wandered into the town of Santa Elena de Uairen, which looked as if it had dropped from the sky onto the hilly slopes, forming neatly to its contours. I'd been told Portuguese and Spanish were similar and that while I learnt the new language most Venezuelans would understand my Portuguese, but they were wrong. My Portuguese wasn't good enough.

The church there was home to hospitable Franciscan friars who eagerly taught the Spanish I'd need for the months ahead. Asking a Franciscan to pray for unity was a bit redundant. It was already a strong part of their lives. That being said, I hoped the flame might have been re-lit, if needed.

I stayed in Santa Elena de Uairen for Sunday Mass and morning tea in the packed church courtyard, reminiscent of 15th century castles with high sandstone walls, elaborate arches and open hallways lining it. The youth played hilarious games in the courtyard that didn't highlight a victor, but a despondent loser. I was welcomed with smiles and hugs.

I wasn't due to start walking until I was on the northern side of the expansive Grand Savannah wilderness, 236 kilometres away, but I was now aware of what I'd be missing out on and I had a few days to play with, so I decided to walk as far as I could each day, then grab a lift as needed.

I set out under the hot sun, but with a cool breeze blowing. The hills gave way to vast grass savannah surrounded by mammoth 3,000 metre high mountains that rose straight up and were dead flat on top. Even from thirty kilometres away I could make out huge waterfalls cascading off them. The tallest waterfall in the world, Angel Falls, was only a hundred kilometres to the west, but the ones I saw were impressive enough. There was no sign of civilisation. It was absolutely brilliant. Every hill presented a new breathtaking view of mountains, rivers and sweeping savannah between them. I wished a few friends were there to experience it with me. It was an easy place to be drawn into prayer. Those Franciscans were onto a good thing.

I sat my camera down on a guidepost to do a monologue with views of mountains, palm tree clusters and sweeping plains behind me, but when I squatted in front of the camera I got the fright of my life. On the LCD screen I could see a man standing directly behind me. I stumbled to my feet. Where the hell did you come from? The young indigenous man, dressed in a colourful handwoven vest, just stood there staring at me. He smiled and raised his hand for a split second. It took a while for my heart rate to slow down. All he wanted to know was what the thing on the guidepost was. He was as innocent as could be and genuinely inquisitive. With a few of my muesli bars in hand he walked back out into the vast open grasslands, leaving me wondering where on Earth he'd come from. The nearest trees were kilometres away and the steep, grassy hill I was on swept down smoothly without anywhere to hide. I was at a loss.

I walked on into the evening where a few soldiers at a checkpoint organised a large meal for me, and then a lift in a large rickety 1960s truck that had just rolled in. The driver didn't want to give me a lift, but he was less keen to argue with a semi-automatic toting soldier. I scored a night-time ride to the next town.

There was so little in the settlement that all I was able to secure for breakfast was water and a bottle of lemonade. Walking on across the plains with a sloshing stomach was not nice. The scenery was magnificent—amazing waterfalls cascading through the savannah—but all I wanted was food. Pushing on for hours with my stomach turning itself inside out, I prayed a rosary to draw my focus away from the hunger. It mostly worked.

After three hours I was able to scrounge a bread roll from a national park ranger, but was unable to secure a lift. I had to wait until one-thirty in the afternoon for some breakfast at a roadside kitchen. I was exhausted. A town called Km88 was my official starting point for walking again, but it was still more than a day's walk from there. I'd seen enough of the unscheduled Grand Savannah, so I tried to hitch a ride …

… without luck.

After an hour of waiting I lay down in the middle of the empty road. It was surreal, laying there with no traffic for miles, staring up into the blue sky watching a wispy cloud turn itself inside out. I lay there a long time. No breakfast followed by a huge lunch zapped my energy reserves.

Eventually two chatty men picked me up and drove down along a steep winding mountain pass sweeping into steaming jungle. I'd been looking at massive mountains while walking, but had no idea that the savannah itself was so high up to start with. Rounding successive tight corners through overhanging jungle, the men warned me of its dangers, pointing to the edge of the jungle and shaking their fingers, "Panteras y pumas". They mimed the action of the big cats swiping and killing a person. They made their point.

Km88 had 'wilderness frontier' written all over it. Jungle hung out over the one solitary street lined with houses as if trying to swallow it back up. All the cars were either beaten up four-wheel drives or random coloured 1970s petrol guzzling V8's with absurdly wide tyres—and they were everywhere. The town strip rumbled to their beat. To top it off, everyone looked like a stereotypical bandana wearing, goatee-toting, drug trafficking gangster: only, smiling.

The next morning I walked into their bank to withdraw some money, but I knew I was in trouble when I handed over my debit card and the teller looked at it quizzically, trying to figure out what it was. They had no electronic facilities. All the other customers carried little blue bankbooks. After some negotiating, the bank manager kindly agreed to exchange my last Brazilian cash for Venezuelan notes at an inflated price.

The stinking hot humidity and thickness of the jungle defied description. I was only an hour out of Km88 when I walked past a couple of purple leaves beside the road. It took a moment to sink in, but the bigger picture came into focus and in a heart-stopping moment I scampered to the middle of the deserted road with my legs nearly giving way. The 'leaves' belonged to the camouflage pattern of a four metre long boa constrictor. Only then did I realise that it was road kill.

Even dead snakes scared me.

I prayed a rosary as I walked on until reaching a small village tucked into the jungle. I stumbled through Spanish trying to order a few things at the shop, but the ten-year-old behind the counter piped up with, "What do you want? You can speak in English. We all speak English." I couldn't believe it. Guyanese refugees had settled the entire village … they were West Indians!

I was invited into a house for lunch and a hilarious discussion on cricket with the mother of the home. She was a huge Ricky Ponting fan. She gave me a big kiss on the cheek for Valentine's Day, so I, in turn, extended the invitation to pray for unity. It led to a more serious discussion about their lives as refugees from a persecuting government. They lamented that many of those who forced them out of Guyana called themselves Christians and attended church. Praying for unity wasn't a magic fix, but it was also more than just a start. Their hospitality was beautiful.

After a restless night in my hammock under an outdoor awning in the next village, I hit the road under the cover of darkness with the first morning light not far away. Enjoying the near silence of the jungle-clad road, I wondered if pumas roared in the mornings like lions do. I kid-you-not, within one minute, a deep domineering roar rumbled through the jungle. It was exciting and frightening. I quickened my pace, keeping an eye on the jungle. The big cat let rip with a deep raspy roar every thirty seconds or so until I'd left the area.

By lunchtime, I'd met another Guyanese refugee named Daniel. He was a quietly spoken, shirtless, proud-looking native Indian with long black flowing hair tied back with a bandana. Daniel invited me to his home and on the way he climbed a coconut tree and threw down a couple of yellow coconuts, then made an incision in them with his machete and offered me a sweet drink. His timber house overlooking the village was simple.

I told Daniel about the puma I'd heard that morning and he acknowledged that they were around. I imitated the low, raspy roar and Daniel stopped smiling. With his sternest West Indian accent he corrected me, "That's not a puma, man. That's a jaguar. There aren't many of them, but they're here. Be even more careful of them!" Jaguars added a little spice to the area. Daniel taught me the difference between the two big cats' roars, and what to do if I encountered either. It essentially came down to, "Stand tall, don't run, make a lot of noise and throw at it anything you have."

I walked on from there watching the side of the road intently, all the way to the town of El Dorado. I was given a hotel room with dirty sheets and no running water. It was uncomfortable after such a humid day.

My feet were hurting the next morning so I carried my boots and wore flip-flops through the town. No one was at the church, so I grabbed breakfast and sat on the side of a large flowing river. The rough gold-mining town was in full swing, transporting workers and petrol up to the mine sites using narrow longboats. The shore was abuzz. I hadn't been there long before a young man walked past and announced for everyone to hear, "Bye, bye gringo!" Everyone laughed. Gringo was a term used either to identify a person from the United States, or as a derogatory slur at a white man. Only a few had the decency to even look at me while they laughed. He lowered a large fuel can into his boat and turned back to me, reiterating sternly, "Bye, bye gringo." There were a few smiles, but no laughter this time. He turned to his friends and smiled as he stepped up to the front of his longboat and flicked his hand at me with a gesture of 'get lost'.

I'd never been harassed due to my skin colour and, as minor as the incident may have seemed, it ate at me. I stared him down while he continued leering at his friends. I couldn't stand it. I called out to him in Spanish, "Idiota!" and then let fly in English with what I thought of his attitude, education and lack of love. Not one person was taller than my chest so when I stood up they pushed right back. I kept a firm stare on him. The foreshore ground to a halt. He kept sniggering at his mates, so I approached the boat, maintaining my angry lecture in English.
I knew he couldn't understand what I was saying, but I knew he understood the sentiment.

As the people in front of me stepped aside his smile vanished and he scampered to the back of the boat. My toes dipped in the river's edge as I asked him in Spanish, "What's the problem?" He hastily tried to start the engine, so I picked up a stone from the river. Everyone took a backwards step thinking I was going to throw it, but I called out, "Hey!" and pointed to the rock, holding it up for him to see, and drew the comparison between the rock and his heart. I think he got the message. His mates on the foreshore just looked at the ground.

I tossed the rock into the river and walked back up through the silent crowd, leaving the fellow in the boat continuing to try to start the engine. Having stood in the edge of the river my flip-flops were wet and I could feel them slip with each step so, to save the embarrassment of slipping over in front of everyone, I sat down in the middle of the entire El Dorado mining workforce and put my socks and boots on. The crowd maintained their stare at a distance.

I walked off seething, not knowing how to deal with it. I started walking the forty kilometres to Suasua, but on the way out of town I again caught the brunt of racial slurs: men drove up and down the road yelling at me. I felt unsafe, but once I'd passed the town border they left me to walk on alone. I had a long time to ponder the wisdom of picking a fight in such an isolated town.

The jungle gave way to swathes of dry farmland, banana plantations and simple tin and mud-brick homes. Remnant jungle existed in pockets and metre high grass stretched along the road. Every time traffic passed by I had to step into it and my legs were scratched to smithereens. I prayed while covering as much distance as I could by sunset, stopping only once at a small roadside restaurant with an enormous anaconda skin stretched across the wall inside. The owner asked if I knew where the anaconda skin had come from, then pointed out the window,

"In that swamp. Be careful."

I lost my appetite.

When night fell, Suasua was nowhere to be seen. To conserve my torch batteries I opted for the silence of the dark night, but it was so dark that I couldn't even see my hand in front of my face. I wasn't sure where I was headed, but had a sense that God had me covered somehow. Time dragged out miserably and after a few hours dense jungle again lined the road. In the darkness I was unaware that I was passing an unlit hut until a large guard dog charged me, barking ferociously.

I nearly peed my pants. I scampered into the darkness, not being able to see a thing, but not wanting to flick my torch on in case I drew more unwanted attention. The dog drew back and I pushed on nervously. Then, in a frantic split second, I heard something of substantial size half a metre in front of me and frenziedly jagged back in near-paralysing fear. I stumbled towards the centre of the road away from the animal as it also recoiled from me. I flicked my torch on and with unfathomable relief I shone into the eyes of a very scared human. We had very nearly head-butted each other. He had no torch, so could see nothing but my blinding light as he backed away fearfully.

I shone the torch back on myself, half-blinding me, and spluttered an apology. When I flicked the torch back on him two little heads poked out from behind him: his sons, Fernando and Junior. They were trailing José, their dad, to their jungle home. I turned the torch back on myself and smiled a hello as I backed out further onto the road, giving them space. José hesitantly smiled.

"Where is Suasua?" I asked. He pointed back down the road. Apparently I'd passed the turnoff to Suasua ten kilometres earlier. I was so despondent. José tried to overcome the language barrier, asking why I was out on that lonely road. I explained with my poor Spanish before asking how much further it was to the next town. His answer was succinct, "Too far to make tonight." He insisted that I be their guest.

José and his two boys lived half a minute down the road at the little hut cut into the jungle. Under the guide of my torch we approached the now happy black Labrador guard dog. I told José I'd 'met' the dog a minute earlier and he just laughed knowingly. Their hut was incredibly basic. In Australia we'd call it a chicken coop. It was a double-roomed, dirt-floored, wire-mesh-for-windows, tin-nailed-onto-posts-for-walls home, but it was theirs. José lit a diesel-fuelled lamp and prepared dinner while Fernando and Junior sat beside me enthusiastically asking questions about the mission and journey.

We shared a simple Devon-sausage-on-bread dinner around the flickering lamp, before José invited me to sling my hammock. They disappeared into the adjacent room to a homemade king-size bed with three individual sleeping spots. There was no mattress, just blankets on a wooden platform. I swung to sleep with a view through the chicken wire of the quiet jungle and star-filled night sky.

After a splash-shower from a drum behind a banana tree I ate breakfast with José. He produced a large knife and told me he carried it to defend against pumas and jaguars. He warned that the puma, in particular, would sit low in the grass and swipe its claw at the leg of passers-by. He was firm, "Watch the tall grass on the roadside."

Fernando and Junior took turns riding the black Labrador like a horse, until it grew tired and lay down, so they grabbed what appeared to be their only toy; a small plastic ball. They placed a rock on the ground and took turns trying to hit it, all the while nagging José for something, persisting in holding out the plastic ball while Junior stood by frowning. José excused himself to the other room saying, "Okay, okay. I'll get it for you." The boys celebrated as José ducked into the other room and then returned, placing onto the table roll-on deodorant. He pulled out his huge knife and cut across the top of it before pushing down hard, "Pop!" Out shot an identical plastic ball to the first one. They now had a toy each. The boys ran around, picked it up, high-fived each other and drew a large circle in the dirt floor to play marbles and each victory was celebrated as though they'd won the World Cup. They had so little, yet somehow had more than most.

I handed José half my food supply as thanks for his hospitality, which he exchanged for his entire stash of fresh fruit and a ten Bolívar note, "For the mission." It was worth about half an Australian cent. I found a shiny Australian $2 coin in my wallet and handed it to him, much to Fernando and Junior's fascination. It was a long goodbye and they stood at the roadside seeing me off. Their simple life and hospitality to a complete stranger left an indelible mark.

I arrived late in the small town of Tumeremo and slept the night on top of my sleeping bag on the concrete floor of a cement box attached to the local church. It was muggy and uncomfortable. I didn't sleep well and the stifling hot thirty-nine kilometres to El Callao the next day was incredibly difficult. The heavily trafficked narrow road, with foot-high thorny bushes alongside it, made it practically impossible to step off. A number of drivers hit their horns aggressively and yelled out, "gringo!" until one driver actually swerved at me, forcing me to leap into the thorn bushes. Others then followed suit and even took to throwing projectiles. Sometimes they missed, sometimes they hit. At first I reacted in a way that had me apologising to God. By mid-afternoon I was bleeding, badly bruised and struggling in the heat.

I was nearly ready to go home.

As I entered an even narrower section of hillside road seven kilometres from El Callao, darkness fell. A beaten-up four-wheel drive approached from behind and without warning a full can of beer exploded into the bitumen between my legs, mid-stride, showering the grass in front of me for at least ten metres. I was so angry that I fastened my backpack straps and gave chase as he rumbled past. Did I think I was going to run down the speeding vehicle? No, I didn't think at all, I just ran until a car approached from ahead of me and in the darkness, with the headlights glaring, I slowed down and stepped off the road … unaware that the road dropped away sharply for a few metres. My left foot 'fresh-aired' and I crashed to the bitumen with a thud. I sat there in darkness holding my cut hands. I felt defeated.

I picked myself up slowly and walked on singing, 'The Lord is My Shepherd', partly for me and partly to ward off any lurking big cats. When I caught sight of the town lights tucked in behind the hills I began to run and prayers of thanks flowed.

The town's population had swollen three-fold and the town's streets were alive with music, dancing, food and cheer. It was Carnivale! I couldn't have cared less about Carnivale. Every hotel was booked up, but I passed an Anglican church with people cooking barbeques and socialising in the front yard and the Reverend Adams welcomed me with open arms, showing me to a safe, quiet space inside to sling my hammock. I soaked in an overdue shower and curled up in my hammock, bruised, aching and my ego dented, but safe in the Anglican church.

Welcome to Venezuela Sam, welcome to Venezuela.

After the short seventeen kilometres to neighbouring Gausipati, and another beer can hurled my way, I decided to take a good old-fashioned rest day, beginning with a huge breakfast the next morning at a small bakery. The Catholic priest was busy, so I extended the mission and headed off quietly, passing a group of teenagers playing with water bombs and water pistols. The adults lounging back in their street-side chairs yelled out, "gringo!" with accusing stares. The pressure built fast. I decided to not react as I'd done previously, but instead smiled and yelled back, "Venezuelans!" A few cracked a smile. In my best Spanish I explained why I was there. The teenagers motioned towards me and one teenager asked, "What are the poles for?" I showed him how they worked and handed them over. There was laughter and the mood lightened. The young man tried to use the over-sized poles with little finesse.

A young kid ran at me and pegged a water bomb into my chest, saturating me, so without a moment's hesitation I shoved my water tube into my mouth and shot the water straight back out onto his feet as he ran off, drawing cheers from the adults. I may have started to win the locals over, but I was now fair game and they wanted me drenched. I filled my mouth with water again, threatening to spit, warding the smiling

Carnivale in Venezuela!

assassins off, but they only grew more excited at the prospect of getting the Aussie gringo. A girl let fly with her water balloon and in a moment of surprising coordination I caught it safely and in one motion flung it back, bursting it across her back. It was on. Water flew everywhere and the adults joined in with massive buckets. It looked like getting out of hand. And it did. To my delight though, the poor kids were done-over by the adults who used me as bait to draw their attention away as they crept up from behind and emptied the buckets on them.

We sat around for the rest of the afternoon, sharing stories back and forth.

My 4 am start began with a hitch. The iron bar front door of the posada I had slept at was locked. I quietly searched for an exit in the pitch-black, but found nothing. "Lord, how do I get out of here?" I flashed my pen-torch around and suddenly lit up a man standing in front of me. He scared me half to death. I turned the torch onto myself, "Dónde está la salida?" (Where is the exit?). The man, who wasn't the owner, ushered me cautiously through the private residence attached to the side and out the front door.

The small town disappeared into darkness as a walked out under a moon-less, star-filled night with the Southern Cross sitting just above the horizon. The sweeping road through tall tussocky grass was lit up softly under the lights of the odd random car, but for the most part it was just in the company of stars. Ever so slowly, night faded until, ten kilometres into the day, the intense sun burst across the plains.

Monkeys in a cluster of intertwined trees chattered to me while the morning reprieve ended with a surge of commuters between towns. I stepped off into the tussocks and then back onto the road for as long as the traffic permitted, but was again forced to leap into thorns—or the hedge from hell—to dodge apparently homicidal drivers. Stinging dark-red Venezuelan acupuncture dots covered my legs, head and neck after I literally unplugged myself from thorns.

Praying as I walked on, I had the strangest sense. It felt like God was asking me a serious question; one I'd preferred not to hear. "Do you want the stigmata?" In the silence that pursued me afterwards I didn't know how to respond. The wounds of Christ would, well, make it difficult to walk! In any case, I seriously doubted my sanity or that God would ask that of me. I couldn't shake it though. I pondered the proposition. I concluded that if, in fact, God had asked me then I should trust Him. I took a settling breath and said, "Okay Lord, yes." I wasn't sure what to make of the uneasy prayer, but soon found a distraction: the roadside kilometre marker. It was marked 466 kilometres and, in an attempt to not think about that prayer, I repeated it over and over again, "Kilometre 466. Kilometre four sixty-six. Four sixty-six."

The road wound up through stunning small hills towards my destination of La Cruz (The Cross). My map showed it to be a town of 500–1000 people but, when I approached the forty kilometre mark on a sweeping corner, there was nothing but continued rural scramble. Where is La Cruz?

I met a young man selling drinks from a roadside caravan and I asked, "Where is La Cruz?"

He pointed back down the road, "It used to be down there, but there are no homes now." He then offered a warning. The surrounding hills were home to many pumas and they moved around a lot in the early evening. The sun was setting. Not exactly news I'd hoped for. I grabbed a few drinks and headed off, but looked back over my shoulder and noticed something written along the top of the caravan; Unidad en Cristo, meaning, Unity in Christ. "You've got to be kidding me?" I thought. I'd told him about the mission, but have no recollection of inviting him to join in that prayer. Perhaps he already was.

With the sun setting behind billowing clouds, sending streams of light in all directions, I was soon passing three-foot caiman lounging on the side of the road. I walked down the middle of the road singing Louis Armstrong's 'What a Wonderful World' to deter any nearby animals. They gave me a wide berth.

The next town was fifteen kilometres further on and when I arrived in darkness I was dumbfounded. The 'town' was nothing more than an unmanned power sub-station. I sat on the side of the road scouring my map under torchlight. It was another twenty kilometres to the next town, but I was out of food and water, fifty-five kilometres into the day and tired. The trees along the road were too small to sling a hammock from, so I studied my surroundings. The night sky had clouded over. There was no moonlight or starlight—it was very dark—but on the western horizon I could just make out the glow of lights on another hill. They looked like streetlights, but it was too far away to know for sure. I needed water, so I pressed on into the night.

Every so often I heard movement in the grass and generally managed to guess the animal before I turned the torch on: a rabbit, three cows, a large snake. My feet tired significantly until each step pained me. The walking poles became essential, so I tucked the torch away and continued on in darkness along the dead straight road.

BOOM! A gunshot ripped through the night and I nearly stumbled to the ground. It was so loud and so close. I was panicked, but remained silent in the darkness, scampering on down the road fast. From within the bush, off to the side, a vehicle started up and voices could be heard. They were hunters. I scurried on into the night as invisibly as I could.

The dehydration worsened to the point where my saliva glands stopped working and my organs began shutting down. The skin on my feet felt like it was lifting off the bone in one enormous blister, but the lights on the distant hill kept creeping closer. When I drew alongside I was shattered. It was a roadwork's depot with two very angry German Shepherds behind an enormous security fence.

The dogs smashed themselves into the fence at me, throwing foam from their snarling jaws. If I had any fluid left in my body I may have even cried. I was so thirsty, so hungry and so far from home. Ignoring the irate dogs I sat at the gate under the glow of an orange light and stared into the night. I prayed for a short time, but then staggered back to my feet. To where or why, I didn't know, but I hobbled on. I couldn't just stay there hurting so much.

Right on midnight, on that secluded country road, I realised I wasn't alone. Something moved in the tall grass two metres in front of me and I froze. It was of significant weight and made a sound through the grass like no animal I'd heard before. I knew what it was. It was as though I could see the shape of it through hearing alone. I fumbled for the torch, flicked it on and there, crawling slowly towards me through the dry grass, was a puma. Low to the ground, its paws inched forward—one at a time—and the only sound to be heard was the slow grate of grass opening up in front of it.

I've never been more scared in my life. The hair on the back of neck stood up on end and the errant thought ran through my mind, "Wow, it does stand up on end when you're really scared!" One walking pole was ready to poke and the other ready to whack in case it jumped. I obscured its vision with the torch, but even I had trouble seeing it amongst the tall grass. It had perfect camouflage. I shoved the emergency whistle on my top backpack strap into my mouth and blew it loudly, hoping to discourage it … but it kept creeping closer.

It was at least a good minute before I realised it was a good idea to walk backwards. I was so set to fight that the option of flight hadn't kicked in. Still blowing the whistle and keeping the torch fixed in its eyes I backed away on jelly legs. At that point it laid low in the grass. Paranoid that a second cat might be lurking nearby I flashed the torch around to make sure the coast was clear and then shone it straight back on the one I actually knew existed. I backed away one step at a time until I was well over 100 metres from it.

Three cars rounded the corner behind me, breaking the darkness. I stepped to the side and frantically waved them down, but the first two shot past without even slowing. I stepped out onto the road for the third car and pleaded for it to stop. They slowed to crawl, swerved to the side and accelerated past. I was alone in the night with a puma, which then let out a powerful roar. It sounded nothing like a lion. It sounded more like a house cat on steroids. It gave me more than enough incentive to keep shuffling back towards the orange glow of the roadwork's depot. The mangy German Shepherds were just as displeased to see me, but at least they couldn't get to me.

I tallied up the distance walked that day and figured it to be sixty-six kilometres. For the first time since it happened, I remembered kilometre four-sixty-six, and that question. I was exhausted, severely dehydrated, starving and scared out of my wits. Within that, I thought, were the wounds of Christ; unrelenting physical pain, complete mental anguish and feeling completely abandoned.

I caught sight of a security guard peering out through the window of a small cabin inside the depot, so I yelled in desperation, pleading for his help. It was agonising without saliva. He just shut the blinds and flicked the lights off, along with any hope of water.

Afraid and alone, I pulled my sleeping bag out and flicked it out over the ashen ground along the security fence. I figured the now calming German Shepherds would at least deter nearby pumas. It was February 21st 2007: Ash Wednesday. Twenty-one hours after the day had begun, I lay down to sleep, but stayed awake for a further three hours praying: "Jesus, I trust in you," until I closed my eyes and fell asleep at just past 4 am.

I doubt there has ever been a sweeter dawn to wake up to than the one on that Thursday morning an hour later. I could barely move, but the hope that the glimmer of light across the eastern horizon offered was unshakeable. I may have done serious damage to my feet and kidneys, but relative to a puma, those problems seemed tame.

I propped myself up against the gate, aimlessly watching the odd car pass by until one pulled over at sunrise. The whole ordeal appeared to be over. The driver opened his door and motioned for me to come. It was such an agonising struggle to rise to my feet and once up I lacked balance. With compassion, the man said he'd seen me the night before and thought, "No one will stop for him; he'll be there in the morning." He handed over a plastic bag full of bread-like doughnuts and a packet of eucalyptus lozenges and smiled, "Breakfast." I was so incredibly grateful, but could only manage a weak, "Gracias," before he closed the door and drove off leaving me standing there. "No, no, please! I need a lift. Please."

I slumped back down against the gate with the breakfast, but couldn't eat it. I had no saliva. I sat the bag on the ashen ground, unwrapped a eucalyptus lozenge and popped it in my mouth. It stayed there for a long time. I needed water.

An hour later I heard footsteps and turned to see the security guard and his wife approaching. Keeping their distance they asked who I was and what I was doing. Hardly raising my eyes I answered matter-of-factly, then begged one last time,

"Please, I need water." It came as a surprise to the wife when her husband walked back to fetch some. He slipped a bottle through the wire, giving no words, just a nod of the head. I drank only a tiny amount, not being able to stomach much more. He stood back with a solemn face, while his wife asked angry questions, making it clear that I wasn't welcome. When she returned to the cabin, her husband moved in closer, but not a word was spoken. His entire demeanour was apologetic. Whatever his wife saw in me, he saw something different.

I slowly consumed the water and then passed the empty bottle back through the fence. He nodded silently and returned to his guardhouse. Struggling back to my feet I stood at the roadside trying to thumb a ride. No one stopped for a few hours. It was so taxing. The car that did eventually stop carried a husband, wife and two children. There was no room for me, but that didn't matter. The kids squeezed over and they welcomed me in. "Gracias."

I was dropped on the edge of the next town of Upata, where I staggered to a small restaurant and ordered my first meal since midday the previous day. Fighting off sleep deprivation I struggled through the vegetable soup. My body resisted taking in any food, so it was a slow process. I was a wreck and fell asleep next door in a hotel for most of the remaining day.

When I woke, I finally had the energy to search for a church and carry out the mission. Standing upright was a struggle, but a warm shower sure helped and, after the evening Mass, I met two Polish Palotine fathers who spoke fluent English and welcomed me in for a barbeque dinner and beer. I hate beer, but this time it tasted fantastic.

With the sun having just risen, and feeling pretty good despite the previous forty-eight hours, I walked on for the thirty-five kilometres to the city of San Felix, being warned numerous times from people I met that it was the sort of place where a bullet to the head wasn't out of the ordinary. I moved cautiously as I ventured on further into adjoining Ciudad Guayana and then up to Ciudad Bolívar. The mission was received well everywhere I stopped.

I was biting off more than I could chew by walking on foot in that part of the world, and what lay ahead didn't fill me with any sense of security. I didn't even want to think about Colombia. It was one day at a time, and often one step at a time. I struggled to trust anyone: gradually I had started to assume danger everywhere. I had to keep finding innocence, or risk being crippled by fear.

I walked down to the Orinoco River for the longboat-ferry ride across the mighty river. It looked calm but, in the middle of the vast river, the current ripped under us, forcing the ferry off at an angle. A golden sun rose over the Orinoco through Ciudad Bolívar's hazy mist; it was a beautiful sight.

The riverside township of Soledade was a hive of activity; there were hundreds of students gathered to catch buses. I towered over them and they began chanting, "Hey Americano! Gringo! Gringo!" They gee'd each other on, except for the ones directly in front of me who backed away with wide-eyes. I said good morning to the students I made eye contact with, but the sound of, "Bye-bye gringo!" overpowered the small talk.

I pushed out into a long, hot, dead-straight and dead-flat fifty kilometre day with no civilisation apart from a few tiny stand-alone farmhouses. The intense heat was too much for the few litres of water I carried, so the few cashew trees growing along the road with their ripened fruit—bursting with juice—were a saving grace.

I slung my hammock at a roadhouse at day's end and then continued on to the rural city of El Tigre. I was stuffed when I arrived there, so I remained in El Tigre for a rest day. I found a fellow capable of nailing a new heelpiece onto my worn boots, then sat in a bakery owned by an energetic ex-USA citizen. I ate my three meals there and he joined me each time. He warned me sternly about El Tigre, "Two British tourists were mugged here last week. Be careful."

There was no staff present at the churches except for Freddie, a teenage boy considering a call to the priesthood. He was praying at his church when I rocked up, and I met with him twice that day for prayer before meeting the parish priest at evening Mass. Freddie did a bunch of introductions for the mission, and the padre did some during Mass.

Rested and backpack-laden with supplies, I set off from El Tigre at 4:30 am, crisscrossing the heavily trafficked country road seeking paths through the grass and bushes. There was no space to walk on the road's edge and without shade or opportunities to stop and rest; it was tough going.

At the twenty kilometre mark I found a clearing to sit down and eat my lunch at a pine tree bordered farm entrance. Five minutes and half a can of tuna later, thinking I was all alone, I was startled by a very soft, "Oi," from behind.

I swung around to be looking down the barrel of a pump action shotgun.

A frantic-looking wiry farmer was thrusting the firearm into my head while I stumbled to my feet, throwing my arms in the air, sending the tuna flying. He was so jittery I was worried that he might accidentally pull the trigger, let alone do it on purpose. I stepped away, knowing that the further I moved away from the shotgun the less damaging the lead-shot would be. The fence prevented him from walking after me, but he didn't back down.

I pleaded in Spanish for the gun to be lowered, but there was no light at the end of the barrel. He pumped the gun and sighted back along it. I cringed at every flinch. Time ground to a halt. Backed up to the edge of the road, with cars and semi-trailers hammering past, I yelled out in Spanish, "Please! There's no problem! I'm a Catholic missionary from Australia. I'm walking around the world praying for the unity of Christians. There's no problem!" I repeated it over and over again, but his sights remained fixed.

He yelled back angrily, "Gringo, go!"

He was giving me the chance to walk on, but it would be without my backpack or walking poles, which sat at his feet. I pleaded, pointing at the pack, "I have nothing else. Please sir, I need my bag. I'm a Catholic missionary from Australia. I am no problem for you."

He lifted his head slowly from behind the gun and asked, "No gringo?"

"Soy Australiano," I replied. He hesitated for a moment then lowered the gun. I repeated everything I could in Spanish and with a backwards nod he gestured for me to walk back over and reclaim my gear. But he didn't back away. I took the first step towards him with my hands still raised. I was so nervous that the only thing I could think to do was hold out my open right hand, smile

Mistaken identity in El Tigre

and enquire: "You want half a biscuit?" He grinned and declined when he saw the fist full of crumbs.

I reached down to grab my gear and he struck up a conversation with me; "What are you doing here?" I explained the mission again and as I stood back up I asked, "What was the problem? What did I do wrong?" He flicked his hand at my walking poles and muttered something about me being an American robber. Being a westerner in that country, I was discovering, was not favourable. He looked me up and down and smiled, "You are Australian!"

A padlocked chain was wound tightly around his front gate so I pointed to it and asked, "Why?"

He answered sternly, "It's dangerous around here."

Yeah, no kidding!

I pulled the backpack on, but he asked softly, "Why walk for unity?" My heart was pounding, so after a few calming breaths I removed the pack again and pulled out my itinerary, explaining from scratch why I was passing his property. He asked inquisitively, "How have all these towns treated you?" He was glad to hear I'd been received well in some and just smiled knowingly when I pointed out the places where I'd encountered racial abuse. "You look like a gringo," he said. "That's not good for you." He gestured to the ground and in Spanish said, "Sorry. Please sit down and finish your lunch." I'd lost my food and my appetite, so I thanked him and indicated that I'd walk on.

After only a few steps I turned back to him and asked, "Excuse me sir, that's a nice gun. May I take a photograph of you with your gun?" He didn't say a word. He just held the gun mid-chamber, rested the butt on his right hip and placed the other hand on his left hip, striking the quintessential gunman's pose. I couldn't believe it. I lined him up and took the shot.

On a massive adrenalin rush I walked on, praying through the sorrowful mysteries, thankful for getting out alive with a cool photo, and for Calvary. A gun to the head clears it a little.

In the hours to come I collected thirty-three random silver coins littered along the road, presumably from the badly rusted 1960s cars thumping past with holes in the floor. It was enough to cover the cost of my lost lunch.

I was out of water when I arrived in Meso de Guanipa and there was only one solitary locked building. There was, however, a broken down van full of workmen who reached into their cooler to fetch a beer for me. Funny how a non-beer-drinker like me ends an encounter with a puma and being held at gunpoint with a beer in hand. They assured me there were a few churches a couple of hours further on, so I ambled on to much appreciated hospitality and chicken and vegetable soup. The mission was received well by both the Pentecostals and Catholics in that town. They all said they'd keep me in their prayers, and I was grateful for that, because all I could see when I closed my eyes that night was a very dark gun barrel.

> *You have heard that it was said, 'You shall love your neighbour and hate your enemy.' But I say to you, Love your enemies and pray for those who persecute you.*
>
> Matthew 5:43–44

Total walked: *1,383 kilometres*

# Stonings, Rats & the Witness of Unity
*March 2007*

Each passing week presented a story I didn't particularly want my family to read on my blog. Their trust was significant. As it was, I walked into a new day with a huge smile. A close friend, Dave, had sent me a tongue-in-cheek email about pumas, having taken it upon himself to be my resident big cat expert. In brief, it read:

> Sam, I found some stuff on pumas. I've inserted my own advice—*highlighted*. I am, in fact, a puma expert (consider me your personal 'David Attenborough'), as you will see from my sound and well thought out logic.
>
> - Avoid hiking alone—*you will probably struggle with that one, unless you take my advice with the child: see below*—especially between dusk and dawn. This is when the puma usually does its hunting.
>
> - Make plenty of noise (e.g. talk) so as to reduce the chances of surprising a puma. *You will probably look insane although, judging by the niceness of the locals, you won't be losing any reputation points.*
>
> - Always keep children within arm's reach in areas that could conceal a puma. Pumas appear to be drawn to children. *A better idea would be to always have a child with you, so you could use it as bait, as you get your butt out of there.*
>
> - Pumas will normally avoid human contact at all cost. *You were probably wearing Lynx—puma deodorant.* If a puma is encountered, always remain calm and maintain eye contact.
>
> - DO NOT run away, this may trigger an attack response. *You are pretty fast, and trying to outrun a puma would look great on your blog ... and would also make a great epitaph.*
>
> - Make yourself look bigger by raising your arms. *You already look big—don't waste energy with your arms, maybe just make an angry face.*

- Small children should be lifted to avoid them panicking, this will also make the person look larger *and provide a terrific photo opportunity with a puma jumping two metres into the air to eat the child.*

- Avoid bending over or crouching. *As you may look like an attractive mate and death would be a better option. Although if you have the decision between a Brazilian man in the middle of the night, and a puma, just ask yourself: what would the blog-readers want? WWBW*

- Install motion-sensitive outdoor lighting. *It will probably require a budget of A$12,543,768.59 to pave your whole journey with lights but, hey, it'll get some media attention.*

- In the event of an attack, the only advice offered is to fight back. *In these situations, try to think about the movie* Crouching Tiger Hidden Dragon. *A better option would be* Conan the Destroyer. *Remember when Arnie punched the horse and knocked it out? Just do that.* People have, on many occasions, successfully driven off attacks with rocks, sticks and even their bare hands. *Guns are better.*

- Fortunately such attacks are rare. *And successful attacks often go undocumented, as the puma population is largely illiterate.*

If you have any more animal related enquiries Sam, just email.

Cheers, Dave.

I smiled all day.

A joyful family invited me to set up my hammock in their backyard and join them for dinner, and we sat out there late into the night, deep in conversation and Spanish lessons. The difficulties of the past few months were catching up with me. My reactions were changing. While leaning forward in my chair, the huge family dog jumped up and hit me in the face with his head. It hurt, but my reaction shocked me. I grabbed the dog around the throat, jumped up and threw him off to the side. He landed clumsily and trotted away with his tail between his legs. I snapped back to reality and was so embarrassed. Dogs aren't treated well in South America, so the family just laughed, but I had never reacted like that in my life. I quietly flicked pieces of food to the dog for the rest of the evening, slowly regaining his trust. I just wasn't sure that I trusted myself anymore.

The next day I made it to Santa María de Ipire. There was no padre, so I checked into a hotel and after reading for a while, I cut my toenails, but accidentally cut the left big toe nail a little short on one corner. I didn't give it a second thought, and if it didn't become so important later, I wouldn't even mention it.

By the time I'd walked thirty-six kilometres through stifling heat to the tiny roadside settlement of San Domingo, I was stuffed. I sat out the front of the shop on an old wooden bench under a tin veranda, removed my boots and rested my sore left big toe. The edge of the nail was rubbing against the skin.

I still didn't think it was much to worry about.

Sitting nearby was a frail old man watching the world go by. He fascinated me. He nodded hello when I sat down and as people visited the shop he said hello to them too, but most of them ignored him. When the local cheese man rocked up and weighed out 100 kilograms of the stuff, the old man tried to ask a few questions but, again, everyone was too busy to talk. He returned to watching the world go by. Customers came and went. A carload of young guys pulled up in front of us. The old guy said hello as they walked in, but they were too engrossed in their conversation to notice his greeting.

The young driver hadn't accounted for the fact that his car didn't have a reverse gear and he'd parked too close to a veranda pole. When they were leaving, he swung hard on the wheel and drove forward. I yelled out, "No!" but he bounced off the pole right in front of me, Bang. The car rolled back a metre and he again released the clutch to try again. "No!" I yelled, but again, Bang! His car bounced off the pole. To my complete disbelief he tried a third time. At least on the third attempt he took it slowly and merely became stuck in front of it. The men stepped out and pushed the car back a few metres for extra room, while the old guy sat off to the side with a grin on his face that said, "I may not move much, but I'm not that dumb."

We wished each other well with a handshake and I walked on praying for him. It wouldn't take much for someone to extend the hand of unity to him.

It was fifty-three kilometres to El Soccoro and I ran out of water half an hour from the end. My mouth dried out and my body ached. I still managed to move pretty quick when a congregation of caiman rushed into a farm dam very near me.

I was already watching for snakes, but was now all the more wide-eyed.

I wasn't welcomed at the church—I wasn't even allowed to introduce the mission—so I asked two teenage girls on the street outside for help. One of them, a beautiful young lady by the name of Gabriella, convinced her reluctant friend to walk me to the town's posada. I was thankful for her generosity. She chatted the whole way, asking questions about Australia and praying for unity. Her friend remained nervously quiet.

I stayed in El Soccoro for a quiet rest day, but the locals steered well clear of me … other than to voice gringo slurs. One girl sitting in the central park with her friends stood up and berated me with gringo calls across the park while her friends laughed. I just walked on and found a quiet step on a side street to eat lunch.

From there I saw a baffling sight: a woman shading herself from the midday sun with an umbrella walked down the street and through an open door, but failed to close the umbrella first. Yoink. The umbrella caught on the doorway and yanked her backwards. I smirked, but the smirk became baffled chagrin as I watched her rotate the umbrella and try to pull it through again. "You didn't just rotate a round object to pull it through a square frame did you?" Sure enough, she rotated it a second time and pulled with greater force. My jaw dropped. She stood in the doorway looking at the umbrella, perplexed, and rotated it a third time, pulling hard.

To my great relief, a person from within the house came to her aid and angled the umbrella through the doorway. I was left on that step contemplating the reality of 'umbrella rotations'. Do we do that? As humans, do we continually rotate round objects to fit through square holes? I hoped that what I'd observed was a one-off anomaly and not indicative of our tendency to not learn from history.

I walked on before dawn towards Valle de la Pascua, but the sunrise brought with it kids hanging out of bus windows yelling racial abuse. It was difficult to not react. An hour later I approached a rural school set amongst overgrown bushes with a handful of students gathering for class. I cringed, expecting the same reception, but standing at the road was a humble teacher named Ramon. He smiled as I approached and asked where I was from. As soon as I explained the mission he called to the students, bringing them in for an impromptu class atop the town's water supply pipeline running between the road and school. It was a mix of geography and religion with some social studies thrown in. It was fun trying to communicate and I enjoyed their enthusiastic questions. All it took for respect to be shown was for one person they respected, Ramon, to make the first move.

It was so hot and the inflamed big toe was now numb. On I walked, praying and extending the invitation through Valle de Pascua and dusty Chaguaramas, but I walked clean through Carrizalito without realising it; apparently it consisted of only two houses.

At an equally tiny rural settlement sat a humble little shop where the shopkeeper gave me permission to sling my hammock under his front veranda. While counting out my coins to buy dinner, the shop door closed and the dead bolt slammed shut behind it. "No!" I called out to the shop owner, but there was no reply. He appeared at the side of the shop and I explained my situation, pleading for the shop to be reopened. He nodded, "Okay, momento," and disappeared out the back, so I walked back to the front door and waited …

… but nothing happened. He'd walked on out across a field to his small home, leaving me alone at the locked-up shop on the edge of the dusty settlement with nothing more than a mango, half an onion and three cracker biscuits. I had to be grateful to at least have something, I guess.

I was so hungry and having walked thirty kilometres from Chaguaramas my body cried out for more. Throughout the night my stomach ached. I felt horribly insecure too, waking at the slightest sound. Having not showered after sweating it out through the dusty countryside, I felt disgusting and was ready to move on when the shop reopened in the morning. I practically inhaled the food I bought as I walked on with my backpack squishing around on a revolting layer of sweat.

Late in the day I met a young man intrigued by the walk. He asked questions with great sincerity. I pulled out my itinerary to show him the plan and he caught sight of a small picture tucked into a clear plastic sleeve of Saint 'Padre' Pio, an Italian saint from the mid 1900s. St Pio had short grey hair and a neat beard, but the young man stared at it intently, shook his head and pointed at me then back to the picture asking, "Osama Bin Laden?" I nearly choked with laughter before correcting him, "No. Not even close. It's Padre Pio!"

He was so confused. "Not Osama Bin Laden?"

"No mate, not Osama Bin Laden."

He nodded approvingly.

My left foot worsened to the point of hurting every step. I booked into a hotel in El Sombrero and, when I removed my boots and socks, I found the skin along the edge of the left big toe had split at the centre of the inflamed lump. I hit the shower, then elevated my foot and flicked on the TV. The station was broadcasting a live speech by Venezuela's President, Hugo Chávez, from a rally elsewhere in South America. I wasn't interested, so flicked the channel. The same thing: Hugo Chávez, live. I flicked again and found some cartoons but the next channel was, guess who, Hugo Chávez. Five out of seven channels were broadcasting his speech. I was now interested and became even more so when I spotted a massive communist sickle and hammer flag waving in the crowd of cheering fans adorned with red socialist shirts. It was intense.

Chávez ranted Hitler-like to the fanatical crowd about the evils of the USA. He labelled George Bush as satan and likened Americans to the spawn of satan. I was pretty sure he then encouraged them to rid Americans from South America like rats from a sewer. A massive banner at the back of the arena read, "Assassinate

Bush!" And if that wasn't enough, he then ranted on about the countries that had befriended satan. Second on his list was my dear Australia. I was officially an unwanted rodent, 720 kilometres into the sewer with 640 kilometres to go. I was in the heart of a country that despised me and was being encouraged by El Presidente to be driven from their land like plague-ridden pests. I felt very alone. The few times I'd gone without shaving, the locals hadn't associated me with the USA, but with either France or Russia. I put the razor away. The beard would be unleashed.

After a rest day, I attended evening Mass and made my way forward to meet the padre, but an over-zealous woman wouldn't let me pass. She stood near the altar, demanding to know what I was doing. I explained who I was, but she was defiant, telling me to get out. Not even my official letters helped. The invitation went no further in El Sombrero.

I left the next morning under the cover of darkness, but not enough cover, obviously. A guy and his girlfriend in a truck, plus a guy sitting in the tray, jeered at me, "Hey gringo!" I ignored them, but the guy in the back just wouldn't let up. He leant over the side and went off his nut at me. He was so close that I wanted to reach out and reef him off; I had to fight the desire so hard, continuing to walk and pray. Once they'd driven off and all seemed peaceful, they came back again … twice. Each time they jeered at me, they pulled faces; they were begging for a reaction. I was concerned about walking out onto the blackened open road away from civilisation. I made it to the narrow highway and in a scream of smoking tyres they turned around and let me be.

The toe-split widened further on the thirty-eight kilometres to Dos Caminos and nearby Ortiz nestled in the hills. An English-speaking lady named Elsy, and her son Jonathon, showed me to the Catholic church. They weren't even from the area, so had to ask for directions as we went.

The vibrant Padre Vladimir bounced around excitedly while talking up the need to pray for unity. He cracked open a bottle of wine while peppering me with questions. Elsy and Jonathon translated. Elsy wasn't Christian, but was interested in the church because she'd built a small chapel on her tourist eco-farm. She started asking her own questions of Padre Vladimir and he enthusiastically answered while encouraging her in her faith journey. He even gave us the grand tour of the church, explaining to Elsy what meant what so she could create a sacred space within her newly built chapel and, by the end of the tour, she invited him to take the drive out to their property to bless the chapel. He responded passionately, "I'd love to!" When Elsy and Jonathon said goodbye Padre Vladimir patted me on the back and declared, "Let's get ready for Mass, Samuel!"

If the church was an amazing building while empty, it was a slice of heaven when jam-packed. The padre introduced the mission at the start and then invited me forward at the end while he led the few hundred parishioners in singing a blessing song for me. I at last felt reasonably safe again and was counting every blessing. While standing up there I hoped that the split Church wouldn't resort to rotating umbrellas through square doorways in order to reunite and that, through the power of prayer, God might just tilt us on an angle and lead us into complete unity.

The road from there snaked along the Orinoco plains at the base of sheer hills. The temperature soared, again, and I struggled to put solid two-hour walking blocks together. My mind ticked over about the televised Hugo Chávez speech and, after a sweltering time in prayer, I nutted out a film script in my head for an Ocean's Eleven type film where a crew of renegades would be assembled to abduct the world's leaders, throw them all into one secret location and berate them with the consequences of their flawed leadership ... and so on. During a break I pulled out a piece of paper from my itinerary and wrote on the back a detailed timeline of how such a story could unfold and what the plot would be. I needed a long rest from the heat so I then went on to do a mathematical problem involving the weight distribution of a pyramid of oranges that I remembered encountering at university.

Pretty random and nonsensical stuff but, nearly a year later, that piece of paper would land me under arrest.

I copped a lot more racial abuse and death-stares in the days to come and my body basically hated me for undertaking what I was doing. I was very anxious in my surroundings too. I felt like I'd become a wild animal, not capable of eating or drinking without firstly scanning my surroundings for danger.

At one rest stop, just beyond a large farm entrance with a guard on duty in a small guardhouse, I sat on cool cement bench bus stop under a tree. I glanced back down the road and saw the guard standing on the viewing platform above the guardhouse loading his rifle. "What the hell is he doing?" I reached for my camera, sat it on my knee and flicked the LCD screen up so I could watch as I zoomed in. He finished loading, crouched behind the small wall and lined me up. "You've got to be kidding." I was not in the mood for it and couldn't be stuffed moving. I knew he could see me through his telescopic lens so I smiled broadly, held up a tomato, bit into it and held it aloft again. I looked back down at the LCD screen and watched him pop his head up over the scope to look at me. He stood back up, stared at me for a moment, unloaded the gun and stepped down. "Give me a break."

I needed to cover a mammoth sixty kilometres to reach the town of Tinaco from a military checkpoint, where I'd slept the night in my hammock strung between two lemon trees. I was up at 4:01 am with a bounce in my step, striding out along the narrow pitch-black country road, zigzagging from side to side depending on what direction any cars approached from I was happy to see a small store alongside the road at morning-tea time, but their husky guard dog wasn't happy to see me. It hit out hard against its chain and snapped it. He charged. The owners screamed for him to stop, but he wasn't listening. I stood my ground and at the last moment cracked a walking pole down across his nose sending him diverting to the side. I grabbed a drink and kept moving.

I prayed my way towards a dauntingly massive hill while facing the oncoming traffic (of which there was none) but I could hear a large truck approaching from behind on the other side. Just before it passed I thought, "That sounds really close," and in a frightening moment my body was sucked road-wards. A huge dump truck was overtaking a semi-trailer and it thundered past only a few centimetres away with a Whoosh! As much as I tried to keep my head and right arm from being sucked into the body of the truck I just couldn't hold my balance and with the thought of, "I'm done," I overbalanced into the speeding mass of metal with my eyes clenched.

My right foot thumped down on the road. I'd stepped right in behind it as it hurtled on towards the hill, leaving me standing on the road trying to make sense of what had flashed by.

While sweating it out under the blazing sun up that huge hill, an enormous explosion ripped across the countryside. I rounded the hill half an hour later to an awesome view across a lake with mountains surrounding it, and another explosion rocked the landscape.

At a turnoff was a military training base with tanks lining its driveway. A solitary family-owned shop at the hillside turn-off provided a good elevated spot to eat and scope out the army base. Rapid gunfire echoed from beyond the hills. President Chávez had been flexing his military muscle with naval exercises in the Caribbean Sea, but what concerned me was his openly voiced view that Venezuela, Colombia and Ecuador should unite to form a superpower to rival the USA. Chávez, of course, would be its leader. It was a sobering view.

I reached for a can of hot sauce clams that had been sitting in the top of my backpack all day and I cracked open the lid.

Poomf! It exploded.

Hot-sauced clams shot over every inch of my shirt and face. It smelt disgusting and, to add insult to injury, a chunk of sauce dropped from my hair, clipped my nose and landed fair in my crotch. Canned hot-chilli sauce clams shouldn't be placed in the top of a backpack on a 39°C day. Lesson learnt.

I plodded into Tinaco at 8 pm in total darkness after sixty hard-fought kilometres and having just run out of water. I'd consumed fourteen litres in total. I was so tired and sore but, as I passed homeless men sheltering around campfires on a river's edge, I could only be grateful for what I had. The Tinaco padre put me up for the night in a hotel in nearby San Carlos. We went by car but, as I tried to exit, I had to sit straight back down. In fact I laid flat on my back on the pavement. I was burning up and could feel my temperature rising by the second. I gently rose to my feet and tried to make it the hotel room, but my ability to focus suddenly wavered. I was passing out. A cooled water bubbler in the hotel was all that saved me. I fell to my knees and drank, quenching the fire within. It took a long time before I was able to stand back up and, with incredible concentration, walk on to my room.

A youth group member travelling with us generously fetched two hamburgers and two iced teas for me. Once eating, they were satisfied that I'd be okay and said goodnight. I ate one and a half hamburgers, but then had no energy again. I lay down on my side on the bed with a bottle of iced tea, trying to muster the energy to unscrew the lid, but fell asleep.

I woke at 10 am the next day with the iced tea still in my hand. I felt like death. I stayed in San Carlos to rest for a few days and visited three churches: the first two being unreceptive. At the third, they welcomed the mission and invited me to stay a night. They were hosting a German gap student named Philip, who I was to share a room with, but I went to bed early while he attended a party and when he arrived home he attempted to sneak into the room without disturbing me. I was a light sleeper by this stage and I woke in a panic with no recollection of where I was. I was ready to fight him to the death and was out of bed in a flash as he backed away with a stumble. I scared him as much as he scared me. Finally waking up enough to realise what was going on, and with no physical contact made, we were able to nervously laugh it off and wish each other a good night's sleep.

While in San Carlos I received an email from Patricia, the girl who'd danced the forro with me in the town of Malta, Brazil. She delivered sad news. The two girls who had greeted me enthusiastically with cue cards at the Malta parish office had tragically drowned in a boating accident. They were fishing with the padre and parish secretary on the nearby lake when their boat sank, forcing all four to swim. The two girls weren't strong swimmers and while trying to help each other they only succeeded in dragging each other under. I can only imagine how desperate and panic-filled that moment must have been as they drowned hand-in-hand. The news hit me hard and I spent a lot of time in silent prayer.

During an evening Mass, one of the padres surprised me by inviting me to share the mission without a translator. He handed me the microphone and smiled. I looked at him with wide eyes, "No hablo Español." He smiled again and indicated with his hand for me to try. He'd heard me speak enough Spanish to know that I could and so—with great trepidation—I slowly addressed the packed church. To my surprise, I talked for a few minutes and, gauging by the applause, they understood.

Walking on at last, I hadn't made it more than an hour out of San Carlos when I passed a man sitting on the front veranda of his farmhouse, well set back from the road. I nodded hello to him, but received nothing in return. I continued on and without warning a fist-sized stone flashed in front of my eyes and crashed into the scrub nearby. I'd felt the rush of wind as it flew past my nose. From about forty metres he'd missed by only millimetres! It would've been a death shot had it connected. The man stood on his front step defiantly. I stared back and muttered "Coward," while flicking my chin up at him. I backed down the road a few steps, maintaining eye contact, and then turned on my heels, walking on while keeping an eye on every direction. I prayed for him, plus the few other people who'd recently 'tossed a stone' my way, but I really had to force them out.

I walked on to arrive in Apartaderos after sunset and attended Sunday Mass there the next morning. I found a spot off to the side and knelt down to pray, but was soon being stood over by two very stern men. They asked straight off the cuff, "What are you doing here? What do you want?" I looked around. A great number of the parishioners were looking in my direction. I screwed my face up and answered, "For the Mass." The two men looked at each other, nodded with acceptance and walked back to their seats. It turns out that they suspected me of being a disruptive Evangelical.

The padre's sermon centred on President Hugo Chávez and I wished I could have understood more Spanish. He spoke passionately, comparing Chávez and

Jesus, asking everyone to make a choice. I cheered on the inside. The padre happily accepted the request to pass the invitation to pray for unity on to his congregation and offered his assistance to get me moving that day with all I needed.

A few hours into the scorching hot day I was struggling and longed for a cold shower, or, even better, snow. It made me wonder though, "When I'm in Canada during winter, if I make it that far, will I miss the tropical heat?" My answer was succinct, "Nope." I was determined to remind myself of that if I ever found myself in freezing conditions longing for warmth.

I arrived in Agua Blanca late in the afternoon and was straight away called over to a house by a rowdy family drinking beer under a tree. When they found out I was Australian they yelled to the neighbour's English-speaking guest, who was sitting in his front yard also enjoying a beer. He happily translated for me and in the end invited me to stay at his house for the night. I was sceptical. None of them were overly taken with the "Praying for the unity of Christians" part and were all verging on just-past-tipsy. I decided to at least go with the offer for the time being.

I felt more comfortable with his offer when we walked into his home and the first thing I saw was a huge painting of Jesus, followed by his smiling, motherly wife who welcomed me with a hug. She showed me to a room and handed me a fresh towel for a fantastic cold shower, but in pulling my gear out of the backpack I found a bottle of apricot juice I'd bought that morning. Without any second thought I flicked the lid off and sculled it. It was disgusting. It'd sat in the top pocket all day in that tropical heat and was hot. The taste was foul.

I showered and joined them for dinner before being introduced to a few young locals. A kind introduction goes a long way: no rock throwing or name-calling. I learnt more about Chávez as we chatted, but from a different perspective. For them he was a hero; a man who gave the wealth of the nation back to the poor, gave them a voice and an identity. One of them wore a red Hugo Chávez "V for Victory" t-shirt and produced his Chávez youth identification card. It was obvious that having the status of belonging to something empowered these guys, bringing a sense of dignity. For some it would be a difficult choice between a socialist President and a crucified Christ.

The hot apricot juice lingered as the young guys took me on a night-time bicycle tour of the town. By the time we'd arrived back home I was nauseous and struggled to hold my balance. Concerned at my rising temperature my hosts sat me out on the grass in the cool air, where I sat in pain with my head between my legs, breathing heavily and trying to stay awake. One of the young men appeared with half a lemon and indicated for me to sniff it. I looked at him confused, "Do what?" He sniffed at it again and handed it to me. I had no idea what he was on about so just did as he'd asked. My stomach immediately rumbled and with two fists full of grass I held on for dear life, vomiting towards complete exhaustion.

At some time around midnight I crawled into bed and curled up to sleep, praying that God would accept the pain, the prayers and the joys so far for the complete unity of Christians. Security had become a thing of the past, but there was also plenty to be thankful for. "Please unite us," I prayed, and fell asleep.

While recovering in bed the next morning, half the Agua Blanca school kids popped in for a visit. I had no idea who they were. By 2.30 pm I felt up to walking on and, after a long farewell, my hosts jammed my pack full of food and water, sending me off with the aim of walking as far as I could before nightfall. A number of locals joined me for the walk to the town's boundary, but I walked on alone from there, praying and keeping a conscious eye on my health.

I walked on for thirty kilometres, well into the night, all the way to a military checkpoint. A friendly soldier allowed me to sling my hammock under a semi-trailer, but I double-checked with him: "This isn't going to start up and drive off with me underneath it is it?" He laughed and shook his head. It wasn't going anywhere.

I got going early and enjoyed the tranquillity of walking on along a pitch-black, under-construction freeway. In the darkness I could just make out a few large parked earth-moving vehicles, but I failed to see either the guard dogs underneath or the armed security guard perched on top. The dogs launched into aggressive barking and a massive spot light flicked on nearly blinding me. I figured my best option was to act completely innocent, so I continued walking and waved at the intensely bright light while smiling. I had no idea what was going on behind the bright light, but with a flick it was off and the guard dogs were told to shut up. Walk on.

Sunrise revealed amazing views of the Andes Mountains rising sharply three to four mountains deep to a height of over 3,600 metres. They induced a cool, crisp breeze and as far-fetched as my hope of snow the day before was, its benefits were right there. With no traffic to contend with I was offered some of the best physical conditions possible and, despite an uphill climb for most of the day, I covered fifty-one kilometres by sunset to the sprawling mountain city of Barquisimeto, where I wandered the night streets from church to church, passing on the mission. At my hotel, I hopped into my first hot shower in eighty-one days. It was brilliant.

I rested a day in Barquisimeto before setting off along the shadowy pre-sunrise streets towards the surrounding mountains. A fellow who'd just stepped off a bus showed great interest in the simple mission and introduced himself as a Christian. When I invited him to pray for unity he took it on, immediately. With cars flying past he raised his arms and prayed. It took me a bit off-guard, but I smiled and joined him.

By lunchtime I'd walked to an isolated church perched on a small hill in a vast sweeping valley amidst towering peaks and pushed on into the mountains. The traffic dropped off to a big fat zero. With only an hour of sunlight left, the one twisting road marked on my map
forked in front of me ... without signage. Making the wrong choice could lead to a very dangerous night. I chose the road less degraded, but it headed straight up into the clouds.

A sheer mountain soared to my right and fell away into a massive valley to my left. The first vehicle in a few hours, a four-wheel drive, approached from up ahead so I tried to wave him down to ask for directions, but he slowed enough to pass me by before accelerating away. My only company were a few mountain goats scampering down the valley wall.

At 1,400 metres above sea level I crossed a narrow divide cradled between two peaks. Clouds swept through a mesmerising sunset of orange hues across a multitude of valleys and mountains for as far as I could see. I proceeded hastily down the narrow road hugging the edge of a dry valley stretching out into the twilight.

I arrived in the town of San Pablo in fading light, but was all alone. The highland breeze whistled through the ghost town of crumbling houses and scattered roof tiles. It was an eerie sight. Terrified of meeting another puma, I walked on into the darkness praying fervently, but on a quiet bend a shadowy figure suddenly appeared in front of me. I nearly leapt clean off the road. It was a woman walking back to her home and she just stepped around me and kept walking. I put my heart back in my chest and did likewise.

Halfway between Barquisimeto and San Pablo, across the northern tip of the Andes

After a massive sixty kilometres in a day across the Andes, and with a toe on my left foot bleeding badly, I limped to within sight of an Evangelical church. They were starting their Thursday night service and the doors were wide-open, flooding light into the darkness. I was so exhausted that I could barely stand, but the pastor ushered me inside and the tiny congregation received the invitation to pray for unity gladly.

Pastor Roberto and his wife welcomed me into their home where we shared as best as we could with my poor Spanish. He was a marathon runner, so knew exactly how I felt, and how to feed me, both for dinner and breakfast.

Over the next few days, my toe worsened. It burnt every time my left foot touched down and bled unceasingly. It wasn't healing. I walked a miserly fifteen kilometres on the Saturday and a 'why did I even bother' three kilometres on the Sunday.

In the town of Carora, where I'd ended up, a padre inspected my credentials, listened to my spiel, made a phone call and left without any instructions. Fifteen minutes later a mid-thirties man walked in and asked in English: "Are you the walker?"

Raphael wasn't a member of the Church; in fact he'd stopped attending many years ago. He was the local English teacher and explained that he had no idea why he was there, only that the padre had called asking for him to come and take care of a walking Australian. I explained what I'd already said to the padre and Raphael turned his hands up saying, "What am I supposed to do? I don't even go to church!" He was annoyed that I'd been palmed off to him, but made his sentiment clear that although the Church wouldn't look after one of its own, he would make sure the mission I carried made it to those who would listen. He wasn't a practising Christian, but he understood why I was there, and would help.

Raphael served me lunch and made a couple of calls to the two other Christian groups he knew of in Carora and in the open courtyard of an Evangelical family's home ten locals gathered waiting to hear what I had to say. I spoke in Spanish initially and then reverted to Raphael's translation. They were sceptical of the Catholic inviting them to pray for unity and a number of probing questions were asked like: "Do you believe in the action of the Holy Spirit?" and "Do you worship Mary?" But they eventually accepted me as a Christian and accepted that perhaps not all Catholics were as idolatress and superstitious as they had suspected.

Having accepted me, I went on the front foot and explained in no uncertain terms how scandalous and opposed to the Gospel the broken Church was. I pleaded that lukewarm Christians who believed it was okay to just accept each other and let each Church believe what it wanted to believe had hijacked unity. "We are not the Church of Pontius Pilate who says, 'What is truth?' and then lets each other believe whatever they interpret scripture to be. Unity must be founded in truth and one truth alone. We must compel each other deeper into truth, but always with love. We must stand in truth, never waiver from it, and continually and humbly seek to love one another into it, but allow ourselves to be corrected into it as well." I added, "You and I have different beliefs, we know that, but the call to unity is not about glossing over the differences, but embracing what we have in common and purifying the differences openly until we are one. There is one Church, the body of Christ, and it's broken. The greatest evangelisation tool we have is our unity; our love of one another."

They nodded in agreement and affirmed their intention to set a foundation of praying for unity. One woman stared at me intently and muttered something, causing everyone to laugh. I looked over at Raphael for help, but he was also laughing. The woman pointed at me and passionately said the same thing again. Everyone nodded in agreement. "Raphael, help me here. Why are they laughing at me?" He leant in close, "They think you look like Jesus." My beard had come along nicely. Still laughing, they gathered in to take photographs. One woman even tugged at my beard. I flicked her hand away, "I'm not Santa Claus!"

The gathering concluded with us standing in a circle in that courtyard and praying for the complete unity of Christians. They prayed in Spanish, and I did in English, but we interceded together. Raphael stood with us quietly with his head bowed.

Raphael organised for me to stay with his friend, who in turn introduced me to a second Catholic padre the next morning. Padre Jaime Vivas spoke English, was young, animated, opinionated and ready to fight anything for the Gospel. He was brilliant. He took me under his wing and used my presence to teach the seminarians what unity looks like and why unity means standing as one against the tyranny of the world. He had a few choice words to say about his President too. "Communist! He's a communist and he's ruining our country!" He didn't hold back.

When it came time to leave, Padre Jaime checked my itinerary and shook his head. "You can't walk there. That direction you are headed, you can't do it." I'd heard that before and explained that I'd been through dangerous parts of South America already, but he wouldn't let up, persisting with, "I realise you've walked a long way and can cope with bad roads, but you have to believe me, you cannot walk on that road." He pulled out a more detailed map and pointed out the massive section of that day's walk cutting through forested mountains. "There's a lot of traffic, the road is very narrow and there is absolutely no space along the side. You can't even walk off the road. I'm paying for you to take the bus today." I thought about it, but out of trust in his character I accepted the alteration. My bleeding toe celebrated.

Padre Jaime was right. That road would have been deadly. It was narrow and it was without space to walk. Each tight corner posed a new challenge for the driver and, as beautiful as the steep forested valleys were, the continuous stream of traffic would have made it perilous on foot.

I stayed the night in El Venado and hit the road a few hours before sunrise along a similarly bad road, jogging from side to side to avoid the traffic. By the time the sun rose I'd emerged onto farming plains and passed the immediate danger. The humidity was back with a vengeance and the roads in that part of Venezuela were repaired one continuous layer at a time. They dropped off on a steep angle anywhere between one to four feet into long grass and thorn bushes. It was horrible. I could only walk on the road when the lane was free of traffic and had to keep a keen ear out for overtaking cars from behind. It was a strenuous workout up and down for a forty-five kilometre and then thirty-five kilometre day. My thighs were shot and my big toe scythed with pain.

Lake Maracaibo is a massive body of water that passes through a narrow neck from the Caribbean Sea before ballooning into a basin to the south. Connecting east and west at the neck was the single longest bridge I've ever seen. It was over eight kilometres long! It was also out of bounds for pedestrians, so I hitched a ride across in a roof-less four-wheel drive and continued on foot from the western bank.

Gringo taunts rained down on me from kids hanging out of bus windows.

The Maracaibo Catholic Church received the mission and I was directed to a posada run by a parishioner, where the woman in charge paid extra attention to me, inviting me to eat with her family.

After a second night in Maracaibo I moved on to the north, stopping at a number of churches along the way. The humidity was crippling and I only made it to the city limits before finding a Saturday vigil Mass and deciding to finish up. I was able to invite the padre and a few parishioners to pray for unity, but they weren't overly interested. I asked around for the nearest posada or hotel, but they just shrugged their shoulders and I was left to my own devices.

I asked a middle-aged, thin and scraggly man passing by on the street if he knew where there was accommodation. He smiled and said, "I saw you in church. You need a place to sleep? You are welcome at my house." I was wary of accepting accommodation from a complete stranger, but in reality, a stranger provided nearly every second night's bed. I shook his hand and followed. His home was a kick in the teeth for my privileged upbringing. He lived alone in a tiny two-room house smaller than most people's garages. Through the rickety door sat a black-plastic-for-a-tablecloth covered table hard up against a cabinet with a stash of used plastic bottles ready for recycling and little nick-knacks that seemed to have no connection to each other sitting across the top. There was a mug and saucer, an empty beer can, and a wilting rose in a small vase. The wooden floor was dusty and a dead bonsai tree sat on top of the rusty fridge. It was a poor man's home, but he never stopped smiling or offering hospitality; there was richness there. It was overwhelming.

There was no spare bed so he gathered a few old rugs together, folded them and laid them on the floorboards as a bed for me. I unfolded my sleeping bag on it. It was perfect. He disappeared into the other tiny room and I laid there with a street light down the road throwing a splattering of light into the room. After a few minutes something moved beside me. I flinched, swinging my head to the side, but couldn't see a thing. I waited a moment and then, patter, patter, patter, a rat scampered from the stove to the fridge, then, patter, patter, patter, another scampered along the side of my bedding. There was no point turning the light back on and there was nowhere else to go. I lay there wide-eyed as the rats went to work in the darkness. I was pretty sure there were four of the sods running around and occasionally they stopped to stare at me before running off again. I did not want to fall asleep—I might've lost an ear! It was time for a trick I'd learnt when I was a kid. I slinked into my sleeping bag and pulled the covers over my head.

In the middle of the night a rat walked across me inducing a knee-jerk reaction that propelled it airborne across the room into the adjacent wall. It may have ended up with a nasty headache. I was so tired in the morning, but after a cooked breakfast and a good laugh at the rats he couldn't get rid of, the man wished me well and offered his prayers for unity. I offered him mine, but also some money for his next groceries.

For all the madness that the month of March had produced, it had also brought something very special. Simmering in the background was Carora's Raphael. The more he'd translated, the more he'd learnt about the mission and the angrier he'd become at the Catholic padre who had palmed me off. He was angry because that sort of reaction was exactly what he expected from the Church, it's why he had nothing to do with it, but in that courtyard with three Christian faiths talking openly, laughing and importantly praying together, years of disdain and shunning of God undid. Raphael emailed me:

Dear Sam,

I want to thank you for visiting us in Carora and to tell you what happened after you left. I'm so sorry that the padre dismissed you without really listening. It made me angry, but by the end of the day I was angry with myself, because that was exactly how I have treated God. The day you left, I sat down at the table alone to eat dinner and realised that I hadn't thanked God for the food I ate for many years, so for the first time since I was a teenager I prayed a small prayer thanking God for my meal. Then when I went to bed, I realised I

hadn't thanked God for all the blessings of my life, so before I went to sleep I knelt down beside my bed like I used to and prayed. The next morning I couldn't
get out of bed until I'd prayed and by the time the end of the day came I was walking back into the church for evening Mass. Do you realise that at no stage did you invite me to pray for unity? I just want to let you know that I am praying and will continue to pray for the unity of the Church. God bless, Raphael.

> *I in them and you in me, that they may become completely one, so that the world may know that you have sent me and have loved them even as you have loved me.*
>
> John 17:23

Total walked: 2,022 kilometres

# Colombian Assault, Glued Lips & Fireflies
## April 2007

The fertile wetlands merged into grazing land along the quiet road to San Rafael, and a quiet country road is not the place you want three shady men to drive past you, in their 1970s jacked up V8 sedan, glaring darkly. A few minutes later they returned in the same manner. I nodded hello, but received nothing more than a raised chin from the driver. I was on edge, hoping they didn't stop and step out. I walked and prayed and, for whatever reason, after a third passing, they left me alone.

The padre in San Rafael organised accommodation for me in a stunning, up-market holiday posada with sweeping view across Tablazo Bay. A strong wind whipped up short waves against the rocky bay while the setting sun cast orange pastels across the sky. A full moon rose over the distant peninsula. The owners weren't happy that the padre had assumed I could stay without a booking, but he fought for me and secured a room. I was thankful.

Within two days I'd be crossing into Colombia, and even the Venezuelans shook their heads at that idea. The posada owners suggested an alternative route to the heavily trafficked and dangerous Colombian border approach, pointing across Tablazo Bay by longboat to the distant peninsula where I could walk on in relative anonymity. It would add extra distance, but offer forty kilometres of uninhabited beachfront wilderness.

I raced along in the high-powered longboat through choppy sunrise waters to the isolated fishing village of La Mohan and walked out across the peninsula onto the deserted and windswept Gulf of Venezuela/Caribbean Sea coastline. The water was the colour of washing machine discharge and it crashed ashore along the sloping sandy beach that curved to the north in an unbroken line to the horizon. I'd consumed copious amounts of water before leaving La Mohan and carried four litres for the day. If I ran out, there was nowhere to refuel.

My only conversation all day was with two native Venezuelan Indians who rode down the beach on horseback and stopped to check me out. At lunchtime I removed my boots and washed the bleeding big toe in the salt water. It felt so good standing knee deep in the Gulf … eating a banana. But I made a big mistake: I applied sunscreen and then immediately took a sip from my water bladder tube. The tube and water washed the sunscreen off my bottom lip and over the rest of the day it fried under the hot sun and sea's dazzling reflection.

The sunset left me to navigate the twilight wilderness with no water and a hot salty wind until I struck civilisation in the form of a coastal settlement of wooden homes with coconut palm thatching and sand flooring. I was so thirsty that I drank a litre and a half right there and then, much to the public-kitchen owner's amazement. While eating the battered fish they served though, I noticed for the first time that my bottom lip was burnt.

I was directed towards neighbouring Paraguaipoa for accommodation where I met a parishioner at the church and asked for directions to a posada, or just a place to sling my hammock. The young indigenous woman, named Sonrie, smiled sweetly and ushered me to follow her, walking me back to her home. I was taken aback by her generosity.

Sonrie was a gentle soul who cooked up a huge egg and bacon breakfast in the morning and wrote a blessing for me on a napkin, signing it off in her indigenous language. I still don't know what 'Akoyojüshi Wattapünaa i' means, but she farewelled me with one last smile and I walked on and out of Venezuela.

My passport was stamped and I walked on across dry, arid terrain covered with thorn bushes and low-lying scrub. A man sitting on the side of the road up ahead of me rose to his feet and stared at me groggily. When he started yelling aggressively it became apparent he was drunk. He held a large torch and, while venting at me, he lifted it aloft as though wanting to hit me. I moved out onto the empty road and jogged past, but he stepped out after me. I put in a few quicker steps and pulled away as he established, without too much doubt, that he hated me for some reason. He came after me, but I stayed one step ahead, switching back and forth across the road as traffic passed. I left him behind, continuing his scratchy-voiced abuse.

I thought I was in the clear until a small truck passed by, pulled over ahead of me, and the drunk jumped off the back. Clever boy, I thought. You may be drunk but you can still keep up. He staggered back towards me across the empty road and launched into another angry lecture. He was ready for me this time and wasn't about to let me dash past. The torch came out and he moved in closer, corralling me to the side. I yelled at him to get out of my way, but that was futile. We moved in eye-ball-to-eye-ball and he lashed out at my head with the torch. I grabbed his arm with my left hand and scruffed him around the collar with my right, forcing him backwards in an ugly tango of shirt punches: "Back off!"

Suddenly, a camouflaged soldier brandishing an automatic rifle jumped out of the scrub and held us both at gunpoint. We let go of each other and raised our hands as the soldier moved in cautiously, sharply alternating his aim between us. It was going from bad to worse. I kept my mouth shut, but the drunk didn't know how to. The soldier pointed the rifle at the drunk and told him to, "Shut up!" He obliged. Holding the rifle with one hand he put the other out asking me, "Passport?" I handed it over and he flicked it open, checking the stamp I'd received an hour earlier and asking in Spanish "What are you doing in Colombia?" It was the one answer I knew fluently. He handed the passport back saying, "Have a good walk. You can go," and with that I was off. The drunk was promptly arrested and bundled into an army vehicle that roared onto the scene half a minute later.

I knew God was watching over me, but in Colombia, apparently camouflaged soldiers were too.

By mid-afternoon I'd made it to the bustling rural city of Maicao, which was crammed with electrical wires streaming above the motorcycle-clogged streets. The mission was received well and two young soldiers kindly showed me to a posada, but when I woke the next morning it was with a scare. I was breathing through my nose, but when I tried to open my mouth, I couldn't. It was jammed shut. My jaw worked fine; the problem was my lips. They'd become one and wouldn't open. Panicked, I stumbled to the bathroom mirror and was met with a horrible sight. Dried blood surrounded my mouth, sealing the lips tight. I splashed water onto my face, working it into the lips as bloodied water dripped into the sink. Prising them apart was painful.

After cleaning the blood away I could see the full extent of the sunburn from two days ago. It was a third degree burn and the majority of the skin along the bottom lip was missing. I sought out a chemist and bought skin treatment for burns, but eating and drinking was going to be a challenge for a while.

I walked and prayed on into the dry hot days from there through vast scrub wilderness, with my mouth gluing shut a few times. After a hammock wilderness sleep I made a discovery down a side road. I couldn't believe it: out in a scrub wilderness village sat a massive missionary boarding school. The number of students easily outnumbered the tiny town. The principal welcomed me excitedly and gathered the seniors to hear the mission. I hadn't always explained the 4:01 part to people, as it was difficult to explain its significance in a foreign language, but with their full attention and a lot of time I was able to get the meaning across and they enthusiastically took it on. They asked questions left, right and centre and I had a lot of fun answering them. One kid asked, "Before coming to Colombia, what did you know about our country?" The first thing that came to mind was the drug trade, but I didn't want to say that straight off the cuff. Instead I named the second most famous export, "Shakira!" The students roared with approval and started singing as an impromptu dance broke out.

It was the right answer.

I walked on and pain pierced through my body from the injured toe. I even began to grunt and groan ... so long as my mouth wasn't bloodied shut. After sunset, and forty-six kilometres, I limped into the coastal city of Riohacha and up to a cathedral on the edge of the Caribbean Sea. Franciscan Capuchin friars ran it and housed a group of young missionaries in their enormous facility. They greeted me with open arms and sat me down for a big feed. They weren't all Colombian so were interested to know if I'd passed or would be passing through their town. One of the Venezuelan guys was so excited to scour my itinerary and they eagerly accepted the invitation to pray for unity. There was no room for me to stay with them, but a private chat between one of the missionaries and the leader produced an agreement whereby they'd point me in the direction of a posada, but with an invitation to return to them for all my meals.

I rested in Riohacha on that Good Friday and then Easter Saturday, attending the Masses and joining in the celebrations. I could barely walk on the injured toe. It looked disgusting. I desperately wanted to jump into the palm-lined aqua blue beach on the city's edge, but the open wound hurt so much that the thought of even stepping into crashing waves made me cringe. I just sat at the end of a long jetty overlooking the beach and rested, dangling my feet into the salt water and occasionally prying apart my bleeding lips.

Before leaving Riohacha I took the time to track down the local bishop, but not for the purpose of extending the invitation to pray for unity. Between the border and Riohacha I'd stopped at a number of towns and experienced one very isolating and confusing moment that gutted me. One padre had invited me into his office and received the mission gladly, but then asked if he could bless me.

What happened next wasn't a blessing; he molested me.

I was out of that office in a flash, so confronted, disgusted and shocked that he was still smiling at me as though everything was fine. I didn't know how to react other than to get out of there. In the hours that followed, over and over again, I wanted to turn back and with a clenched fist knock his lights out. I didn't know how to deal with it. I couldn't believe he'd done it. I was so angry that I nearly put my fist through a few walls and trees that day. It was the biggest struggle I'd ever had to rationalise and forgive another person. "You bastard," was about all I could muster.

The bishop spoke English, but it was a difficult incident to describe. He was shocked, but almost to the point of disbelief. He shook his head saying, "No. Not that padre. He couldn't. He wouldn't. Why would he?" I didn't care how good his reputation was, I wanted his ministry stripped. The bishop asked a question that infuriated me, "Why did you let him do it?" I blew up at that point, but he quickly calmed me down saying, "This is horrible. I'm so sorry. This is horrible." The bishop was completely stunned. He offered his continued apologies before asking what he could do for me. I asked him, "Please pray for unity and please make sure that padre doesn't touch another person." He nodded slowly.

When I wrote my blog for that week I included the molestation, but within twelve hours it was taken down from Australia due to concerns about the sensitivity of the incident and, in particular, the misconstrued media coverage it may generate. I was disappointed, but at least agreed with the reasoning. I rewrote the blog making only a vague reference to our need as a Christian body to pray for those who are not united with the Church due to abuse or scandal. As I rested over Easter, what resounded within me was that in those moments those perpetrators stood for no one but themselves. They masqueraded as representatives of God, or perhaps represented Him for the most part, but in those moments represented only themselves. Having had an active role in the Church for a number of years I was in a unique position to say, "No, I am standing for Christ and you are not. You don't represent who I stand for." I could distance myself from the padre without distancing myself from God or the Church.

I prayed fervently for those who had departed the Church because of abuse, most of whom had been subjected to far worse experiences than I had. I prayed for the purity of the Church, the witness of it, the healing of those who'd been hurt by abuse and those shamed by it. I also prayed for the grace to forgive and be merciful. It took a long time to not want to thump that padre. It was yet another journey within the journey.

The process of being unified, much like notions of world peace, can be twisted into a soft, placid mind-set, but peace isn't the absence of war; it's love in action. There is nothing placid about seeking unity with those we despise, those we think deserve hell, and those who have proved arrogant or fake. The likelihood is that unity will hurt. Forgiveness and mercy don't flow easily, nor does compassion and constant love to those who've been injured. I really wanted to punch that padre.

I set off on Easter Sunday for a shortish twenty kilometre walk to the village of Camarones. It was hard fought. My toe showed little sign of healing and my bottom lip continued to glue my mouth shut. The toe burst with pain, making me incredibly lethargic. In northern Colombia I would be walking for nearly a full week around the base of one massive mountain called Pico Cristóbal Colón. At 5,700 metres above sea level, it was so extreme that it created its own microclimate: not weather … climate.

It was a tough fifty-five kilometres further on to Campana and, a third of the way into the day, the cactus and thorn bush-covered parched land gave way to flowering bushes, large leafy trees and trickling creeks. The foothills loomed nearby. It was a welcome relief to walk in under the cool shade of tropical rainforest. The excruciating sixty kilometres to make the next small village saw the rainforest continue for mile after mile with glimpses of mountains as I crossed the fast flowing rocky rivers. None of the mountains I could see were anywhere near 5,700 metres in height, in fact only just over 1,000 metres. I hoped for a glimpse of the real deal.

I rested at lunchtime on the banks of a beautiful river with the forest curling over the large boulders lining the edge. It was perfect. I plonked myself down in the shade and removed my boots, dangling my feet into the cool mountain river and momentarily glanced downstream … and nearly choked on my lemon tuna. Two machine gun carrying camouflaged soldiers were approaching. I kept low, gathered my gear and moved fast in behind the bridge. At that moment a few children ran down to the river upstream of me and, after checking me out for a split second, made for a swimming-hole ten metres from the bridge. One of the children looked downstream and gave a friendly wave to the soldiers. That was a good sign.

I wanted to hang my foot back into the water so moved forward with conviction and set up on the edge once more, and glanced back downstream. The two soldiers had stopped dead and were staring at me. "Act calm. Just act as though you're meant to be here." I smiled and gave a friendly wave and they both raised their heads, smiling acceptingly. One stripped down for a swim and the other walked up to check my passport, wishing me all the best with the mission. I walked on completely unaware that the entire region was a guerrilla stronghold. What you don't know can sometimes kill you.

The people of that region were peaceful and, of all the South Americans, the most unafraid of a 6' 5" white guy walking towards them. Instead of running away they'd call out to their family and friends to come and watch me approach. They were typically all smiles and hardly a conversation took place without laughter being a prominent feature. One retired farmer sitting on his veranda was adamant that walking was overrated, and laughed that if I got too tired I could come back and pull up a seat next to him to share a coconut drink. He saw me off with a kind wave.

I was apprehensive about walking at night along the edge of the Colombian forest and my comfort deteriorated when a couple of young men provided the day's first aggressive racial heckle in the fading twilight. I'd been advised that walking at night was a no-no, but I was still two hours from my destination. I pushed on uneasily into blanketing darkness. The forest sounds accompanied me. My torch remained off. Humans were the greatest danger and I didn't want to garner any unwanted attention.

With the night as dark as could be, I passed a house tucked into the forest. The old gumboot-wearing owner—with a leathery weathered face—was sitting on his veranda and watching me pass by under the illumination of his lights. He stood up and called out a few questions, but never paused for an answer. I wasn't sure what to do, and couldn't communicate with him, so politely bid farewell and walked on. He followed. I was concerned at first, but decided that a seventy-year-old farmer in gumboots didn't carry a high risk factor. He walked behind me chatting away to himself for the full hour. He didn't miss a beat. He was elderly, but his step was a lot easier than my limp.

We passed more houses tucked into the forest with owners also out on the veranda enjoying the evening and, each time they heard us walking past, I could see them through the shrubs rise to their feet to see who was there. Without fail, as soon as they heard the rambling farmer come into earshot they sat back down to continue their conversation. The passing noise was deemed local.

Darkness had enveloped the forest and the traffic had thinned to an occasional random passing car, but the forest was alive. At first one, then two, then twenty, then a thousand dancing fireflies lit up the forest floor on both sides of the road, which quickly resembled a dark river through a sea of white dots. Their dance was to the beat of hundreds of frogs croaking in chorus and the faint mumblings of an old farmer twenty metres behind me. I prayed prayers of thanks and walked on smiling, despite the pain.

Having made my destination and hobbling in under the streetlights of a cluster of homes, I thanked the old man for his company. For the first time we seemed to communicate. He said, "Okay," reached into his pocket and pulled out the equivalent of forty cents, saying, "This is so you can buy dinner." He placed the money in my hand and walked off down the road into the night, leaving me standing under the street lamp staring at the forty cents.

The fifty-one kilometre trek to Santa Marta was relatively smooth but, while struggling up a large hill covered in rainforest, I was amazed at what I saw, the sort of stuff a driver passing by would miss. There was something odd. In the dense undergrowth sat two perfectly round dots floating a metre off the ground. I stopped to focus on them, trying to figure out what they were. Then 'it' came into focus. I nearly wet myself. They blinked. Another fully camouflaged Colombian soldier with his assault rifle in hand stared unwaveringly. I nodded a polite, "G'day," but he remained silent, not flinching a muscle. I walked on nervously. I had to laugh that he was probably disappointed to be spotted by the only person to have ever walked past him. At least he didn't have cars pulling over to take family snap shots. That would be deflating.

Still not having caught a glimpse of Pico Cristóbal Colón, I was left wondering how a 5,700-metre-high mountain could hide. The road into Santa Marta twisted on itself through forested hills as another sunset beat me. Still no sight of that mountain. I was satisfied to finish off a massive 166 kilometres in just three days, but I must have been thoroughly exhausted by the time I found accommodation because I have no memory of it.

I think it was a hotel.

The following day I walked along the sea front with beautiful ocean views. None of the churches I passed were open so it was a matter of just praying and extending the invitation to any random person I met, of which there were a few. The forest of the last few days disappeared as the steep climb over a massive headland introduced more sandy thorn bush covered escarpment. The temperature soared, along with the tourist high-rise infrastructure along the beachfronts. Local families remained confined to the inland side of the main road along the thirty kilometre stretch to Ciénaga.

I rose well before dawn with my standard opening prayer of, "Lord, I give you this day. Please come Holy Spirit," and, with the small breakfast in hand that the posada owners had kindly set out for me, I walked off into the darkness disappointed to have not caught a glimpse of Pico Cristóbal Colón over the previous four days. I settled into a rosary with the stars shimmering above the peaceful countryside.

With sunrise not far off I finished my rosary and turned for a random 'danger-check' back down the road. I stopped dead in my tracks, and turned completely around. My mouth hung open. There, on the morning of the fifth day, as I walked away from the mountains across the coastal lagoons, was Pico Cristóbal Colón. All 5,700 metres of it, silhouetted against the dawn sky, towering above the foothill-mountains that had blocked my view of it until then. Cristóbal dwarfed the 1,000 metre high mountains around it so much so that they looked like silly insignificant hills. I stared at it. "There it is." It dominated the landscape. Even there in the tropics its summit was snow-capped.

As a kid I'd seen a large bird fly by while driving around the farm with Dad. I asked if it was an eagle and he replied, "No, it isn't big enough. That's a hawk." I took his word for it, but a few weeks later I saw a larger bird, so asked Dad again, "Is that one an eagle?" He laughed and said, "No, it's just a big hawk." I was frustrated so asked exactly how he could tell the difference. He simply said,

"Believe me, when you see an eagle, you'll know." That annoyed me to no end. No matter how much I pushed, Dad stuck to his answer.

A month later I was out on the motorbike and saw what I thought was a hawk gliding towards the ground ahead of me. I stopped the bike on a hill to watch it drift down to land, but instead of landing in the pasture directly in front of me, it settled on a tree branch over 200 metres away which bent under its weight. The size of the animal suddenly came into perspective! It was enormous and, to be honest, its size scared me. It was unmistakeably an eagle, standing just under a metre in height. There was no way that 'thing' was a hawk. Dad was right, when I saw it, I knew. We can argue back and forth about what unity looks like but, like Pico Cristóbal Colón or an eagle perched on a bending limb, when we see unity in action it's pretty unmistakeable. And sometimes what seems so far from achievable is so much closer than we could imagine.

I didn't make it all the way on foot to my South American end point of Barranquilla that day. One assumption killed that attempt, being that the sixty-five kilometre walk along the coastline would offer at least—at least—one store to replenish my supplies, like every other Colombian day. There was nothing but wilderness. The tourist ventures, salt pan workers and fishing villages, all of them, ceased. I walked alone across the wilds of northern Colombia for as far as I could, but under the blazing sun and with the salty breeze biting at me, my water reserves were consumed by the twenty-five kilometre mark. I couldn't make sixty-five kilometres in that heat without water. I walked for a further two hours, clocking off thirty-five kilometres before my hand was forced. I was dehydrated.

Two men had broken down in their truck with a flat tyre and were having trouble removing the wheel nuts. They had no water, but did hand me a huge spanner to help them. It was a hot and tiring half-an-hour changing that blown wheel. I was afraid of either vomiting or passing out. In return they offered me a lift to Barranquilla and a wonderful service station.

I hobbled on to a few churches, who received the mission well. One particular padre was happy to hear that I wasn't attempting the two-week trek between

Colombia and Panama, a four hundred mile stretch of thick, mosquito infested, and machine gun ruled jungle called the Darien Gap. From Barranquilla I intended to fly across to Panama City and walk north from there. The padre had heard recently that approximately 90% of people who entered the Darien never returned and, of the 10% that walked out the other side, most did so without their clothes or belongings. Even the map I used in my planning had a warning written in red to not attempt the gap. Animals, native Indians, and the drug-running paramilitary had all claimed their fair share of lives. It also averaged an inch of rain a day.

The soles of my boots had worn clean through, so I searched for new ones. I had enough trouble finding size sixteen boots in Australia, so Colombia was never going to be easy. The local storeowners just laughed at me. I jumped online, but even the Australian stores were out. It was a sticky situation.

Colombia had been beautiful and surprisingly peaceful. My first few days in the country were regrettable, but from there I had enjoyed it. The prayer for unity had travelled that little bit further and, with South America behind me, one chapter closed and a new one opened up. I just hoped the foot and my ability to trust would hold out.

*You are the light of the world. A city built on a hill cannot be hid.*

Matthew 5:14

Total walked : *2,614 kilometres*

# Part 2

Central and North America

*The South Americans* had often shown concern about my plan to walk through Central America. Even they were scared of it. In researching the months ahead I confirmed their suspicions, discovering that Guatemala, El Salvador and Honduras, combined, was the most dangerous place on earth at that time. I found that hard to believe considering the war in the Middle East and war-torn African nations, but the figures spoke for themselves. Guatemala City alone averaged twenty-one murders a day, and kidnapping was rampant. An El Salvadorian born missionary I worked with in Australia had warned me of the dangers, but I'd shrugged it off jokingly saying, "A six foot five white guy carrying a red backpack ... I'll blend right in!" Now, having encountered heated racism and confrontations in countries that considered themselves mild compared to the Central American trio, I was downright terrified.

## Surgery, a Drug-Induced Haze & a Pink Dinosaur
*April 2007*

My plane touched down in Panama City early in the evening and I headed straight to accommodation in the city. Panama City was spectacular at night, but all the churches were shut and no one was answering their door, so I found a quaint suburban hotel near a cathedral and settled in. My boots had lasted over two and half thousand kilometres, but with the sole now worn through and the internal heel leather cracked badly I needed to replace them. I used a rest day in Panama City to visit churches and shoe shops. I did better with the churches. I'd been in correspondence with a fellow from Australia's adventure store, Paddy Palin, and James, a Christian, had done what he could to make sure I could continue walking. He searched high and low for me, before discovering a pair in storage at their Sydney warehouse. I emailed through an address for the Catholic church in the city of David, two weeks further up the road, and hoped to rendezvous with the boots there. The pain of the split toe had me wishing I'd ordered slippers.

I set off into Central America toward a town called La Chorrera, excited to walk up alongside the famed Panama Canal. It was illegal to walk across the bridge

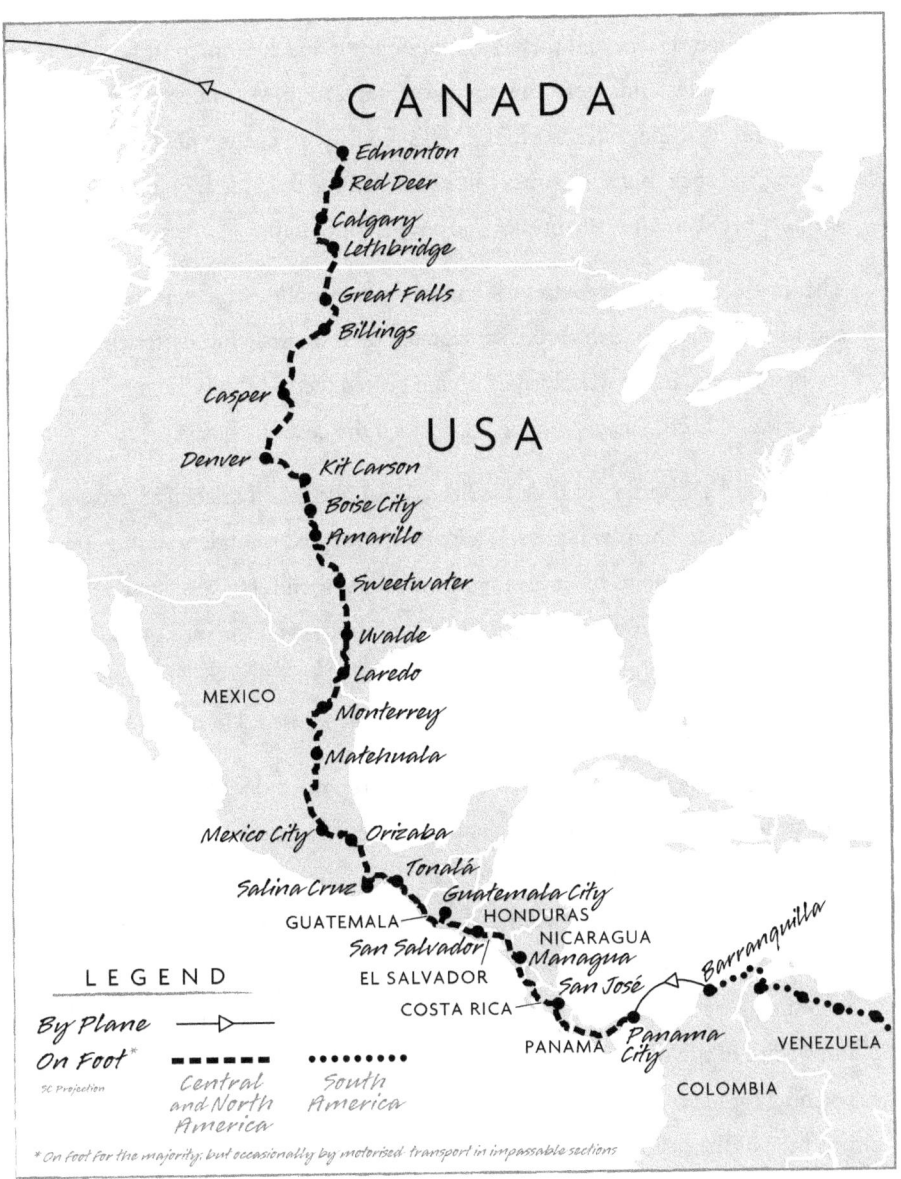

spanning it but when the two police officers who'd stopped me found out why I was there they grabbed their police jeep and drove me across themselves.

The toe reached new levels of pain. I limped on. Edmonton in Canada was over 5,000 kilometres away and there I was hobbling along at 3 km/h. It felt like I had a cigarette lighter underneath my toe every step I took. For the first time the pain actually brought me to tears. I took breaks regularly to change my blood-soaked dressing and sock, but sometimes I just stood on the roadside looking at what lay ahead. They weren't really breaks, I just wasn't moving.

That first thirty-one kilometres took nearly eleven hours, from sunrise to sunset, and I was completely exhausted. I meditated on the sorrowful mysteries and did my best to sing, but it was always through gritted teeth. I think the most heartfelt prayer was: "Lord, please help me." I dreaded the cost of a hospital.

I arrived in La Chorrera in time for Mass. Both sitting and kneeling were welcome relief. The parish priest, Padre José, struggled to understand my poor Spanish, so took me to meet his English-speaking friend. He was genuinely interested to find out who I was and began to understand the mission after a short walk and talk. He enthusiastically asked if I needed anything specifically and, with a hobble, I communicated that my foot was badly injured. He smiled knowingly.

Padre José's English-speaking friend was a doctor and under the padre's request Dr Rolando and his nurse wife Dalia saw me between patients. After a quick inspection he advised that it required a small operation, which he was happy to do straightaway. Dalia swabbed the toe, cleaned it up and injected anaesthetic before her husband re-joined us to begin operating and translating for the padre, who didn't stop asking questions. Dr Rolando didn't miss a beat. Flesh had burst out a third of the way across the nail, which he cut away with a scalpel, before reaching for plier–scissors. Cutting down along the toenail all the way to the nail bed he split the nail in two and reefed the wounded side out.

Thankfully, the anaesthetic did its job.

Padre José gladly agreed to take the invitation to pray for unity to his parish and offered to pay for the surgery, but Dr Rolando wouldn't accept it, "No, no, there is no charge. This is my contribution to the mission." But it didn't stop there. He drove me to the best hotel in town and paid for the night saying, "I know you'll probably just keep walking even if I tell you to stop, so I'm paying for you to stay in this hotel for tonight and then you have to return for a check-up tomorrow lunchtime. That way you can stay still long enough for the toe to at least begin the healing process." I was lost for words, other than a very humble: "Thank you." He swiped his credit card at the hotel and was off.

As the anaesthetic wore off that night I scrambled to down my painkillers. I lay on the hotel bed in agony, holding the foot until I flopped backwards on the bed, accidently smashing my head against the bed-head. The resulting headache at least drew my attention away from the toe for a while.

The late afternoon check-up went well. Dr Rolando and Dalia cleaned the wound, re-bandaged it and made up a travel kit so I could take care of the toe over the coming weeks. Again, they refused payment.

Padre José sent me on my way by bus to the next town to meet the next priest. I don't know what sort of painkillers I was on, but I have no recollection of that night. Nothing was recorded to jog my memory apart from a solitary scribble on my itinerary: Gorgono? The fact that I'd written a question mark suggests that I didn't know where I was. I remember sitting on the bus, but that's it.

The following day wasn't as hazy. The swelling in my toe reduced substantially and with a tedious slow pull I slid my boot back on to be genuinely surprised with not the slightest hint of pain for the first time in months. I laughed. I was supposed to walk to Santa Clara, but the ability to walk painlessly put such a spring in my step that I walked straight on through to Río Hato. Along the way, a brand new silver minivan pulled over and a group of young Franciscan nuns jumped out. They were headed north for a retreat and had stopped at La Chorrera to say hello to their friend, Padre José. He'd spent his lunchtime telling them the story of the mission, inviting them to keep it in prayer, and charging them with the mission to find me, make sure I was okay and hand over fresh fruit, sandwiches and a juice. They were hilarious. Most of them were attractive twenty-something women absolutely full of life and smiles. I felt very cared for in Panama.

I prayed, sang and whistled on to the large town of Penonome, and then further afield to Natá. The Catholic church there was memorable, firstly because it was built in 1572. I checked it out from an engineering point of view and from a tourist point of view, before staying for Mass … for the God point of view. Every part of the building appeared to be the original 1572 beams, concrete walls and iron girders. Mind you, it may have had a facelift in 1750 and I'd be none the wiser. It was a treat to sit there thinking that Mass had been celebrated in that very spot for the last 435 years. The sermons relative to the 'modern' issues preached from the pulpit must have been wide and varied.

The second reason St James Catholic Church was memorable was due to the lady sitting in front of me who read the newspaper through Mass. She put it down to stand up for the creed, but as soon as she sat back down (which included when everyone else was kneeling) she picked it back up and read on. I sat behind her thinking, "What are you doing here?" She didn't listen to the scripture readings, nor participate in the prayers of the faithful or listen to the sermon. Perhaps she was fulfilling an obligation? She was getting less out of the Mass than I was and I couldn't speak the language!

After the final hymn I again struggled with the parishioners. I've always understood a statue to be like a family photo or a signpost that reminds us of God's goodness and work in the world through His Church and Saints but, in Natá, a few women walked around visiting each statue, kissing them, placing their hands on them and stroking them lovingly while looking up at the face and praying. The process was repeated over and over around the church. It's possible they were letting the statue act as a reminder of God's glory manifested through the lives of the Saints, but if I was an outsider who hadn't seen a lot of that sort of thing then it would really look like they were making idols out of them. I felt uncomfortable there.

The invitation to pray for unity was well received at every town I visited, bar one, and I rarely felt threatened; but the further north I walked, the more I had that sinking feeling that I was headed deeper into the jungle. With the surgery having provided amazing relief I bounced on down the road to Divisa, Santiago and then out along the stinking hot Pan-American Highway along the edge of lush farmland crawling up sprawling hills lathered in steaming forest. The heat made that day a slow one and the sun was setting when I arrived in the inconspicuous hillside village of El Higo.

El Higo was not much more than a few rows of houses set on the edge of a dusty town square. There was no hotel or staff at the locked church, and when I went to introduce myself to the locals they just ignored me, or flicked their hands at me and turned their backs. The gringo wasn't welcome. There was a shop in the village, which was nothing more than a window cut into the front of a home, and it appeared to have the village's only television. It was set up on the edge of the window with the evening game show playing. I bought a few odds and ends in an effort to put a full dinner together, but it didn't exactly fill me up. They had very little. A number of young men sat on a log at the front of the shop watching TV, so I took a seat a few metres down from them. A couple of times they went off into conversations about me that I couldn't fully understand ... and they knew it. I felt very out of place and unwelcome.

A young man appeared with his three-year-old daughter and sat between me and the young men, placing his daughter up onto his lap. The guys continued with their raucous conversation, but the new guy just played quietly with his daughter. He looked across at me and said hello, offering his hand in friendship. His name was Adolfo.

Adolfo was excited to hear about the mission and tried to tell the other guys where I'd come from, but they continued to just flick their hands at me. They wanted nothing to do with me. Adolfo was twenty-four years old and he patiently did his best to understand my broken Spanish.

At the end of the night the television was turned off and everyone departed for their homes. I'd resigned to having to put my hammock up on the edge of the forest but, after everyone had left, Adolfo stood up with his daughter in hand and asked, "Do you need somewhere to sleep? You can sleep at my house. I don't think my wife will mind." I was so thankful.

Under the aid of my torch we walked on out of the village, down a hill, across a small creek, through some banana palms and up onto a cleared field. He appeared trustworthy, but as we ventured further into the night I made sure there was always space between us, just in case. His unlit home was tiny. It was a wooden open-faced tin roof shed. It couldn't have been more than three by three metres. Adolfo's wife welcomed me with a smile. There was no running water, no toilet, no electricity and they had no address. They didn't even have a door across the massive doorway, so had to sling their hammocks high from the roof to keep away from dangerous animals. Their daughter had to be placed up in her hammock.

Adolfo asked if I needed anything to eat, but I could see under my torchlight that they had no food. I was so hungry and thought that if he'd offered that perhaps he had a bag of rice stashed away somewhere, so I said, "Yes, please. I don't need much, but anything you have would be great, please." Adolfo excused himself and ran back up into the village to go door knocking, returning ten minutes later with half a bread roll and a slice of sausage on it. I was so embarrassed.

Adolfo's wife and daughter swung to sleep in their hammocks as Adolfo and I sat out under the stars chatting slowly about everything from Australian sports, to how he likes to cook rabbits and how far coyotes came down the mountains. My Spanish was poor, but we communicated with ease. We retired to our hammocks late in the evening and I swung gently, gazing out at the stars until I fell asleep.

At sunrise Adolfo returned to the village to grab a bread roll each for us and then cut a clump of wild lemon grass, which he threw into a pot of water, placed a length of sugar cane in and boiled over a small fire. It made a pretty good lemon grass tea. His wife and daughter walked off hand in hand up into the village, leaving us to chat over breakfast. He'd been chatty for most of the

Adolfo, who would have such an influence on me, and the journey ahead

morning, but as his wife and daughter walked off through the banana palms he fell silent. After a few quiet sips I asked him, "What's it like living here?" He palmed the question off, answering it by referring to his disappointment in the Panamanian soccer team's poor defence.

I changed the subject and instead asked a question about his wife and daughter. He lowered his head. After a long pause he looked back up with tears in his eyes and said, "Sam, tomorrow I'm leaving my wife and daughter. You know last night in the village how no one would talk to you? It wasn't because you are a gringo; it was because you are not one of them, and in this village if you aren't one of them, you're never one of them." He lamented, "I wasn't born here. My wife and I moved here six months ago to be closer to her elderly parents. The locals still won't talk to me though. Her parents are the only people I can beg for food from. That's where I got the bread roll from last night, but I was hoping to get four bread rolls, not one. We hadn't had dinner either, Sam. All they had was one spare, which I gave to you."

I couldn't believe he'd done that for me. He had no friends, no job and no money. I asked about work there and he sighed, "I can't get a job because no one will talk to me. They keep the jobs within the families. I ask for work, but they just flick their hand at me and walk away. I'm so lonely here. You are the first guy I've had a good conversation with in six months. My wife and I have pulled together the few dollars we have and bought a bus ticket to Panama City," which was 250 kilometres to the southeast. "Once there I'll try to find work. I'll probably just sleep on the streets to start with, but I'm hopeful of finding accommodation." Adolfo's plan was to earn as much money as he could and send it home to his wife so that they could eat.

"How long until you return?" I asked him.

Without looking up he mumbled, "Three, maybe four months. I don't know." He was overwhelmed. The conversation fell silent until he rose from his wooden bench seat and indicated that he wanted to give me something to remember him by. He walked inside and picked up his daughters only toy; a small pink Dino doll from the Flintstone's. "She doesn't play with it anymore." Dino had a plastic key ring attached to his head, because he was a McValue Meal Dino. Adolfo wore a thumb rosary around his left thumb, ten beads with a cross hanging off it, and he did all his work with the right hand while holding onto the cross with his left. He slipped it off though and pushed it over Dino's head so that he was wearing it like a necklace. Handing Dino to me he gestured for me to attach it to my backpack.

Adolfo sat back down and looked up through glazed eyes, "I'm giving you this so you won't forget me. I'll never be able to see the world like you will. I won't even get to see all of Panama. Dino might as well go with you. Every day is a struggle just to stay alive. Please don't forget me. Pray for us." I was floored. He was sacrificing everything for his family.

I pulled a postcard of Tasmania out of my backpack that I'd carried to show people what my home looked like. I wrote my details on the back and handed it to him with an invitation to pray for unity and for me, while I prayed for him. We shook hands in agreement and he placed the postcard on his wall next to a cluster of loose photographs of him with his daughter. He accepted some money from me with half a smile and ran down to the creek to cut a length of sugar cane for my day's sustenance.

I walked on from El Higo with Dino attached to the side of my pack, flicking into view every step I took for the next twelve and a half thousand kilometres to Spain. I walked on from that village feeling disgustingly rich. I'd never had to compare my circumstances to someone in Adolfo's situation. It ripped at me, to the point where I stopped walking twice that day and sat in silence, pondering his life and mine. Why on earth was I walking and praying for Church unity? Surely there were more important areas to direct my attention to. It was a struggle to put the encounter with Adolfo into perspective.

For the next 150 kilometres to the city of David everything seemed to slow down. It was hot, it was disgustingly muggy and it was frustrating trying to convince myself that this whole walk around the world for unity was worth ten cents. Having said that, I also wondered how much the divided Church had harmed, rather than healed, the divisions in the world.

On the way to the city of David I stayed at a missionary school filled to the brim with boarding students, each carrying a little of Adolfo's story. There was hardship and sacrifice in all their lives, not that many of them recognised it. They were just happy to play soccer.

After dodging a few more snakes and narrowly missing a massive tarantula that had a few hairy legs already draped across my walking poles when I went to stand up after a rest—ugly—I walked on through beautiful forest with its steep hillsides. From deep within the jungle an incredible sound erupted: a group of monkeys and a pack of coyotes came face-to-face. They made a fantastic racket until the smile was literally wiped off my face by a passing truck that flicked a stone bullet-like straight into my front tooth. "Crack!" I swung off the side of the road holding my mouth before spitting out fragments of tooth. Brilliant. I scanned my teeth with my tongue, determining that two had been chipped.

I'd like to think that if I weren't distracted I would have snatched the rock out of the air with my teeth.

I arrived in David under the dampness of an afternoon downpour. I was drenched from head to toe, but smiling—albeit a dented smile—and buoyed by the prospect of new boots. My current boots were falling apart and I was eager to slip my feet into something a little fresher. A worker's hostel offered cheap beds allowing me to rest before finding the new boots first thing in the morning.

By now, somewhere on the streets of Panama City, Adolfo was alone and searching for work.

> *"To love him with all the heart, and with all the understanding, and with all the strength," and "to love one's neighbour as oneself,"— this is much more important than all whole burnt offerings and sacrifices.*
>
> Mark 12:33

Total walked: *3,020 kilometres*

**walk4one** *Paving a Path to Unity*

# Scorpions, Highway Knives and a Thunderstorm Pursuit

*May 2007*

My boots were nowhere to be found. They'd been mailed to the city's Caritas office, where the secretary struggled to understand my Spanish but eventually accepted that I had mail there. She turned the place upside down trying to find them, but without success. She simply asked me to return the next day to speak to her English-speaking colleague.

I booked back into the dim, warped hostel and unpacked in my tiny cubicle with a ¾ wooden wall and fly-mesh making up the rest. It was sufficient, whenever the lights worked.

The boots never turned up. The manager of the Caritas office was a fellow by the name of Padre Xiegdel and he helped me for five days straight trying to track down the missing boots. When Paddy Palin, the outdoor store back home, emailed through the shipping advice showing that the package had arrived in Panama twelve days ago, we concluded that they'd been stolen. That just made me smile though. The disappointment on the face of a thief discovering he'd stolen a pair of size sixteen boots that wouldn't fit a single person in all of Panama would be priceless. "Good luck selling those," I thought.

Over the five days in David I extended the invitation to pray for unity to every church. A humble Methodist minister invited me to relax with him and his wife over lunch. As I left, he asked me to keep his wife in my prayers while she battled breast cancer. It made their joyful hospitality all the more significant. For the majority of the week I had little to do but attend Mass and contemplate my encounter with Adolfo, glancing down many times at the Dino doll attached to my pack.

An Australian fellow and his Costa Rican wife contacted me via email with an invitation to stay with them as I passed through San José. They'd been following my journey online. Damien and Tatiana led a small youth catechesis group and they were all excited to join me for the short twenty kilometre walk scheduled from San José to neighbouring Alajuela on Saturday the 12th of May, 2007, which was just over a week away. I made the decision to push on from David without new boots, causing a new dilemma: if I walked from David to San José and walked a series of very long days it would take me a minimum of nine days, so I'd miss the opportunity to walk with the group on their day off. Not one person had walked a day with me at that point and, with few people in Panama hearing of the invitation to pray for unity beyond the immediate face-to-face contact, I decided that the opportunity to walk a day with those youths would be a more fruitful option for the mission than to walk the entire distance from David and walk on from San José alone sometime in the middle of the following week. I swallowed my pride and opted to take transportation for the next two days, racing from town to town while extending the invitation to pray for unity.

The Costa Rican border along the Pacific Ocean was one of the most stunning areas I'd seen, making my decision to rush through even more unpalatable. I stopped at Río Claro for the Saturday vigil Mass, where the padre spoke on my behalf and invited the congregation to pray for the complete unity of Christians. They were all very keen to chat after Mass and a bed was secured for me out the back in the youth group room.

In the next town, Villa Colón, I visited the town's churches one by one before deciding to put at least an hour aside for walking and praying. I set out along a country road through forest-covered hills and mountains that swept down sharply to the seaside plains to the west. The tall forest provided relief from the blistering heat and every now and then a beautiful pocket of cool air escaped from its depths. There was very little traffic. Part way through a rosary a bloke on a dirt bike wearing a World Youth Day t-shirt pulled over to say hello. Our conversation became quite animated when he heard I was an Australian because he'd been saving his money to fly to the next World Youth Day in Sydney. He'd attended in Germany and he was getting the students of the small school he taught at excited about Sydney 2008. He happily accepted the invitation to pray for unity.

I wished I was the one on the motorbike.

When I stuck my thumb out to hitch a ride I hadn't reckoned that three hours and fifteen kilometres later I'd still be slogging it out along the edge of the jungle before at last scoring a lift to the tiny beachside tourist village of Dominical. With sunset very near I called it a day and wandered through the towering coconut palms, kicking up sandy soil as I went down onto the edge of the Pacific Ocean. Palm trees curved out over the wild beach; the forested hills rose behind them. It was practically deserted with a brilliant red sunset between enormous thunderclouds on the horizon.

I stripped my shirt off and ran into the surf like a veteran ironman, but I immediately struck rock underfoot and smashed into the water like a bag of dropped potatoes. Struggling hopelessly to gain a footing on the rolling rocks the waves crashed in over me, forcing me to painfully crawl back out over shifting stones.

I dragged myself back up off the beach and searched for accommodation instead.

For a few dollars I could sling my hammock in a wall-less A-frame shelter just off the beach. With hammock hooks everywhere, the sleeping space was an open-air sleeping platform on top of the concrete box building housing all the amenities within the structure. There were no lights in and around the sleeping area and, after showering, I was left to find my way back to the hammock in darkness. I didn't see a lone concrete step and I had thongs on. I slammed my right foot fair into the step. As if shot by a sniper I crumpled to the ground in pain and could feel warm blood running under my foot. Buckled over with my jaw clenched I tried to remain silent, not wanting to wake the other guests. Breathing was difficult.

At least it wasn't the healing left foot, but wow, did it hurt.

I limped back to my hammock and grabbed my torch. The split was deep and ugly. It was rather providential that I was already carrying toe-healing equipment. With the aid of my mouth-held mini torch, and a lot of grimacing, I patched it up, starting by pulling the skin out of the wound. It was exhausting and when I finished the job I slumped back into my hammock to sleep.

The distant thunderclouds drifted towards land that night and each rumble of thunder grew louder. The wind howled, lightning flashed and rain then pelted the A-frame's roof. I just smiled, wearily closed my eyes again and swung to sleep in the cool damp breeze.

I kept moving by bus for one more day, bumping and swerving our way along a treacherous dirt road through thick forest and past huge isolated date palm plantations. It took a few hours on that cramped, hot, motion-sickness-inducing bus, but we made it in one piece to the portside town of Quepos and then on to Damas. From there I was at last within walking distance of San José and capable of arriving in time for the youth group. I had three and a half days to cover one hundred and thirty-three mountainous kilometres.

It was mid-afternoon when I started out on foot for the twenty kilometres to a remote posada, which was filled with lizards, frogs and tropical beetles. I slept well and continued on from there up into the mountains. The dirt road I followed wound up through scratchy farms and a few five-star retreats. I passed no more than five cars the entire day. It was a spectacular, calf-burning ascent with tall forest that was home to playful spider monkeys, observant families of brightly coloured toucans and the odd blue Ulysses butterfly—the size of both my hands—fluttering along the track in front of me.

A few hours into the mountains, I walked through a tiny village tucked into the camouflaging forest. I felt like I'd travelled 100 years back in time. They were lovely people. The temperature dropped with increased altitude until the sky blackened under a billowing afternoon thunderstorm. The difference this time was that I'd walked well over a kilometre above sea level and, instead of looking up at imminent danger, I looked out into it. The track followed a precarious line along mountainous drop-offs on both sides, leaving a narrow link between peaks. An earth-shattering crack of thunder resonated through my body and the conditions deteriorated into a torrential downpour, churning the track into a fast flowing river, filling my boots and saturating my clothes. Lightning bolts crashed into the surrounding mountains and while hustling along a thin mountain link I glanced out into a valley in time to see a lightning bolt strike down through the clouds into the shrouded depths. I was suspended in the heart of a storm and it lashed at me to such a degree that the skin on my fingers shrivelled and I couldn't keep my eyes open for the watery barrage.

With water squishing out of my ratty boots and dripping off my nose, I completed the forty-nine kilometres in darkness and arrived at the town of Salitrales, perched high above a broad valley. There was a pub, an unstaffed church and no one on the street. The pub-owners chatted to me while I drip-dried and were amazed at where I'd walked from that day. They noted, however, that: "The next posada is a few hours' walk from here." I was exhausted, so I just rolled my eyes, decided to let God sort it out, and relaxed with dinner. The accommodation offer came soon after as the owners returned. They invited me to set my hammock up in the entertainment room adjoining the pub. If I could find a place to sleep in there, it was mine for the night. The concrete-floor room was at least indoors. I figured out a way to hang my hammock from the ceiling and, although it was nearly two metres off the ground, it suited me fine.

After a hearty pub breakfast with the owners, I walked on towards San José. I only managed a kilometre before a piercing pain ripped across my back, like a hundred ants biting at once. I flew into a frantic strip, reefing both the backpack and my shirt off. Nothing fell from my shirt when I flicked it so I whipped it over my back to hit whatever had bitten me—if it was still there—but there was nothing that I could see. My shoulder blade stung and pain rifled through my body. My back began to swell. I slid the shirt back on and the backpack over it ... and walked on, praying.

The pain subsided slightly, but remained discomforting. I passed wonderful views of farmland and villages spread along the mountain valleys. After some time I started to feel weak and nauseous. Focussing my eyes became a struggle. My breath was laboured. Pretty soon, I felt like curling up to die. I plonked myself down under a tree, still not knowing what had happened or if the symptoms would pass.

My heart spasmed: stop … restart … it began missing beats. I was in trouble. Every few minutes it spasmed, missed a beat and, with unspeakable relief, fired back up. It was a lonely and sickening time, propped up groggily against that solitary tree, high above sprawling farmland, with a beautifully landscaped garden hanging above me on top of the hill. It was a nice place to die, perhaps, but I preferred not to. "Lord, help me, please. May your will be done."

I glanced up the road to see a man walking my way with a machete in hand. I pulled myself upright as he passed by and he smiled, saying, "Olla." I replied with a very Aussie, "G'day," and he stopped dead.

"Bloody hell, you're an Aussie!" he replied with an Australian accent.

"So are you!" I laughed.

Peter wasn't a doctor, but he was great company. He was born and raised in Sydney, but had moved to Costa Rica with his wife to begin a yoga retreat centre, which happened to be hidden behind those manicured gardens above me. He checked out my back and offered his diagnosis: "It looks like a scorpion sting." There was little we could do so he just sat with me under the tree and kept me talking for half an hour until my heart stopped skipping beats, the colour returned to my face and I was capable of slowly standing back up. I tentatively walked on.

For the past month I'd felt God challenging me to let go of my desire to defend myself and to just accept whatever happened. Walking on with my health returning, I pondered my experiences of verbal abuse in Venezuela and the assault on the Colombian border. I'd often revisited those moments, where more than often I'd fought back, and although most would argue that I had a right to defend myself, it felt like God was challenging me to let go and not fight. It was difficult to grapple with because as much as I could say "yes" to the challenge right there and then, I knew that if I was put back into the same situations I'd do exactly what I'd done previously. Any "yes" to not fighting back would be nothing more than lip service.

The country road gave way to modern, sprawling towns either perched along high escarpments or threaded perilously along thin ridges. The churches were welcoming and I was impressed by a teenage girl who roared past on a quad bike along the main road, dropped it down a gear and power-slid through a sweeping bitumen corner. Seriously impressed.

I'd organised to meet my San José contacts—Damien and Tatiana—outside the church in nearby Villa Colón. It was pouring with rain when I wrapped up the forty-five kilometre day and I was well pleased to see Damien pull over to pick me up. We drove back to their home in San José for dinner and a bed, with the intention of returning the next day. Damien had grown up in Melbourne and he and his wife had heard of my passing through Costa Rica via an Australian World Youth Day publication. From the very outset, as we drove into San José, there was something familiar about him. We both commented that we thought we'd met before, and to our amazement, we had a number of friends in common. Eventually we hit on it. We'd met at a friend's party back in 2006 and, not being party revellers, had taken a seat in the lounge room to chat the night away. I still remember that mechanical engineer who was about to marry the love of his life in Costa Rica, and Damien remembered the tall Tasmanian, also a mechanical engineer, but who was working in youth ministry. Here we were, a year later, introducing ourselves again on the other side of the world!

Their hospitality was incredible and their comfortable apartment in a secured housing complex a delight. They had a toilet.

Damien dropped me back to Villa Colón the next morning for the small day's walk into the hustle and bustle of San José with its incredible mixture of poverty and wealth. Costa Rica had no street names, which made navigation awkward, but I couldn't help but laugh at the unique way they addressed letters. In theory my address could be: Sam Clear, Villa José, 200 metres west of the old tree, 150 metres south of the tavern.

It paid to know your neighbours in San José.

While entering San José I again felt that urge from God to let go of my right to retaliate if anything should happen and to instead be docile. This time I was able to conclude that, as much as I wanted to defend myself, if God was asking me to do something ... I wanted that more. With some sort of conviction my attitude changed and I relaxed, knowing that if I was placed in a dangerous situation I could restrain myself from fighting back. In short, that meant coming to a place where I was content with the possibility of death.

Wandering along the city streets I half expected trouble every time I passed anyone looking at me. I thought God would immediately test me; but, happily, I made it to the central San José Cathedral without incident, and extended the invitation to pray for unity before returning to Damien and Tatiana's.

That night, after Damien and Tatiana went to bed, an Australian radio station called for a ten-minute interview. We talked mostly about my encounter with the puma, and the interview basically went well, but there were two moments that bothered me. Adolfo was still on my mind and I nearly downplayed the importance of unity on national radio when I spoke about the importance of loving one another over the importance of uniting the churches. I still hadn't made the connection between unity and what I saw in Adolfo's village: his fight to support his wife and daughter. Perhaps it wasn't confusion, but anger. The other frustration was the interviewer's closing line. He signed off with, "Yes, well in the end we're all brothers and sisters in Christ and that's all that matters I guess, isn't it?" To which I replied, "Yes, absolutely." It seemed to be a nice ending, but as soon as I'd hung up I thought, "No, it's not all that matters in the end. The fact that we are brothers and sisters in Christ is not an end point, but a beginning, and from there we are called, through love, to unite. Unity isn't about standing back and accepting errors, it's about getting your hands dirty and not giving up on each other." I kept replaying it in my mind and kept hearing the interviewer's comment as a palm-off to the issues facing the Church. The slap-on-the-back, "You're okay, mate" attitude doesn't unite churches: it just allows them to coexist without pressure, possibly in error and at a distance from one another. I wanted to call him back and say, "No, it's not all that matters in the end. Truth is important in uniting the churches. We aren't the Church of Pontius Pilate (What is truth?') and it'll take a lot more dialogue and prayer than a simple 'You're okay, mate' to pursue it." For that interview at least, the moment had passed.

Tatiana called the San José newspaper as well and they dispatched two reporters to travel out a few hundred metres east of the black stump, a few hundred metres south of the pub, and find me for a chat. I was so pleased to have the mission taken across the country, but all my gear was in the wash so Tatiana had to fit me out for a photo in a pair of Damien's suit pants to go with my tight-fitting thermal T-shirt. I threw the boots and backpack on and looked like the best-dressed pilgrim the world had ever seen. The interview was written compassionately, the photo turned out well and the invitation was indeed taken to the whole country.

On Sunday morning, Damien, Tatiana, their youth group and I gathered on the steps of the cathedral for the twenty kilometre walk to neighbouring Alajuela. Damien and Tatiana had invited me back to their place that night, so I'd left a few items of clothing at their apartment, and I was ready for the short walk with a light pack. We gathered on the steps and a television crew appeared for an interview, but so did a middle-aged woman with a large envelope. She handed it to me, saying, "You need to read this." The document was written in Spanish, so I replied, "Sorry, I can't read Spanish." She just insisted that I read it and she walked off.

Tatiana scoured the document. It was a series of attacks on the errors of the Catholic Church and an explanation on why the Growing in Grace Church was the one true Church. I asked Tatiana if she wanted to read it, but she laughed, "No, I know about them and they scare me!" For months after that I saw television programs made by that Church and I agreed ... scary stuff. Any pastor who tattoos "666" on his arm and claims to be the "new" Jesus is always a little different, to say the least.

Once the eight youth group members had arrived in the city centre, all eleven of us hit the road, chatting and laughing. Out on the main road we quietened to pray a rosary (a major point of conjecture in itself for most non-Catholic/ Orthodox Christians) until we approached a large bridge spanning a deep canyon. On the other side of the six-lane highway two young men standing on the edge of a shantytown whistled out to us. They shouted something, but Tatiana told us to just keep moving. Whatever they shouted, it wasn't encouragement. They whistled down into the shantytown and disappeared for a moment before re-emerging along the top of the highway cutting with two more young guys. Their shirts were tied around their heads.

We crossed the bridge as the four men ran ahead of us as and ran through the traffic to our side. Their tied shirts flailed in the wind. In single file they made to walk back past us as we stepped off the bridge, but as they drew alongside they reached behind and each produced long-bladed knives. The leader, who had long dark hair flowing out from underneath the wrapping shirt, looked like revolutionary Che Guevara. He pressed his knife up hard against my abdomen and forced me back, while the other three men did the same with Damien, José María (the only other guy) and one of the girls.

Traffic flowed past as we were lined up against the railing and stripped of everything valuable, one person at a time. 'Che' wanted my backpack, but struggled to undo the straps with one hand, so placed the knife back in his jeans and reached up with both hands. I was over a foot taller and twenty kilograms heavier. With both hands up on my top backpack strap I thought, "I'm going to plummet you." He was wide open for a kick to the groin before slamming his head down onto my knee quicker than you can say, "Where's your knife, Che?" But as open to being smacked unconscious as he was, I'd only just made the decision to be docile in that exact situation. The other three men still had their weapons drawn, so to take out 'Che' may have placed the rest of our group in danger. It was a painful ten seconds standing there letting him fumble with the straps, strip the pack from me and heave it on. "It doesn't even fit you properly," I thought.

The next thief down frantically stripped jewellery off everyone, so with 'Che' struggling with my backpack, I withdrew my hands to behind me, unclipped my watch and flicked it backwards into the tall grass. It was as solid as a rock and hit the ground with a horribly heavy crunch. I cringed, thinking they had to have heard it, but no one flinched. 'Che' stepped in, removed the sunglasses from my head and ripped my sleeves up, looking for a watch. I just raised my eyebrows at him.

The four men took flight down the bridge with four backpacks, a number of cameras, mobile phones, wallets, watches and sunnies. We were left standing on the edge of the highway in shock. We quickly turned to each other to make sure all were okay, and a number of the younger girls fell into each other's arms, crying. I plucked my watch from the grass just as two motorbike police rode down the highway. Damien and I launched out into the traffic to snatch their attention and our short-lived sombre post-mugging reflection turned rapidly into an aggressive bid for justice.

We sprinted through the slowing cars, pointing the police towards the fleeing thieves. Their lights flashed into action as they accelerated between the cars. Within thirty seconds, around ten police vehicles were screaming through the heavy traffic from both directions. Adrenalin was pumping. We gave chase, sprinting through the now crawling traffic, flanking the weaving motorbikes across that high bridge. The thieves were being set upon from all directions, so veered through the traffic and made the end of the bridge just before the oncoming police did. The men turned on a hairpin around the edge and scampered down the steep canyon walls, ducking as the police opened fire.

Damien and I ran on, jumped the traffic divider and jogged over to the gathered police. The thieves had split into pairs deep within the canyon, making off in different directions and disappearing from view. The circus had only just begun.

With six lanes of traffic stopped and police cars everywhere, it wasn't long before a succession of news crew arrived. The media were forced to wait as police cars scrambled to head off the offenders at both ends and the remaining officers gathered to take statements.

Once free to talk with the media, Tatiana sheltered the youth group and spoke with great composure for a person who'd just been mugged at knifepoint. She told them what had happened and then in great detail why we were walking. With so many varied media outlets represented, the invitation to pray for unity suddenly received more exposure than ever before, but it had come at a price for all of us.

One of the girls was more upset than the rest so Tatiana tried to comfort her. What we soon discovered was that the thief who'd held her at knifepoint had gabbled, "Hurry up or I'll pull the gun out and kill you." She was in shock. Most of us had thought that knives were the only weapons present, but the girl who'd been standing next to her confirmed that she also thought that particular guy had a gun. I was lost for words, realising the danger I absolutely would have placed everyone in had I decided to fight 'Che'.

The highway wasn't a good place to debrief. We made the call to stick together and meet back at a country club near Damien and Tatiana's for a meal and to talk through the incident. Little by little we found comfort in being at that country club, talking about being mugged, as opposed to being out on the highway bleeding to death. We prayed that God would use what had happened for His good, and that the muggers would be blessed with forgiveness and faith. I still wanted to hit 'Che' though, so that prayer didn't come easily.

One of the parents, a bank manager, helped me cancel my credit card, but we left the debit card active just in case the police recovered my gear. Being overseas without access to money was going to be difficult.

Damien and I jumped in the car to drive back to the bridge. There was no real plan or intelligent reason for going there, we just weren't content with sitting at home. We drove slowly through the dusty shantytown of tin sheds and mud-brick homes, meticulously scouring every face we passed. Tatiana rang with the news that the police had caught one of them, so we hotfooted it back to pick her up and proceeded to a large police building, close to where we'd walked that day.

The police had apprehended a man in possession of a few stolen goods as he emerged from a field and they found three dumped bags nearby. To my absolute delight, one of them was mine. My poles were still attached and so I was hopeful that all my gear was still in it but, alas, my camera, Antarctic jacket and numerous other items, including cash and my Maglite torch, were gone. The other two bags suffered the same fate and most of the expensive items had been taken. I was thankful, however, that my passport, Bible, and moneyless wallet were still sitting in the top zip pocket, together with my debit card, which would at least allow me to purchase more gear and walk on. I'd lost nearly $2,000 worth of gear.

There was a real sense of loss in having the film and photos on the camera taken from me—particularly the encounter with Adolfo. Staring at his daughter's Dino doll swinging from the side strap of my faded backpack, I had to admit that I was still in a privileged position. My parish priest once spoke about humankind's propensity to want to capture moments instead of simply enjoying them. If I ever needed a reminder, there was always Dino wearing Adolfo's cross.

The young man they'd arrested was being held in a jail down the road and we were asked if we wanted to meet and identify him. We jumped at the chance and drove to the tiny cement building with a solitary holding cell.

The police led out a young man, no more than sixteen years of age, by the name of Danny. He was ashamed, and stood there quietly, looking at the floor. He half looked up at us, but then lowered his gaze again, so we introduced ourselves, one handshake at a time. Tatiana did most of the talking again. She asked him straight up why he'd mugged us and he responded with, "Money for drugs." It was his first offence and he was the youngest of the four. My Spanish was improving by the day so I explained who we were and why we'd been walking, then handed him a World Youth Day postcard invitation from Tasmania that some friends had sent to me. I invited him to come to Sydney in 2008, but Tatiana shook her finger at him, "Only if you raise the money legally." He cracked a smile and nodded. Damien pulled out his rosary beads and asked, "Do you pray?" He nodded. Damien held the beads out and Danny opened his hand to receive them, wrapping his fingers around them and looking up with a smile. He mumbled a "Gracias," and extended his hand tentatively to make peace. We shook hands before he lowered his head and was led back to his holding cell.

It was a sobering moment. I have no doubt there was some sort of malice in the kid (otherwise you don't hold a knife to a person) but, beyond that, there was still a young man struggling in a poverty-stricken area and being conditioned by an older group of guys who didn't have his best interests at heart. I felt sorry for him.

"Did you recognise him?" the officers asked. None of us did. Apparently it didn't matter because he'd been caught fleeing the scene with the stolen gear; we were required to visit the local courthouse up the road to fill out more forms for the proceedings to be official.

We sat in that courthouse hallway for three tedious night-time hours … waiting. Damien placed a cup out in the middle of the hallway and we tried to flip a coin into it. What started as a means of passing the time soon became a focussed competition where every flip was greeted with appropriate applause or jeering. Tatiana was even drawn in and did pretty well, much to her delight. While retrieving one stray flip, the door at the end of the hallway opened and Danny was led across into another room. His head was bowed and Damien's rosary beads dangled from his handcuffed hands with the postcard being held onto firmly. I paused for a moment, raised my eyebrows at Damien, and then flicked the coin back to continue on.

We were so tired when called through to fill out the monotonous paperwork at around 11 pm. Who was I to complain, though? Tatiana did all the talking and writing. Damien and I were just whining moral support.

We arrived back at their apartment sometime around midnight and I called home to let my family know what had happened. It was a quick call, mainly because I reached Dad on the other end.

"I'm just calling to let you know I was held at knifepoint and mugged today."

"Well," he replied, "the fact that you're calling me suggests you must be okay!"

"Yes."

Mum on the other hand had a few more questions to ask, and advice to give.

She'd been at me for some time to arrange people to walk with me for safety, but having now been held at knifepoint while walking with ten people she decided that maybe I was better off walking alone: "You'll probably bring less attention to yourself if you're alone." I agreed.

There was a lot of work to be done to get back on the road. I had no camera, jacket, sunglasses, credit card, or water bladders, I had to attend a court hearing, and I was still walking in very old ratty boots that ripped my feet. I felt more than a little opposition to walking another day. At least I had a comfortable bed and a soft pillow.

I spent Sunday being interviewed by journalists, the only break being provided by the anonymity of Sunday Mass. Damien, Tatiana and I gathered in front of the TV as the Sunday night newsreader began: "He was attacked by a puma in Venezuela, held at gun point in Colombia, and now, Australian missionary Sam Clear, who is walking around the world for the unity of Christians, has been robbed at knife point in San José." In true media savvy fashion their Google Earth map scrolled up from South America to Costa Rica, labelling each incident as they went. The story was being played out across the nation's varied media, though the truth wasn't always adhered to—like being 'attacked' by a puma—but millions heard of the mission.

The court case wouldn't take place for another month, so I was required to provide my testimony to a judge at a closed court hearing, so that I could continue on my way. I needed a few days to purchase new gear anyway, so I wasn't in a hurry.

Damien and Tatiana provided beautiful hospitality, working me into their schedule to run me to the court appearance and shopping centres. I knew I wouldn't find the exact gear I'd lost, but I was hopeful of at least finding something to cover each basic need, and did … except for two items: the flashlight and waterproof backpack cover. However, that night Damien presented me with a parting gift: an LED headlamp. It was awesome. As for the waterproof backpack cover, I was already carrying a strong, orange plastic survival body bag and was pretty sure I could use it to form a makeshift cover for the time being. All up I spent over $1,000 replacing the equipment, which would have wrecked my flimsy budget had it not been for a few business friends back home (Philip Ryall, Marita Franklin, Fr Michael Kelly and Kristen Toohey) who pitched in to cover the cost. The new credit card was to be sent to the San Salvador Archdiocese office in El Salvador, so until then I'd just have to withdraw money regularly with my debit card.

When I was given my chance to speak before a judge I gave my evidence carefully, but it was garbled through translation. They'd learnt American English and my accent threw them all. It took a number of hours to give a ten-minute statement! Danny was also there and any sense of remorse had been replaced with a real gangsta swagger. As much as I thought the mugging hadn't affected me greatly, once I spotted him in the hallway my heart raced. I instinctively scoured the multitude of faces for the other three muggers, "Perhaps they were stupid enough to come with him? Perhaps they knew that I'd be there and have come for some sort of revenge for 'little bros' arrest?" Perhaps I wasn't dealing with it as well as I thought I had.

Tatiana picked me up late in the afternoon and drove me to a town on the outskirts of the city, from where I'd begin walking the next day. We passed over the now infamous bridge; I had no intention of starting walking from where we'd finished, despite any sentimental reasons. The bridge between San José and Alajuela had sufficiently played its part. We instead drove on to neighbouring San Ramón.

The San Ramón parish priest instantly recognised me. He welcomed me inside with laughter and excitedly grabbed his Sunday paper, displaying my photo to the secretary. She sat down to read the story while he ushered me into the sitting room and made a few phone calls. Within minutes the room had filled with the local youth group members. We had a ball of a time. The mission to pray for unity was accepted with humble smiles.

The padre offered me hammock-hanging space in his locked carport so I could rise before sunrise and leave without disturbing anyone. I was very grateful.

That first day back on the road was to be a thirty kilometre walk over a mountain range. I was now four days behind schedule, but I'd already played catch up across southern Costa Rica only to arrive just in time to be mugged. With no one waiting up ahead, I was content to let the walk take its course and tackle the hot, humid mountains.

I was nervous and felt particularly vulnerable. I prayed as I went, and passed numerous smiling local farming kids walking to their school bus, which helped ease my nerves. I was occasionally jeered at, but it was pretty timid stuff.

I walked on into thick steaming forest with small farming plots dispersed amongst it and suddenly heard a rustle in the undergrowth. I was startled as a man leapt down onto the road five metres in front of me, glanced up at me as he landed, turned and then walked on in front of me. I immediately slowed my pace to put ground between us and scoured the forest for any accomplices.

The man's right hand slid into his pocket and pulled out a knife.

My heart raced. "Here we go again." I firmed my grip on the walking poles, intending to use them to defend myself if needed. His grip concealed the knife, but it flashed into view every now and then while he walked. I looked to the other side of the road and considered crossing over, if only to see how he reacted and assess his intentions, but there was no time left. He raised the knife up in front of him, out of my sight.

I took a deep breath. "I'm ready for you."

His left arm lowered. He had a juicy mango. He cut it with the knife and raised a slice of fruit to his mouth.

He was eating lunch.

The man casually stepped out onto the road and wandered across, slicing another piece of fruit off. He straddled a wire fence and walked down a field towards his tiny wooden house, leaving me to walk on.

If I'm honest, I wasn't too far from taking the offensive before he had the chance to get me. If that farmer had simply turned to offer a piece of mango he could have easily copped a walking pole to the head … and that scared me. I was jittery and defensive. The wind flicked the loose length of my backpack strap into view near my waist and sent me into a frantic aggressive spin to ward off whatever had snuck up on me. I was met with nothing but an empty road through beautiful forest. There were a lot of prayers needed to refocus every hour.

I ate lunch at a tiny roadside diner where there was an outspoken ex-United States citizen. The mission captivated him, but I hadn't mentioned that I was a Catholic and he started berating Catholics for all the problems in Christendom. As far as he was concerned all Christians (like him and me) were united in Jesus and it was the Catholics' fault for every problem the Church had. He gloated about how he'd helped a young local girl escape the evils of Catholicism by pointing out to her that having statues in church was a sin. "It's right there!" He said. "The second commandment. 'Thou shalt not bow down to any image other than me.' It's right there." I was about to take him up on his interpretation of the second Commandment, but he moved on quickly to talk about how Catholics don't read their bibles and that they'd be saved if only they would. He then congratulated me on my mission and wished me all the best in converting the Costa Rican Catholics.

The congratulations didn't stick too well.

I was torn over which statement to comment on first, and how to both stand my ground while encouraging him to take up the invitation to pray for unity. I took the diplomatic approach in defending the Catholic Church, but let his gloat slide without comment. It was a side issue that could have led to a theological argument that distracted from the invitation to pray for unity. The radio announcer's closing comments about unity was still ringing clear, so I instead took him up on his notion that all Christians were united and that it's just the Catholics who weren't. I flat out disagreed with him and noted a series of examples that highlighted the disunity amongst non-Catholic Christians. For the many churches proclaiming that Christian unity exists, the idea of unity wasn't so much based around love, but passive indifference, like belonging to a club. He agreed and by the time I left he was setting his alarm for 4:01.

My objection to his interpretation of the second commandment was that it doesn't ask us to not make statues, but to not make an image of anything in heaven or on earth to bend down and worship. By his interpretation, if any image of anything on heaven or earth (whether it is being worshipped or not) is a sin, then a family portrait or a landscape painting could be viewed as sinful. Even God himself commanded Moses to forge two Cherubim out of bronze for the Ark of the Covenant and for the snake on the rod to be placed for the dying Israelites to look upon and be saved. The second commandment didn't forbid creating an image. It forbade worshipping anything other than God. I did agree with him on one point though. I had regularly seen people act around statues or images of Christ with more than just reverence. They did appear to worship the image. That being said, in churches where statues have been outlawed, I'd witnessed what could be described as the idolatress worship of the preacher or music ministry band.

I once had heard it said that idols are not made by hand, but with the heart.

Storm clouds gathered over the mountains and the rumblings of thunder rolled on as the day grew darker by the minute. A tropical storm erupted and saturated me ... fast. By day's end a painful heat rash had developed across my feet. There was no escaping the sticky humidity.

I passed by a village tucked into the jungle the next morning when a large dog trotted out of a house and across the highway. A semi-trailer hurtled past me from behind. The dog looked up and in that split second froze, cowered, and then disappeared to the sound of a sickening thud and pain-filled yelp. The truck didn't even brake. Its body twisted violently underneath before momentum threw him under the trailer wheels, spitting out a half-skinned carcass that slid to a stop right in front of me. I stood there, fixated on the dog's ear as it slowly curled down. It was like watching the last flicker of life fade. It was a jolt: how fragile life is.

The one upside to being back on the road was that a lot of motorists knew who I was. A car horn had previously indicated aggression or hatred, but that had changed. Passers-by even swung off the road to greet me and to take a photo, including two full family portraits. I was regularly offered food, or money for my next meal; nearly everyone that stopped offered an apology for the mugging on behalf of Costa Rica. They had taken it upon themselves to make amends, and often farewelled me with: "We're praying for unity. God bless." The invitation to pray for unity had spread far and wide and every encouragement lessened the difficulties of being there.

The long periods of sustained exercise through intensely humid days, coupled with afternoon storms, caused my skin to remain hot and damp for up to twelve hours a day. My skin didn't like that and, by the time I arrived in the town of Cañas, a stinging heat rash had spread across my back, arms and stomach. The other ailment I discovered was my troubled left foot, which hadn't quite closed up after the operation. My sock was bloodied. Both the operated-on toe and the one next to it bled profusely. It was a mess. My raggedy boots weren't coping with the afternoon rain and the torn leather liner was shredding my feet. And to top it off, the orange survival bag didn't work as a waterproof cover as well as I'd hoped. All my gear was saturated.

I hobbled to a little hardware store and bought a bright yellow roll of sticky tape, which I used to tape both the back of my boots smooth—in a bid to stop further irritation—and the orange survival bag to my backpack. Anything would help, and I had something helping me a little better than sticky tape: Damien. Damien wrote to me with the fantastic news that he'd found a pair of size sixteen Scarpa hiking boots in the USA. He'd ordered them, not that he knew how to get them to me, but he was an engineer—he'd work out a solution.

In the quiet night streets of Cañas, a crowd dispersed from a small Pentecostal church as I walked back to my posada. A few of the members knew who I was and chatted with me on the sidewalk, while receiving the invitation to pray for unity. The road to unity needed to start somewhere and I at least had hope in that starting place of prayer. From that fundamental foundation could stem a desire to be fully united and a willingness to step out, as painful as it could be, to allow God to mend the rifts. The mission had spread far and wide, thanks mainly to Danny and his three amigos. The mugging had produced some beautiful fruit.

People regularly stopped to say hello over the final 150 kilometres, making for a lively trip. The posadas were 'lively' too. I checked into one room only to find that the metal ceiling fan didn't work. I reached up to smack it on its way and … zzzzzzt … electricity surged through my arm. If I'd grabbed it instead of hitting it I may well have never let go alive. The momentum of the hit had brought us apart and as the fan seized up again after half a turn I recoiled to the bed in pain. Oww. It had thumped me. I felt tingly for a good while.

Over the couple of days leading up to Liberia, one driver had sounded his horn and waved a number of times, until he pulled over to introduce himself. Jonathan was the DJ for a local radio station, BeatFM, and he wanted nothing more than to encourage me. On the day into Liberia he pulled up with a work colleague and they opened the back door, allowing me to sit in air-conditioned comfort while consuming a huge lunch with iced drinks. A dedicated support crew would have made the whole journey so much more enjoyable!

I did the rounds at the Liberia churches, ate dinner with 'DJ' Jonathan, and then booked into a cheap posada where the humid rooms resembled holding cells. The one-inch thick foam mattress on wooden slates was not conducive to a good night's sleep. It was exhausting.

I walked on sluggishly into a thick, dry, crackly wilderness, home to a substantial population of jaguars. A man on a small motorcycle pulled over wanting to know why I was out there. He spoke fluent English, but he didn't fill me with any confidence. All he wanted to talk about was how dangerous it was out there, not just due to jaguars, but for the drug trafficking too. "There's a lot of smuggling at the border. It's not safe." He wandered around to the other side of his bike and undid a carryall container on the back as he noted, "A lot of people carry guns out here. It's normal. The thing is, if you're walking all alone near the border anyone could just pull a gun on you and strip you of everything you own."
My hair stood up on end as he reached inside with one hand and without raising his eyes said, "You take a big risk, all alone. If someone pulls a gun on you, what are going to do?" He looked up at me, "All it takes is one gun." I wasn't in a winning position.

"There's not much I can do," I replied. He nodded and lifted out a packet of biscuits, "Do you want a biscuit?" I could have killed the guy. I wish he'd chosen something else to talk about while ferreting for bikkies.

On approach to the Nicaraguan border my plans were altered slightly by a cheerful young padre in the large town of La Cruz. He knew who I was, so fed me and insisted that I stop walking for a few hours to join him in his ministry. He wanted me to meet a few locals who didn't receive many visitors. I was all in, so we jumped into his four-wheel drive and took off into the east along a gravel road. We drove through a wide shallow river before continuing up into the dripping wet green rainforest along the country's northern frontier. It was an amazing detour.

We celebrated Mass with remote subsistence communities tucked away on the slippery slopes and the padre extended the invitation to pray for unity at each of them. I enjoyed being out there. Beauty was everywhere.

The other plus was the padre's driving. The steep slippery rainforest tracks required a certain dedication to acceleration and he wasn't afraid to just gun it. He offered a lift to a lady from one village to the next and she begged him to slow down, but he just laughed every time. "It's the only way! Hang on!"

The joyful padre offered to drive me to the border, but I was happy to walk on through the pitch-black night under the light of my new headlamp. It worked a treat, but my ears did work overtime in the clouded night, listening for any danger. There was hardly a single car on the road, so I sang loudly, hoping to avoid a repeat of the Venezuelan puma. I was a lone voice in a dark wilderness.

I found a posada at the border and crossed over the next morning when it opened up. My boots were only just holding together; I took to using a new mixture of tissue paper and yellow tape to keep them from ripping up my feet. Just trust in God and carry ample sticky tape. I was quickly on my way for the forty-three kilometres to Rivas, and I immediately fell in love with Nicaragua. Beautiful rolling countryside followed the shoreline of an enormous lake with billowing volcanic islands spotted through it. It was breathtaking.

The people, on the other hand, were more difficult to appreciate. Costa Rican news was not Nicaraguan news, and the well-publicised mugging was now history. Death stares, 'gringo!' taunts and women running inside and locking the doors as I approached, were back. I felt very alone. There was no celebrity status in Nicaragua.

In the late afternoon the secretary of the Rivas Catholic Church generously found me a place to stay with parishioners. The hospitality was tainted when I wandered through Rivas to find other churches and returned to discover that I'd been robbed again. The house was secure behind an iron gate and a maid was present the whole time, so it appeared to be someone in the house. They'd lifted a week's worth of allowance, leaving me with only the few dollars in my pocket. With no one in the house speaking English it would have been a difficult conversation to hold without throwing wild accusations around, so I just let it rest and headed to bed.

Verbal abuse intensified the next morning; a number of machete-carrying men yelled at me to get out of their country. Even a four-year-old screamed his nut off at me. I was shocked. He was tiny. I was three times his height and probably seven times his weight, but it didn't stop him expressing his hatred at the passing gringo. I stopped and stared at him, as if asking, "What on earth are you doing little man?" He shut up and looked off to the side but, as soon as I walked on, he launched back into his rhetoric. As if that wasn't bizarre enough, two guys then passed by in a horse drawn cart and launched into a combination of aggressive threats and spits in my direction. There was actually something amusing about being heckled from a horse-drawn cart, even if they did have machetes. On it went for most of the day, both farmers and school kids took their verbal swipes at me.

After the sun had dipped behind a smoking volcano, I arrived at a remote Assembly of God church gathered for their Saturday night service. The thirty-odd members sang passionately, though mildly off-key, before the pastor spotted me and invited me to introduce myself. The mission was received with enthusiasm and the pastor led the congregation in interceding for complete unity.

I pushed on to Nandaime, singing all the way until catching sight of the town's lights. It was late and there was no ATM, so I explained my plight at a cheap posada and handed over my passport as collateral. I'd somehow find cash the next day. The owner kindly let me in. It was possibly the worst nearly-paid-for accommodation I'd had. The humid sweatbox concrete room had no windows, no air-conditioning, no fan and no mattress on the broken steel framed bed. Cardboard and a sheet had been placed over them to add 'comfort'. The communal bathroom was no better. The air was thick with mould, moss and slime growing in every nook and cranny. I couldn't sleep. I sweated non-stop and was grossly uncomfortable on the cardboard and steel rods. The forty-six kilometre-day-induced-tiredness made it all the more frustrating.

I caught a crammed bus the next morning to the neighbouring city of Granada, found an ATM and returned to pay for my cell. The Nandaime padre and a Pentecostal minister received the mission sincerely, while I 'received' a new, cooler and more comfortable room and stayed a second night. This time I slept.

I left Nandaime quietly praying a rosary under starlight, avoiding the pre-work rush of verbal abuse. Maintaining my pace for a good few hours, at sunrise the road split with no sign in view; I was faced with a choice of left or right. When I asked a man waiting for a bus, he pointed to the left, "Las Conchitas is that way."

It wasn't. Las Conchitas was to the right, but I didn't figure that out until I'd walked thirty kilometres in the wrong direction. His mistake, deliberate or not, turned into a beautiful blessing. It was the road less travelled, with space and numerous settlements to stop and rest at. The road rose higher throughout the day until a thick cool mist rolled in. Crude remnants of concrete buildings, with no roofs and a few walls missing, lined the road and the mist flowed freely through the hollowed out memories of a previous life. It was ghostly and silent but, for the first time in a long time, I felt comfortable in my own skin.

From the refreshingly welcoming town of El Crucero, the road wound down off the tablelands into Central America's second largest city: Managua. Lining the hills were stunning houses with flourishing gardens which were tightly secured behind cast iron fences with electric or razor wire atop. The residences were definitely not what I expected.

I continued to stop at any church I passed along the way until I arrived in the heart of Managua. There was no heartbeat. It was in ruins and abandoned. The contrast between the flourishing outer suburbs and desolate centre was overwhelming, like a scene from a Hollywood sci-fi horror. I was standing alone on the edge of the overgrown city park with trees stretching their limbs out through the shattered walls of surrounding buildings. My hopes rose when I saw a massive cathedral, but it too was gutted. Just to the side, looming above me, stood a clock tower. Its hands were frozen at 12:29.

An old man hobbled down the sidewalk, so I asked why the city centre was deserted. Over a few minutes he slowly educated me about the shallow earthquake that decimated Managua in 1972. Thousands were killed and the city centre was left to waste away as new centres were erected on the outskirts in the years of chaos that followed. The old man recalled how he'd run outside to see metre high shock waves rolling through the earth, one after the other, smashing houses. The fires and sickness that followed were just as devastating. The city was still picking up the pieces thirty-five years later. I wandered off across the overgrown, rubbish-filled central park. Two lone girls played on a rope swinging from a tree.

Damien emailed me with instructions to pick up my new boots at the Managua central DHL office, but if there's no central Managua, how could there be a central DHL? While searching for it I found the new massive Catholic cathedral, followed by two boot-less DHL offices until, at last, I found the DHL depot. There was a lot of tiring city walking involved. A huge wire-mesh fence ran along its front and when I pushed against the gate it didn't budge. I pushed again. Clunk-clunk. It was locked. I was livid. When two security guards walked up I thought everything was about to turn out just fine, but one pointed to his watch and shook his head saying, "We close at 4 pm. Special deliveries only."

It was 4:30 pm. It was a frustrating end to a tedious search.

The next morning the gate was open, but there were no boots. "We're sorry sir, but the plane your boots are on has been grounded at San José's International Airport." I said nothing. It was Thursday, so the pressure was on for the boots to arrive soon or I'd be staying for the weekend.

I wandered off and enjoyed some random conversations with old men watching life go by and mothers spending quality time with their kids outside their homes. It was a relaxing day even if it wasn't what I wanted to be doing. The invitation was handed on one random conversation at a time.

I returned to the depot at closing time to find that the boots had arrived, but customs had quarantined them. I was not intent on hanging around for another week of boots-waiting. I took a few deep breaths and asked how I could get my hands on the package. All she could offer was that I return the next day.

I didn't exactly skip down the street to the depot the next morning. I didn't hold much hope, but the lady at the desk smiled as I walked in and said, "They have arrived. I'll fetch them for you." It was an absolute delight to see those boots and they smelt so good. It had taken three months from the first enquiry to have them on my feet, and with no intention of binning the old ones I placed them in the box, taped it up and mailed them home. Three and a half thousand kilometres on foot through the tropics out of one pair of boots was pretty good.

I walked on with a genuine spring in my step despite knowing that it would be a tough journey breaking the boots in while walking thirty to fifty kilometres a day. The humidity rose and drizzle fell as the edge of a small Pacific hurricane pushed inland. Day seemingly turned to night and pretty soon lightning flashed through the strengthening storm. The boots were to receive their baptism in the ensuing downpour. The streets emptied and the water level rose rapidly, spewing out across the road up to two feet deep.

The storm wasn't the only danger.

Standing under a shop awning ahead of me were the only two men still out on the street. When one of them noticed me through the pouring rain he grabbed his friend's attention. Their glare was all too familiar. I stopped dead in the downpour, peering out through squinted waterlogged eyes, and turned my sights to cross the wide nature strip running down the middle of the road. The two men moved towards me, but stopped short of walking out from under the awning. They called out, "Hey gringo! Come here!" while gesturing as though they wanted to help, but there was no smile and no compassion in their invitation. They stepped out into the rain, "Gringo! Come this way."

My decision was made.

I stepped out and crossed over towards the median strip. "God, help me please." The two men stepped onto the road and their invitation through the pouring rain became more forceful. "Gringo! Stop! Come here gringo!" Their walk turned into a jog. One of them reached to the back of his jeans, clutching at a something. I ran. I ran hard across the wide median strip fearing the sound of a gunshot ringing out. It was a horrible feeling. The two men gave chase. Water splashed up over our legs and rain was belting us in the face. I scampered across the road to a small grocery store and, as I made the shelter of the doorway, I checked back through the watery shroud. Not wanting to follow me into the shop, the men had pulled to a stop in the middle of the median strip. They made a final gesture at me and turned back through the downpour, repeatedly glancing back my way.

The few locals in the grocery store stared at me nervously and kept their distance from the tall, saturated, heavily breathing gringo. I felt sick. When the heavy rain eased to a misty drizzle I nervously stepped back into the dark afternoon, scouring the waterlogged streets. The now natural tendency to contemplate worst-case scenarios suggested they'd potentially lay in wait further down the road, so every street corner was given a wide berth and every movement that caught my eye, scrutinised. Prayer was a non-stop conversation.

Rain slowly set back in and after a few hours I was close to leaving Managua. A young man sitting in the shadows of a veranda behind cast iron bars called out, "Hey, Americano!" Without breaking stride I nodded hello and went to walk on, but he was on his feet in a flash, peering out through the bars, and in perfect English asked, "Where are you from? And where are you going in this storm?" His English caught me by surprise. I stopped and replied, "I'm from Australia and I'm walking until I find somewhere to stay."

Cesar was a boxer. He was of average height but built ... well ... like a boxer. Half-Nicaraguan and half-American, he quickly invited me to stay as his guest and the iron gates were swung open. I was so scared that he'd pull out a knife and do me over, but his smile, enthusiasm, beautiful wife and one-year-old daughter soon had me at ease.

The house was simple, but standard for that part of the world, except for one glaring oddity. A sheet of tin, three foot wide by seven foot long, was missing from the roof. The downpour outside continued right on through to the living room and kitchen making the cement floor a war zone. Everything was up off the ground, stacked high on the benches and cupboards, while sand bags and towels encircled the flood. Every so often Cesar or his wife stepped into the lake to sweep it out the door with a broom.

I asked the obvious question: "Cesar, where's the tin?"

"It's in the backyard," he explained. "We have a double bed now and it was too big to fit through the doorway, so we took the tin off to lower it through."

"A new bed? Nice. Did you bring it in today?"

Cesar shook his head, "No, about two weeks ago."

Having watched them dedicate so much time to the flood over the last half an hour I blurted out, "But it's been raining in Managua every afternoon for the last week! Why haven't you put the tin back on?"

Without much thought he responded, "We just haven't had the time."

"But Cesar, it'd only take ten minutes to put the tin back on. Then you wouldn't have to do any of this."

His mind ticked over before he responded with, "Yeah, I guess it would."

The lights were flicked off and I was left to curl up on the couch to the sound of random drips on the flooded floor. Looking up through the hole in the roof into the dark night sky I saw a similarity between that roof and unity. Like shifting furniture around or dealing with floodwaters there were so many areas in the world requiring attention, but more problems would surface in time because the tin is missing. Our propensity to seek solutions to individual problems rather than looking for ways to prevent them, and numerous other related issues, could be a sign of the disunity that exists within the Church and society. To be united with those around us would be like fixing a length of tin to the roof. If we could find no reason to distance ourselves from the individual but cared so much that we were involved in each other's lives, we would have a Church, and society, so quick to respond with love that despair, fear and loneliness would rarely be given the opportunity to gain a foot-hold. The drip, drip, drip of, "It's not my problem—I'm right with God" filled the flood of indifference in the Church. Hopefully the tap, tap, tap of prayer, like nails into the tin, would clear the way for God to bridge the gap.

> *If then there is any encouragement in Christ, any consolation from love, any sharing in the Spirit, any compassion and sympathy, to make my joy complete: be of the same mind, having the same love, being in full accord and of one mind.*
>
> Philippians 2:1–2

Total walked: *3,603 kilometres*

# Swindlers, Stalkers & Salmonella

*June 2007*

Cesar saw me off in the morning with a warning. "My friend, be careful today. There are violent gangs in the area you are passing through. Watch your back." Great. It was ironic that my mission specifically had to target the very thing I now feared: people. While passing the outlying satellite city of Sandino I received a few derogatory—"Hey gringo!"—calls, but they never eventuated into anything more. My theory was that criminal gangs weren't in the business of rising early to make the most out of the day.

It took two days to reach La Paz Centro and, even though they weren't long days, the new boots had caused a blister to form under each foot. I arrived at the 6 pm Mass ten minutes early, but was confused to find the church packed and the service already underway. I kept my head down and took up a spot halfway down the aisle while they sang the opening hymn. Launching into the final verse, I looked up to watch a bride and groom walk back down the aisle followed closely by the priest. The song concluded, everyone applauded and the church was promptly vacated, leaving me standing alone applauding in bewilderment. I waited patiently for the scheduled Mass.

The long and hot forty kilometre trek to the rural city of León was disastrous. I made a horrible mistake. Instead of stopping immediately to tend to some foot soreness I pushed on to my next scheduled break over an hour away and, by the time I stopped in the entangled dry-season wilderness, the two blisters sitting in the arch of both feet had grown substantially. I was gob-smacked at their size. I did what I could with them, ensuring they wouldn't grow further over the remaining thirty kilometres, but no amount of tape or tricks would stop the pain. The stiff boots pushed hard against a part of the foot that hadn't seen pressure for five months.

In an attempt to ease the pressure I subconsciously adjusted my foot position each step, and consequently by lunchtime the outside of my left leg, at the top of the boot, was painful and I began to limp. My pace dwindled and by late afternoon when I reached León I was reeling. Every movement was laboured and I couldn't place my foot down without cringing.

The founder of a local religious order had just been canonised and León was celebrating. The centuries old cathedral overflowed for the vibrant Mass and the 'afterparty' of hymns, church bells, police sirens and fireworks created a deafening, but intoxicating blend. The town was alive. In pain, I just sat back on the cathedral steps with a local man, who chatted away while his boys clambered over the lion statue nearby.

I tended to my injuries that evening. The blisters were huge and a lump had formed on my leg just above the boot line. I couldn't apply any pressure to it and it had all the makings of being a stress fracture.

The overnight rest served me well and I left León at 5 am with only a slight niggle. At dawn, I pulled up in disbelief. Ahead of me was a man flogging his horse to make it move faster, but its legs were tethered to stop it running. The ropes had cut through the skin, creating weeping blood-socks, and the horse reacted to each whip with a sickening staggered lurch. I couldn't just walk by.

I unceremoniously stepped in between him and the horse while telling him what I thought of his weak and undignified actions. I let rip. I was over-stepping my tourist boundaries. He backed away with a scared stumble, heading quickly to the front of the horse, taking it by the reins and leading it on slowly. I didn't know if I'd overreacted, but maybe I shouldn't have stopped until the ropes were off.

The road to Chinandega passed below the ominous San Cristóbal Volcano, rising 1,745 metres above sea level and smoking gently under the clear blue sky. The blisters grew over the next two days, and then split. The real concern though was the lump on my shin. Pain shot up my leg. I tried massage, hoping it was muscular, but my heart sank when I pushed in and felt a localised stabbing pain. I hoped it wasn't a stress fracture, but it didn't look good. I was exhausted when Chinandega emerged.

The rising sun silhouetted the smoking San Cristóbal Volcano as I continued out along the fifty kilometre trek to Reyal the next day. Halfway there I found a roadside settlement and made a path straight for the general store. After polishing off a tub of yoghurt I tossed the container basketball-like into a nearby bin, but my perfect shot was met with looks of shock and dismay. I'd unwittingly 'three-pointed' my yoghurt tub into the settlement's dried corn kernel supply. I blurted out an apology and retrieved the tub, but as I stood back up the cross around my neck hooked on the side of the bin and literally popped the figure of Jesus right off! More shock and dismay. One woman sounded like she was about to faint. I fetched the Jesus figure from the corn and discovered it had little nails in the back. Without any thought, I hammered the figure back onto the cross with my fist.

The locals just stared in silence at the sight.

I found the real rubbish bin and bade a quick farewell.

My leg thumped with pain and directly ahead was an even bigger problem; an enormous black storm sent rapid-fire lightning bolts into the Nicaraguan plains. With the volcano towering off to the side, I stood on the edge of the settlement and weighed up my options. The storm was massive. I knew my leg needed a lengthy rest, I had to stop, but I wanted to finish Nicaragua on foot. I wanted to walk at least one country in its entirety. I stood there facing the storm, knowing there'd be a price to pay if I wanted to complete the remaining 100 kilometres.

I looked down at my new boots and muttered, "God please, let me at least finish this country." There was pride there, but also a desire to do the hard yards for unity. I limped forward down the dead-straight road, praying a rosary into the veil of darkness. The outer spray of the raging storm hit first before lightning bolts surrounded me. I felt like a steel pole on a skyscraper and flinched at every strike.

Then … it happened.

Without any prior indication, the storm split fair down the middle and the dark veil of hammering rain parted like the Red Sea. A one-hundred-metre-wide path emerged through the centre allowing me to walk on in amazement for nearly a kilometre, clean through the storm. I still flinched at every crack of lightning, but received nothing more than the storm's light drifting spray. I prayed non-stop and when I emerged onto the wet farmland beyond, the dark passage closed up behind me and continued to belt the fertile countryside.

"Absolutely awesome."

The next twenty kilometres were horrible. The pain shot through my leg as if a thumbtack was wedged between the top rim of my boot and shin. It was agonising. I placed so much pressure through the poles in an attempt to take the weight off my feet, but my arms eventually gave way. I stopped at one point and just cried. The pain was too much and when the sunset sank me into darkness, I was holding on by a thread.

After praying for a few hours, a single distant streetlight flickered into view. It was a roadside restaurant that offered nothing but stares, except for one young man named Neilson. He smiled and in decent English offered me a place to sleep. I struggled to accept his invitation, wary of sleeping in a stranger's home, and so stalled him for a while to gauge his character. At no stage did he become aggressive or forceful, but just maintained genuine concern with his invitation. I peered out from the roadhouse along a side road lined with houses and asked, "Neilson, is this a town?"

He smiled broadly, flashing a silver tooth, and replied, "You are in Reyal!" I accepted his offer and we headed inland on his tricycle-taxi along a bumpy dirt road to his simple home where he lived alone. Neilson willingly agreed to pass on the invitation to pray for unity to his local Baptist Church.

I continued hobbling on, determined to make the border on foot but my leg deteriorated further. When I struggled into Somotillo, a further forty-three kilometres to the north, I was limping badly. After the padre agreed to pass the invitation on to his congregation I turned to backtrack a kilometre to the only posada, but my leg had seized up. A man on a tricycle taxi pulled up and asked in Spanish: "Where do you need to go?" I jumped straight in.

After the five-minute ride we arrived at the posada and I went to pay him, but was taken aback by the price. It was a lot higher than I'd anticipated. I handed over the money, but while checking into the posada the lady there confirmed with remorse that I'd been charged nearly five times the going rate. With gritted teeth I pushed back outside to be met by a mass of tricycle taxi riders laughing at me from up the road. One called out, "Hey my friend, where do you want to go? For that many pesos I'll take you anywhere!" They roared with laughter.

I marched with a limp back through the town and 'my man' happened to ride up alongside again. I didn't recognise him at first, but he made the mistake of opening his mouth and saying, "I just dropped you at the hotel my friend and now you are back! Where do you want to go now?"

I smiled, "Did you steal from me?" I placed my hand firmly on his shoulder, and the blood drained from his face. He reefed my handful of money out of his pocket and threw it at me. I released my grip, took back two thirds and gave him one, which was still well above the going rate. He took it with a humble, "Thank you," and rode off, but anger got the better of me and I kicked his rear tyre, bouncing it off the ground. It free-spun, throwing the chain off the back spoke and my moment of lashing out only made me feel guilty. The young man threw the chain back on in a flash and rode off even faster, leaving me to make my apology to God and limp back past the jeering tricycle owners.

I managed to pace out the final seven kilometres the next day to the Honduras border with a lot of prayer and grimacing. The 399 kilometre crossing of Nicaragua was done. A moneyman exchanged my currency, but over morning tea a couple of friendly locals informed me that he'd short-changed me by a hefty 30%. "Here we go again." I limped back to the border, grabbed a policeman on the way and searched for him. He was nowhere to be seen, but an honest man stepped forward and happily gave me the owed money, saying he'd seek out his friend for the difference later. The policeman and I were very grateful for his generosity.

I could hardly move. I grabbed a room at the border settlement and, after a conversation-filled dinner at a roadside grill, headed to bed. I was so tired, but couldn't sleep. Soon the contents of my stomach were pushing up and a terrible lethargy set in. I'd eaten something bad. A deep pain set in and I curled into a foetal position, sweating profusely. The pain intensified over the next hour until I scrambled for the toilet and vomited my way through the night until 5:30 am. Only then was I able to release my fragile embrace of the porcelain and lay back in bed with a thumping headache.

"God, if it's okay, I'm taking the bus."

Honduras was a write-off. I was to pass through a thin three-day's-walk slice of the country, and the headache was set to stay with me the whole way. The short bus ride to each church to extend the invitation was excruciating. I did little more in Honduras than sleep, re-hydrate and pray.

On my final night in Honduras I was offered accommodation in a basic complex with a chapel opposite my chicken-wire-windowed room. I still felt awful and headed to bed early, but didn't remain asleep. Waking lethargically from a deep sleep at an unknown hour the dark reality set in that a man was slowly getting into bed with me. I flinched to fully awake and the dark shadowy figure retracted to the middle of the room. I was terrified. Lying motionless I had no idea what to do or if he carried a weapon. I acted as though still asleep, although controlling my breathing was difficult. He didn't move for a few drawn out minutes, but then backed away and slipped out the door.

I prayed for help, jumped up and approached the ajar door. His soft footsteps moved through the open-air corridor, paused for a minute, and then returned. I waited, staring at the door as it was pushed back open. I flicked the light on and seized the slightly built teenager by the shirt with both hands and carried him at pace across the corridor, bursting through the adjacent chapel door. He was terrified and his feet desperately struggled to touch the ground as I ploughed straight through the chapel's plastic chairs and flung him in front of the altar. He landed on his knees and thinking I was about to belt him he pleaded, "No, no, don't hit me! Jesus is here!"

I yelled at him, "Yes and he's the only one allowed in my room. Goodnight." I picked the chairs back up as I walked out and, with him beginning to pray, I locked the chapel from the outside, giving him a free evening with God. Securing my own door shut with a propped up chair, I headed back to bed in pain and *seriously* incensed.

By morning, the chapel was unlocked and the teenager gone. I was happy to move on by bus to the El Salvadorian border, fighting sleep deprivation. At least my leg felt better. The compounding mistrust of everyone and everything made it impossible to relax. I was so edgy. I checked the exchange rate with three exchangers before making a transaction with the first guy and looked over my shoulder at every turn. Every stare was a threat.

Spain was so far away.

To make matters worse, El Salvador and Guatemala had been proposed as the two most dangerous countries I'd visit. I prayed, "God, if you want a martyr I'm okay with that, but please protect me. I'll just keep walking, okay?" The leg pain had reduced enough to at least attempt El Salvador on foot but, in all honesty, I wouldn't have minded flying over it.

I began with a short walk to the town of Santa Clara. A Pentecostal and then Baptist church received the prayer for unity really well and a bed was provided for me but, at every sound, every flicker of light, every half an hour it seemed, I woke from sleep in panic. Trying to sleep was tiring.

I set out nervously from Santa Clara amidst a tangle of forest, farmland and mountains for the six-days' walk to the capital city of San Salvador. The thirty-five kilometre first day took my leg straight back to excruciating pain and by the second day it had deteriorated to a point where I was practically hopping on one leg, not able to put any pressure on it, even while standing still. El Salvador on foot was dying miserably.

I sat on the side of the road for an hour until a bus to nearby San Miguel came along. I waved him down and headed straight to the hospital. The limp around the block to the hospital was interspersed with long breaks with my left foot raised. I spent the day filling out forms, seeing doctors, taking x-rays, waiting, seeing more doctors and eventually hobbling back onto the street none-the-wiser. The doctor's only advice was, "Señor, stop walking." I agreed.

I hopped along to a few churches before curling up in a posada for the night, contemplating that the journey might be over. I wasn't ready to go home yet, even if I could no longer walk, so for now I'd just keep moving from town to town by bus, visiting the churches and extending the invitation to pray for unity.

Drug-related violence and murder was rife in El Salvador, so perhaps it was a Godsend to visit each town by bus and not on foot, although the bus wasn't exactly safe either. Ruthless armed hijackers had recently stripped a few buses. The territory generally came with an element of risk.

I bussed to the beautiful mountainside village of Mercedes Umaña and then San Vincente, where I found a bed and flicked on the TV. There, in that little room, the encounter with Adolfo began to take shape. I found a show in English, being an interview with filmmaker Michael Moore (Bowling for Columbine & Fahrenheit 9/11), and he was elaborating on his latest film, SiCKO. During the interview he noted that when he arrives at the pearly gates, "I expect to be asked by Jesus if I fed him when he was hungry, clothed him when he was naked and nursed him when he was sick. As a Christian it's my responsibility to stand up for those who cannot stand for themselves." It struck me on two counts, firstly because I didn't know Michael Moore was Christian and, secondly, because up to that point I'd believed unity essentially hinged on truth, but now realised that unity and loving your neighbour were intrinsically linked. The lesson was now ticking over.

I travelled by bus the next day to Cojutepeque and then to the sprawling capital of San Salvador. Hearing the tale of a young boy whose arms had been cut off the previous day with a machete by a gang who wanted his mobile phone only solidified that fear. The city scared me. I visited a few churches, including the tomb of Bishop Oscar Romero who was assassinated while elevating the chalice during the consecration in 1980. I found the archdiocese office, introduced myself and asked, "Do you know if my credit card has arrived?" The secretary stared back at me with a look that said: "Your what?" It wasn't there. The upside was that I was able to meet the archbishop and share a cup of tea with a few priests there. I ordered a second replacement credit card, this time to be sent to the Basilica of Our Lady of Guadalupe in Mexico City.

I ended the day at a Dominican parish in the heart of the city where a huge German priest standing at around 6' 7"—and on a step—answered the door. His bushy beard made him even more intimidating. When I explained the mission to pray for the unity of the Church, that all Christians would be united and proclaim one truth together, he responded bluntly in his thick German accent: "I don't care for what you're doing and I don't think God does either."

Taken back, I bumbled out, "But, it's in the bible. Jesus prayed for the complete unity of people of faith in John 17:23. What do you mean He doesn't care for what I'm doing?"

The huge German didn't budge, "I don't care for inter-denominational unity when there is such disunity within the Christian world socially. The rich and the poor are not united. Jesus didn't pray that we'd agree with one another, he prayed that we'd love one another. There's a big difference. The world needs love." In sombre silence the penny continued to drop. All around San Salvador's city centre was evidence of division, from the bullet holes in the Dominican church doors where twenty-one people had been massacred, to the hundreds of homeless folk on the street and reports of an average twelve murders a day.

The Dominican preached to me from his doorstep for thirty minutes before inviting me inside for dinner and a bed for the night. We continued talking over the course of the evening, but he wasn't telling me to go home and stop the futile mission. He wanted me to see that there was a lot more to the mission than I was presenting. It was the first time I'd genuinely recognised unity to not just be about truth, but also—and primarily—about love. Truth without love would be like faith without works: dead. The two couldn't fully exist without the other and ultimately the unity of the body of Christ, the Church, in order to be living in unity had to express it as love in action.

The priest's words ate at me. The following day I read a series of quotes from Blessed Teresa of Calcutta. She expressed a similar thought to that of Michael Moore with her own take on what would be asked at the Pearly Gates saying, "Jesus will not ask you how much you have done, but rather how much love have you put into what you have done." I'd walked and prayed well over three and a half thousand kilometres, and travelled by boat, bus and plane a few thousand more, for the sake of unity, but it was all now cast in a different light.

Unity was theological, philosophical and social—it was complete. Unity was love, not as a sentiment, but personified as Christ-centred action. What I could see was Adolfo, and that there were Adolfos everywhere in the Church: those who felt abandoned, misunderstood, unloved, unworthy, uncared for, and on their own.

I hobbled on slowly through the city to Nueva San Salvador. I shouldn't have been walking, but I needed thinking space. With so much disunity in the world that I could apply myself to for the rest of my life, would I ever make it back to Australia? My prayer for unity overflowed into prayers for those around Adolfo and his family to be united with him, and likewise for the people I'd met along the journey that were cut off or unwanted. The prayer for unity nagged at me to take responsibility to reach out to everyone in Christ's love.

I set off on the bus to the stunning village of Concepción de Ataco nestled in the forested mountains to the north. During evening Mass the division within the church was graphic. The wealthier parishioners sat up the front and the dirty street-clothed poor sat down the back. And during the sign of peace they didn't mix. At the end of mass the wealthy jumped into their cars and drove off to their secured homes while the poor flooded back onto the streets. I'd seen that many times over, but it just hadn't hurt as much as it now did.

I headed around to the priest's home to introduce myself, and a short smiling Franciscan friar opened up. I explained who I was, but he gently cut me off saying, "I know you."

I paused, unsure of what he meant. "Sorry?"

He smiled a cheeky grin, "You are the Australian walking for unity. I know you." My eyes were wide open. He grabbed my arm, ushered me inside for dinner and continued with excitement, "I'm visiting from Costa Rica to fill in for my friend here. Back home we all talked about your journey over dinner one night after you'd been mugged at knifepoint." He stopped, grabbed both my arms and looked up at me, "I can't believe you've made it to El Salvador!"

I grimaced a little, "Yeah, but it hasn't all gone to plan." The friar fed me and encouraged me to no end. I recounted the journey in depth from Costa Rica to his front door. He reaffirmed the German Dominican's, Mother Teresa's and Michael Moore's points. "Keep walking in that direction, Samuel. Keep walking that way."

I visited a few beautiful but empty churches in Ahuachapán, and I also ordered rooster soup for lunch.

I'd regret that.

Crossing the Río Paz Bridge on foot from El Salvador into Guatemala with a pronounced limp, I boarded a bus to take me further north to a rural town called Jalpatagua. The locals and padre welcomed me, receiving the now slightly altered invitation to pray for complete unity in truth and in love, but I wasn't so welcome at the Evangelical church. I waited for the Sunday service to wrap up before making my way through the large crowd to the heavy-set preacher. He looked at my credentials and called over an associate, then turned back to me, raised his eyebrows and said: "Let's get religious." He and the associate clamped a hand each on my shoulders and with the other hand wrapped over my skull they pushed me to the ground and onto my knees. I resisted at first but they easily overpowered me so I just knelt as they began praying loudly. They cried out with a prayer of repentance on my behalf, or an exorcism. I don't think he liked my Catholicism. Their painful grip felt like it was about to crack my skull. I prayed silently, "Jesus, what's going on here? Please have mercy on us. Please unite us."

When the men let go and the blood rushed back into my shoulders and head, I gingerly rose back to my feet. The huge preacher eyeballed me, nodding his head triumphantly. I shook his hand and wrapped up sarcastically with, "Well, thanks for that. I guess that's a no to the invitation then?" Not understanding a word I'd said the preacher just continued nodding.

I departed on a bus the next morning to a few towns, before reaching the outskirts of Guatemala City, population: three million. The friar in northern El Salvador had written down an address for a friary on the approach to the city, which I found nestled in peaceful forest.

Two Irish friars, both named Gerard, spoke matter-of-factly about the struggles of being missionaries in Guatemala. The older of the two noted that, "One of my friends was shot dead the other day. He'd gone out to dinner with a friend and some men walked up behind him and, without saying a word, shot him in the back of the head. Then stole his wallet."

"They didn't even hold him up?" I asked.

Gerard senior shook his head, "All for $50." Gerard junior stood off to the side in his brown habit and a tight fitting hand-knitted beanie. He was young, but there was a steely determination in his gaze. He spoke up, saying, "Just a few days ago, a few kilometres from here, not far from where you passed today, a young girl was found dying with her abdomen split open and her organs removed. The townsfolk suspected three women and without any proof dragged them out into the street, doused them with petrol and set them alight. They burned to death." Gerard junior's steely gaze came into focus. He was a man in the thick of darkness. "The scary thing is, Sam, that if you go back into that town today everything and everyone will be back to normal. Life goes on as if nothing is wrong and nothing had happened. Everyone looks happy, but there's an undercurrent of tyranny and fear."

"Why?" I asked, bewildered.

Gerard junior continued: "Sacrifice was a normal part of a lot of indigenous groups in the surrounding areas, and that disrespect for human life has filtered through to the current generation. There's no respect for life. That's our mission here, to restore it."

Gerard senior tipped back his baseball cap revealing a wisp of white hair. "Some don't think it's even worth $50."

Gerard junior asked me, "Sam, will you speak to our seminarians about your journey and why you're doing it please?" With their encouragement to speak in Spanish, I stepped into a room full of Franciscan seminarians for my first public lecture on the need for unity, particularly expressed as Christ's love in action. I'd picked up enough Spanish to explain the mission more extensively than I thought, because I spoke for five minutes without drawing breath. The twenty-odd young men agreed to take on the mission before firing out questions, one after the other.

After morning Mass I decided that the seven days of rest had me in a good place to try walking again. I told Gerard junior that I intended to walk that day through the city and then up to the Mexican border over the following week, but he warned me, "They're averaging twenty-one murders a day in the city. One of the worst areas is out on the other side where you're headed tomorrow. Watch your back."

I walked on down the road to a view of the sprawling metropolis cradled on all sides by mountain ranges. I sang and smiled excitedly just for being able to walk comfortably again. A police utility drove past with three handcuffed men under armed guard sitting in the back. I smiled, "Well, they've already caught those guys. They're no longer a problem."

As I reached the heart of Guatemala City I began to feel tired, but put it down to not having done a great deal physically for a week. I grabbed an ice cold drink to pep myself up only to suddenly feel every ounce of energy drain from my body. I sat on the steps of a pedestrian overpass and struggled to stay awake. My bowel churned and I was caught in a horrible place of needing a toilet, but not having the energy to even stand. "God, help me please." I roused the strength to stand and stagger up an alleyway to a public toilet, which was staffed to maintain safety and cleanliness.

I held on desperately while ferreting around for coins to pay the guys, and was finally shown to a booth. There was no relief though. My body screamed with an intense mixture of crippling pain and lethargy as though I'd been hit with a baseball bat and tranquiliser dart at the same time. I attempted to leave, but had to relinquish my hold on the door handle and sit straight back down. That point of, "I'm in trouble," set in. I struggled to hold my head up.

Dipping in and out of consciousness my longer than normal stay drew one of the staff members to knock on the door, asking me to hurry up. I reached out with an unsteady hand and unlatched the door, pleading, "Help me, please." The man took a confused step backwards, but then called the staff members over and with great care eased me to my feet, propped me in a chair off to the side, sat my backpack underneath me for safety and sent for an ambulance.

A crowd gathered outside as my condition worsened. I shivered uncontrollably in the tropical city, so they threw a blanket over me. I pleaded in agony for the workers to let me lay down on the floor, but they insisted I remain upright. After two hours I was still there, immobilised and fading in and out. Two armed soldiers checked in on me to make sure everything was okay, but I must have passed out again because one moment they were there and then they'd disappeared, along with most of the crowd. The generosity and care of the toilet workers was humbling. They kept me upright, fed me bottled water and continually asked how I was doing.

It was torture sitting there for five hours until the ambulance arrived. The paramedic apologised in response to something said by one of the toilet workers, "Sorry sir, you weren't a priority. You haven't been stabbed or shot." These guys were really overworked. They slotted in under my arms and guided me down the stairs through a crowd that stood back with amazement when they saw how tall I was. I said hello and many of them smiled back, wishing me well as I was laid down in a mini-van ambulance.

I began slipping unconscious as we raced through congested traffic with the siren wailing and the horn honking all the way to the St John of God Hospital. The paramedic persisted in telling me to not close my eyes. I was nearly crying with frustration at not being able to just let go. The freezing cold had passed and I now baked on high, breaking into a lather of sweat.

I rolled my head to the side as Guatemala City flashed past, just in time to catch sight of a huge statue of Jesus, arms outstretched. I have only faint memories from there. I was soon lying in an under-resourced, cluttered, high-ceilinged emergency ward with machines hooked up to me and needles being poked in. "Mr Clear. Mr Clear! Can you hear me?" I opened my eyes to see a young doctor standing over me. "You've been assigned as my patient. I'm from Belize, but my parents are Scottish, so I grew up speaking English."

I gingerly extended my hand: "Nice ... to ... meet ... you."

"Have you eaten anything bad recently? We think you have salmonella poisoning and a subsequent typhoid fever."

Halfway through eating that El Salvadorian rooster soup three days earlier I'd noticed the flesh was a little red. I didn't eat any more, but apparently I'd eaten enough. I smiled at the doctor. "Bad ... rooster," I managed.

He hooked me up to a drip and pumped a couple of litres of antibiotics and fluids into me throughout the night. I felt like death on a stick. The symptoms wouldn't back off. Diarrhoea persisted and with the ward being understaffed no one was available to take me to the toilet. I begged for assistance, but had to wait for fifteen agonising minutes before a nurse was able to help me into a wheelchair and, with me holding onto the drip, push me to the toilets. As we approached the toilets she stopped to talk to someone, but my body was giving out, "Push me, please!" She thrust me forward through the door and I stood up out of the chair, vomited into the sink and then fell back onto the toilet. There was nothing pretty about salmonella and typhoid.

The nurse had left me so, holding onto the drip stand, I heaved myself back into the wheelchair and with one footrest up, pulled myself along with one leg, cleaned the sink I'd vomited in, washed my hands thoroughly and groggily dragged myself back down the hallway to my bed.

By morning, the emergency ward had filled with student doctors. They were run off their feet, but enjoyed their work more than most enjoy a football match. In my hazy state I watched two interns arm wrestle next to their bloodied shot patient, a nurse do the rounds to all the doctors with a funny SMS, and a male intern try to find a date for a female intern by asking all the patients if they liked her. And then there was Gigantor. I have no idea what his real name was but that's what everyone called him. He was huge. Gigantor spotted my size sixteen boots under the hospital bed and picked them up with laughter. He then took them on tour around the ward.

Having stabilised, I was discharged later that day, but asked to stay close by in case I needed to return. I walked tentatively down the street to a posada a block away and remained there for two days, showering, eating and sleeping.

The challenge of being united in love, not just truth, weighed on me so in an attempt to put it into action I bought dinner for two homeless guys sitting out on the street. It was late and the temperature was dropping, to the point where they cuddled up for warmth. I sat next to them and handed over the food stash. One of them introduced himself. I asked if he had anywhere to stay and he replied, "No, I have no home, but there's a shelter down the road. I can stay for (the equivalent of) $5." It didn't come easily, but I handed over the money for them to stay the night there. The guy I'd given the money to though wouldn't hand over the other guy's share. I watched wide-eyed as they fought before I snapped back to reality with a thunderous, "Hey!" They stopped and stared at me. I looked at the first guy, "What are you doing?" He lowered his gaze and reluctantly handed over part of the money to his friend. I couldn't believe it, one moment they were cuddling for warmth and the next they were fighting like dogs. It was hard enough for me to prise the money from my wallet, but the challenge of loving them was somewhat more of a challenge. I needed God's grace.

The posada was expensive so, after two nights and with energy returning, I visited some churches and then found a hotel for three more nights. That Sunday night was to be my last on the road alone. The next day at 10 am I was to meet a friend at Guatemala City's International Airport. I looked forward to seeing a friend, but was apprehensive as to how the coming months would pan out with someone beside me. My leg was healing and the salmonella and typhoid had passed, enabling me to focus on the one struggle I knew I was plunging into. I was travelling as a Catholic missionary with my life on display for the world to see and I had my own boundaries and morals to uphold, so how would I cope, day in day out, walking across Mexico with Nikki, a fit, gorgeous blonde woman with a cute smile, active faith and adventurous spirit? "Um, Lord, thanks for pulling me through this time of sickness, and all the guns and stuff, but I think

I'm going to need your help again. A lot."

On the Monday morning I set out on foot early from the shifty Guatemala City hotel to the international airport. I didn't want to leave Nikki waiting, holding her backpack and wondering if she'd arrived in the right country. I'd known her for a number of years and we'd shared a year serving on Youth Mission Team Australia back in 2003. While ambling across the Americas she'd set out across the 780 kilometres long Camino de Santiago in Spain, but feeling the pull to walk and pray for unity she'd sold up, shipped out and was headed to Guatemala.

I arrived at the airport late and found Nikki standing out the front holding her backpack and wondering if she'd landed in the right country. She was jet-lagged and I was exhausted, but I'd made arrangements with Fr Gerard junior to stay the night back at the Franciscan friary in the mountains for the night.

We were set to go the next morning, but not on foot. I was well behind schedule to fly out of Canada to Russia in a few months' time, my body was still recovering and I felt the pressure of leading Nikki through the very place Fr Gerard considered *seriously* unsafe. We'd steam ahead by bus, visiting the churches along the way, to where I should've been by then: the Mexican border.

The bus trip was perilous. The driver roared through tight corners, overtaking semi-trailers and forcing on-coming traffic onto the gravel edge. That was except for the one semi-trailer that had nowhere to go so simply locked up with smoke billowing from the tyres. We squeezed agonisingly through a vanishing gap. Nikki strangled the bar across the seat in front of her while I looked on wide-eyed ... "We're going to die." The traffic slowed to a near standstill and our driver didn't like that. He reefed on the steering wheel and accelerated up over the median strip to the wrong side of the road and powered on, not even bothering to adjust his speed. We dodged oncoming freeway traffic for over a kilometre until he swung through an intersection to the correct side of the road and roared on to victory: being disembarking alive.

We crossed out of the country on foot—happily. In the late afternoon, we walked into Mexico's Ciudad Hidalgo and were offered accommodation by a padre. Nikki was adamant that she'd do the hard yards and wanted no special treatment. We set off before sunrise along a quiet country road for the nearly 2,000 kilometre stretch to Monterrey in the north. It was soon evident that Nikki was in better condition than me. And that suited us fine: the pressure was taken off her to keep up and put squarely on me just to finish.

One behind the other we walked down the road praying a rosary. Half our journey that day to Tapachula was along tiny laneways crisscrossing lush, flat farming land where locals happily helped us find our way. Nikki's Spanish wasn't too bad so we were able to translate pieces for each other, and while she revelled in the enculturation I quietly kept an eye on everyone and everything for the next possible threat. Her lack of suspicion was odd at first, but it helped to relax me.

Near the end of the thirty-seven kilometre day the humidity spiked and our backpacks squished from side to side. A dark thundercloud billowed up above us and a mighty bolt of lightning seemed to open up the dark ceiling above us into a torrential downpour. It was refreshing, but we were saturated when we entered Tapachula.

We had to laugh when we spotted tequila in a shop refrigerator right next to the milk. "We're definitely in Mexico."

We found a room each at a hotel near the picturesque town square, which possessed a cleanliness that I'd forgotten existed. The rural city came to life that evening: well-dressed locals filled the place with laughter and smiles while men played trumpets and guitars. The customary stares at the tall white guy continued, but they were now accompanied by a succession of lingering stares at the blonde beside me.

Nikki screwed her lips up. "Way to make a girl feel welcome."

With the temperature soaring, stifling humidity, my fitness waning and a blister each, we only covered twenty-four kilometres the next day to a dusty settlement called Huehuetán. There was only one option for accommodation, but we were left confused when we opened up the door to find one queen size bed and a cement floor. Nikki just laughed. I jogged back to the office to sort it out, but the lady shrugged her shoulders and said, "It's the only room."

Nikki and I searched for hammock space for me, but with nothing available we negotiated. I offered to sleep on the concrete floor but she refused and said she'd sleep on the floor. It went back and forth until the stand-off concluded: a pillow was placed in the middle of the bed and each of

Striding out across southern Mexico with Nikki

us nominated a side, prayed night prayer, and laughed at how awkward it was. We took our sides respectfully above the covers in the hot room for the nervous sleep. I was more concerned about moving during the night and waking her up than I was about laying a metre from an attractive woman.

When my alarm sounded at 4 am, I clumsily reached out and flicked the light on. On the wall directly in front of my nose was a huge scorpion staring right at me.

I calmly woke Nikki and her dazed disapproval at waking morphed into a wide-awake flurry of arms and legs. I pulled my head away slowly. Once clear I grabbed a walking pole and prodded the deadly centruroides scorpion. It thrust its tail at the pole, standing its ground. I left it alone.

What really amazed me was that, despite our venomous 'friend', Nikki wanted more rest. "I'll grab a lift and find you later." She slipped back into bed under the gaze of the scorpion and fell back asleep.

I walked on through the quiet morning until the countryside slowly emerged from darkness. A sharp sunrise punched over the jagged jungle-covered mountains to the east. A small truck delivered a refreshed Nikki a few hours later and she joined me in displeasure of the tropical heat and lack of space. We marched on in single file, dodging a massive black snake as we went.

I was relieved to be walking freely and was enjoying Nikki's company. She was fun, fit and even randomly joined in my meandering singing. I did have a twofold struggle though. The anger from past experiences was heavily influencing my reaction to situations where I'd have reacted differently in the past, and the second issue eating at me was the poverty. Every day, across northern Guatemala and southern Mexico, we were passing desperate poverty and were seeing more 'Adolfos'. The struggle to survive was everywhere, yet so much of it was avoidable. It didn't have to be there in all its guises, but through greed, apathy and acceptance it continued. The two issues combined into a struggle with a call to grow in mercy and in love. "If you want unity Sam, are you willing to be a part of the fix?"

A 'wake up call' southern Mexico style...

> *I am now rejoicing in my sufferings for your sake, and in my flesh I am completing what is lacking in Christ's afflictions for the sake of his body, that is, the church.*
>
> Colossians 1:24

**Total walked: 4,044 kilometres**

# Refugees, Earthquakes & the Kiss

*July 2007*

On Sunday 1st of July we walked to the town of Escuintla, and then headed across a river to neighbouring Acacoyagua. As we walked along the footpath a middle-aged man and his wife swung off the road at speed in front of us and into a service station, missing Nikki by a matter of millimetres. She flinched out of the way to avoid being collected. It was a frightening miss. I dashed across to the man as he pulled to a hard stop at the bowser. Nikki shouted out, "Sam! Don't do anything stupid! It doesn't matter!" I wasn't really listening. In a flash I was at his open window letting loose with what I thought of his dangerous driving. We'd begun copping more verbal abuse each day in Mexico and I was dealing poorly with the mugging in Costa Rica. I kept replaying that mugging in my mind and how I could have beaten all four of them. In my mind I was incredible at Kung Fu. I was angry. Whether this guy at the petrol station meant to drive close to Nikki or not, I couldn't remain silent. "Your driving is dangerous! You nearly hit my friend! Do you understand? You … are … dangerous."

The man just ignored me.

Everyone at the service station ground to a halt and Nikki caught up to me, grabbed my arm and pulled me away, "Sam, leave it! It doesn't matter."

I backed away and we rounded the vehicle towards the road as the man reached in behind the seat and grabbed his rifle. "Oh, not again." We headed straight out to the road and left him standing behind the car glaring at us with the gun slung low.

We bore the brunt of more abusive slurs from passing cars as we marched out of there. I was paranoid that the man at the servo would come after us so my gaze regularly swung southwards. Once I'd calmed down I tentatively turned to Nikki and apologised. I'd placed her in even more danger than walking across Mexico already offered. She pressed on me that it was okay.

The racial jeers continued through the long muggy days to come, but we kept our heads down and focussed on extending the mission. The views were spectacular. Crystal clear fast flowing rivers lined with smooth creamy-white boulders rushed out of lush jungle-clad mountains across farmland sweeping down to the Pacific Ocean a few kilometres to the west.

At the end of the sweltering forty-four kilometres to Pijijiapan we had heat rash, blisters and saturated sweaty clothes. Nikki withdrew some money and I sat on a concrete step to rest. When I stood back up she burst out laughing. "Look at that!" She pointed to where I'd been sitting and there, on the concrete, was a perfect backside sweat mark. I was slightly embarrassed. Every inch of our clothing was disgustingly wet.

We found a hotel with two single beds and Nikki showered while I grocery shopped. By the time I returned, the shower was mine. Peeling out of those clinging clothes was fantastic and, when I tossed them onto the shower floor, they landed with the most grotesque sloppy suction sound.

Blisters, heat rash and an air-conditioned ice-cream store halfway along the forty-four kilometres to Tres Picos slowed us down. We had a few ice-creams. Walking on through the tormenting heat and more racial taunts we became anxious when the sun began setting and Tres Picos was still nowhere to be seen. We walked on into isolating darkness.

A farmhouse light glinted through scraggly trees, and we could hear voices. I flicked my headlamp off and peered through the trees. A few people were saying goodbye at the front door, so we decided to do something I'd avoided to that point; enter a property at night to ask for help. Nikki stayed at the front gate as a safety measure, and I cautiously started down the dirt driveway. An aggressive dog immediately charged me, and the conversation at the front door swung towards the stranger emerging from the darkness. I turned the headlamp on myself so they could see I was no threat and the owner called his dog back with a snap. It obeyed, but maintained a barking vigil from a few metres. I yelled out in Spanish, "Hello! I'm a Catholic missionary from Australia. I am walking around the world praying for unity, but I'm lost. Where is Tres Picos?"

We were welcomed in with huge smiles.

Tres Picos wasn't even on that road. It was out to the west under the shadow of a three-peaked mountain, but the two young adults leaving excitedly asked if they could drive us there to meet the padre. It was out of our way, but we could hardly refuse. We jumped in the back of a black Volkswagen beetle and took off, rattling our way west towards Tres Picos.

Their padre friend welcomed the call to pray for unity and offered accommodation, but added, "There is basic accommodation, but you not sleep alone. Okay?" We weren't sure what he was trying to say, but when he showed us around the corner we understood. Under the shelter of a church awning, lying on blankets spread across the concrete or huddled together talking softly, were fifteen El Salvadorian refugees. A few nervously looked up as we walked in, but the rest just kept their gaze low. The padre reiterated: "Basic accommodation, but you not sleep alone." He was concerned about Nikki sleeping outside on the ground, but she stubbornly refused anything else. "If it's good enough for them, it's good enough for me," she said.

We stayed the night under that church awning with the fifteen men, sharing a meal the local church had cooked up. The padre spoke to me quietly off to the side, saying that refugees often passed through. They were genuinely scared and looking for any help they could as they headed north to the USA, hoping to hitch a ride on the freight trains. Many were murdered before they reached the USA. "They are in dangerous territory."

I remembered Adolfo with tears in his eyes saying, "Sam, if you're not one of them, you're never one of them." The padre described a recent incident involving a local head of police who led a vigilante gang. They'd stopped a freight train at night in the mountains to the north and executed the Central American refugees clinging to the trucks. I was aware of the problems refugees faced crossing the US border, but was ignorant of the problem Central Americans faced in crossing Mexico first. The padre asked me, "How have you been treated by the locals?" I recalled the constant verbal abuse and he nodded saying, "They are angry at how their countrymen are treated in the USA. They think that you are one of them." Dinner was a sombre affair.

I lay on my sleeping bag staring up at the awning. "The Mexicans are treating us in the exact same way they despise their countrymen being treated," I thought. "They've become what they hate." Ever since central Brazil I'd heard apologies for each country's taunts with the added comment, "They just think you're from the USA." It was amusing at first, but with the taunts worsening over time the justification sounded more like, "Sorry, your skin isn't the right colour for you to be treated with respect from the start." I once heard Bono from U2 say, "Don't become a monster in order to defeat a monster." It was a modern take on Jesus' call to, "Turn the other cheek", "Love your neighbour", and "Feed the hungry and visit the imprisoned". It's easier said than done.

A few younger men respectfully enjoyed Nikki's company over breakfast. I'm sure the company of a beautiful woman with sincere interest in their journey was a welcome change to their daily struggle. They even smiled a few times.

With great thanks, and some financial assistance to a couple of the men, we headed off for the hour-long walk back to the highway, and out through overgrown countryside for mile on end. One of the refugees trailed us at a distance, ducking in and out of the bushes every time a car came into view. Wherever he was headed, he was headed there slowly.

After thirty-six kilometres we arrived in the hillside town of Tonalá where a group of Franciscans at the Catholic church received the mission with joy. They invited us to join them for dinner, but while sitting in the centuries old stone building at the kitchen table an odd sound filtered through an open window overlooking a steep laneway. It sounded like a semi-trailer was trying to drive up it. The increasing roar drew everyone's attention and we motioned towards the window to see what was happening. BANG! Everything jolted violently; a 6.2 magnitude earthquake ripped through the village. The cry of "Terremoto" (Earthquake!) resounded through the friary. The roar hit with such force that the entire house lurched half a metre in one direction before jolting back and forth. Cups, vases and plates rolled in every direction and we lunged for anything solid to brace ourselves. I couldn't move. It was impossible to run outside because the back-and-forth shunting toppled us, too. I feared the old place would collapse under the violent shaking.

Half a minute later the roar subsided to the sound of tinkling crockery and the head Franciscan calming everyone down, "Tranquilo, tranquilo!" Stay calm? I was a wide-eyed Aussie who'd never experienced an earthquake and for some bizarre reason I waited with a beaming smile for more. However, there wasn't even a noticeable aftershock. There were plenty of stories to be shared amongst the locals who had filled the streets. Earthquakes are quite the social event and with no reported injuries or significant property damage everyone was smiling: slightly flustered, but smiling.

The next morning Nikki and I walked on to Arriaga in the north and, with sweat-induced blisters, we walked straight to a roadside café. In there we met a once-were-Texan family; over an iced chocolate we were invited to stay the night at their home.

Jason and Amanda had sold everything to move to Mexico to serve in a fledgling church with a special mission: an orphanage. Their job was to simply love the children who had seen everything in their lives except love. We appreciated their basic-but-neat home and over the first hour I showered, washed my clothes in a washing machine (quite a novelty) and ate toasted sandwiches with their two kids. It was beautifully relaxed.

We drove to the orphanage to meet the crew. The guy in charge was a middle-aged American named Bill, whose shaved head and grey goatee gave him the appearance of an emperor in civilian clothes. He was gentle and smiled heaps, but spoke in a way that meant there was no doubt as to who was in charge. He'd moved to Arriaga to teach fifty students, who later formed the basis of a non-denominational congregation. He'd previously worked in Romanian orphanages and brought that experience with him to Arriaga. The team of American and Mexican workers worked hand in hand to love the thirty-odd kids into adulthood. The demand to take on more children was growing. The orphanage was a beautiful home and it was buzzing with laughter. The kids took to playing with Nikki particularly.

The lives of the refugees and orphans were humbling, and the realisation of the need for unity in love, not just truth, was blooming. It wasn't a bloom that initially brought joy though, but sorrow. My world had been rocked in more ways than one.

We swung westwards from there, rounding the Pacific's Gulf of Tehuantepec into dry, sparse and exposed territory. More aggressive racial slurs followed us for the hot two-days-walk to Santo Domingo Zanatepec and when I sought directions to the church from a few locals they fled from view, taking cover in their homes and bolting the doors behind them. "I guess we'll keep walking then." It frustrated me so much.

We found an unmarked family-run posada before being received particularly well by the Sunday Mass youth group. They were keen to invite us into their lives, so our evening was spent roaming the streets as one large group, learning languages, hand games and group dances before sampling the food of one of their mums from a sidewalk barbeque. I little hospitality went a long way.

Nikki and I were carrying bad blisters, heat rash and aching joints, so our first rest day in eleven days and 368 kilometres was grabbed with both hands … and feet. We spent the day with locals in a wide sparkling shallow river soothing the heat of the day away. It was wonderful.

Falling asleep that night was a battle. I couldn't shut my eyes. I really enjoyed Nikki's company and it was now undeniable that I was attracted to her. I didn't know what that meant for the mission and wondered how I could continue on with her and maintain boundaries. We practically lived in each other's pockets. While bearing the brunt of ongoing verbal abuse, it wasn't hard to see why we'd take solace in each other, but on the off chance that she liked me, to pursue a relationship there in Mexico under those circumstances would have been fraught with danger. I stared wide-eyed into the blackened room.

It was a blurry-eyed walk and rosary on to Niltepec the next day. The local Catholic Church greeted us and, after Mass, the padre handed me the microphone. My Spanish was poor, but when talking about the mission it was now a well-honed monologue. The adults were happy to chat for a few seconds afterwards, but the bright-eyed teenagers were set on spending quality time exchanging cultures and playing impromptu games for hours on end. I slept better that night.

The increasingly dry, windswept cattle grazing plains to the west produced such strong gusts of wind that they blew us off the road a few times. Not surprisingly, we walked into a landscape of over one hundred towering wind turbines towards a town called La Ventosa, or 'The Windy'. It was a tough slog for those thirty-seven kilometres with the wind at no stage behind us. "Gringo!" jeers, plus the odd middle finger with a pre-packed cuss, followed us all the way there.

There was nowhere to stay in La Ventosa, so we rested at the front of a small supermarket and inspected the map. I turned to Nikki with a proposition, "With a little more rest do you think you could walk on to Juchitán? It's fourteen kilometres further on." Nikki, like me, wanted the day to be over, but after taking a moment to gather her thoughts she said, "As long as we can have a few minutes to rest here, I'm up for it. Sure."

As difficult as it was to stand back up, the highway at least swung south and the wind finally edged us along. We bathed in the cool twilight temperatures, but it was well and truly night-time before we wrapped up a total of fifty-four kilometres and Nikki's longest day. I was so tired that I barely remember falling asleep at the hotel in Juchitán, and I didn't stir once. It had been a long time since I'd slept all the way through a night without waking to check my—and now our—safety.

We continued to visit churches with a good response, but in Santo Domingo Tehuantepec our planned route changed. In scouring the map I noticed an alternative path up to Mexico City and another from Mexico City to the US border. The first alternative route allowed us to arrive a day earlier while passing through more hospitable areas, even if the first half was sparse. And instead of taking the coastal route from Mexico City to the USA, the second alternative route was a more direct line fair up the middle. The distance was longer, but the spacing of towns allowed us to arrive a few days earlier. I was supposed to take the bus from the northern city of Monterrey to the US border due to a combination of drug-related violence and a desolate environment, but now that I'd seen as much as I'd seen I wasn't so concerned about walking it. Danger was everywhere.

Nikki and I ducked down to the Pacific Ocean for a quick a swim before continuing on. The deserted beach dumped curling waves onto the beach's edge and it didn't look particularly safe. We ventured out only to just above knee depth, but still managed to be dumped. A massive wave caught me by surprise, tumble-washed me up onto the sand and unceremoniously dragged me back into the surf on my belly while I clawed back to my feet. I stood up just in time to be smashed back into the sand by a second wave. I'd discovered Mexican all-in-one exfoliation.

I'd ripped one of my shirts and it was widening, so I hatched a plan. We wandered from the beach to a sport's store and I said to a young fellow working there, "I need a Mexican soccer shirt, something that will make me look less 'gringo', if you know what I mean." He smiled broadly, agreeing that a soccer shirt would indeed un-gringo me. He showed me the two most popular shirts: the Mexico City Pumas navy blue with a gold puma, and the Guadalajara Chivas red and white stripes. I asked him, "Which of these two teams do most rural people support?" He pointed to the red and white stripes of Guadalajara saying, "The Pumas are supported by rich people. We like to see Guadalajara beat the Pumas. Guadalajara Chivas is for the working man." I liked it.

Nikki and I found a small posada, where the owners straight up explained the horrific dangers of being a gringo in that part of the world. They scared us and then directed us to our room. Something was lost in translation though because our request for two single beds had produced one double bed. The owners locked up behind us so we didn't have much choice and just laughed it off while allotting sides. After concluding the day with night-prayer the light was flicked off.

We managed fine last time, but our relationship had deepened since then and I was now lying next to a girl I really liked. I again just stared up at a darkened ceiling. It was only a matter of time before one of us broke, and as it turned out, it was both of us. Nikki rolled her head in my direction and stated the obvious about the situation. Within a good … say … three seconds, we'd broached the ten centimetre gap and kissed.

What was at risk was the mission. If I was travelling and in a relationship with a cute blonde, but not married to her, it could easily provide for situations that would become a stumbling block to any number of churches or individual Christians we met. The real or perceived impurity of my own life could easily dominate the call to pray for unity. I didn't want to place myself in a situation where the invitation was discarded because of the one carrying it. It was only one kiss, albeit drawn-out, but it could so easily erode the foundations of self-control. We soon pulled back from each other, but I wanted to kiss her again. That first boundary had been crossed and would be so difficult to re-instate. Despite what I may have felt in the moment I honestly didn't know if we had a future as a couple, so I also didn't want to just act on impulse. The kiss wasn't the problem; it was that it was with a girl I liked, in a pitch-black room, 20,000 kilometres from friends and family, while undertaking a specific mission. It was like lighting a match in an oil distillery. It felt like everything was on the line.

Stupid black ceiling.

The next day was a sombre affair. Everything we did was impersonal and 'work' related. It was obvious that we both recognised the danger of beginning a relationship there.

The change in itinerary had us backtracking to a town called Matías Romero and back into lush humid rainforest on the windward side of the mountain divide. I felt awkward in the new soccer shirt but it proved useful. We passed a group of men sitting on a veranda and one stood up, yelling aggressively, "Hey gringo!" I turned to him, expecting the usual abusive rhetoric, but his face lit up with a smile and he thrust one hand in the air, exclaiming, "Guadalajara!" I tugged at the club's emblem and smiled back while the other men laughed and applauded. It had worked.

If only shared humanity united us as easily as football ...

Nikki and I needed to chat about the kiss, but neither of us was about to break the ice. We walked on in silence. By late afternoon, I'd had my fill so I took a breath and said, "Nikki, I'm not quite sure how to do this or what exactly to say but ..."

She laughed, "No, it's fine, I know we have to talk I just wasn't sure what to say either."

We offloaded our feelings and agreed that a relationship was dangerous for the mission, but that we did have mutual admiration for each other. We walked on with random conversation opening back up. It was a time that so easily could have been defined by a kiss, but I was relieved that self-control and joyful purpose had re-emerged.

We were well short of Palomares as the sun set beneath a brooding thunderstorm. Brilliant lightning struck the ground every few seconds and the downpour engulfed us. There was nowhere to hide and nothing to do but keep walking. The last remaining light seemed to flee in fear. The darkened road turned into a watercourse and the cracking thunder rattled us. It was frightening and awesome at the same time.

"I hate this!" Nikki screamed from a few metres behind me.

The torrential downpour made it near impossible to hear her, so I turned with my headlamp flashing and yelled back, "What?" But the flashing lamp picked up something. I stopped and turned around while pointing to her boots, "What the hell is that?" She wiped the rain from her eyes and looked down. Two growths of billowing foam had enveloped her boots. I laughed uncontrollably, "What is it?" Lightning cracked around us and the torrent sprayed up over her boots, carrying a trail of foam downstream. "Argh!" she screamed. "I washed my socks in shampoo last night because I ran out of washing powder. I don't think I rinsed them properly!" As much as the road torrent swept away, the pounding rain just kept churning out more.

"That's brilliant!" I shouted.

Nikki walked on past me, "Shut up. It's not funny!" I trailed along behind laughing at her sparkling boots dropping foam-floats into the storm torrent. "Sam, seriously, shut up, it's not funny."

A remote winding road took us from Palomares through thick rainforest for a few days, past tiny settlements. The locals happily returned our greetings and the soccer shirt worked a treat. At one forest village some young guys playing soccer on the road were eager to say hello. One of the boys was also wearing a Guadalajara Chivas shirt, but his had a collar. I commented to him, "It's a good shirt. I should've bought one with a collar too." He smiled appreciatively and resumed the game with his friends, but after walking on a hundred metres the young boy came running after us, calling for me to stop, "Señor! Señor!" He ripped his shirt off and held it out to me. It was well worn and mine was brand new, but his did have the collar and would be a much better asset for the miles ahead. "You want to swap?" I asked. He shook his head as I motioned to remove my own shirt and simply handed the shirt to me saying, "It's yours", and ran back up the winding road, shirtless. I was speechless. Nikki laughed, "That is the cutest thing I've ever seen!" There I was, the proud owner of two Guadalajara Chivas football shirts because an amazing young kid literally gave me the shirt off his back.

After another day's walking, in gentle rain, we stopped for morning tea under a half-collapsed palm-leaf-roofed bus stop outside a farm. We hadn't been there long when I heard footsteps approach from behind. I was immediately on edge … then a massive pig rounded the corner. It was looking for shelter too and wasn't fussed about our presence. It sniffed around and took up residency alongside.

However, being a pig, it could smell the food in my backpack and proceeded to try and eat through it. We shooed him off, but it became aggressive and tried to eat everything—my bag, my boots and the walking poles. Everything was a potential meal. He even tried to bite my hand. When it again tried to eat through my backpack to my food I figured I had only two options. One was to punch the pig … which I didn't want to do. Surely there was a more St Francis method of dealing with this. So … I attempted to try and befriend the big lump of pork. I flicked a biscuit on the ground so that he'd turn away from me and, when he did, I quickly scratched him behind the ear. The pig forgot about the food and pretty much collapsed on the spot and stretched out. I continued scratching and he closed his eyes. I went from food supplier to long-lost buddy.

I began massaging the pig's shoulders while saying softly, "If you don't stop eating my bag I'll make you into bacon for lunch." It grunted and groaned, and then eventually fell asleep.

Nikki's face lit up. "Oh my goodness. I think it's snoring!"

The hungry pig

Indeed he was. The rain eased so we picked up our bags and said goodbye to our solid friend, who half lifted his head acknowledging our leaving and lay back down to resume his siesta.

We walked and prayed into the middle of nowhere where we passed an obscure gravel road just as a farmer hopped through the fence on the other side. It was close to sunset so I introduced myself with a smile and asked, "My friend and I have walked and prayed from María Lombardo de Caso today … do you know where there is any accommodation?"

He smiled and nodded back, "Si, mi casa. Vamos!" ("Yes, my home. Let's go!") So we did … along the gravel track with the chatty middle-aged farmer to his three room bush hut in the isolated village of Niños Héroes. It wasn't even on my map. The farmer, his wife and their two daughters eked out a meek existence, but welcomed us in with wonderful hospitality. Nikki was given a hammock next to the parrot and rooster and I was offered a wood-plank bed with a blanket over it for softness. They even introduced us—and the mission—to their neighbours.

The long-drop outhouse fifty metres away was … not so welcoming. The smell alone induced a mixture of nervous giggles and gagging. While standing in there, holding my breath, I heard a faint sound emanate from the dark reaches below. My headlamp was handy so I flicked it on and shone it down. There was less giggle and more gagging. Metres below, the entire cesspit rolled and shimmered under the weight of a thousand worms and beetles churning through years of festering sewage.

If I'd lit a match it would have wiped out half of Mexico.

The mission was received well by pretty much everyone we met, from farmers to hotel receptionists, road workers to church workers. An interview with an Australian Christian radio station was set up for that evening, so I had to find a telephone in the rural city of Tuxtepec and call home at 6 pm. The difficulty was that fifty-eight kilometres still separated us from Tuxtepec. We set off at 4:30 am. It was a tough ask. We pushed hard all day.

In one section, where the forest grew right up alongside the road, I stopped. I could hear a strange sound, coming from the forest, like a large dog panting. I turned to Nikki, "Listen to that." It was close, even within a few metres, but the forest was so thick that we couldn't see a thing.

We opted to not hang around and find out what it was.

In the next village, an extroverted Evangelical Christian man invited us into his house for lunch with his wife and three daughters. I asked him: "Do you have any dangerous animals around here?"

All of them responded in unison, "Jaguars."

"So," I continued, "Do they pant like a dog when resting? Like this …"

The father smiled knowingly, "Si, si". In fact they saw up to fifty jaguars a year along the edge of that forested hill we'd passed. I still wonder what view that possible jaguar had of us as standing there like self-serve take-away staring into the forest. After closing lunch in prayer we were again warned to watch our backs due to kidnappings, mutilations and murders. Jaguars weren't at the top of the food chain. The irony was that nearly everyone warned us of these dangers with a warm smile. The warnings made little difference to how I already viewed each day, but having Nikki with me did cause me to be extra vigilant.

We walked hard, but after a leg-numbing fifty-four kilometres it became obvious that we'd finish half an hour late for the interview, so the mission took precedence and we jumped in the back of a truck for the final stretch. In a state of exhaustion, I searched for a telephone ... and the interview went ahead right on time and the invitation to pray for complete unity was spread across Australian Christian radio.

A mixture of racial slurs and compliments for my soccer shirt followed me for the days ahead, while Nikki attracted a bombardment of graphic sexual verbal abuse. The young to middle-aged men just couldn't hold back from propositioning her. She handled it with humility and just kept soldiering on with a smile and prayers for them.

Tierra Blanca ushered in the welcomed second Mexican rest day, which was spent printing and cutting out calling cards for the journey ahead to leave with those I met as a reminder of the invitation, or at unattended churches. The slip of paper read in Spanish, "Please pray for the complete unity of Christians—John 17:23" and included the walk4one website. It was pretty simple.

I slept horribly that night. It was as though my body was saying, "Why are you trying to sleep? You haven't done anything today!" I fell asleep only a few hours before my alarm sounded and I headed off into the dark morning tired and disgruntled, praying a rosary with Nikki.

More racial taunts were thrown our way, plus more sexual propositions to Nikki, and after entering the overgrown countryside beyond a village it turned even more ugly. A voice yelled out from behind us, "Hey gringos!" A young man dressed in suit pants, ridiculously out-of-place shiny black shoes, a white dress shirt with a black jacket and his hair slicked back, paced out after us. He meant business and, as far as I knew, there was only one business in Mexico that people dressed like that for, and it wasn't legal. He shouted an angry, hate-filled jibe and increased his pace. I told Nikki to keep walking. The young man became more infuriated and bellowed in Spanish every conceivable swear word. His anger and gangland manner was downright scary.

We walked on, maintaining vigilance over our shoulders, but we were headed away from civilisation and the only obstacle I could think of for him was that his shiny black shoes would give him a blister. If he carried a gun ... that would be that.

He marched on shouting abuse, but when he began to charge us down a passing car pulled over between us. We scooted on. The car windows wound down and the four young guys inside extended their hands to our pursuer to 'lay some skin' with a not-so-normal handshake. Checking over my shoulder it looked like they'd asked the obvious question, "What are you doing?" because his sights quickly rose to us and he pointed aggressively while explaining something. Our opposing numbers were rising. I frantically tried to figure out an escape option.

The friends talked to him from their car and he frustratingly glanced our way a few times. Whatever it was they had to say to him, it must have been important because the passenger door flung open, he hopped in and they drove off in the other direction. I hadn't come up with a single escape plan, so it was a get-out of jail free card. We were on edge for hours to come while we marched towards La Tinaja with the sun setting behind ominous mountains to the west. We were mentally and physically exhausted.

Heading out from La Tinaja under the cover of night, with a thunderstorm flashing periodically on the horizon behind us, we linked onto the side of a massive split freeway cutting a beautiful path through forested hills and across deep watercourses. We prayed with the stunning sunrise behind us.

A man on a bicycle rode down the other side of the freeway with his dog trotting behind him. When the dog saw us it barked at us and ended up running out aggressively at a speeding four-wheel drive ... and misjudged his lunge. The front wheel collected him flush across the head with a sickening thud and sent him spinning, legs sprawled, for ten metres down the road. The dog was killed instantly. The owner was forced to swerve the skidding carcass, but then glanced back at it before looking over at us with a smile as if it to say, "Oh well, what can you do?" and rode on without missing a beat. The whole scene was disturbing and only underlined the undercurrent of little value being placed on life in general.

When we'd entered Mexico we were granted a three-month visa with the condition that within a month we'd pay a nominal fee at an immigration office. Nearly a month later we still hadn't found one of those offices. At the end of a fifty kilometre day, we searched Córdoba, at the mouth of the Orizaba Valley, for an immigration office, but again found nothing. Córdoba was gorgeous: clean European-style squares, landscaped sidewalks, tiny parks and tightly packed well maintained villas. The backdrop of lush forested hills rising into towering mountains clipping through the clouds was even more impressive. We had three days left on the visa, so continued west into the Orizaba Valley to its namesake, the city of Orizaba.

Towering mountains guarded each side and through the crisp air we could view the highest peak in Mexico: the 5,760-metre snow-capped volcano, Pico de Orizaba. There was something significantly different about the people there. They were gentle and their smiles were always followed by a, "Hello" or a "How are you?" I'm not sure if there's any basis to this, but it felt like the lush environment, fast flowing clean rivers, deep valleys with misty waterfalls and clean city streets were directly contributing to the locals sense of contentment. It seemed that beauty manifested peace.

The Orizaba padre was quick to accept the invitation to pray for unity and then introduce us to an intelligent, good-humoured young man who took us out for a meal. That evening I read a frustrating comment left on my weekly blog. I'd finished the previous week with, "... my resolve is stronger now than when I started that the Lord's heart is for unity. True unity. It's a long road ahead though." Someone unknown to me, a fellow called Miguel, read the blog and offered his advice through jumbled scripture quotes and incoherent sentences, citing that there was no mission to pray for Christian unity if that person was from any church he believed were unbiblical. I apparently couldn't experience unity until I was a homeless Christian. How homeless do you want me to be?

I was at a loss as to how I earned his posting and the comment ate at me for the rest of the week. My possible response waxed and waned between rebuke and a humble acknowledgment that my faith did need a shake up every now and then. I flipped between defensive dominance and humble submission, unable to find a suitable response.

I hate internet conversations.

Nikki and I walked on. Snowy Pico de Orizaba glowed in the morning light well before the valley beneath emerged from darkness. The invitation to pray for unity was welcomed in the neighbouring towns and, by mid-morning, we'd stretched out across the last of the valley's flats to walls of mountains closing in on all sides. The freeway (somewhat pathetically) attacked a monstrous climb to the plateau two kilometres above, winding through a succession of tunnels and a few hundred corners. The higher we pushed the more difficult it became to breathe. It almost caused me to shut up, much to Nikki's delight. Many hours later, after sunset, we finished off the forty-five kilometre day, walking across highland plains at the foot of the 5,760-metre high snow-capped volcano glistening in the moon light. There was a peaceful sense of gratefulness to God for such a difficult yet beautiful day.

At an isolated roadside restaurant there was no accommodation, but the burly unshaven man running the place told us—not invited us—to sit off to the side until he'd finished his shift and he'd drive us to a posada. The guy was scary. I reckon he could've crushed us with his bare hands. Even his bristling five-day growth looked dangerous. When he'd finished up he ushered us out the back door into the darkness to his beaten-up old car. We jumped in and took off down a dirt track in the complete opposite direction to the township we could see inland of the highway. We'd joked about the scariness of the guy, but now it was very real. We were in the back seat with a guy who still hadn't smiled and was speeding along a dirt track surrounded by thorn bushes into no-man's-land. We quickly became terrified that this guy was about to rob us and dispose of our bodies without fuss. Where do you draw the line between trusting someone despite their physical appearance and being discerning about character?

Amidst a cloud of dust he rattled around a sharp corner and accelerated hard. We held on. We were nowhere near civilisation. The dirt road approached the highway we'd walked along and shot down underneath it with a thump, then out across the plains towards a tightly clustered village. As we drew closer to the village we offered each other looks of, "This might be okay." He drove straight up to an old two-storey building, jumped out and knocked on the door. A woman answered and the burly Mexican explained briefly who we were. She looked past him to us and ushered us in with a smile. Hairy-Scary turned, shook our hands, jumped back in the car and tore off back out of town. He was trustworthy. He just didn't smile, shave, drive cautiously or do small talk.

We called into the beautiful old Esperanza church in the morning and the padre welcomed us for Mass and a hot breakfast. There were no visa offices in either Orizaba or Esperanza, but the padre assured us after some quick research that we could pay it in the city of Puebla, ninety-six kilometres further on. It was D-Day though. Our visas were set to expire at 5 pm and we couldn't cover that distance in that time. We walked hard that morning to cover thirty-two kilometres. Just as we noted that it was time to find a lift, we walked up alongside a parked bus that was about to start its run to Puebla ... very convenient indeed.

We couldn't find the immigration office and eventually burst through its doors at ten minutes to five. After waiting in line, it was well past five. After all other patrons had exited, we were called forward and explained our situation. The immigration guy smiled broadly, "You've made it here. Just." Technically, we were now officially in the country illegally, and that caused some issues when trying to enter our data into the computer. With the aid of his superior, they figured out how to override the system and, by 6 pm, the nominal fee was handed over, our passports stamped and hands were shaken. We were on our way again. We'd cut it fine.

When I went to write the next blog I was still none-the-wiser about how to approach Miguel's comment. I didn't want to ignore it, so I simply clarified my position in case he'd misunderstood, "… I don't completely understand the rebuke because my comment was simply intended as a reflection on my deepening of faith over the duration of this journey and the utter hopelessness I've felt at seeing so many underprivileged people suffering, coupled with the infighting amongst churches. Having seen what I've seen and heard what I've heard, the scriptures regarding unity (from the Gospels and Paul's letters particularly) are coming alive for me. My resolve is stronger. I haven't been blessed with the wisdom to unite the faith world, but I have been blessed with prayer, so this is my role out here on the road: to pray and bear witness."

In hindsight I'm not so convinced that Miguel's problem was with what I wrote, so much as with my Catholicity. In either case, it highlighted the very real unwillingness of many Christians to pray for unity.

We headed off bright and early across the dry plains towards two enormous snow-capped volcanoes separating us from the sprawling metropolis of Mexico City. We stayed in San Martín Texmelucan, and then continued on to Río Frio along a meandering thirty kilometre road past small farms, sprawling villages and the ever-present smouldering volcanoes. With the mountains rising to 4,000 metres above sea level, we pushed on through light mist that lingered within the pine forests leaving a dripping dew to accompany us for the first few hours. It was cool, fresh and inviting. We walked up to 3,240 metres in elevation. My body was so used to sweating through the hot tropics that the lower temperatures and increased altitude had an unexpected impact. I had to duck off into the pine trees to relieve myself nearly every twenty minutes! It really tested Nikki's patience.

By early afternoon we were descending into Mexico Valley and ever-increasing urbanisation. Despite the hot sun, Mexico City was still high enough that the air remained cool. We visited a couple of churches with mediocre responses and continued on the next morning after a small argument. I hadn't wanted to join Nikki as she peered into someone's car at their headrest TV sets, while the car was fully occupied, and she cracked it at my timidity. It was a stupid argument and we moved on in silence.

I wasn't seeing the poverty I expected. A lot of work had gone into housing developments and the slums were difficult to spot, but the pollution, on the other hand, was difficult to avoid. We manoeuvred through some disturbingly grotesque wafts and even passed a bloke wearing a gas mask while riding a pushbike. Not a dust mask: a full-on World War II gas mask. The smell we were saturated in was a mixture of rotting flesh and sewage. It was difficult to breathe.

Having to stop at streetlights every few hundred metres made the thirty-odd kilometres into the heart of Mexico City difficult, plus we often needed to ask for directions. The closer we drew to the city centre the more traffic, the more pedestrians, and the more road choices we had to contend with. Up and over, round and back around we seemed to go on weary feet until, at last, beyond the swarming mass of people filling a colourful market alleyway, we caught sight of the Plaza de la Constitución and the enormous Catholic cathedral. The five-foot tall locals stepped back like the parting of the Red Sea as I approached. The same thing happened for Nikki, except it was only the men who stepped aside to gawk. The impressive plaza— a dead flat, paved city block with a huge Mexican flag in the middle—had a few hundred people walking through or sitting in it enjoying the architectural sights.

The cathedral's padre, Padre Francisco, welcomed us and offered passionate encouragement to continue the mission. He was agitated about the severe lack of unity in truth and the obvious lack of unity in love within Mexico and the wider Church. Nikki and I had walked past a few shrines to the angel of death, so I seized the moment and ask him what on earth it was all about. He shook his head saying, "It's a cult. It's a combination of fallen away Catholics and indigenous beliefs, but they have lost sight of Jesus and worship the Angel of Death spoken of in the book of Revelation."

"But why?" I asked.

He raised his eyebrows and said, "They believe that if the Angel of Death is the one to take their life then if they are on his good side their souls will be safe."

I replicated the raised eyebrows, "Have they forgotten who he works for?"

He laughed, "As I said, they have lost sight of Jesus."

> *Therefore, if food is a cause of their falling, I will never eat meat,*
> *so that I may not cause one of them to fall.*
>
> 1 Corinthians 8:13

Total walked: *5,028 kilometres*

# A Racing Heart, a Dislodged Hip and Border Security

*August 2007*

Nikki and I walked the two hours north through hectic suburbia to the most significant shrine in the Americas: the Basilica of Our Lady of Guadalupe. Unlike the Angel of Death shrines, this one was centred on one basic call, "Come to Jesus." The basilica was incredible. In the 1500s there were still significant indigenous human sacrifices taking place when a poor man named Juan Diego was visited by the Virgin Mary. The series of miracles and the building of the shrine on that spot led to mass conversions to Christianity and the bloody sacrifice of what they now understood to be God's children became all but obsolete. They'd come to believe that there was no need for human sacrifices, as Jesus had sacrificed himself for all. On Juan Diego's cloak was left an image of the Virgin Mary, which has baffled and split the scientific community since, and it was still on display, unchanged, on the wall behind the basilica's altar.

The call is still as true now as it was then: "Return to my Son and stop the slaughter of innocence." In South and Central America the slaughter of innocence was apparent in the newspapers every day, but in western society it usually took the ugly guise of the unborn. In today's world there was no slaughter to 'appease the gods' so much as it is to appease ourselves. They were the unseen Adolfos.

I'd organised for my second replacement credit card to be forwarded to the basilica, but the main office was again void of any mail addressed to me, "Sorry, it has never arrived." I wondered if the Commonwealth Bank back home would consider sending a third replacement card, but after yet another email they responded kindly and a third one was to be sent. ATM cash remained my lifeline.

With the second half of the new itinerary kicking in, we took aim at trekking straight up the middle of the country, setting off through sprawling, twisting suburbia. The slums now came into full view, but the people we met along the way were gentle-hearted and humorous. What they lacked physically they made up for in character. Halfway through the day we emerged on the side of a highway and were able to stretch our legs out for the rest of the forty kilometres up to a town called Coyotepec, overlooking the Mexico City plains.

A cowboy-hat-wearing padre welcomed us in and introduced his two Rottweilers and Chihuahua. He revelled in the art of hospitality and offered us a room each with a license to relax. None of us knew quite what to do with one of the very amorous Rottweilers though. The more the padre learnt about the mission the more he wanted us to stay for Mass in the morning to meet the congregation and, after obliging, they happily received the invitation to pray for unity. One old woman slapped my back, too short to tug at my cheeks.

We walked out across a patchwork of rolling farmland to the cute valley town of Tepeji del Río. Nikki had to increasingly grit her teeth through some major foot and leg pain. A local directed us to the padre's house, but an enormous fence enclosed it. As we approached, the huge front gate opened up and a car pulled out. The gate remained open so we just walked up along the gravel driveway and rang the doorbell. The confused padre opened the door, wondering how we'd entered the property, particularly when he looked back down the driveway and saw that the gate was now shut. He didn't even know who'd left through the front gate, there was no one visiting him, so he just put it down to God's perfect timing and welcomed us warmly.

In packing my gear away I realised that one of the walking pole's tungsten tips had fallen out. It was a blow because it drastically limited the life of the poles. The remaining two-inch hard plastic spike would still work, but wear away fast.

After praying with the padre in the morning, we departed at sunrise along a yet-to-be-opened empty dual carriageway and then back along the main road past ever-increasing piles of litter: beer bottles, pornography, used condoms … and a handful of abusive slurs. The soccer shirt brought some smiles and waves, but didn't sway everyone. One slur did make me laugh. A young man hung out the window shouting, "There's no snow here you idiots!" It was directed at our walking poles. Later, a passer-by managed to hit a nerve; amidst the graphic litter, and other random verbal abuse, it was the straw that finally broke Nikki. A semi-trailer rushed past and I caught a glimpse of the driver's focus set in on her twenty metres behind me as his hand rose off the steering wheel. A few seconds later I heard Nikki scream in frustration. She ripped her backpack off, hurled it into the side of the road and turned around to face the past truck, screaming, "No! No! No! That's disgusting! Just leave me alone!"

She threw her poles into the grass, sat down and cried.

I jogged back to her. "What happened?"

Nikki screwed her face. "He put his hand up to his mouth and acted out a blow-job. I'm sick of this! I'm sick of it!" Blazoned across the back of the semi was a sticker reading, "Jesus". His action spoke louder than his word. Sitting down beside her I apologised for what she'd landed in. Before she came, I bore the brunt of everyone's aggression, but now it was as though 90% of the male population couldn't see me. Mexico had been mostly conflict free and I was adamant it was because the one thing young aggressive men wanted more than to fight a gringo was to stare at a beautiful woman. Nikki hadn't chosen to cop all the abuse in my place, but I thanked her anyway.

Pushing on slowly, our conversation centred on what people say compared to what they do. I was eight years old when my family left Flinders Island and I'd rarely seen Brian and Maureen—Mum and Dad's friends—since then until I ran into Brian when I was in my mid-twenties. While catching up on the years that had passed I noted that I'd only recently discovered that he was a Christian. He laughed with a hint of embarrassment. "That's not good. You'd hope it was obvious!" Here was the deal though; Brian didn't have a Jesus sticker on his truck or wear a flashy gold chain with a cross on it, but if there was one couple on the island that I trusted as a child and looked up to, it was Brian and Maureen. I loved having them around. He always smiled and made us feel like we were worth something. His actions were louder than his laugh, and that's saying something. At the end of the day I found internet access and jumped online to check out the prayer page that listed all those who'd signed up to pray at 4:01 every day. Lo and behold, the brand new names sitting at number 154 were Brian and Maureen. I laughed, "God is good. Their actions still speak loudly."

We set off towards San Juan del Río—fifty-six kilometres away—well before sunrise, hoping to make it in time for Sunday evening Mass. We weren't even sure if there was an evening Mass. We pushed hard, interceding as we went, but due to continued leg pain, and with the pace quickening, Nikki opted to grab a lift after forty-one kilometres. In my stupidity, I decided to take on a challenge of increasing the normal kilometre rate to finish off the final fifteen kilometres in the remaining two hours before what we suspected would be the start of Mass. Having already walked forty-one kilometres it was not a moment of wisdom. I increased my pace and worked the poles hard while praying away. It was a seriously tough task and I even induced a sweat in the cool afternoon, keeping one eye on the watch and one on the kilometre markers, figuring out my needed speed.

I knocked off the final fifteen kilometres in one hour and fifty minutes to rendezvous with Nikki outside the church minutes before evening Mass. The satisfaction of making it turned quickly to regret: my body went into meltdown. I'd pushed so hard at the end of an already long day that my heart rate and temperature soared. I slinked to the cool slate floor at the rear of the massive church and just tried to hold on. My heart rate rocketed and my whole body felt like it was about to catch fire. I couldn't stop it. Nikki ran out to grab cold water while I focussed on staying conscious. She returned fast and as I drank, the burning within my abdomen abated. I no longer felt like I was about to self-combust, but my heart rate remained dangerously high. Mass came and went, but I remained stationary. Over the next two hours my temperature slowly dropped and my heart rate slowed back to fifty beats/minute.

By nightfall the scare faded and we finally cracked a smile when Nikki spilt an entire drink onto her crotch. With the appearance of having wet herself we ambled across the town square to accommodation and a solid night's sleep.

At a more sane pace, we continued passing the invitation on one church at a time all the way to El Colorado, and then on out into prickly pear, cactus and raggedy Joshua tree covered hills. It was a long dry few days. The constant drum of sparse dry wilderness with horses roaming free and farmers on donkeys was peaceful … until we stepped into the grass for a break. I trod smack-bang in the middle of a festering dead dog. I jerked my leg out of it. Nikki was mortified and walked on ahead to a cleaner place to rest while I scraped my boot clean in the grass. Nikki placed her backpack down and her water bladder mouthpiece slipped down onto the ground just as I stepped in to take a seat and trod fair on top of it, leaving a dirty 'dead dog' footprint along it. She screamed, disgusted beyond description; I apologised profusely. I attempted to wash the mouthpiece with water from my own supply, but as I removed my mouthpiece to increase the flow the water shot straight out over her mouthpiece and into her open backpack. Half-crying, half-laughing, she shoved me out of the way saying, "Stop, please. No more."

You just can't win sometimes.

There was no offer of hospitality at day's end; we were informed that the only hotel was out to the east on a quiet country road. We stuck our thumbs out and set off to find it. A young man picked us up, but was too eager to get home … as I tried to squeeze into the back seat he took off, not realising I wasn't in. My right leg was planted firmly on the ground and the sudden lurch forward rotated my foot such that the sole of my boot faced the rear tyre and, in that split second, the car mounted my sideways boot, jacking the car up a good ten centimetres. I was dragged out the door. Nikki screamed at him to stop. He stomped on the clutch, and the car rolled back onto the road with a thud.

Had the car driven just one more inch forward it would've rolled on my ankle and surely snapped my leg like a twig. My dirtied sideways Scarpa boot had held steady with a car parked on top of it and I walked away with nothing more than a wrenched knee and a dusty tyre mark imprinted on the boot. I limped slightly for the next few days and it ached, but it still worked.

The further north we pushed the more frequent the verbal abuse became until it matched that of southern Mexico. The arid region contained a few delightful surprises though, like roadside stalls of fresh hothouse strawberries with cream. Not once did we walk past without stopping to do our bit for the local economy. Anything with water and sweetness was right up there with owning my own tropical island.

My crippled walking pole wore away a few millimetres each day and the dry sparse terrain wore on us. While stocking up on supplies at a service station I took the Mexican plunge of purchasing the hottest chilli on offer and eating the stupid thing. It nearly killed me. Tears ran down my cheeks, my nose ran and to my surprise, so did my ears. "What has this done to me?"

I ate, I learnt … I've never returned.

A little-used winding road led us down into dusty Santa María del Río. We were singing Queen's 'Bohemian Rhapsody', which echoed off the surrounding hills, as we approached the town, but we quietened down as we drew near the first scattering of homes. It wasn't just us quietening down though. The streets fell silent as we walked along. The locals refused to return our hellos. Some looked away, while others just kept staring. A huge local ensemble of guitars, trumpets, drums and singers played an upbeat Mexican tune in the town square while a throng of locals looked on. As we approached the tune came to a thunderous climax, but not a single clap was heard. Every pair of eyes stared at us, wide-eyed, following every step with unnerving caution. I smiled hello to one guy and with confusion he turned to his amigo for moral support. The only movement in that whole square was a solitary pigeon taking flight from amongst them.

The church workers were equally apprehensive and we were left without any hospitality, not that I'd asked for it. I'd only ever ask if they knew of a place where we could find two beds. Some people would offer directions, others would offer their own hospitality, but these guys just offered a, "No."

We found a hotel fifty metres away.

At the end of the next long hot day, we walked on into Villa de Pozos for Sunday Mass, followed by a rest day. We visited a few churches with a reasonable response and then set about doing a number of chores. I organised for a third credit card to be sent ahead of me to Amarillo in Texas, and took my damaged walking pole to a do-it-all workshop on the side of a dusty street. A kind gentleman fashioned a steel nib into the pre-existing slot, which was fastened with glue and some of the old yellow Costa Rican sticky tape. It worked a treat. We were both very satisfied with the finished product.

That day I checked my blog to find that Miguel was back. My apology was off target. He hadn't been offended by me realising how much God's heart was for true unity, but that I was indeed a misguided Christian mixing with fake Christians. His new comment ticked me off to no end and only firmed the need for the invitation to pray for unity to go so far beyond those who already agreed with each other. The need to be united in love was still at the forefront regardless of who I met, but unity in truth between the varied and, at times, hostile Christians was still were I felt a deep passion. It was to people like Miguel that I wanted more than anyone to take the mission to, but he was unlikely to pray for something when the person asking wasn't, in his eyes, even a converted Christian. I didn't belong to the Church as he did. Truth or not, if it comes from an enemy it sounds like a lie. God hadn't explicitly asked me to walk cross-country inviting people to pray for unity, but I was confident that I had been asked to put my time towards prayer.

Not according to Miguel though.

That evening Nikki pulled me aside with news I didn't see coming. "Sam, I was checking my bank balance today and I don't have enough money to continue much further. I'm heading home from Monterrey." I hadn't known how long she'd walk with me, but I thought it would be at least well into the USA. The fact that she'd mailed cold weather gear to Denver was probably part of that thinking. Her news was met with a mixture of sadness and relief. We hadn't talked as freely in northern Mexico as in the south and our relationship had 'chilled'. She'd also become frustrated with me a few times. Nikki hadn't become any less attractive though, and I was impressed with her combination of beauty and toughness, so there was a sense of relief that she was heading home. Nikki had been a kind of summer on an otherwise winter mission. She'd booked her flight and was heading home, hoping to look into a few missionary ideas that had been sparked during her time in Mexico.

We set off at 4:30 am, trying to find our way through the darkness along a dirt track with little LED headlamps. It was awkward when multiple options opened up. "Left or right, Nikki?" I was nervous about rattlesnakes and kept a keen eye on the side of the track as we chuffed along through loose dust. There was, however, a full showing of stars and the fresh air of the overgrown countryside made it a refreshing pre-dawn amble. It was with great relief that our little dirt track eventually met the wide-open freeway and, as a gentle sunrise beckoned in a new day, we were able to stretch out for the next three days across an enchanting wilderness of stark mountains and massive sweeping plains thick with stands of Joshua trees and prickly pears. The strawberry stalls disappeared, replaced by families in makeshift rickety stalls selling cactus and splayed dried rattlesnake.

Yes, they were for eating.

"I'll take the cactus, please."

In Entronque El Huizache we found a remarkable old church sitting behind the town on the edge of a hill. It looked to be the original building in the dusty, sparsely populated town. The new freeway, a few hundred metres away, had drawn the town towards it, leaving the church oddly alone in the rocky field. The parishioners happily took on the mission.

At the town's family-run posada, the owner's three young boys were mischievously intrigued by the two Australianos. They hung back for a while, but then started chatting and, within minutes, we were engulfed in a game of tennis ball soccer on the loose blue-metal driveway. They didn't stop smiling. The more competitive Nikki and I became the more fun they seemed to have. One asked what sports we played in Australia, so I grabbed an old fence post for a bat and set up a plant against the fence for wickets. We enthusiastically launched into their first ever game of cricket! They smacked the ball all over the place, but it always somehow returned to us, careering off the fence, trickling off the posada roof or bouncing off the neighbour's trees back into play. I loved it.

Day 245 began with a 4:30 am alarm followed by a 5 am wake up holding the alarm. We hit the road under the cover of darkness, rounding a hill to be met by an amazing sight: car headlights stretched in a dead straight line across the plains below all the way to the northern horizon. The other end of the visible road was so far away that when a car appeared on the horizon with its lights gleaming in the arid darkness, it stayed in full view for over half an hour before flying past. From that hill, the entire sixty kilometres straight to the distant hills was visible, and the surprisingly heavy traffic split the night in half with two seemingly motionless flickering red taillights and white headlight pinstripes. I'd never seen anything like it.

The sun rose once we were out on the plains and ushered in another dry, hot day through cactus, prickly pear, tough grass and white sand wilderness. By the time we tipped past forty-five kilometres there was still no sight of a place to stay and the locals at a tiny settlement indicated that we wouldn't find a hotel until Matehuala, eighty-two kilometres from our starting point. Nikki was still struggling with leg soreness, so she travelled on by truck to find the hotel. I wasn't sure how much further I'd walk, but for some reason I didn't want to finish there. I knew I'd need to find a lift or risk sleeping on the side of the freeway with rattlesnakes that were yet to be splayed for sale. I felt good physically and was eager to do some solitary prayerful miles. I pushed on with sunset imminent.

Fifty kilometres came and went, then a sign marking the Tropic of Cancer. I'd hit a brick wall at the thirty-five kilometre mark then gained a 'second wind' before again hitting a brick wall at the fifty-five kilometre mark. A 'third wind' kicked in along with darkness and, before I knew it, I'd dashed any possibility of catching a ride. I didn't really care, and just walked on praying. Apart from the cars and trucks rumbling past it was quiet out there and incredibly peaceful. I blocked out the traffic and revelled in the calmness of everything else. It was a beautiful place to be.

While rounding a small rise I looked back over my shoulder to stare back down the sixty kilometre stretch of seemingly stationary white and red car lights from the other end. My mind flashed back to a certain February day in Venezuela when I walked sixty-six kilometres and came face to face with a puma, when for only the second time I visited kilometre sixty-six. This time I walked on without a hitch and in much better condition. It felt strange to push past that mark into new territory.

Praying and singing softly, my spirit was high and my body hurt less, but that was mainly due to an increasing all-over numbness. I could barely feel my feet. After seventy-three kilometres I was able to stop at a service station to restock my food and water supplies. Nikki had my wallet and I'd taken a $20 note in my backpack hip pocket for the night ahead, but on arriving at the petrol station I reached for it and it had gone. Oh, the agony! I must have knocked it out when I pulled out a small packet of biscuits an hour earlier. It was crushing. After seventy-three kilometres I was now on an empty stomach and there in front of me was a shop full of food and drinks. I couldn't buy a single thing. To rub salt into the wound, I was busting to go to the toilet, but needed a $2 coin to open the door. After a moment of staring at the door in disbelief I turned on my heels and walked on, praying.

My stomach churned inside out and my mouth gaped for a drop of water. I narrowly dodged a snake soaking up the heat of the road when it shot out from under my approaching foot. I clicked past eighty kilometres. With inexpressible delight, I approached a lit sign saying the one word I longed to see, 'Hotel'. The front desk clerk pointed me towards room number one where, after a few knocks, Nikki groggily appeared asking, "What time is it?"

"It's 2:30 am," I replied.

She stared out through sleepy eyes: "You idiot." She then smiled and pointed to my bed.

I couldn't help but point out, "You should be thanking me. I've just walked tomorrow's day. Tomorrow's now a rest day."

She just shook her head and slinked back into her bed, "I'm glad you're okay."

My day wasn't yet over. I was hungry and dehydrated, so I offloaded the pack and wandered down the main road half a kilometre to a twenty-four hour service station, bought them out of house and home, ate well, returned, showered and then turned to bed twenty-three hours after starting the day. I curled up with a prayer at 4:01 and fell asleep.

I have no idea what time I woke the next morning, in fact it may not have been morning. Nikki had been waiting a while. We finished the final three kilometres into Matehuela that afternoon and all was well apart from basic muscle soreness. We stopped at a few churches, grabbed two beds in a cheap central hotel, and spent some down time in the city square where we met an English-speaking evangelical missionary. He shared his mission in Matehuela before asking about our reason for being there. I told him in very simple terms what the mission was and how it had unfolded, for which he was very supportive but then, not realising I was Catholic, he ripped apart those 'Whore of Babylon' Catholics who'd strayed so far from Jesus. He was on a roll. My mate Simon once advised me, "Sam, always defend people behind their back. Voice your objection to their face, but defend them in their absence." I sat there listening to that guy go on and on about the atrocities of those 'other' churches. He overstepped the line a few times, so I corrected him, but that only led him to ask the inevitable question of, "What Church are you from?" He didn't like me so much after I answered and didn't care for the invitation to pray for unity one bit. Our conversation ended with him inviting me to an impromptu preaching to take place on the cathedral steps before the Saturday vigil Mass. He wanted me to hear the truth being preached. I turned up and listened to his fast, shouted, angry Spanish for a few minutes, didn't understand a thing, and walked into the cathedral with my bible in hand to pray quietly before Mass.

We were more easily accepted forty-two kilometres deeper into the north at a small settlement where a family very warmly offered assistance. They had a key to the chapel next door, so invited us to sleep the night there. Nikki took my hammock, slung it from the rafters, and I took the concrete floor with both our clothes folded up to form a sort of mattress. It did us fine. To top it off, the family invited us next door for some animated conversation over a huge pot of soup.

After 240 kilometres of prayer on foot in one week, a couple of hearty bowls of soup and a bunch of smiles go a long way.

By mid-afternoon the next day we were watching a storm brew before deciding to rest under a solitary tree outside a neat, modern isolated house. We took our boots off to relax when all of a sudden the house flared into a frantic confusion of screams. A rattlesnake had slithered through the front door and taken up residence in the lounge room! We watched on as the mum swept the snake out the door with a broom while the dad ran around from the side with a shovel and, "Thwack!" disposed of it unceremoniously. The thundercloud we'd been watching suddenly split open and the torrential downpour had us hastily gathering our gear together. The family standing over the disposed snake called out through the unleashing storm and ushered us in to shelter with them. The snake had gained us entrance into their home.

The Mexican father was an American citizen and Pentecostal preacher. He, his Mexican wife, and daughter all spoke English. They were rapt to meet two random Australians walking across Mexico praying for unity and invited us to stay the rest of the afternoon and evening. We happily did.

While learning to use a corn grinder, the conversation about Christian unity deepened. He was sceptical at first, but the more we talked and the more corn we ground, the more he warmed to the mission, understanding that I wasn't inviting people to join the Catholic Church, but to pray for complete unity in truth and in love, whatever shape that took. When we started talking about the need to sort out theological differences for the sake of evangelisation and the need to encourage each other to be united with those around us in love, we found ourselves agreeing ardently on the need to travel the distance separating us, rather than looking across the gap accusingly.

We were afforded a solid sleep-in before praying together and parting company, thinking we needed to cover forty-nine kilometres that day, but I'd miscalculated by ten. Extra kilometres beyond what was expected always carried double-weight. The end of the day dragged on through a baked landscape well into darkness, past another five foot black snake soaking up the road's warmth. In the crisp night air we searched every rounding corner or hill for the town we thought we should have already arrived at. After fifty-nine kilometres had passed, we at last strolled into a town with no church, no hotel and to be honest, I wasn't sure there were any people. It was dark and silent. Nikki had been praying for somewhere to stay so I asked the Lord, "Okay, what's the deal? Where are we staying?" A building off to the right caught my eye and I felt God tug on my conscience saying, "You're here." I told Nikki and she didn't question my sanity, just wandered over with me closer toward the darkened lifeless building. I admit, I was thinking, "God, you've got to be kidding me. You are not going to have me knock on this door in the middle of the night in northern Mexico. I'll be shot!"

At that moment a man stepped out onto the street through a side gate, glanced up at us and took a hesitant step back, as did we. He asked, "Can I help you?" We introduced ourselves, but he reached behind for his back pocket. I felt the blood drain from my face, but his hand emerged holding out a police badge, not a gun. He was knocking off work and was also a Catholic. Without hesitation he invited us to his place for the night. Officer Hector was on deployment at the outpost and spoke openly about missing his wife and children, who he saw only on weekends. He was happy to share his workhouse with us and cook up a huge dinner for three. "Thanks Lord, nice solution. Thank you."

We hit the road an hour after sunrise, entering a fifty kilometre stretch of thriving inquisitive gopher communities that checked us out from the security of their burrows, calling loudly to one another with peeps and squeaks all day long. The massive sheer mountains of the region offset the flat plains we walked along and I was so engrossed in the mountains that I trod straight into a shallow hole. Crunch! The jarring rotation of the backpack hurt my back. It wasn't walk-ending, but it hurt. Nikki was slightly sympathetic, but thought my rubbernecking was probably bound to get me into trouble eventually. She launched into an impersonation of me striding out with big steps, lifting her chin up and swinging her head from side to side, looking at absolutely everything except for the road ahead. It was slightly exaggerated.

We were exhausted when we arrived at an Evangelical church in dusty San Rafael. We were welcomed by a missionary preacher who was regularly on the move setting up massive tents in the highlands to hold huge rallies to, "… set people on fire for Jesus and then send them back to set their churches alight!" He was encouraging of the need to pray for unity and said that he didn't have a big problem with the Catholic Church, only that many of its members were asleep in Christ, not alive in Him. The Pentecostal Church though, well, he didn't have much time for them and went to town on what he saw as biblical hypocrisy and straight out unbiblical teachings. It felt odd to be the accepted one while other Christians were slammed.

My back continued to hurt as we descended off the highland plateau into fresh valleys filled with green pastures and irrigated crops over the next few days. Jagged valleys and narrow canyons gave way to the mid-level plains housing the city of Saltillo, before we entered a region of mountains of such intricacy: a constant ebb and flow of valleys, peaks, canyons, vegetation, cliffs and blunt abruptness against the flat sweeping plains. It was difficult not to rubberneck.

In the Monterrey outlying district of Santa Catarina we ended up at a hotel that was equally as abrupt. I asked for two separate beds, but got a jaw-dropper of a room. We were chatting as Nikki unlocked the door, but fell silent as it opened up. The carpet was deep red shag pile. So were the walls. There were no windows, just a row of continuous mirrors, and off to the side of the king-sized circular bed was a red pole. Its function was not structural. We cracked up laughing, embarrassed to even look at each other. Nikki pointed at the bed, "It has love hearts on the wall behind it!" I grabbed the pole while looking at it, stunned. Nikki stared at me as if to say, "Move away from the pole." It was horrendous. I then reached out and touched the shag pile walls, "Hey Nikki, the shag pile carpet on the walls is really soft."

She convulsed with embarrassed laughter. "Don't touch anything! You never know what you might catch!"

We prayed night prayers and agreed that taking one 'side' each of the circular king-sized bed would be okay. We hadn't needed to share a sleeping space in a long time, but if anything, the grotesque room actually helped uphold purity. We slept comfortably a couple of metres apart, rose early and got out of there.

For Nikki, after nearly 2,000 kilometres on foot, her last day had arrived. It was a smooth entrance out of the final slopes, past the spectacular Unity Bridge, and into gorgeous Monterrey. Now only a few hundred metres above sea level, the views back towards the enormous mountains we'd walked out of reminded me of Cape Town and Hobart. It was a phenomenal sight. Had Nikki and I not taken a wrong turn and ended up on top of a hill at the historical bishop's residence instead of the real deal, it would have been a slightly shorter day too.

We received one rejection of the mission at a church, but for the most part it was extended fruitfully, all the way to the Monterrey Cathedral. Miguel was back online for the very last time and he went out with a bang. A couple of blog followers had written comments in the mission's defence against Miguel and he wasn't happy. He responded, "If I have spoken evil, bear witness of the evil: but if not, well why smitest thou me? It is hard for thee to kick against the pricks. Lest haply ye be found even to fight against God. You could ask … Where dwellest thou? You'd find it most helpful. 'Come and see.'"

Saying goodbye to Nikki, with her Mexican patch

For the first time I took the chance to respond directly in the comment's section and as humbly as I could, I stood my ground then moved on. Within an hour Miguel offered his final 'food for thought', a half page dumping of scripture verses that I thought backed up what I was doing, as opposed to pulling it apart. I left it alone and quietly reaffirmed my submission before God, asking for His mercy, and continued on, with or without Miguel's prayers.

It felt like the 'end of the school year'. After nearly ten months I was within a whisker of crossing out of Latin America into western culture and Nikki could almost smell the salty sea back home. She sewed a Mexican badge to her backpack, gave me a hug and we said our goodbyes. It was as simple as that. Walking on in separate directions was bizarre. A few times I even did shoulder checks to see how far back she was, but of course there was nothing more than an empty street each time. I missed her company.

The change of itinerary back in southern Mexico had reaped the reward of arriving five days ahead of schedule. I'd been told that the territory between

Monterrey and the border was inhospitable and dangerous for foreigners, but I'd seen so much since Brazil that I now chose to walk, drug traffickers or not.

In the northern suburb of San Nicolas I asked for directions to a church from a well-dressed young man who'd run out of petrol in his lowered black Volkswagen Beetle. Alexis was an attorney, spoke fluent English and he and his friend, Edgar, were hilarious. They were so enthusiastic about the mission that my initial question turned into a fifteen-minute conversation. They objected to one aspect of the journey though and pointed at my red and white Guadalajara Chivas soccer shirt. "What is this? Do you know what this is?" Alexis reached into the Beetle, pulled out a blue striped Monterrey C.F. training shirt and threw it at me, "You must wear this and get rid of that stupid top!" The major sponsor plastered across the front was the local bread company – BIMBO! The shirt was a keeper.

After checking into a hotel that night I checked out the sore spot on my lower back in the bathroom mirror to find that my left hip protruded by about two centimetres. "That's not good." Two hospitals and a number of specialists later it was concluded that an injury of that nature could only be caused by a serious accident, not by me jarring my back in a pothole. I explained that my pelvis had never protruded from my back, but they shrugged their shoulders and discharged me. It ached and it was disconcerting to reach behind and feel that lump.

While remaining a further two days in Monterrey to assess the injury I stayed with a group of young missionaries. The padre in charge took me on his rounds to a few rural villages to the north—where I should have been walking. However, through his invitation, the mission was passed on further than my meandering would have achieved. He was a lot of fun. I wore the new soccer shirt as we visited each village for Mass, but it drew his ire. At day's end he called me aside and shook his head, "You should not wear this shirt. It is not good for a missionary to be seen in it." I thought he was serious until he produced the rival Monterrey Tiger's yellow and blue shirt and thrust it upon me to the cheer of the missionaries. One of the girls raised the stakes further by then handing me the Monterrey CF purple training strip. I was inundated with soccer shirts!

Hearing of my plan to walk into the north they all warned of the drug-associated dangers and rebuked me, telling me to stick to the original itinerary. Having now visited a number of the northern villages, I heeded their warning and reverted to the original plan, not that choosing the responsible option was necessarily part of the 'job description'.

I arrived in nearby Nuevo Laredo by bus, excited to be crossing into the USA. It was also daunting to think that for the first time in ten months I'd be able to speak English daily and read the road signs. I almost expected culture shock from my own culture. My Spanish had improved so much in the last month alone that there was also a sense of sadness in leaving Latin America before I'd progressed to fluency.

Nuevo Laredo looked like a bomb had hit it. Streetlights were smashed, storm water drain covers in the middle of the road were missing, raggedy lawns were a foot high and graffiti covered a good portion of the rusted tin lining the rickety back street houses. The dangerous border town made me nervous.

I found the crossing over the Rio Grande into the USA and filmed myself at arm's length as I went, but that fostered a cold reception. A woman waited for me with a serious frown. "What were you filming, sir?" My first encounter with Border Security wasn't shaping up as nicely as the previous eight borders. I showed her what I'd filmed, which thankfully ended up being nothing more than my bearded face. She scolded me. "Put the camera away and don't pull it back out until you are well clear of here."

In the Border Security office it went from ignorant to worse. The distraught young lady in front of me was picked up for carrying a fake passport, which turned out to be real, before I was invited forward and asked to explain my reason for entering the country. The look on the officer's face when I told him what I was doing was priceless. He stopped typing and looked up asking, "Sorry sir, could you please repeat that?" It didn't help that I had no idea where I would stay that night. I wanted to sarcastically say that, "I often thought it was a problem too, but I'm still going!" but I kept my mouth shut.

As the officer spoke privately with his superior I had a blood-draining moment as I realised that in all my planning I hadn't once taken into account the ninety-day visa restriction I'd be under in the USA. I had no idea if my planned thirty to forty kilometres a day itinerary had me entering Canada after seventy days or one hundred. The officer returned and with no hint of humour asked, "Sir, could you please come through to the back here."

I was escorted into an interrogation room, my backpack was placed to the side and they conducted a body pat down with two armed soldiers standing over me. "Okay, take a seat sir." A second officer sat opposite me and began firing question after question, scrutinising every answer. For more than an hour we sat there until I thought I'd completely hit rock bottom. He left the room and re-entered fitting blue rubber gloves. He gave the final glove a flick on his wrist as the door was closed. I blurted out, "Oh no!" But the confused officer looked at me and then smirked: "No, no. I need to search your bags. You're okay." I breathed a very long sigh of relief. Every piece of equipment was pulled from my pack and inspected.

"Why do you need so many soccer shirts?" he asked, curiously.

After ninety minutes, my passport was stamped and I was free to go. I didn't see it coming and must have looked completely bemused because the interviewer smiled and said, "You come from a visa-waiver country, so you can enter the USA without a visa. That means we have no idea who you are. We just needed to be sure you are who you say you are. I hope you have a great trip across the States."

I was happy to have that stamp.

After I hit the road, I grabbed my itinerary to check the number of days allotted for the crossing. "Oh stuff it." I'd budgeted for 102 on a ninety-day visa and it was already a solid schedule. I prayed, "Father, I'll just keep walking, but I'll need a lot of help to make this distance in ninety days."

Twelve days behind schedule from the outset, any thought of enjoying some

US comfort was dispelled immediately. I quickly visited two churches, but both were sceptical until I turned on my heels without asking for accommodation and walked on. On both accounts I was then called back with an invitation to come in for a drink and a bite to eat.

Within the hour I'd set out along a quiet access road alongside the busy freeway, stopping only once for a policeman wanting to see my passport. He handed it back with his best wishes for the mission ahead and I continued on into my first sunset on US soil. It was stunning. Deep orange hues silhouetted a massive arching ranch entrance and I felt much safer at sunset than ever before. I almost wanted to bend down and kiss the ground. The darkness of night hadn't stopped me before, but the weight of 'what might happen' had lifted. I could've skipped had my back and feet not hurt so much.

I turned off along a country road and walked into the silence, praying prayers of thanks for being there. At 10 pm I prayed, "If it's okay, I'll walk as far as that random lit up sign in the distance and then look for a house or shed to sling my hammock in." The random sign was a huge advertisement, but down low and off to the side sat a barely visible smaller sign pointing down into a paddock to an RV Park: a caravan park. "Yes!" I secured a cheap hammock swinging spot, palmed off one amorous resident who offered some 'extra warmth during the night' … "Thanks, but it's plenty warm enough …" strung my hammock up between two trees and swung to sleep under thousands of stars with coyotes howling in the distance.

When I rolled out of my hammock before sunrise I caught myself just in time before stepping into a swarm of red ants. "You're kidding!" They'd made a nest in my backpack! The clean-up was tedious and fraught with danger. Un-stung, I headed out into the middle of nowhere. The middle of nowhere in Texas sounded exciting.

A massive thunderstorm ripped across the countryside that day with lightning flickering back and forth. Texas was a lot greener than I expected, but if it rained like that (even once a week) it wasn't hard to see why. By nightfall I'd completed fifty-five kilometres and found a picnic area. I slung my hammock in a barbeque shelter and slept an inch above the picnic table. It worked well. My water supply was low, so I needed to show self-control and not scull it if I wanted to make the next town in the morning.

I slept okay, except for the mass of howling coyotes ... and one cowboy who pulled into the darkened picnic area at 2 am to relieve himself. I scared the life out of him when I rolled over in my hammock and chirpily said, "G'day mate. How are you doing?" He jumped into his pick-up and sped off at pace, leaving me to fall back asleep.

My original schedule had me bussing from Monterrey to Carrizo Springs, my next day's walk—not to Laredo—but I'd ditched the schedule and instead walked from the border out into no-man's land. I'd begun my assault on knocking off twelve extra days by adding three more. So it goes. I couldn't stop smiling. I was in Texas at last.

> *Remind them to be subject to rulers and authorities, to be obedient, to be ready for every good work, to speak evil of no one, to avoid quarrelling, to be gentle, and to show every courtesy to everyone.*
>
> Titus 3:1–2

Total walked: 6,055 kilometres

# Bolting Snakes, Sex Crimes & a Tornadic Storm
## September 2007

I was dehydrated when I marched into the settlement of Catarina just after sunrise and drank their little store out of juice and lemonade. Just about everyone that popped in for their morning paper and coffee engaged me in friendly conversation and I felt almost like I'd returned home after so long away. Well ... almost. Twenty kilometres further on, in the sparse township of Asherton, I wanted more fruit juice so asked a woman on the sidewalk: "Do you have a shop in town?"

She looked at me with confusion, "Oh no, we don't have a shop. What would you want a shop for?"

"I just want to grab a drink."

Her eyes lit up, "Well why don't you go to the store?"

'Shop' equalled a place to fix your car, not a place to … shop. I found a store and drank my juice on the spot. Then I asked the young lady behind the counter: "Do you have a rubbish bin?"

She stared at me blankly and asked, "Sorry, a what?"

"A rubbish bin."

She leant to the side and looked past me down the store aisle, then apologised, "Sorry, I don't think we've got one of them."

I held up the empty bottle, "A rubbish bin, as in, for rubbish."

"Oh!" she exclaimed. "You mean a trash can."

I then tried to ask, "Do you have internet in town?" but she just stared at me. I moved my fingers as if typing on a keyboard, "Internet, as in emails, websites …"

Her eyes widened, "Oh! You mean inner-net. No, we don't have inner-net. I tell you, I don't know where you're from but you're sure hard to understand!"

Indeed.

I covered forty-four kilometres by day's end to vibrant Carrizo Springs, where Spanish was the prominent language and, ironically, everyone understood me. The Hispanic community was throwing a festival in the streets surrounding the beautiful church and there was singing, dancing and more food than I could've hoped for. It took some time to locate the parish priest in the crowd, but he was just as welcoming as everyone else and invited me to extend the mission to pray for unity to the revellers right there and then.

"Now, Samuel," he said. "We need to organise a bed for you I guess?"

A young Anglo-Saxon man chimed in with, "It's okay, I'll put him up in the hotel for the night."

"Done!" said the priest and he wished me well. Tanner was an oil exploration and legalities officer working in the area. He and his boss checked me into the hotel and half an hour later came knocking back at my door, holding aloft a Texas University Longhorns cap, "This is your ticket across Texas. Wear it and you'll be fine. Just make sure you take it off before entering Oklahoma."

The same hospitality was extended in the next town of Crystal City, where a young husband and wife asked me where I was from. I obviously didn't look Texan despite the Longhorns cap. Upon hearing of the mission they excitedly introduced themselves as Pentecostal Christians and asked if they could at least buy my meal for me. We shared a late lunch while discussing the need for unity, misconceptions of what unity is and the disunity within Christianity. We agreed, for the most part, but I voiced concern at his statement that all we needed to do was have people read their bibles and then we'd be united. "There are many Christians who have read their bible and don't agree with each other's interpretation. We need to read our bibles, but then seek truth together." He thankfully nodded in agreement. They also paid for a hotel room for the night and prayed with me in the car park. I was so grateful.

After a good sleep I woke early in the muggy Brazilian morning, daunted by how much walking still lay ahead. I looked around at the room, confused, thinking, "This is really modern for Brazil …" Then it dawned on me, "Ha! I'm in Texas! Yes!"

A misty rain enveloped me as I wandered down a country road without my jacket, enjoying the cool conditions, when a pick-up suddenly pulled off on the other side of the road. A man jumped out, raced around to the tray of his pick-up, grabbed a thick yellow workman's raincoat, ran halfway across the road and under-armed it through the air to me. "Just so you don't get sick, son!" And he was gone. I stood there in the middle of nowhere holding the huge jacket, "But I already have one. I'm just not wearing it."

The memories of abusive drivers were fading fast. I pulled the jacket on and continued on my way.

The town of La Pryor was noticeably different to the other towns I'd visited. It was quiet, sombre, everyone moved slowly and there was no idle chitchat on the streets. A warm-hearted Catholic priest welcomed the mission and invited me to sleep the night in the parish hall, before explaining why tiny La Pryor was so glum. It was devastated. The previous night a fourteen-year-old girl had been accidentally shot and killed by her eighteen-year-old brother who'd been playing with a gun at a party. Unaware that it was loaded he'd accidentally shot her. It was horrific for the tightknit community.

I joined the school's memorial service next door, where there was a massive outpouring of grief. She was well-respected and loved. Her brother was there too and it was for him that I felt the most pain. He was shattered, but the town stood by him. Everyone I spoke to only had compassion and concern for him. Killing his sister was sentence enough.

The wider community gathered in the church afterwards to celebrate Mass and everyone went out of their way to welcome me. Some even thanked me for being there to pray with them. The priest could so easily have palmed me off, and I would have understood, but he didn't. He walked up at evening's end with half a smile and said, "Come on Sam, let's go find some dinner." They were amazing people in La Pryor.

I walked north praying a rosary the next morning through lingering misty rain and approached an older Hispanic man standing at the end of his driveway, waiting for a lift. He was noticeably uncomfortable in the rain without a jacket. He smiled through raindrops dripping across his face, so I asked, "Do you need a jacket?"

He acknowledged with a laugh, "Yes, yes, I need a jacket. I know."

I corrected him, "No, I'm asking; would you like a jacket? I have a spare one."

He stared at me without a word so I said, "A guy gave it to me yesterday, but I already have one. You can have it if you like."

He motioned towards me with a smile and said, "Yes please." His jaw dropped when I pulled the huge yellow workman's coat out. It was a lot better quality than he expected and he accepted it with appreciation, wrapped himself inside and flicked the hood over his head, beaming out a smile.

Delivery complete.

Rain set in heavily that afternoon and my feet were killing me by the time I entered Uvalde. The churches responded positively to the mission, particularly the Baptist minister and three smiling Teresa of Avila sisters, who offered me a room for the night. My wet socks had rubbed against my feet all day and it looked like I had the plague. Skin was missing from my toes and all were imprinted with smears of blood and black tanning agent from the boot's internal leather. It looked disgusting and no matter how much I delicately scrubbed, they stayed blackened.

The journey on to Junction was scheduled to take five days. I decided to tape my toes up and try to make up a few days with distances of forty-nine kilometres, sixty kilometres and fifty-six kilometres back-to-back. As I headed out of Uvalde, I ran into a lady who'd seen me walking the day before. As quick as a flash she was on the phone to the local newspaper which led to another interview. The invitation to pray for unity was on its way to the front yard of every house in town.

I hiked on through sprawling green farms, up into a hidden jewel of the Texas landscape: the Hill Country. The range was covered in elms, oaks and silver birches with clear bubbling rivers cascading through them. It was beautiful. I made it to the Garner State Park well after sunset to find it all closed up. I considered slinging my hammock from the visitor centre picnic area, but when I spotted two sets of eyes staring at me from the bushes nearby, reflecting in the visitor centre's spotlight, I decided to find something safer. By the size of the two animals and the way they moved my best guess was that they were wild boar.

I found a cabin with an ensuite … it was just missing the cabin part. Most people would call it a public toilet, but beggars can't be choosers. The State Park office had an unlocked, spacious, very clean and air-conditioned disabled toilet alongside and it was glistening white. I was so thankful for the person who'd kept it in such prime condition. I sat my survival bag down on the floor, filled it with clothes and placed my sleeping bag on top, locked the door and slept uncomfortably. The constant ducted air conditioning made it chilly in the middle of the night, so I just reached up, tapped the hand dryer a few times and enjoyed the blasts of warm air. Seriously, that place was convenient!

More eyes followed me the next morning as I headed on before sunrise. There were pumas in the area, too, so I was extra watchful. With the relief of sunrise came the rural town of Leakey and, over breakfast, I discovered that those hills in fact contained boars, pumas, black panthers, bears and squirrels.

The day stretched on and by 8:30 pm I'd made it to the only shop along a ninety-nine kilometre stretch. It was closed, but the smiling owner opened back up for me so I could top up my supplies, and offered me hammock-swinging space on his veranda. He was a Texas gentleman. The painful fifty-six kilometres in prayer from there was past some eye-opening ranches containing ten species of deer amongst the low-lying woodlands, plus the iconic African wildebeest. We stared at each other for a good minute before I turned and walked on with them following me down the fence line.

What ever happened to ranching cows?

The final kilometres into bustling Junction were horrid. Parts of my feet were skinless and the 165 kilometres in three days left me aching all over; although, it was more than just satisfying to knock off two days from the lagging fifteen. I hobbled on to a few empty churches and then checked into a hotel for a hot shower.

I took a scheduled rest day in Junction before continuing on a little fresher through real cattle country to the town of Menard, fifty kilometres away. The distances were pushing me to the limit, but I enjoyed it. I'd walk and chat with

God, sometimes apologising for stupid stuff, sometimes thanking him for great stuff, but always leading back to asking for His help with the big stuff. "Lord, please unite us in truth and in love, for the salvation of souls and for the glory of your name. Amen."

Blooming purple flowers scattered amongst lush long grass separated Menard from Eden, where an elderly couple by the name of Ivy and Red invited me to stay the night and fussed over me. They knew a lot more about Australia, and Tasmania in particular, than I'd have given Americans credit for. It was exactly the same for nearly everyone I'd met. I told them about my apparently false preconceived ideas of Americans being naive of the rest of the world and they palmed it off saying, "That's because the media is focussed on California, Florida and New York. We're a different a breed out here." They didn't fly their American flags because they wanted to say, "We're the best and you're not," but to say, "We stand for something as a community and we'd like to uphold it." I liked that.

After dinner we stepped out onto their darkened property while Ivy walked me through the northern hemisphere astronomy, star by star, so that I actually knew what I was looking at as I trundled along in the twilight hours.

I headed on to the town of Paint Rock filled with anticipation. An Australian friend was flying to Houston that day and driving up to visit, bringing new socks and a book for me to chew through. My socks were absolutely shredded by the rain. I spent the entire day looking over my shoulder wondering how much longer it would be until he pulled over. He never turned up. After six months of planning it became evident that we'd stuffed up. I'd told him where I was going to be and he'd told me what airport he was flying into. I'd presumed he'd checked on the map to see where Paint Rock was and he'd presumed that the name of the town I'd given him was going to be close to where he was landing. He'd stepped off the plane, hired a car with his brother, entered Paint Rock into the GPS and … they both had a hernia when it told them it was 655 kilometres away.

He wasn't coming.

While Paint Rock dozed off to sleep, and with no accommodation available, I stepped back onto the road in my not-so-good mood and walked on for another thirty kilometres to the next day's destination. I marched the whole way in darkness without making a single stop, venting my frustration in the first half and then focussing back on praying for unity and a rosary for the second half. I rolled into the Ballinger hotel at 2 am.

I bought a three pack of durable socks in Ballinger, which were incredible to slip on. I'd forgotten what soft padded cotton felt like. Two ex-servicemen, who'd given their lives to the Church as priests, invited me to have a meal with them and stay in the spare room for the second night, which I thoroughly enjoyed.

I'd only made it a kilometre out of Ballinger when a Sheriff pulled up behind me, requesting my ID. Apparently, someone had seen me walking down the road and thought I looked suspicious, so rang the police. He let me continue on, but a few hours shy of my destination of Wingate I ran out of water and rang the doorbell at a roadside farmhouse hoping to top up my water supply. There was no answer, so I took a photo of the old rusted vintage pick-up sitting pride of place in the front yard and moved on. Fifteen minutes later a second Sheriff's car, with lights flashing, pulled in behind me. He jumped out and similarly asked to see my ID, querying, "Why were you ringing the doorbell and taking photographs of the house a few miles back?" The owner was home. I explained the situation, showing the sheriff my photo of the vintage pick-up, and he just laughed, reached into his car and pulled out a bottle of fresh water for me. It'd be nice if people talked to me before talking to the law …

Wingate was quieter than I'd hoped for. The grocery store, café, post office and bank had all closed permanently, leaving only a cotton storage shed. Not much help. I stood on the edge of town for a minute and decided to swallow my pride and just knock on the door of what looked like the most welcoming house. At the very least I might end up with a bed at the sheriff's place. A fit-looking, elderly gentleman opened up and when I explained myself and asked if it would be okay if I strung my hammock up in his front yard he smiled and said, "Sure, no problem." He gathered some food up for me and wandered out to help me string up the hammock. Their guard dog even added an extra level of safety. He occasionally woke and poked his head up over the hammock, resting his head on my belly with a moan, wanting some of the venison they'd given me, but he'd then rest back on the ground and continue snoring.

I was ready to hit the road by 5:30 am but, frustratingly, I discovered that I'd left two of the three brand new pairs of socks sitting in the bedroom back in Ballinger. I could have strangled myself. "Stupid, stupid, stupid." The guard dog followed me for a good distance until we parted company and it was just God and me once more. With a full container of water, but only a tiny amount of smoked venison left, it was set to be an interesting fifty-seven kilometres to Sweetwater.

I was praying my way through the largest wind generation tower array on the planet and I stepped within a whisker of a five-foot bull snake. It launched itself away from me at lightning speed, bolting through the tussocky grass with such speed that it hurled itself airborne over a small bush! It was insane. I'd never seen a snake move so fast and it left me wanting a sheriff's car to pull up and get me out of there.

Battling hunger pains, I heard the dreaded no-water gurgle at around midday out in the middle of nowhere. I stopped at an intersection and looked down the side road wondering if water and food were straight ahead or to the right. A fellow driving by slowed down and asked if I needed help. I explained the situation and he smiled, "Jump in buddy. There's a remote restaurant set up for the wind turbine workers just down this side road." Dale Finch, I later discovered, was a well-respected local farmer and integrity was a word often associated with him. He drove me the seven kilometres to the outpost of Nolan, bought me lunch, organised my lift back and headed on his way with a handshake. I was blown away when the owner then came over and handed me the money Dale used to pay for the meal. She smiled, "It's on the house. Make sure you fill up proper before heading off." The local workers chatted about the mission while the town's 'grandmother'— a woman named Mary—encouraged me to continue on, reassuring me that she'd been praying for unity for a very long time.

The sun set an hour before I'd completed the fifty-seven kilometres to Sweetwater and every church was locked by the time I arrived. Yet another sheriff pulled in behind me, but before he could say anything I piped up with, "G'day, I'm from Australia. Is there a hotel in town here anywhere?"

He smiled and opened his passenger door, "You've passed it by a good mile. I'll take you back."

The following night I arrived in the highway town of Hermleigh with the only suggestion offered for accommodation being to try my luck finding hammock-slinging space at the football ground. I wandered through the dark streets looking for the field, but couldn't see a thing. In the darkness I spotted a guy sitting on the back of his truck outside his house, so I asked if he knew where the field was. He just sat there without saying a word. It was awkward and unnerved me. I flicked my headlamp on. Turns out 'he' was a gas cylinder. No wonder he was so tight lipped.

I found the field and perched myself up in the open bleachers, spread my survival bag and gear out on a step and slept very uncomfortably. Barely awake, I walked on groggily for the eighteen kilometres to Snyder, and arrived just in time for morning Mass. I was careful not to stand too close to anyone as I was pretty sure I was the only one who'd walked sixty-one kilometres since their last shower. The parish welcomed me openly and one family invited me back to their house for food, a shower and a bed. They continued the brilliant Texan hospitality, but over dinner an inevitable questions arose, "If you walk so far in one day, where do you go to the toilet if you need to go?"

"I just have to find somewhere out of sight," I explained bluntly.

Some of them laughed, but the mum and dad showed concern. "Do you realise that if you're caught urinating in public you can be arrested and placed on the sex offenders list?"

My eyes were wide open. "You can't be serious?"

Oh, but they were. It was indeed a chargeable offence that carried with it a listing as a sex offender. The Texas panhandle's flat cropping land had few places to hide, so I began concocting tactics to better disguise the unavoidable necessity. It was a tough ask. I'd picked up another two days on the lagging fifteen over the last week, so that was a positive. I had seventy-four days left on my visa and was eleven days behind schedule. But it wasn't looking any easier. I hurt. After that massive eighty-one kilometres in northern Mexico, the middle of the sole of my right foot ached and it had continued to worsen. I feared it was a stress fracture, but whatever it was the pain was increasing, like a pin being driven right through. Coupled with the precarious pain my back still produced, I was left wondering how on earth I'd ever reach Canada on time.

A bull snake, getting ready to say "Hi".

I left Snyder with a tub of blueberry yoghurt and was so engrossed in it that I didn't see the well-camouflaged chunky five-foot snake curled up on the road ahead of me. The first thing I saw of it was between my chest and forearm as I lifted up the first scoop. Something on the road turned pinkish-white as the flip top mouth opened up and the snake launched thigh-ward in a flash of brown and tan speckles. In the split second between launching and landing its strike I instinctively leapt into a Kung-Fu-like rotation, sending the snake rocketing between my legs at an uncomfortable height. It brushed my inner thigh as I spun mid-air and landed facing the snake. It smacked down on the road a metre from where it took off. It recoiled and puffed itself in and out while hissing loudly.

I was happy to have not spilt my yoghurt.

Over the course of the week I saw more snakes than ever before, particularly at sunset when they sprawled out across the road to soak up its warmth. I nerve-rackingly walked through the world's largest rattlesnake population with my eyes peeled. There was little time to relax.

After forty-eight kilometres, I arrived at the remote settlement of Justiceburg right on twilight. I found a neat spot for my hammock outside the closed Jesse Jane's bar, sitting all by itself waiting for the distant ranchers to visit on Friday and Saturday nights. There were no taps around Jesse Jane's, so I summoned up the courage to wander across the raised railway line towards the lights of a solitary house. I was very tentative about approaching a house at night and did so slowly, trying to gauge what sort of person lived there. All I could figure out in the dark was that he didn't like gardening.

I knocked and stepped well back. A solid guy wearing a well-worn cap answered and after my apology he casually invited me in to fill up my water supply. A shotgun leant against the wall; coming from Australia, where guns have to be under lock and key, it looked grossly out of place. "What's that sitting there for?" I asked. He shrugged his shoulders, "Just in case I need it fast." I laughed nervously. I was happy to receive a few shared crackers and a lengthy chat instead.

It was a horrid night swinging in my hammock. Rain fell on just enough of an angle to render the protection of the veranda negligible and everything was soaked, even the sleeping bag that was inside the waterproof survival bag. When the first light of day emerged amidst continued wispy showers it was far too early. I'd hardly slept. I packed up the soggy gear and sniffled my way towards Post, twenty-four kilometres away.

Having dried out and slept well, it was a further 129 kilometres on to Ralls, Floydada and then Plainview, through cotton field plains and cattle pasture stretching on for mile after mile. Enormous trains powered past at a distance and their drone could be heard lingering on the warm autumn day breeze. On the way to Plainview, I headed out under the cover of blissful starlit silence until magnificent deep red and orange hues pushed back the veil of darkness. I'd never seen so many sunrises and sunsets back to back in my life. They were constant gems.

Trying to pray a rosary was tedious at times: my mind wandered off on tangents, "Focus, Sam! Yes that's a big tractor, but you've seen hundreds before." I was even distracted while apologising to God for being distracted. You just can't win some days. I set aside an hour every day to simply pray and 'be' with God and, halfway through that hour, as I approached Plainview, an army veteran pulled over to check on me. After hearing of the mission he not only offered to pray for unity, but to pray for the next half an hour with me as he continued on in his car. It was uplifting to know that for the next thirty minutes we were interceding together. It gave me a boost. He pulled back over an hour later, flew open the car door and invited me to enjoy a meal with him that he'd bought at the next town. We ate and chatted for a considerable time. Texans are right up there with sunrises and sunsets.

In Plainview I visited a few churches, including the Hispanic community gathering for Mass. The parish priest invited me forward to share about the mission, so I asked, "I presume it's okay to speak English?" There were a few blank faces. One man laughed, "Only if you want the few of us who speak English to understand you!" And so I unexpectedly had to revert back to the Spanish I'd missed speaking.

To my delight a huge family threw me in their car afterwards and drove me home for a wonderful feed. I had also missed Mexican food. I thought their hospitality was fantastic, but I was about to learn that Texans always take it one step further. With a knock at the door a woman walked in amidst a flurry of hugs and kisses before presenting me with an envelope, "We took up a collection and everyone chipped in so you don't have to pay for hotels or food for a few days." I was stunned. She kissed me on the cheek and left amidst more hugs and kisses from the family.

Alarms were being set for 4:01 all over the place as I pushed north up to Tulia, Happy (whose slogan was, "The town without a frown!") and Canyon; and the hospitality remained superb, particularly from a Church of Christ preacher who invited me in for Sunday lunch with his family and organised for new socks to be delivered to me before I walked on.

When I approached a young rattlesnake, my fifth for the week, it wasn't bothered by my presence at all, so I spent a few minutes watching. I'd never seen a rattlesnake rattle, so I reached out with my metre and half walking pole and placed the end close to its head. It recoiled into a striking position with its tail rattling away beside it. That was all I wanted to see, so I left it alone from there and walked on humming and praying.

I dropped a prayer slip at a number of empty churches in Canyon before calling it a day, having pushed beyond the illusive 300 kilometre mark in a single week for the first time. I'd caught up on another three days to be only eight days behind schedule. I was tired, sniffling and grimacing from the piercing pain caused by the thing under my foot (not to mention the on-going back pain) so it did come at a cost.

I sat on the end of my hotel bed with a Subway in hand and channel-surfed various Christian cable TV stations. I was wide-eyed at the array of teachings being served up. It left a bitter taste in my mouth. Over one hour I heard:

*Interdenominational Preacher:* "The Baptist Church is run by a board and that is not in the bible!"

*Pentecostal Preacher:* "Hell does not exist and the bible is not the exact word of God."

*Pentecostal Preacher:* "Hell is very real and the bible, the word of God, describes it vividly!"

*Wisdom Centre Church Preacher:* "The Holy Spirit whispered to me: 'I can get you money anywhere in the world.'" and "The Lord wants to bless you with financial security, so if you send a $1,000 deposit right now, to the address on your screen, you too can allow the Lord to bless you."

*Unknown Preacher:* "We need to make atonement for our sins! Send a minimum of $60 to the address below and begin to make your atonement with God."

*Pentecostal Preacher:* "The Catholic Church seeks to control your life."

*Evangelical Preacher:* "The Pentecostal Church is so legalistic."

It was sad watching the public face of Christianity—a cloudy mixture of truth, half-truth and deceit. For the average Christian there were confused messages dressed up as clarity, rather than a building up of faith. Even worse, for the searching non-Christian the display on offer was one of marketplace-like division and chastisement, even if there was truth amongst it. I flicked the TV off. "God, help us."

It was a short hop along the highway to the major northern Texas city of Amarillo where a V22 Osprey (a hybrid helicopter/airplane in development for the US army) was being tested off to the side of the road as I walked by. I watched in amazement as it was put through its paces.

I visited a number of churches in Amarillo before a Catholic parishioner named Steve invited me to stay at his place for the night, and my rest day. Steve worked on the V22 Ospreys so it made for engaging dinner conversation. When it came to chatting about my journey, he jumped straight on the phone to the major local paper so that the invitation to pray for unity could be stretched that much further.

The Amarillo Globe chief columnist was handed the job. I arrived at the offices the next morning for the interview, then set my sights on finding the Catholic Diocese office. My third replacement credit card, I hoped, was waiting there. It hadn't shown up. It was frustratingly nowhere to be seen. I didn't bother ordering a new one. I just let it go and withdrew more cash.

Every Wednesday, Steve headed to the adoration chapel at 4 am to pray, so I sluggishly joined him for the hour and mostly stayed awake. After breakfast, we headed out to an impromptu second interview with the EWTN radio station. I'd been interviewed a few times on radio, but they'd always been pre-recorded and edited. EWTN was live for the fourteen-minute interview, which provided for a more dynamic conversation. Having two energetic interviewers to carry it along helped to no end.

I was out on the road by mid-morning, heading out towards the Canadian River, where right on nightfall, a fabulous mum of nine running the isolated café there offered one of her absent son's beds to me. The next day it wasn't a snake I was avoiding, but a huge hairy tarantula. It wandered down the side of the road in front of me. I stooped low with my camera and filmed it walking along and it looked fantastic … until the tarantula reacted to my presence and walked out across the road. Phlump, phlump! a pickup flattened it flatter than a tortilla. "Whoops," was all I could offer.

An SUV pulled over a few hours later and the driver asked, "Are you Samuel?"

"Yes, I am," I replied tentatively.

"I have a package for you, from the Diocese of Amarillo." It was my credit card! It had taken four and a half months to reach me, plus a two-hour drive from a generous Amarillo fellow.

The Mexican metal shoved into the plastic nib of my walking pole had worn away, but that day I found a mini screwdriver and a nail on the side of the road. I prised the old bit out with the screwdriver, but it slipped and I jammed the screwdriver up under my thumbnail, producing blood and a jaw clenching shot of pain. With lots of trusty yellow sticky tape I fixed both the pole and my thumb.

Car horns tooted and friendly waves were offered throughout the next morning. I thought everyone was just being nice, but when I walked into a highway truck stop they produced the Amarillo Globe newspaper, with my picture on the front page, and asked me to sign it. Despite the mission spreading fast, it was a sombre walk on into the night to finish that fifty-four kilometre day to Stanford. Back home my youngest sister was about to walk down the aisle and I was the only extended family member not attending. On top of that, it was also the Australian Football League grand final and my team, the Geelong Cats, were playing for their first premiership since 1963. I was born in 1979.

My sister married and the Cats won emphatically.

After a solid sleep I set off along a phenomenally straight road towards the Oklahoma border. It was sickening how corner-less it was. The road was alive with scooting tumbleweed backed by roaring wind packing gusts exceeding seventy km/h. A doctor, and member of a nearby Methodist Church, pulled over after lunch with her two teenage kids and one of their friends to brave the wind and walk with me. The wind made it difficult to chat about unity and our roles in the Church, but we persisted, and I was impressed that they walked with me out across those sweeping plains for as far as they did. Their car was no longer in sight. They had a long walk back. It was a wonderful Texan send-off. Many Texans had commented on how difficult they believed it would be for Christians to unite completely in theology and love, but they were almost always happy enough and humbled to pray for it.

I crossed into the Oklahoma panhandle late in the day, tired and with increasing back and foot pain. The windy day produced nothing but blue skies and wispy clouds, which faded into the evening twilight. As darkness set in, I failed to notice the stars above disappearing.

On approach to Oklahoma's rural town of Boise City a few lightning bolts flashed over the western horizon, followed fifteen minutes later by a sweeping electrical storm across the north. The wind howled from the east at 80 km/h so I assumed those storms wouldn't come near me, and they didn't. But in the darkness, a third front curled in behind me. Its first lightning bolt cracked into the plains a kilometre behind me and I swung around to realise that the storm had encircled me. And it was ramping up. Lightning flickered to the north, south, east and west in a dazzling show that lit up the sky every few seconds. Some bolts cracked into the ground, others flew up into the clouds and a few flashes sparked their way across the under belly of the storm in a mesmerising stream of iridescent purple. Out of sheer instinctiveness I repeatedly ducked.

A sheriff, with lights flashing, pulled up and yelled out through the howling wind, "Do you want to be out here?"

I smiled and yelled back, "Yes sir!"

He just raised his eyebrows and said, "Okay," flicked his lights off and drove away. I didn't mind the storm being around me, but that soon changed. The show-stopping moment flashed in front of me as a distant bolt struck in just the right spot to show up a funnel cloud twirling down out of the storm. I peered into the darkness waiting for another appropriately placed flash. Bang! A massive tornadic spiral lit up. I had no idea if it would hit the ground and I had no idea what direction it was headed. In the event that it came my way the only thing I could spot under the hypnotic lightning flashes were stormwater drains every two hundred metres running under the adjacent railway line. I marched on with one eye on the distant funnel cloud and one on the distance to the next drainpipe.

The wind swung to the opposite direction and picked up in speed causing my backpack to act like a rudder, forcing me into sudden turns. Heavy rain bulleted in at in excess of 100 km/h on a near horizontal plane. I wanted that sheriff back! I struggled to remain upright and my waterproof backpack cover fluttered violently until suddenly it went quiet. I turned in time to see the fluoro-yellow cover disappear in a flurry out across rural Oklahoma.

I kept my head down and prayed my heart out until 11 pm when, with a hairstyle to rival Albert Einstein's, I scurried along the last few kilometres into Boise City. "That was dumb, but absolutely fantastic at the same time. Thank you, Lord, for letting me make it here in one piece." I ambled up to the first hotel, sopping wet.

I was happy to relax at Sunday morning Mass the next day before slowly stretching out for the remaining forty-four kilometres across to southern Colorado with more enormous trains ploughing across the landscape.

A rustic sign welcomed me, "… to colorful Colorado." It was absurdly ironic. Other than dead brown grass stretching to the horizon, there was no colour! The plains wouldn't take up the entire state though; the Rockies weren't far off. A member of the Campo Assembly of God Church unlocked their little church hall for me to sleep in. "Just make sure you turn the gas off when you leave," I was told. I was left to count my blessings. I was seven days behind schedule, but felt that I was right where God wanted me to be.

> *For he will command his angels concerning you to guard you in all your ways. On their hands they will bear you up, so that you will not dash your foot against a stone..*
>
> Psalm 91:11–12

Total walked: *7,229 kilometres*

# Night Sprinklers, Agape & the Imposing Shirley Basin

*October 2007*

Colorado's coarse cattle-grass plains were being tossed back and forth in blustery pre-dawn winds. I set my sights across them. Autumn days were numbered. In my first stop of Springfield, while visiting a few churches, I spotted a motel at the end of town. As I headed towards it I passed a small Quaker church with a matching house and was forced to weigh up my priorities. "I should go say hello and invite them to pray for unity but … I'm tired and want that motel." There was a gentle encouragement to just do my job, so I turned and plodded over.

The pastor engaged me in positive conversation about unity, but as I departed a gentleman across the road waved from his front door, yelling, "Oi! Oi! Come here!" He was abrupt, but the bald late-fifties man with a round weathered smiling face also had a softness about him. Gerry and his wife, Rita, were the Pentecostal preachers at the church I'd slept the night in at Campo. They offered me dinner and their spare apartment upstairs. The motel would've been a poor decision.

An animated dinner conversation went on long into the night. I asked about their respective journeys to being Pentecostal preachers and Rita's answer surprised me. She'd lived elsewhere and was married to an abusive alcoholic. She was Catholic and sought help from the parish priest, but his response was to slap her on the back and say, "Just pray three Hail Marys, you'll be okay," and walk off. She was gutted and never stepped foot within a Catholic church again. She found acceptance, love and help in a neighbouring Pentecostal church and it was there that she went on to study to become a preacher.

Rita paused and shook her head. "Sam, I don't understand why the Catholic Church teaches such a thing. How can it teach that if you just pray three Hail Marys everything will be okay?"

I was angry at the priest's response. "Rita, that isn't the teaching of the Catholic Church. You just had a heartless priest who didn't care." I explained Catholic teachings on alcoholism and abusive marriages, while highlighting the various organisations that worked in those fields to help and protect people. In the end all I could do was apologise. "I'm sorry the Church let you down. I'm really glad you found help and grew in faith."

She grabbed the back of my hand and shook it lightly. "God moves in mysterious ways."

In a similar fashion, I'd meet two men in two towns over the next few days who also invited me in for dinner. One was a lapsed Christian whose father was once an Evangelical preacher, and the other wasn't lapsed, he just never was; but both invited me in and showed great interest in the mission to draw the Church into prayer for Christian unity. Incredibly, both men asked the exact same question, "So, you're a Catholic? Why do you worship Mary?"

"We don't." I replied. "We just hold her in high esteem as the perfect role model of how to follow Jesus. On top of that, Mary has appeared to people throughout the ages with a repetitive call to repent and return to her son, whose heart aches for us. Nearly all the time, Mary has said, 'And if you want my prayers, just ask for them', so we ask Mary to pray for us in the same way we'd ask a friend to." I added, "Any Catholic who worships Mary has lost sight of the destination and stopped to admire the signpost pointing to the destination." Even more incredibly, both men, twenty-four hours apart, nodded slowly and accepted my explanation with, "It kind of makes sense now."

I wondered how a major Catholic/Protestant division could be answered so quickly. Perhaps their acceptance wasn't typical. At the end of the night with the lapsed Christian I asked him to pray for me as I continued on. He just smiled, saying, "I already have," and shook my hand.

Halfway along one seventy-six kilometre sprawl between towns I knocked on a rancher's door at sunset to ask for permission to put my hammock up somewhere. A solid man by the name of Greg opened up. He owned a 30,000 acre ranch, wore shorts and a t-shirt and, with great ease, agreed to me tying the hammock up in his front yard, but he then added, "Do you want some dinner first? I've just cooked up meatloaf and mashed potatoes if you'd like some."

Greg and his wife, Valerie, offered wonderful hospitality and, before too long, I'd been offered the spare room. At the end of the night Valerie headed off to bed, but Greg wanted to chat. "You have some tough gun laws over in Australia. You can't even have pistols can you?"

"Not unless you're in a gun club," I replied.

He walked into another room and returned brandishing two of them, "Have you ever fired one? You want to go outside and do some target practice?" I struggled to contain my excitement! We set up a tin can in front of old railway sleepers and jammed a maple leaf between two sleepers a few feet above the can as a secondary target. In the chilly evening Greg's first two shots were mild sound-wise, but the third nearly blasted my eardrums out. "What happened then!" I asked.

He smiled. "That bullet was different to the other two." Yeah, no kidding. Greg handed me a pistol and I lined up the can, yelled at the cat to get out of the way, zeroed in and, "BANG!" The leaf went flying. It was a good thing it was dark and Greg couldn't see my confused expression. With no idea that I was shooting for the can he was mightily impressed and congratulated me, "Good shot!" I think my mission was similar: what I aimed for and what I hit weren't always one in the same. At least my aim improved as the night progressed.

Greg and Valerie organised for me to see their chiropractor in the next town and he took me straight in for X-rays. What was evident from them was that my left pelvis was badly rotated, causing it to stick out of my back by a few centimetres. Little could be done right there and then. It was a case of just hoping to have it seen to back in Australia in a year's time. He worked on it for a while, but sent me on my way with a few exercises to keep me mobile.

I trekked up Highway 287 to Eads amongst farmers rushing around carting hay bales in before the forecast first snowfall hit in a few days' time. I simply tried to stay on the road: fierce warm crosswinds tipping 100 km/h buffeted me for the exhausting long days. When the wind swung to the south at one point the tumbleweed began overtaking me. I'd fallen a few notches in the highway food chain.

On the two-day walk to Hugo the wind was head-on again, forcing me to work the walking poles overtime to maintain forward momentum. I covered forty-three kilometres by sunset, but there was nowhere to sleep out there and I'd run out of water. I pushed on – avoiding a sprawling bull snake – all the way until 11:30 pm. I was in the middle of nowhere. The wind eased off momentarily, but without warning it then smashed me from the north. It felt like the freezer door had been opened and the temperature dropped by 10°C in thirty seconds. My skin rapidly tightened.

The cold front had arrived and I was a sitting duck.

Dehydrated and pining for water, I was approaching a gravel truck pull-off area when a car drew to a stop. He opened up the passenger door, "Are you okay? Do you want a lift?" I was more than happy to take the ride to Hugo, and find my way back the following day. The gentleman dropped me at the Hugo service station at ten minutes before its midnight closure. I nearly bathed in the drinks.

The hotel was already shut so I wandered back through the town looking for a spot to sleep. On the edge of town I found a small public building with thick green grass surrounding it. That was good enough. I laid my sleeping bag down, slid in to it and prayed the day to an end. It was 2°C.

At precisely 2:10 am the reason for the lush grass became apparent. I woke with a fright to the sound of a rattlesnake perched right beside me, but as water drenched me I realised it was in fact a pop-up sprinkler. I scrambled, tumbling out of the bag only to be hit in the face by the sprinkler. I gathered my drenched belongings in one swoop and ran to the road, dripping wet and shivering. "God, this isn't nice. Really. Not at all." A stiff breeze took the relative temperature below freezing and I struggled to breathe without sounding like I was fitting. I threw on all the clothes I had and started walking back eastwards into the night for the fourteen kilometres trek to that gravel truck stop.

Mile 401 in Hugo, Colorado

I was close to falling asleep while walking, but the cold numbed the pain and the chance to sacrifice everything as an offering for unity was compelling. A crescent moon, with Venus following underneath, rose dead ahead of me, growing higher in the night sky as the hours ticked by. By the time the horizon began glowing under the first hint of dawn, I'd stopped shivering, feeling hungry, and feeling tired. I'd basically just stopped feeling anything. With a weary smile I spotted the truck stop emerging as a rough silhouette against the dawn sky.

I plonked myself down on a picnic table and pulled out my bible to pray for half an hour while watching the sunrise. I felt capable of just turning around and walking back to Hugo. So I did. At 9:30 am I passed mile marker 401 to arrive back in Hugo, slightly late for Sunday morning Mass. I suspect I looked close to death, but they welcomed me and the 4:01 invitation was carried on. A few parishioners bought me a huge breakfast, which I knew I needed to eat, but I felt sick. It took great concentration to stay awake and eat it. I was so grateful when they then paid for a hotel room for me. I'd paced out eighty-nine kilometres with a one and a half hour sleep in the middle. I was now only five days behind schedule.

With the temperature dropping significantly I rugged up and set off from Hugo on the Monday morning into battering winds. The sharp needle-like pain in my right foot intensified. I'd passed nearly a train a day since Amarillo and, as I approached Limon, another huge yellow freight train thundered in from the south. This time the train engineer was hanging out the window with a gleaming smile, sounding the horn and waving me on encouragingly. I think I'd made a new friend.

The 4:01 invitation was passed on to a couple of churches in Limon before a local journalist rounded me up. A lot of people had seen me walking down the road without any idea of why I was there, but most of them read the newspaper, so the invitation eventually arrived on their kitchen table. I was doubly grateful for the generous journalist who also fixed up my accommodation at the motel for the night.

My next night's accommodation, after a fifty-five kilometre day to Deer Trail, didn't end so well. While looking for a place to sling my hammock I passed a few trailer homes and spotted an abandoned one with an ideal front porch. I approached the trailer home next door to ask what the deal was with the empty one, knocked and waited. Sitting on their front porch was a big old couch and I wasn't looking forward to spending a cold night in my hammock, so without giving it any intelligent thought I changed my plans. A young man opened up and I introduced myself before enquiring about the possibilities of me curling up on the couch for the night, perhaps even at cost. He responded with, "Just wait here a minute. I'll check with my wife," and closed the door. I stood on the front step waiting for ten minutes growing increasingly uneasy. Suddenly the door flew open and his wife screamed at me to get off the property just as a car power-slid into the gravel car park and their skinhead friend jumped out. He ran to the porch as I backed away apologising. The skinhead, with his mouth partly open as if he wanted to take a bite out of me, stepped in between the woman and me as I backed up to the road. The wife said to the skinhead that the police and sheriff were on the way, so I turned and shouted back, "Why did you do that?"

She stepped past the friend and blurted out, "Because you wouldn't leave!"

I was flabbergasted, "But … your husband said to me, 'Wait here'. I did what your husband asked me to do!" She then told me what she really thought of me. I have no idea where the husband went, but he didn't show his face again. It was just his screaming wife and a scary malnourished skinhead.

Now I didn't want to put my hammock up in Deer Trail anywhere. I moved on into the night across the countryside for my next day's destination. There was little traffic, but for the few cars that did approach I tactfully removed myself from the road and hid behind whatever I could find. I didn't mind if it was the police, just not the skinhead. I prayed on and on through the cool still night.

I reached Byers in the wee-hours of the morning, wrapping up a seventy-four kilometre day. I was thankful to the hotel owner when he woke to the late night doorbell and welcomed me in with tired eyes. He was genuinely happy to receive a tip for having had his sleep interrupted.

Over the next two days the Rocky Mountain peaks slowly broke the western horizon beyond harvested wheat fields. Clouds hid the top of the snow-covered mountains towering over the plains below, where the highways grew larger and connecting roads increased until my path became cluttered with street poles, signs and pedestrians. I was approaching Denver.

Homeless men were scattered along my route, some of whom were intoxicated, and it was only 3 pm on a Friday afternoon. I chatted to some of the homeless guys and shared some of my food, often they would take over the conversation, sharing about their faith and standing with God. Huge brand new cars continued to rumble past as we chatted and I couldn't help but acknowledge what side of the divide I grew up on.

A rough looking character with a tooth missing and a buzz haircut walked straight at me, stopping me in my tracks, "Do you wanna fight?" He was in my face and because of everything that had happened from Brazil to that point I was immediately clenching my fists.

I stared back and replied in the same matter of fact tone, "No."

He was surprised that I hadn't taken him on, tried to run or sworn at him. He looked around as if searching for someone to help him out with what to say next. He leaned in closer. "Why not?"

I leaned in even closer again, "Because I'm trying to walk around a good portion of the world while praying for the unity of Christians. Bashing the stuffing out of you or you bashing the stuffing out me would hardly help me achieve that goal. I'm a Catholic missionary. I don't want to fight you."

He stepped back and thought for a second. "Really? You sure? 'Cause you're kind of a big fella and I feel like having a real good fight."

"No," I replied again.

To my astonishment he then backed away and let me walk on saying, "Okay then. That's a long walk!" and wandered back to the bar from whence he'd come.

I visited an Ethiopian Orthodox church, before finding the Catholic cathedral where a bishop was conducting a Rite of Christian Initiation of Adults class. The RCIA program is the means by which adults become practising members of the Catholic Church by learning what they are saying yes to with their lives, not just their words.

The room was packed, with the majority of participants being non-Catholic Christians with a sound knowledge of scripture. The questions came thick and fast. One question, "What good is tradition? Shouldn't we just believe in what the bible says?" gained some impromptu support from the participants. The bishop agreed that we should believe in what the bible says, but added, "We need Church tradition to enter into the scriptures more fully." He didn't win everyone over so he proposed a test. "I'm going to read a scripture verse and I'd like you to tell me what it means." Everyone nodded in agreement. He read aloud John 21:15–17:

> *When they had finished breakfast, Jesus said to Simon Peter, "Simon son of John, do you love me more than these?" He said to him, "Yes, Lord; you know that I love you." Jesus said to him, "Feed my lambs." A second time he said to him, "Simon son of John, do you love me?" He said to him, "Yes, Lord; you know that I love you." Jesus said to him, "Tend my sheep." He said to him the third time, "Simon son of John, do you love me?" Peter felt hurt because he said to him the third time, "Do you love me?" And he said to him, "Lord, you know everything; you know that I love you." Jesus said to him, "Feed my sheep"*

The Bishop asked everyone, "What does this mean?" and hands flew up everywhere. Each person's interpretation was given with authority: each tried to out-trump the other. Most believed it tied in with Peter's denial of Jesus, but once the Bishop had received everyone's comments (some very blunt as though it was so obvious) he trumped us all. He noted that the bible wasn't written in English and that much is often lost in translation. "It requires the tradition of the Church to help us understand what is happening here. There are a number of words that describe what in English we call love. The two we need to know for this translation are 'Philios', to love someone as a brother; and 'Agape', pure self-sacrificing love. The bishop picked his bible back up and drew it all together, "This is how it actually reads:

> *When they had finished breakfast, Jesus said to Simon Peter, "Simon son of John, do you agape me more than these?" He said to him, "Yes, Lord; you know that I philios you." Jesus said to him, "Feed my lambs." A second time he said to him, "Simon son of John, do you agape me?" He said to him, "Yes, Lord; you know that I philios you." Jesus said to him, "Tend my sheep." He said to him the third time, "Simon son of*

*John, do you philios me?" Peter felt hurt because he said to him the third time, "Do you philios me?" And he said to him, "Lord, you know everything; you know that I philios you." Jesus said to him, "Feed my sheep."*

You could have heard a pin drop in that room. The mental cogs were turning. A voice in the crowd murmured, "Jesus came down to Peter's level." There were a few raised eyebrows and looks of bewilderment. I think every single one of us, Catholic or not, learnt something new about that passage. The Bishop concluded, "The tradition of the Church is supposed to bring the scriptures alive and make Christ manifest in our lives."

I walked on through Denver pondering the sacrificial proposal Jesus offered Peter, and his consequent lesser counter offer when Peter turned out too weak to accept. Jesus met him where he was. I wondered how often Jesus needed to meet me where I was, rather than me meeting the call he'd initially placed. A chatty homeless guy helped me find a cheap hotel above a pub and, with Philios love looking far less attractive, I paid for a room for him as well.

I spent a jam-packed rest day in Denver, beginning with a visit to the Denver Archdiocese offices to collect a package. The secretary stopped me and said: "Archbishop Chaput has meetings all day, but he asked me to let him know when you arrived so that he could at least say hello." Archbishop Charles Chaput was a well-respected man and one of the few American archbishops I'd heard of before entering the States. I'd read a number of books and listened to a number of talks that he either commissioned or sponsored, plus a few statements on hard-hitting topics he'd penned. He was a humble doer who was renowned for bringing Christ-centred life into the Church. The secretary whispered, "He has five minutes before his next meeting if you'd like to go through."

It was a pleasure to receive his encouragement. "Keep seeking Christ's leadership and love in the mission. We used to transition from adolescence to adulthood, but some now believe that a lot of people are making that transition through a period they've termed, 'Odyssey'. You're on your odyssey." He turned the conversation to home, asking: "How are your family coping?"

"They're glad I made it through Central America alive," I answered.

He smiled, "They're on this mission with you, only they didn't choose it. Keep them in prayer."

Before leaving Denver, and with my new credit card in hand, I bought a one-man tent, thick gloves, waterproof trousers, a ski jacket and, at long last, walking socks. In a hotel just north of downtown Denver I familiarised myself with the brand new tent, setting it up on the floor a few times, just in case I ever had to pitch it in the middle of a snowstorm at night.

It was nothing but suburbia for the twenty-eight kilometres north to Broomfield, where a Pentecostal and then Catholic church welcomed me in and accepted the invitation to pray for complete unity. At the Catholic church I made it just in time for the Saturday vigil Mass and took a quiet spot down the back, but after the opening hymn and prayer the priest asked if there were any visitors. I looked around as a couple of hands went up and so I slowly raised mine. The priest asked a woman up the front, "Where are you from?" then made his way through the few out-of-towners. Everyone was from elsewhere in Colorado and he quickly made his way back to me, pointing over the top of the congregation, "And how about the big guy back there? Where are you from?" The packed church turned as I yelled back respectfully, "I'm from Tasmania, in Australia." There were a few wows, a couple of comments and a lot of welcoming smiles. The priest pushed further, "And what brings you to Broomfield?" I paused with all one thousand eyes on me before yelling back, "I'm travelling around the world, predominantly on foot, from Brazil to Spain praying for the complete unity of Christians and stopping in every church I pass to invite them to pray for unity. I stopped here just to go to Mass though." The congregation laughed and the priest extended his hand to the people, "Well, you've all received the invitation now. We all should be praying for the unity of the Church anyway!"

Job done. On the walk towards Longmont the temperature remained dismally low at 3°C: heavy, cold, icy rain fell. A frigid north wind provided a taste of what was to come as I headed deep into the heart of a North American winter. It was brilliant to wear the brand new winter gear, which kept me warm and dry all day long.

The pin-like foot pain escalated, it had become like a nail being driven through it. I was limping badly, with gritted my teeth, when I arrived in Longmont. I visited a few churches including one where the youth group was gathering. It was the first church of its kind I'd come across. It was Ecumenical Catholic, not Roman Catholic. The parish priest was originally a Roman Catholic priest, but he'd fallen in love with his now wife, left the Church for a more liberal community and pastored there with his wife and two children alongside. As far as I could tell, the main difference between the Ecumenical Church and its origins was that it had severed all ties with the Vatican. It made for a deep and gritty conversation about the need for unity and what that would mean, but it was always undertaken with a lot of fun banter between the enthusiastic youth.

I was halfway across the USA and only three days behind schedule, but hurting badly. I had to keep reminding myself to reply with agape and not philios. I saw a doctor before leaving Longmont and the pain emanating from the sole of my right foot was diagnosed as nothing more than a corn. The doctor prescribed a means for fixing it and sent me on my way, but the patch he placed on my foot caused even more pain, to the point where I couldn't take another wincing step. I removed it. It didn't really matter: I'd eventually find out that his diagnosis was incorrect.

Under the glistening snow-covered slopes of the Rocky Mountains I paced out the long distance to Loveland and the welcoming Church of Christ. The next day, in the small city of Fort Collins, a Presbyterian pastor was less enthusiastic. There was a hint of possibly taking the invitation on, but nothing more than that. I bumped into a young man at the Catholic church and asked if he knew where the priest was. He smiled and replied in a Polish accent, "That would be me." Young Fr Peter laughingly invited me to join him for dinner at the Outback Steakhouse, an Australian-themed restaurant, where the menu was anything but Australian. However, the conversation about mission, Church and prayer was very authentic.

Fr Peter organised for me to meet Robert and Melanie, a young once-were-couple who were walking with one another towards entering the seminary and a Benedictine monastery respectively. Their commitment and support of one another in putting Christ first was incredible. It was wonderful to spend time with them.

A massive 106 kilometres lay ahead to the next major town of Laramie in Wyoming, but Melanie worked at a secluded Benedictine Abbey at roughly the halfway mark, so I walked on with her assurance of at least trying to organise a bed for me there by the time I arrived.

Red and yellow autumn leaves lined the westerly road that headed straight up into the mountains. In the unbelievably deserted landscape the temperature dropped with every passing hour until it was well below 'crisp'. Snow fell on distant peaks while the sun set across the wide-open wilderness with deer grazing nearby. There was no traffic. I pulled my balaclava on to combat the freezing winds and prayed a rosary by moonlight, all the way to the Abbey. When I was near the Abbey's front gate, my headlamp picked up the reflection of two solid lime-green eyes watching me from a small cliff off to the side. I kept the headlamp fixed on it. It moved a few metres, stopped and stared again. It wasn't a deer. I'm pretty sure it was a mountain lion, but in the dim moonlight it was difficult to tell. It backed away and I moved on, happy to put some distance between us. I kept my eyes peeled, but the cold was so intense that I actually struggled to focus. My eyes hurt.

My arrival at the warm Benedictine Abbey was met with relief and a lot of motherly hugs. After morning Mass I was sent on my way with more hugs and lots of food as I prayed my way on through the undulating mountains. The powerful Arctic gusts sliced through my balaclava making it too painful to walk head on into it; at times, it was so incredibly strong that I was stopped dead in my tracks and forced to just hold my position. The ninety km/h winds drove the relative temperature down to −22°C. I ignorantly removed my gloves to rummage through my backpack at one point and the cold stung my hands badly.

They ached for the next hour.

I made it across the border into Wyoming, continuing on across frigid plains towards Laramie. A sheriff pulled up alongside me after sunset to check on me. He did the usual request for identification and an explanation, but then did the very unusual thing of driving back to Laramie and returning fifteen minutes later with a receipt for a hotel room he'd booked me into. "Are you sure you'll be okay out here?" Trying to hold back shivers I nodded. He smiled, "Welcome to Wyoming!" Marshall Fritzen was the sort of guy I'd love to have keeping the peace in my town.

I jumped straight into a hot shower at that hotel. After five minutes I realised it was actually a cold shower. I was numb. Weather warnings were current for a large cold front to move in, but I figured I had just enough time to cover the day and a half's walk to Rock River before it hit.

A dog began following me as I walked on and wouldn't leave. I tried to get him to go home, but he just looked at me with puppy dog eyes and trotted on. I waved down a passing truck and asked the guy to take him back, but he was reluctant and left us to walk on together. I scolded him a few times to try and scare him home, but he just kept following until he wandered straight out in front of a speeding truck and was brutally mowed down. He was killed instantly. I was so deflated. As the solitary truck drove off I was left to quietly wander out and carefully remove his lifeless body from the road.

I pitched my tent on the edge of an abandoned settlement with the moon shining and I crawled in for some headlamp-assisted dinner and reading. I didn't feel safe out in the open, but I felt comfortable enough to close my eyes and sleep. Not surprisingly I dreamt that I was walking around the world.

The remaining thirty-one kilometres to Rock River was a race against time. I set off at dawn with the wind increasing and the temperature dropping as the cold front neared. Icy spits of rain began to fall when tiny Rock River came into view, but the motel was closed! I wasn't looking forward to sleeping in my tent through a snowstorm. A voice bellowed at me from the pub across the road. A large man with a trimmed black beard waved me over and, in a rough voice, apologised: "The motel's closed for winter. I have a five-wheeler back home that you're more than welcome to stay in if you like?" It sounded like he'd offered me a bed, but I had no idea what a five wheeler was. It was an absurdly big caravan. I was incredibly grateful.

I woke the next morning to an amazing sight. Winter had arrived and ten centimetres of snow blanketed the now frozen wilderness. Another twenty was forecast for the day and I was invited to not be stupid and walk on but to stay put for the day. I was happy to visit the town's small Baptist church with their teenage son, Josh. He didn't normally go to church, and I'd never been to a Baptist service, so we were both welcomed warmly. I missed not being able to make Mass for the Eucharist, but was appreciative for being able to attend the service with the fifteen rugged up faithful.

Elk Mountain, on the southern edge of Shirley Basin, Wyoming

I waited nervously for the day ahead. I'd be pushing out into wintery Wyoming wilderness just as the old wound from the surgery in Panama was on the verge of opening back up. Putting ice on it at least wouldn't be a problem. I headed out just after dawn into howling winds that scoured the barren landscape. Snowdrifts whisked along in waves, bombarding everything, including me. It was −14°C with a horrendous wind-chill factor on top of that. My gear just wasn't up to it. A gust blew between my balaclava and jacket straight onto my neck causing me to let out a high-pitch shriek that I wasn't even aware I was capable of producing. I was forced to shelter in a culvert for a while and while there I tried to take a drink, but after a few icy squirts the tube froze solid before my very eyes. "Stuff it."

Fighting on through the deep freeze I made it in one piece to tiny Medicine Bow and the famed antique Virginian Hotel. It still held its old-time charm, and prices at only $27 a night. It was daunting from there though. The nearest population centre of Casper was 148 kilometres away across Shirley Basin and my map indicated that it was nothing but wilderness. No service stations, no stores, and no help if I landed in trouble. It would take three full days at a taxing pace, with a small backpack capable of carrying only a day and a half's worth of food and my water supply frozen solid. On top of that I'd have to sleep in my tent for two nights. At the current night temperatures, I had approximately thirty to sixty seconds worth of breathing time before my lungs froze, causing permanent damage.

The locals at the bar noted that there was a snow shelter halfway and then a ranch further afield at the 104 kilometre mark. If I got into trouble I had to make it to one of those two points. They were adamant though that the bus was the only option. One cowboy stepped in and said, "Gee-whiz, you know what? You walked all the way from Brazil! That's awesome! But don't do it. Catch the bus. You don't have to prove anything. Catch the bus into Casper and walk on from there. Don't risk the mission."

I relented and agreed that it would be irresponsible of me to walk across the basin for three days through life-threatening conditions. I grabbed a meal and sat off to the side eating slowly, quiet before God. I wasn't praying, just sitting there eating in God's presence, trying to rationalise my decision due to the potentially fatal weather conditions. Hypothermia and dehydration would be somewhat inevitable. In that pensive silence I pondered my way out across the next three days into the lonely, cold wasteland. My plan to walk in excess of 1,000 kilometres further north to Edmonton in Canada and then from Moscow across western Russia—in the dead of winter—would most likely leave me just that … dead.

I'd bitten off more than I could chew.

In the quiet of my thoughts I felt God say one thing, succinctly and clearly: "Trust." As in, "Trust me."

I'd been through so much at that point that I didn't dismiss it or argue. I recognised 'that' voice, so there was nothing left to do but do as I was asked. "God, I'll do it, but if I die out there, it's your fault."

I slept well and woke a few hours before sunrise, rugged up with a towel wrapped over my mouth and nose to assist the balaclava, and slipped out quietly into the blustery, freezing night. Darkness and the sub-zero temperatures were all-consuming until a spectacular glow of warm deep red sunrise hues slowly exposed a winter wonderland of snow and mountains under a crisp clear sky. The arctic wind taunted me from head-on for hours, then momentarily died, coughed and spluttered, and swung around to the west, hitting with full force. It nearly blew me over. It was what the native Indians called a Chinook wind, which meant 'snow-eater'. It was a dry warm wind that didn't just melt snow: it evaporated it.

The Chinook strengthened over the course of the day, blow-drying the grassed wilderness clean and sending the temperature soaring to well above zero. I was gob-smacked at the vastness of the mountain-guarded basin filled with herds of antelope and white tail deer, strewn out before me. I felt very insignificant out there.

The sun was setting after fifty-one kilometres and it was there that I found a hay bale spread out alongside the road. I formed it up into a type of mattress, pitched my tent over it and then sat on a small hill with my tuna-on-crackers dinner. As though someone flicked a switch, the wind stopped and it was dead calm. Antelope grazed nearby, a whistling bird flew back and forth playfully, and on the still evening air the faint cry of coyotes rolled in from far-off foothills. It was spectacular.

I snuggled into my sleeping bag for the night ahead, but by 2 am was awake again and struggling due to plummeting temperatures. I was in the middle of a massive basin with snow-capped peaks surrounding me with no breeze and clear skies above. The cold air had sunk into the basin, freezing it back over. A very real threat of hypothermia set in. By 4 am it was unbearable and despite wearing full thermals and being inside a thermal inner, inside my sleeping bag, inside a survival bag, inside my one-man tent, I just couldn't stop shaking. I shuffled my head out of all the gear and pulled the balaclava down, fumbling with a shaking gloved hand to turn my headlamp on. It lit up icicles hanging from my tent caused by my breath freezing to the material directly above me. There are few scientific tests that can illustrate how cold it is better than breathing on your tent and watching it freeze.

I'd been shivering for so long that I knew I needed to move on immediately, but I was too tired to move. If you've ever woken up in the middle of the night needing to go to the toilet, but you're too tired to get out of bed and just want to fall back asleep, but you can't because you need to go to the toilet, then you'll understand the predicament. I couldn't move, but I couldn't sleep. With one final thought of, "Th … th … this sucks," I began the arduous task of shaking the ice from my tent, packing the rock-hard water bladders into my pack and walking on fast, trying to warm up.

It took a good hour before I stopped shivering. Praying on through the sunrise, the temperature rose only marginally. Five hours later my water supply was still frozen and I was now dehydrating. A red pick-up rumbled across the basin and pulled to a stop alongside. The driver wound his window down and looked out at me quizzically, "Now what in the hell are you doing out here?" I thought about telling him I was just walking to Casper and leaving it at that, but I had his attention, so I gave him the full spiel. I half expected him to wind his window up and drive off, but he smiled, shook his head and exclaimed, "Hallelujah Jesus!"

Gary was travelling with his wife and son to Casper to buy a vacuum cleaner, and Gary was one of the most full-on Evangelicals I'd ever met. Nearly every sentence ended with some sort of faith sentiment. He asked me where I was from and when I said I was from Tasmania in Australia he responded with, "Wow, you're from Tassie? Praise you Jesus!" Gary asked if I needed a drink and produced a huge bottle of Gatorade saying, "I bought this earlier today, but

I'm not sure why I did. I don't even like the stuff! Here, it's yours." He then ferreted around and found Snickers bars lying on the truck floor and threw me those as well. To top it off he offered to take the invitation to pray for Christian unity back to his church that Sunday and, with a prayer on the spot, we parted company. I walked on praying, rehydrating and on a sugar high.

Walking up out of the basin through the surrounding mountains I caught sight of a slight movement on a distant hill. It was a mountain lion and it powered on up the slope, stopped momentarily to stare back at me, and then continued on out of sight. I was on top of the world after that.

Late in the afternoon, for whatever reason, I had a craving for peanut butter. Gary's red pick-up came rumbling back down across the basin towards me and he pulled over, excitedly saying, "I wanted to get you something while in Casper, but I got no idea what you like, so I bought you a handful of Reese Buttercups!" I'd never heard of them, but accepted them gratefully and walked on, sinking my teeth into the chocolate cupcakes filled with peanut butter. "Yes!" I savoured each sweet one.

I made it to the 104 kilometre mark, and the front gate of the ranch I'd been told about, after sunset. With a near-full moon rising above the ragged hills I walked up along the track to ask for permission to pitch my tent at the front gate. Most ranches had a house, some sheds and maybe a windmill off to the side, but this cowboy had a house, some sheds and a full-on indoor rodeo stadium. The ranch was a hive of activity. Men were welding broken gates, leading horses around and unloading steers from trucks under the stadiums outer floodlights. I asked a welder if he was the owner, but he pointed to the rodeo arena, "Nope, the owner's in there talking with two other men. Just push through that door, you should see him."

I pushed through the side entrance, emerging fifty metres from three chatting cowboys standing with a foot each up on the bull release gate and decked out in hats, chaps, spurs and one guy with straw hanging out of his mouth. They made John Wayne look metro. They looked over at me and took a hesitant step back when, BOOM! The arena was plunged into darkness with a blown fuse. I flicked my headlamp on, lighting up our area and the head cowboy, Jhett, swaggered towards me with a grin on his face, "I got no idea who you are, but I'm sure glad you came!" While the guys outside tried to fix the fuse box, Jhett welcomed me and, being a Christian, he said he'd take on the mission too. He added, "Please don't put your tent down at the front gate. Put it up around here anywhere you like. It's a lot safer."

I set up as everyone headed home, but when I climbed into my tent I thought, "Sam, you're an idiot!" It was the end of the second day and all I had left was one solitary muesli bar. I was sure that if I'd asked Jhett he would have found me something to eat. While I was sitting there pondering my hunger I heard footsteps approaching. I unzipped the tent to make sure it wasn't a rogue cow and there, fumbling through the darkness, was Jhett, with his arms laden with food. "Just thought you might be a bit hungry!" There was enough food for dinner, breakfast and a light lunch the next day.

Sleeping on the rough ground without an airbed was difficult and my sleeping bag was damp from the previous frozen night. It was a weary set-off before sunrise along a dirt track, road 401. Knowing there were pumas in the area and walking at that hour was unnerving. If I wasn't so tired I might have cared more.

I pressed on through rolling hills along stark, steep ridges that dropped dramatically into ravines on both sides. I was hurting from the fifty kilometres a day pace. A chest infection had set in and nearly six months since the operation in Panama, my left big toe split open again. It bled badly and the naked flame pain returned.

Tired and wheezing from the chest infection, and my left foot squelching in blood, I limped on into the city of Casper. The first thing I remember seeing on the edge of the city ahead of me was the Super 8 Motel. I was in love with the idea of a hot shower, a fresh meal and a huge king-size bed. I wasn't praying at that point, in fact I was far from it—I was in love with a hotel; but as I zoned in on it I felt a deep sense that God was over-riding my thoughts of comfort by saying, "Sam, you didn't come here to go to hotels, you came here to go to churches. Do the mission." I was indignant. I couldn't believe that I was even contemplating it. I hadn't showered in three days! "No, you can't ask this of me. No!"

Desperately wanting to stop I fought that sense internally as I continued towards the Super 8. It wasn't until I reached the Casper boundary, right in front of it, that I relented and prayed, "Okay God, whatever. I'll do it. I don't care." I was reluctant, no denying it, but I walked on squelching and wheezing past hotel after hotel and empty church after empty church. It was nearing 5 pm and, with little energy and perhaps less motivation left, I prayed, "Lord, please, I need to stop. I'll find one more church and then I have to stop. I'm getting a hotel."

I limped up alongside Our Lady of Fatima Catholic Church and knocked on the presbytery door. A solid priest with a neat grey beard answered and after I'd explained who I was and extended the mission's invitation to him he replied with a non-committal, "Okay." I wasn't up for trying to start a conversation so I asked, "Do you know somewhere cheap to stay?" He glanced back over his shoulder into the house and then turned back to me saying, "My dinner's in there on the table getting cold, my team is about to play off in the world-series baseball final and I have a meeting in an hour and a half. This is the most inappropriate time possible." He paused for a second. "But God only puts people in my life at inappropriate times. Can I find you somewhere to stay?"

Fr Fox left his dinner on the table and drove me through Casper to the 5-star Hotel Marriott and swiped his credit card for two nights. He had one condition though, "Sam, meet me in the foyer here at 8 am." For two nights in the Marriot, done.

The room was enormous and I felt so out of place. My boots weren't shiny enough! I dropped my clothes and blood-soaked socks into the washing machine, showered and promptly fell asleep.

Fr Fox whisked me off to Mass the next morning and at the end of the service he introduced me to the large congregation, inviting me to extend the invitation to pray for unity. The congregation received it with smiles and nodding heads but, as Fr Fox and I walked down the aisle during the recessional hymn, he leant across with a grin and said, "I have a confession to make. I've made a few phone calls." My confusion must have shown because he added with a chuckle, "It'll make sense in a moment."

The wonderful Fr Fox

We walked out into a press conference. He'd rung the state newspapers, television crews and radio stations, plus the local pizza guy. Fr Fox stood in the background with the pizza guy while the media asked their first question, "Why'd you walk across Shirley Basin in winter?" But when one reporter dismissively posed the question, "Why is unity so important?" Fr Fox stepped in front of me before I'd said a single word. He answered the question succinctly, nailing them about the scandal of disunity on both the Church and society. I was left standing behind him, slightly dumb-founded, thinking, "Where did that come from?"

The journalist nervously leant forward with his little microphone and asked, "Sorry, who are you?"

Fr Fox replied, "Sorry, I'm Fr Fox. I'm Wyoming's Catholic delegate for the unity of Christians."

I laughed quietly, "Of course you are." He turned and gave me a wink. He led a group consisting of most of the Casper church leaders who met regularly to debate theological issues, pray together, and then discuss what mission work they could work on in the city together. From that press conference the mission went out across the nightly news channels, newspapers and radio stations. I wouldn't have to introduce myself in many towns from there on. People learned of the mission well before I arrived, and it was set to travel a lot further than I could have carried it.

The media coverage, very slowly, would snowball.

I look back at the crossing of Shirley Basin and can't believe how close I came to missing one of the most important moments of the journey. I nearly did what faith-filled people were telling me was the responsible option, to take the bus, instead of doing what God was asking of me. And I nearly ignored Him to take that Super 8 Motel. Undoubtedly, it would have been so much easier and less painful to catch the bus, which would have dropped me well past the Catholic church, but in comparison to going through the hard yards of trusting God, it would have been comparatively fruitless and far less satisfying. I still wonder how many times I'd previously closed off to those simple requests to not 'take the bus', and in doing so, missed beautiful examples of His providence. The easy option was often masked as the responsible one, but perhaps a mission lived isn't meant to be easily lived. I was grateful for not having caught the bus or having stopped at the Super 8 Motel. The Shirley Basin lesson rang clearly: How much do I trust that God does know what He's doing? How much do I agape Him?

From a mountain lookout over Casper Fr Fox asked me, "Have you discerned your vocation?" I spilled the beans that for the past few months I'd been contemplating my vocation, and was keen to head back to Australia to join the seminary. Normally a priest would jump at that discernment, but he didn't. He just smiled and said, "I don't think you will."

I was taken aback: "Why not?"

Without any hesitation he explained, "Well, I think you'd make a great priest, but God has called you so strongly towards unity, and the strongest sign of unity we have in the world is that of a man and a woman coming together as one. I think the journey God has you on will lead you to marriage." The more I pondered that comment the more I saw marriage in a new light and the more beautiful that sacrament looked. I was still a long way off making a decision, but from where I stood, well above Casper on the mountain lookout with Fr Fox, I had a great view of two beautiful options.

I left Casper on the Saturday morning under the watchful lens of a newspaper photographer. I felt like a goose as cars passed by with him lying in the ditch, standing on fence poles or running on ahead of me to get his shots.

By midday I was back in Wyoming wilderness and feeling the effects of the lingering chest infection. I was so lethargic and lightheaded that the day became a bit of a blur. I took rest breaks nearly every hour and my ability to stay focussed was miserable. I fought hard even to pray.

At 9 pm I was still stumbling along when a couple pulled over to offer a lift back to Casper. The motel at Powder River, seven kilometres ahead of me, had closed for the winter. Back in South America I would have taken the lift at that point, but the blessing of Shirley Basin was prominent, so despite being exhausted I declined the lift and limped on to an imminent tent pitch.

Roxie, the raccoon, and her carer

After sixty-three kilometres of mind-numbing agony, I staggered into slumbering Powder River, where a few dogs took a disliking to me, barking incessantly. They persisted until they'd drawn a young man from his house to check on the racket. "What are you doing there?" he asked. He kept his distance.

I explained my circumstances and he slowly felt comfortable enough to wander over and make an offer. "I know where the key to the motel is if you want. It'd be a lot warmer and more comfortable. You'll just have to make sure you're out early 'cause no one's supposed to be staying there." I nearly melted with thanks.

I woke on the Sunday morning just in time to hobble next door to the Baptist church for the only weekend service. There were about twenty people there, but they filled the building with pride, welcoming me in. The rural congregation's service was a mixture of liturgy and intimate conversation between friends. I was asked to introduce myself and to share about my journey to Powder River, which was promptly followed by the pastor and his wife inviting me to stay the night at their home. I wanted to push on, but Pastor Chris pressed on me that I wasn't well and more importantly, "It's the Sabbath, rest." So I did. Their hospitality was generous, not just in what they did for me, but in the space they offered for me to recuperate.

It was 101 kilometres to the town of Shoshoni, which required a night in my tent halfway; a coyote chorus ensured I slept lightly for most of that night. I was off before sunrise. A few hours later, amidst the sparse saltbush plains, I at last caught sight of one of those coyotes. The beautiful animal, with its stunning silver and grey coat, stared back at me from thirty metres away before timidly slinking away through the low vegetation.

While the animal population was engrossing, it was the constant flow of well-wishes from passers-by that really had me smiling, particularly the one guy whose travelling companion was a mischievous pet raccoon. It clambered all over the pick-up's seats, before leaning out the window, grabbing hold of my camera with both paws and licking that lens clean.

Near Shoshoni, the couple that offered me a lift on the first night out of Casper pulled over again and the wife declared, "I've prepared you a comfort pack!" I associated comfort packs with moisturiser, face washers and lavender scented soap, so I was very happy to find that this comfort pack was filled with fruit, oven baked pumpkin seeds and a drink. Mind you, lavender scented soap would have been good too … The couple knew roughly where I was because: "The radio station has been giving hourly updates of where you are! A few passers-by have phoned in with progress reports."

I just hoped people were also taking on the prayer.

A cold front swept in without warning two kilometres before I reached Shoshoni and I copped an absolute battering. The pumpkin seeds were blown right out of my hand and the temperature dropped to near freezing within a minute. I scrambled for my beanie and gloves while struggling to stay on the road; the wind slammed me with icy sleet that stung my face. Wyoming: beautiful one moment, deadly the next. The wind was so powerful that the few cars passing by were knocked off course, making me jump well clear. I raced on into Shoshoni shivering and a guy filling his car at the petrol station yelled out through the storm, "Hey, Aussie! We're prayin'!" The mission had beaten me there.

From Shoshoni I turned north again and set out through the most spectacular piece of land I passed through in the USA: the Wind River Canyon. The river itself cut straight through the Owl Mountains creating a sheer canyon through the heart of the snow-covered peaks for nearly fifty kilometres. I walked alongside the fast flowing river through the 900 metre high rock-walls draped in snow. The river disappeared behind mountain after mountain. It was amazing. I had trouble praying because I was so distracted, other than, "God that is brilliant." When I finally broke the day's silence with U2's "Beautiful Day" it reverberated off the canyon walls with a thunderous echo.

Walking into the township of Thermopolis was funny—there were kids running amuck everywhere. It was Halloween. I received directions from plenty of wizards. The Thermopolis Baptist Church was aglow in the twilight with their Wednesday prayer service and one of the pastors agreed to pray for the unity of Christians. He then added that if I hurried I'd also catch someone at the Catholic church bible study.

I moved fast and caught Fr Hugo, who immediately invited me to join the bible study and offered the church's guest room for the night. After so much quiet contemplative prayer it made for a welcome change.

Fr Hugo checked in on me as I settled in. After walking 216 kilometres in just four days he found me sitting on the floor trying to detach my sock from the bleeding big toe. They'd become one. I gave up and left it dangling, much to his horror. He sat himself down in the doorway, tired from his day, and our conversation moved on to life and faith. He asked what my journey was like day to day, so I shared how the long days on the road had allowed me to spend a lot of time alone with my thoughts and that there wasn't a single aspect of my life that hadn't been scrutinised.

He asked the obvious question: "Have you found that helpful?"

"Yes, for the most part," I replied. "In the end it's helped me to know why mistakes were made and be able to recognise the signs of poor choices so I could make the right one. The hardest thing to deal with has been the choices I've made that have hurt others."

We spoke about it for a while before he made an astute observation, "You know what your biggest problem is? You've never forgiven yourself." There was a pause in the conversation. I wasn't able to justify myself any further.

"Yeah, I guess I haven't." I'd sought forgiveness from others and from God, but never from myself. He stood up in the doorway and added, "If Jesus forgives, who are you to not forgive yourself? There's your evening prayer."

Sitting there on the floor I prayed quietly, with that bloodied sock still attached.

*He said to him again a second time, "Simon, son of John, do you love Me?*

John 21:16a

Total walked: 8,318 kilometres

## Surgery, Thanksgiving & Homeland Security
### November 2007

Fr Hugo allowed me to stay in Thermopolis for two days while I organised a Russian and Belarusian visa for January and February. I was only three days behind schedule and felt comfortable in being able to catch back up.

I walked on to Worland with only a slight limp, and then on past wide-open ranches stretching back for miles in the cool winter air. Late in the day the southern migration of Arctic Geese filled the orange glow of sunset and the multitude of flying Vs honked their way southwards. Thousands of the little guys worked side-by-side, but I spotted two of them break the formation and swing back into the north. "Wrong way guys!" I shut up when I realised what was unfolding. To the north of the thousand-odd geese came one lone goose, struggling to catch up. The two breakaways headed straight for it, circled in alongside to form their own three-geese V and, with one of the two taking the lead, powered on back to the main group. They tacked onto the end just as they disappeared from sight beyond the southern hills. It was brilliant. Honking geese were living out unity better than many of us.

There was nowhere to sleep in Manderson so I opted to continue on into the night to the large town of Basin, fifteen kilometres further on. I wanted a hotel. After painfully searching up and down the streets of Basin … I found zip. There was nothing there either. A random driver pulled over and informed me that the town's hotels had all shut for winter. I was despising seasonal hotels. The nearest open hotel was another ten kilometres further on in Greybull.

Punctuated by involuntary sounds resembling an aggravated bear, I completed the sixty-three kilometres into empty Greybull at 1 am. Signs hanging from storefronts swung in the breeze and the town's traffic light moved through its sequence for an empty road, but the small motel's late night call button thankfully brought a big fellow to the door, who welcomed me in. Before going to bed I had to surgically remove my boots and bloodied socks. The split along the edge of the toenail had opened wide, allowing flesh to spill out across the nail, and the two middle toes bled freely with no skin left on the knuckles. I was so exhausted and pain-riddled that when I laid back on top of the bed with my feet hanging off the end I fell straight asleep.

I hardly moved the next day, except to hobble over to the Catholic church and meet the African priest, who welcomed me and the mission.

It was a hard fought fifty-two kilometre limp across vast, undulating, dry, frostbitten farmland to Lovell. My pace dropped painfully, but the odd passer-by hitting their horn and offering a friendly wave provided needed encouragement.

I shuffled into Lovell aching and reaching for the first bed. I decided to grab a meal first and I was glad I did. The lady at the restaurant recognised me and called the local priest, Fr Eckley, who was just finishing up a prayer meeting. He drove straight down and when I went to introduce myself he stopped me with a smile and said, "I know who you are." He sat down at the table to join me for dinner.

Fr Eckley was an educated man from the deep south. He spoke cultured English with clever wit and was under no disillusionment that I wasn't tired or sore, so as I finished eating he simply offered, "I'll drop you at the hotel and we'll catch up at Mass in the morning."

The invitation to pray for unity was extended to the small congregation and, once everyone had left, Fr Eckley asked off-hand if I sang while walking. "Usually, as long as I'm not too tired or in pain," I replied. He smiled and divulged his love for music. He was an opera fan in particular, but had written his own country songs, which had been recorded on compilation albums. His mother wanted him to pursue a career with his voice, but he instead chose the priesthood. Music was now just a healthy outlet. I laughed, "Yeah, well, whenever I sang my mum told me to shut up." He laughed slowly and reassured me, "You're in Wyoming now. There's lots of space where no one will hear you."

The thirty kilometres crossing to Frannie was subdued—much like the town itself—with nothing more than a solitary bar. The few locals sitting at the bar knew each other like family and invited me into their conversation about the up-coming presidential elections. Wow, were they strongly opinionated. The lady behind the bar was a church-goer and was more eager to talk about the mission. She took up the invitation to pray for unity and offered to pass it on to her friends that weekend.

At the end of the bar sat a huge bloke named Terry. He hadn't said much until he spoke up saying, "You shouldn't be out in your tent with the night temperatures dropping below freezing. I have space back at my house. You can sleep there." There was no fanfare, no fuss: just honesty and beer.

Terry lived in a simple house with no beds and few modern conveniences. It was home for him, his teenage daughter and a very large pooch. They offered me the floor in one room while he and his daughter made space on the floor in the other. It was so basic, but a lot nicer than a freezing tent. I hadn't expected to see poverty in the USA, but his simplicity and humility seemed to make up for the lack of furniture. I smirked at the sticker plastered across the bedroom door, "I love God. It's his fans I hate."

For tonight at least, one of his 'fans' was in.

Terry sent me on my way with a sturdy handshake. I tightened my backpack straps and headed on across the isolated Montana border under the gaze of the Yellowstone National Park mountains with wild mustangs galloping across the dead-grass plains beneath and two bald eagles circling above.

I made it to Bridger by nightfall, slept in my tent on the concrete behind the steakhouse, and then continued on for the fifty-six kilometres to Laurel. I wanted to stop walking permanently, but each step seemed to agonisingly find its place in succession until the small city of Laurel came into sight, along with sunset. I tried to visit a few churches, but was never sure exactly where I was. I did stumble across the Catholic church just as a weekend retreat commenced; and the Laurel Bible Church, whose youthful Pastor Chris was working late on his weekend preaching. He put his work to the side and invited me into his office to chat for some time about what unity really is. I think we found ourselves handing it all over to God's grace. He shared that he often met with the Church leaders of Laurel to pray and build the bonds of unity, but that despite almost always being fruitful it was often challenging. I agreed that seeking unity amongst those with differing beliefs was an uncomfortable setting. The tough thing about unity is that we seek it with those we aren't united with. Discomfort comes with the territory.

Despite Ozzie Osbourne and Rob Zombie playing a concert twenty-five kilometres away in Billings, and every hotel consequently being booked up in Laurel, a young hotel receptionist pulled some strings and somehow had me checking into a room after an hour's wait. Somehow.

I finished the short trot from Laurel to Billings at St Patrick's Cathedral for the Saturday vigil Mass. While hanging out with the youth group in their decked-out basement, the Harris family offered me a place to stay. I was tentative to accept because my younger brother, Chris, was touching down in Billings at 10:30 pm. He was taking advantage of his university break to walk across the rest of Montana and Canada with me. I'd arrived right on schedule to meet him, but didn't want to put the Harris's out. Bob insisted that he run me up to the airport to collect Chris and we both stay the night, so that's exactly what happened.

I hadn't seen family for nearly a year and after a year apart; I didn't recognise him at first. I looked straight past him. Mind you, he didn't have a beard when I saw him last. At the Harris's he introduced himself as the funnier and more handsome Clear brother—he'd never been shy—before likening his journey into Billings to descending into a spiralling hole. Nice entrance.

Chris had just finished end of year exams and done no training at all. He'd always been fit though, but had no endurance. He was concerned that his sprinting fitness might make him soft when it came to the open Montana roads, but he was looking forward to the challenge and hoping to experience the faith on that side of the world. We stayed up until 1 am in our shared room chatting, laughing and planning our assault on the weeks to come. Chris was halfway through his nursing degree so he inspected the split toe, which no longer hurt only while walking, but with every pulse of blood.

It was decided, "Yes, it's infected."

Bob dropped us at St Vincent's Hospital the next morning and I was ushered through to a young doctor. After a bit of agonising poking and prodding she shook her head and informed me, "You know, kiddo, I'm gunna have to cut that out." Chris wasn't particularly interested in his older brother, but more in acquiring a few tips. He happily opened up the camera and filmed proceedings while interviewing the doctor.

The doctor tried numbing the toe with anaesthetic, but the severity of the infection caused a lack of blood flow and stopped the anaesthetic spreading. She chatted with her colleagues at the end of my bed and then turned to me, asking, "What's your pain threshold like?"

I hesitated, "Umm … average."

She raised her eyebrows, "I'm going to have to operate without full anaesthesia. Don't flinch. I'll be as quick as I can."

"Suck it in you big sook," Chris laughed unsympathetically.

He filmed as the doctor picked up a scalpel and cut away the over-hanging flesh while giving her commentary. She then reached for cutting shears. I closed my eyes. Chomp! I arched my back in pain; the nail was split in half from the tip to the bed.

"Now, now Sam, you heard the doctor. Don't move," Chris chimed in with a smile, followed five seconds later with a more sincere, "Are you okay?"

More handsome? Hmmmm...

The doctor took hold of a set of pliers, took a firm grip on the nail and yanked hard. The breaking crack was coupled with a spine-numbing shot of pain and Chris noting matter-of-factly, "Gee, there's a lot of blood, isn't there?"

"Yeah there is, but see how I didn't get all of the nail?" she replied.

He leaned in closer. "Oh yeah."

I was close to passing out. She yanked again, ripping the remaining nail from the toe-bed before quickly patching it up. Chris was given all the instructions of how to take care of the toe, but I listened intently. I wasn't letting him anywhere near it.

We checked into a motel across the road and Chris ran to the shops for food supplies and dinner. Remarkably, by 6 am the next morning, we were ready to go and, for the first time in months, my left foot was pain free. I wrapped the toe neatly as instructed and hesitantly slipped the boot on. Plonk. I was wide-eyed and breathing normally. I laughed, "It didn't hurt!" It was an amazing feeling.

We headed out of Billings into a head-on bitterly cold wind that sent tumbleweed racing across the flattened landscape. Only a few kilometres out of Billings, Chris stopped to tend to a developing heel blister on each foot and it just went downhill from there. It slowed him down so much that he believed he was walking at the same pace as an old guy he took care of in a nursing home in Australia.

We sat on the roadside out in the windy countryside, twenty-seven kilometres from Billings, to inspect Chris's skinless heels. Who's the patient now? We decided to head back to Billings, somehow, and get him on the next bus to Great Falls, nine days to the north. I'd then walk on from Billings again.

A classic white Mustang thundered past us and I stared down the empty stretch of road and prayed, "Lord, please, can you provide a lift for us?" Suddenly, the Mustang pulled up on the other side of the road having turned around. "You guys need a lift to Billings?" The V8 roar was sensational.

We booked back into the same motel and set about sussing out a plan for the next nine days. Early the next morning, I headed off back into the darkness to re-walk the same twenty-seven kilometres. After two hours, the sun popped up over the mountains to the sound of thunder … Mustang V8 thunder. The same guy pulled over again and dropped me back at the twenty-seven kilometre mark to walk on.

My new toe was incredible. I flew through the day like a dog let off its chain and genuinely felt light on my feet. I just hoped Chris was okay. Locals had seen me walking along the road out of Billings on both mornings and were wondering, "Where's the other one? What happened to the other tall guy?" Our incomplete first day turned into a blessing: drivers stopped one after the other and the invitation to pray for unity was accepted.

In the rural settlement of Broadview I was shown to the local fire brigade shed for accommodation. The gentleman pointed to the three old trucks lined up inside and noted that, "It won't be luxurious, but it'd be warmer than your tent, and safer. They all have bench seats so I'm sure one of them will do you okay." The gas heating was clicked on and I settled in for the night. It was the most brilliant hotel room in Montana.

The truck bench seat provided a good night's sleep and I was on my way again through freezing pre-dawn darkness to cover a massive sixty-two kilometres to Ryegate. Back in Venezuela, when I'd met the puma, I began walking at the same time and walked sixty-six kilometres, but finished somewhere around midnight. Times had changed. I strolled into Ryegate an hour before sunset.

I was again directed to the local volunteer fire station, where I wasn't offered a truck, but tent pitching grass off to the side. It was a good thing too, because a huge grass-fire broke out sixty kilometres away that night and the volunteer fire brigade launched into action. My little spot on the side of the shed was the only safe place to be as the commotion continued for hours on end with private vehicles coming and going amidst rapid shouted instructions. I couldn't help but laugh when I overheard that the Broadview fire brigade was helping to fight the fire. Twenty-four hours earlier and it would have been a very interesting wake up. "Argh, this truck's taken."

The long walk to Harlowton began with a misty sunrise shadowing Black Angus grazing along rolling frosty ranches. Two youth-filled mini-buses drove past and gave a big wave that said, "We're young and will wave at anyone to make our trip more enjoyable." We'd actually meet in a few days' time.

In Harlowton I stumbled upon a bizarre sight. In an old playground there was a swing, a see-saw and a gazebo, but something in the gazebo seemed out of place. I couldn't work out what it was at first, but then it came into focus. I was staring at two antelope, gutted and hanging upside down from the rafters. In a kids' playground. The Montana hunting season had begun and the motel next door was full of hunters. After stringing the two kills up in the gazebo, did the hunters unwind on the see-saw?

I did the usual church rounds, leaving a unity calling card at each. The only place with anyone present was the Catholic church, but the parish priest was sceptical. He hardly opened the door as I introduced myself and offered little in the way of acceptance. I extended the invitation to pray for unity, thanked him and wandered back to the hotel, but he called out to me, "Hang on a moment. You mean you're for real? You're really doing this?" He smiled and opened the door wider. "Can I at least buy you dinner?"

The priest apologised for his scepticism about my motives for knocking on his door, but I reassured him that most people were sceptical at first, "That's why I don't ask for a bed or food any more. For most people the invitation to pray for unity is lost by any subsequent request." The invitation had to stand on its own.

The walk out to Judith Gap was stunning with the road lunging across sweeping hills that abruptly thrust upwards into jagged snow-capped peaks. At the end of a rosary I ambled into Judith Gap well before the evening Mass and decided to wait. It was nice to have people coming to me rather than wandering the town finding them. Everyone at the 5 pm vigil seemingly belonged to one of two families and the youngest couple, Brian and Sarah, invited me to dinner at their place, while an elderly lady named Margaret offered me her spare bed. It was a wonderful evening; even the six kilometre jog between the two houses. The night was clear, crisp and silent. I loved my new toe.

With accommodation teed up at the end of the fifty kilometre day ahead I marched on towards Moccasin. I stopped at the Eddies Corner roadhouse for an early lunch and, as I left, a young man asked from behind me: "How far have you walked, and why are you doing it?" I turned around and there were two mini-buses full of youth disembarking for the diner. A heap of them rushed over with the same question. My answer was met with cheerful applause. They were a youth group returning from a Christian youth conference in Billings and they were more than happy to take the prayer for unity back to their church. We even prayed together in the middle of the diner before continuing our separate journeys north.

I approached Moccasin at sunset with a low-pressure system sweeping in and the howling wind sending splinters of icy sleet into my face. I re-kitted the gloves, balaclava and snow-goggles, put my head down and pushed on into ensuing darkness. The storm rolled in fast, but I thankfully only had to shiver it out for a couple of kilometres before walking up alongside a parked pick-up being driven by my host for the night, Greg Grove. He threw open the door and I jumped in for the short drive down a side road to his ranch. He and his lovely wife, Karen, were faith-filled in every way and made me feel welcome. We went from complete strangers to good friends in a matter of minutes. Karen even encouraged me to think about future job roles within the church and, although her suggestion of me becoming a priest and then the Australian cardinal one day was tantalising, I really wasn't sure what God had in store for me. "What would you call yourself if you became pope?" she asked with a grin.

I laughed, "My hero is St Francis of Assisi. I think the church could do with a Pope Francis."

Apparently a certain Argentinean cardinal was thinking the same thing …

Chris was doing well by all accounts and enjoying being a tourist, but he was sick of sitting in hotel rooms while his feet mended. I'd arrive in Great Falls in three days' time and Chris was confident of being ready to go by then. My visa was due to expire in eleven days and I had over 300 kilometres to cover. It was achievable, but with one of those days needed for a rest and winter roaring in, the race was still on.

I couldn't believe my eyes the next morning. The dry, wind-swept plains were covered in a foot of snow and it was still falling. Karen announced triumphantly, "Doesn't look like you're going anywhere today! Make yourself at home." So I did. The whole region was in lockdown due to the thirty-five centimetre snow dump. All I could do was bunker down with a hot cup of chocolate and watch a movie on Pope John Paul II. The only work I did was a phone interview with a *Denver Post* sports reporter, who wasn't so much interested in the mission, but the walk itself, and to speak that evening at the pub to the Moccasin prayer group.

With a break in the clouds the next morning, and my visa running out, I pushed on fast. Karen rang ahead to her friends, in the next town—the Sloans—and they happily offered me a bed. Montana was a white winter wonderland, but I was at least assured of a hot drink at day's end. The temperature was a miserable −11°C that day and the wind chill caused by semitrailers hurtling past pushed that much lower. Walking down the edge of the road was possible, but the gap was thin and I was sometimes forced into knee-deep snow.

A freezing wind picked up at lunchtime and it became unbearable. My gloves weren't thick enough and my hands stung relentlessly. Taking a lunchbreak with nothing but flat, snow-covered ground was going to be a challenge, but the rest stop came to me. Karen pulled over and offered me a warm seat, a hot drink and steaming hot food. She'd also brought a pair of Greg's massive elbow length mittens made for stupidly cold temperatures. They were on loan until Great Falls, where I could buy my own and Greg could collect his at the family's Thanksgiving dinner.

Karen wasn't happy that the Wyoming media had covered the walk but Montana's hadn't, so she took it upon herself to ring the *Great Falls Tribune* that morning and they were on their way out for an interview, ensuring that the mission would again extend further than I could carry it.

Walking on into the frozen wilderness there was one solitary car on the vast stretch of road and, as it drew near, it slowed. The driver wound his window down slightly and yelled out, "Are you the guy walking around the world?"

I pulled the balaclava down: "Well, part of it." The *Great Falls Tribune* had arrived. They interviewed me in the car, allowing me to enjoy a few extra minutes of warmth, and they seemed to understand the purpose of the mission, showing excitement at having a great Thanksgiving story. They then asked me to step back out into the snow and walk on while they drove back and forth taking photographs.

Under the protection of the balaclava and ski goggles I was eventually on my own again and prayed my way into Stanford and their Lutheran church. It didn't go well. The woman I met was suspicious at first and then defensive after discovering I was a Catholic. She cited that unity would exist if we Catholics searched for and found the truth as she had done. The invitation to pray for unity was lost.

The Sloan family welcomed me into their house with that hot drink and also phoned ahead to their friends—the Hills—who were equally as happy to take me in at the end of the next forty kilometre stretch.

The next day's temperature didn't ease much, but a tiny town halfway offered shelter for lunch. It looked like it belonged in Alaska. The town of Geyser was plastered in snow, the roads were only partially cleared; it was wind-swept and there wasn't a single soul outside. I struggled repeatedly to stay upright on the thick ice build-up.

Mr Hill pulled up late in the day to check on me, and not long after that the Sloans pulled over with two hot chocolates. They'd been searching for me after Mr Hill tried to find me on his lunch break, but came up empty. "Sorry guys, I was in the Geyser pub having a good chat with a farmer." It was wonderful to know that my back was covered … and to land two hot chocolates!

The Hills went out of their way to make sure I ate very, very well and sent me off on the final forty-seven kilometre stretch into Great Falls. Thanksgiving day was a day to savour. I had no idea that I was the *Tribune's* front-page article with three photographs, but soon twigged that something was up when car after car sounded their horn and waved frantically. Eventually a passer-by pulled over and produced the paper with its full-page story and a classic side on photo of me in full stride, decked out in the winter gear and with the sweeping snowy wilderness behind me. One of the smaller photos made me cringe though. I was used to walking with trucks whizzing past, but the photographer had taken a snap of me from a few hundred metres down the road just as a semitrailer rushed past. The gap between us was a lot smaller than I thought it had been. The article itself was well written and represented the mission clearly. The festive twist on it was that this would be my very first Thanksgiving; after the journey I'd endured, I had a lot to be thankful for.

Cars stopped left, right and literally centre for the rest of the day. It was slow going, stopping every fifteen minutes, but more individual invitations to pray for unity were received that day than any of the 341 preceding it. The icy wilderness and warm-hearted people were in stark contrast. On one hill, the Sloans, the Groves, and the Gees (more friends of the Sloans) pulled over in succession just as I'd finished a meal in the other's vehicle. After finally saying goodbye to the Gees, the Sloans reappeared half an hour after they first stopped, now on their way home from the shops. They had even more food for me. It really was slow going.

I scooted along into a jog as Great Falls emerged from the twilight and Greg Grove and his brother-in-law, Scott, met me on the roadside to guide me back to Scott's house. I was met with a rousing applause from the Grove and the Donisthorpe families, before a resounding, "Boooooo!" thundered from the lounge room. Argh … they'd found Chris. He popped his head out from around the corner with a smile, then he copped it from the families for his un-brotherly welcome! He'd been picked up a few hours earlier and had practically become one of them. Scott's wife, Vicki, asked if she could adopt him. I was more than okay with that. They'd been playing 'Catch Phrase' and by all accounts Chris had managed to break the ice in more ways than one by offering controversial mimes for various phrases. He had a knack for pushing boundaries without offending and ultimately won an offer of adoption instead of the excommunication it would have landed me.

My very first Thanksgiving dinner was brilliant. Out of the five Groves, five Donisthorpes and two Clears, there were seven of us between about eighteen and twenty-eight. After dinner we slinked into the steaming outdoor hot tub in the frigid sub-zero night and, after a long cold week, it was wonderful to just soak. There was a lot of conversation, but I was distracted by the fact that the night air was freezing my wet hair solid. Chris and I submerged and then quickly shaped our hair into different forms before it froze, creating incredible mohawks, slicks, afros and dangerous spikes, all capped off with glittering ice crystals. We were warned to be careful not to mould the hair while frozen, as it would snap. It made for a cheap haircut.

While resting the next day Vicki ran into the lounge room announcing that she'd found people at our next destination who would love to house us the following night. She didn't even know them! That's generosity ... on both parties' behalf. That afternoon we shopped for ski mitts to go over our gloves and then relaxed in the evening with the eldest daughter, Nicole, and her conversational university friends.

While resting three weeks earlier in Thermopolis, I'd mailed my passport to the Russian Embassy to secure a visa. The passport was supposed to be forwarded on to a Catholic church in Great Falls, well before I arrived, but there was no sign of it and the visa company I was working through was on holidays for Thanksgiving. I had just six days left in the country, with six days' worth of walking to go; I just didn't have a passport. It was unsettling, but I knew God could make it happen if it needed to, so I wasn't at panic stations ... yet. I at least had a photocopy of the passport page, so I was sure it could be sorted out.

Chris and I left Great Falls under the morning darkness of Saturday the 24th of November, walking north out across the Missouri River for the fifty-one kilometre haul to the small town of Power. Chris's boots were fitting snug and he felt good, but it was a huge day to re-enter the walk.

Not long after the sun rose behind a blanket of low-lying thick cloud, a pick-up pulled over and a spritely man introduced himself: "Hi, I'm Marcus! You're staying with me tonight!" We memorised directions to his house and wished each other well. He departed by saying, "I'll have dinner waiting for you!"

I loved Montana, much like the states to the south.

If Chris didn't know how far fifty-one kilometres was, he was about to learn the hard way. We rested after ten kilometres and when he realised he had to repeat that four times over he was … well … disgruntled. We walked on and he joined me in prayer, then asked: "Sam, I've gone to Mass all my life, I lead the youth group back home, and I know how to pray a few set prayers, but really, how do you pray? I don't really know how to pray."

I once asked a similar question to our parish priest, Fr Yard, so I relayed the conversation to Chris. "He said he prayed the set prayers of the Church, but tried to make every day one long prayer by making at least one hundred small prayers over the course of the day. If he was walking down the street and saw someone who looked like they were struggling he'd pray, 'Lord, please help them. Please bless them with whatever they're going through.' And then if he saw a cool palm tree he'd pray, 'God, nice job! I like that palm tree!' He basically tried to stay in constant communication with God."

Chris and I agreed that it was easier said than done, particularly when it came to listening rather than just speaking.

Singing on across the plains, with Chris chiming in from behind in b-flat with, "Shut up," we somewhat triumphantly arrived at the house of Marcus, Pam and their recently returned thirty-year-old son, David. He was simply one of the most interesting and artistically gifted people I'd ever met. He was a mixture of St Augustine and St Francis. Despite the icy conditions, at evening Mass he removed his shoes at the door and walked in with bare feet because it helped remind him that, "I'm entering a holy place, not just a building." Indeed.

Chris's legs hurt from the fifty-one kilometres so he stayed to hang out with Dave while Marcus laced up the boots and joined me for a brisk walk to morning Mass in Dutton, four hours to the north. The invitation to pray for unity was extended through his introductions and from there he returned to Power leaving me to push on down the highway for as far as I could. Dave and Chris drove up alongside me at a secluded frozen truck stop at sunset, picked me up and took me back to their place for a second night; and yes, they'd already arranged the following night's accommodation. It was sad sometimes to keep moving. In that week alone I'd met plenty of people I would have been more than happy to have in my life regularly.

When Chris and I departed the next morning from the truck stop, David presented me with a card he'd handpainted. It was an eye-catching Montana landscape with a deep-rooted tree shooting out a thousand green shoots, silhouetted by a sunrise casting a red and white American flag across the sky. It was brilliant. On the back he'd written:

*Come, Oh blessed Trinity,*

*Join hands around my heart.*

*Introduce:*

*Your light to its darkness.*

*Introduce:*

*Your strength to its fear.*

*Sing songs, breathe "The Word", into this deflated soul.*

*Mend this broken body, My shelter, My earthly home; ... And I shall be sure to leave the door open, to you, my Lord.*

*Sam, May we always be inspired by the Unity of the almighty Trinity.*

*David*

Chris fared well from his day off—physically and spiritually. We walked on into a freezing wind with a prayer on our lips and three layers of gloves on our hands. We pulled the ski goggles down. That day would be the warmest for the week at a miserly −8°C. The moisture from our breath froze to our balaclavas producing ice crystal five o'clock shadows. Early morning temperatures dropped to −15°C, and colder days were forecast; every millimetre of skin had to be covered up. Any exposed skin, particularly if the wind was blowing, was subject to frostbite, including our lungs. A layer of cloth hanging over the balaclava mouth section was warmed by our breath and consequently warmed the cold air up as we breathed back in. It was simple, but could easily be the difference between life and death.

The town of Conrad's young Catholic priest welcomed us in with a big smile and a fantastic baked dinner after evening Mass. Marcus had also phoned a second friend in the next town of Shelby, so beds were waiting there as well. We began in mild conditions but, as the sun rose higher, the temperature dropped lower. A low-pressure system swept in and with an increasing wind buffeting us from the north-west. This induced a wind chill factor that bottomed out at a staggering −33°C! It was unbearable. We were skating on thin ice … so to speak. The balaclava mouthpiece and three layers of gloves with heat pads inserted barely kept us in the game.

It was so cold that we couldn't even stop to rest. We had to keep mobile and completely covered up. Eating was more of a circus trick. Without removing any of the protective gear, we retrieved muesli bars from each other's packs, fumbled with it trying to open them up, and then turned our backs to the wind, pulled down the balaclava, took a bite, pulled the balaclava back up under the goggles and walked on. Leaving the balaclava down for more than ten seconds allowed the mouth section to freeze and become a tight ball of material. It was nearly impossible to then pull it back up.

Our inability to rest took its toll on Chris, and as kilometre thirty clicked by he began limping. I wanted to film his predicament, but it was impossible with all the gloves on, so I ripped off the right outer ski mitt, leaving the inner two, just to get a shot. Bad idea. The outer mitt was only just holding the hand above a dangerous temperature and the thirty seconds my hand was out of the mitt was too much for the two layers of insulted gloves. An incredible sting raced through my fingers for the next half an hour as I battled to encourage circulation back. There was Chris, hobbling with a worsening limp, and me running back and forth around him, trying to heat my body up. It was absurd.

By 4 pm Chris's leg had seized up and he hurt beyond what was reasonable. We couldn't pull the balaclavas down so all communication was shouted from close range. He agreed with a grunt to make the top of the huge hill in front of us before attempting to hitch a ride. He pushed on to the top, undid his pack and dropped it onto the roadside, "So what are we supposed to do now!"

I unsympathetically yelled back, "You'd better say a prayer that someone picks you up!" I couldn't tell what his expression was but he yelled back, "I just did!" At that very moment a car pulled in ahead of us and the driver waved for us to come and jump in. Chris laughed, "If I knew it was that easy I would've prayed an hour ago!"

A middle-aged man stepped out smiling broadly, "Are you Sam and Chris? I'm Wally – a friend of Marcus. You're staying at my place tonight!" Chris jumped into the heated pick-up with both our packs, but I said I'd see them in Shelby, and finished off the remaining hour and a half's worth of freezing prayer.

Wally and Marlene were also exceptionally welcoming and offered plenty of hot food and drinks. Wally, a huge ZZ-Top fan, was a character and a half. Christmas lights were plastered across his neighbour's house, so he rang them and with a booming voice yelled with a smile, "Hey! You're giving us a brownout over here! Stop stealing our street's electricity!" Marlene just sat there shaking her head.

Chris's leg ached so, after a good night's sleep, Wally offered to drive him to the final US destination of Sunburst, while I continued on by foot. Having entered the country on the 30th of August with a ninety day visa, I needed to cross the border by the 29th of November. It was now the 28th. I was on target to make up the lagging fifteen days on the final day. I was very satisfied. I still didn't have my passport, but I was still hopeful.

A sloppy-dressed, overweight fellow pulled over in an old car for a chat. Upon hearing of the mission he told me with great joy about a man named Brother

Branham who was appointed by God to usher in the second coming and bring the real Church back to the people. "This will be interesting," I thought. Branham had apparently corrected all the errors of the 'modern' churches and declared that God was using him as his instrument of prophecy. The guy on the side of the road spoke about Branham's miracle workings and how he was a prophet from God but, frankly, I found him just a bit strange. Not Branham … the guy on the side of the road. Whoever Branham was, he sounded a little self-ordained by the man's description, but the guy handed me a book on Branham's life, which I took. As he climbed back into his car I asked what his name was.

He smiled sincerely, "I'm the Archangel Gabriel."

I responded with a blank stare.

With a dead straight road ahead, I walked on while reading the book, but didn't find anything particularly compelling. It's always dangerous when a man makes prophecies and predictions that have either passed in time without occurring or can't be proved. He seemed to just create a lot of excitement amongst some very devout followers before passing away in 1965. Many of his followers were still waiting for his return. It's difficult to strive for Christian unity when some Christians appear suspect or heretical; but to them it looks like the real deal and, in turn, my faith probably looks ridiculous and unholy. It was to extremities like this that the prayer for unity was truly a prayer of surrender.

I pulled out an energy bar and fumbled through opening it only to discover it was frozen solid. The midday temperature was −15°C and there was no way of chomping my teeth through it. I pulled the balaclava down and clamped my teeth down and worked it up and down with my right hand, but it wouldn't budge. After well over a minute of tiny movements—BANG!—it snapped on an upward motion and sent my clenched fist straight into my right eye socket. I staggered sideways off the road and slinked into the snow as stars skipped across my vision. I tried in vain to stand back up a few times before gingerly being able to stand back up. I have no idea how many passers-by witnessed my right-hook.

I made a call from a warm roadside diner to Vicki in Great Falls who informed me that the passport still hadn't arrived, but it had been tracked down. The visa issuing company had accidently placed it in 'the wrong pile.' It was being express posted to arrive the next day and Vicki's sister, Karen, had offered to drive to Great Falls, pick it up and keep on driving all the way to the border to hand it over. The nearly 600 kilometres round trip was offered without any hesitation. I was humbled by their continued loving help.

I hit the road again and, as is expected in those areas, was checked up on by a Homeland Security border patrol. The officer asked for identification. I offered him my driver's license and a photocopy of my passport page, explaining where the passport was and that it was being delivered the next morning, but he looked at me blankly saying, "You must have your passport on you at all times while in the USA and, as such, you are in breach of your visa conditions by not having it with you."

I was stumped. I'd been following the advice of the Australian embassy regarding securing a Russian visa by using a US company to secure it, and they'd in turn noted that I needed to send the passport to them. At no stage was I told that meant I was in breach of my US visa conditions. The officer just shook his head, "I don't care what they told you. You can't be in this country without a passport. If they asked you to send your passport to them they are asking you to do something illegal."

I stayed calm, "Okay, I didn't realise I was breaking the law. Sorry. How is a foreigner supposed to obtain a visa to another country while in the USA?"

"The only way to do it legally," he replied, "would be to fly to San Francisco (the nearest Russian Embassy) and sleep inside the Embassy foyer while they organised the visa." In other words, there was no legal way to obtain a Russian visa while in the USA.

I was invited to take a seat in the back of his patrol car while he sorted it out, so I squeezed into the tight caged rear seat. He jumped in the front and asked me, "Who's bringing the passport for you? Do you have a phone number I can call them on?" I reached into my bag to pull out my little notebook with Greg and Karen's number in it, but it wasn't there. I rummaged through my bag, becoming very aware that it was starting to look bad. I apologised, "Sorry, I have no idea where it is. I had it only an hour ago to make a call. I must have left it back at the roadside diner."

At that point the officer turned the photocopy of my passport over, which I'd carried since the beginning of the walk. His eyes widened. I had no idea what he was looking at, but when he held the back of the paper up to the wire mesh and asked, "What's all this?" my heart sank. I was in trouble. I took a deep breath and answered, "Well, it's a film script idea." The officer just stared at me. I continued, "While I was walking across Venezuela I had a couple of ideas for a story. That one was for a political version of Ocean's Eleven, where instead of hijacking a casino, the people in question would hijack world leaders."

I'd penned my first idea for that story on the back of my passport photocopy, complete with a detailed timeline of when hijackers would be placed into government positions, when vehicles would be hired and when specialised training would take place. At the top of the page was a comprehensive list of world leaders to be targeted and lo and behold, number two was Mr President, George W Bush. I tried all I could to explain what it was and that I had an extended version of the script idea along with a stack of other ideas in my little notebook. The officer looked me in the eye, "Which you can't find."

I lowered my gaze, "No sir, I can't."

I couldn't believe what was unfolding. The officer understood that the odds were stacking up against me and apologised as he locked me in the patrol car. He radioed through to Homeland Security and they replied in coded language. He turned to me and said, "Your visa expires today."

Without my passport I couldn't prove anything but insisted, "I entered the country on the 30th August and the issuing officer wrote in pen across it that my last day was the 29th November. Today is the 28th so my visa can't be expiring today."

The officer didn't even look up. "That means you have to be out of the country on the 28th. A ninety day visa is only valid for eighty-nine days."

"You're kidding?" Crammed into the back seat we set off to Border Patrol Headquarters and I was escorted to an interrogation room with an armed soldier standing over me. Interrogators came and went for over two hours and it looked like worsening when they informed me that they believed the company I'd sent my passport to was an identity theft scam. The team of interrogators asked me to open up all the backpack pockets for them, one by one. I opened up the side pocket and wouldn't you know it, there was the stupid little notebook, "Argh! There it is!" The interrogators took it and flicked through the multitude of addresses, phone numbers and story ideas.

I was left alone for a while with the armed guard, so I smiled and asked how he was doing, just to see if he'd respond. He did, and joked about how 'in-trouble' I really was, even suggesting that I burn the photocopy of the passport page if they ever let me out. I agreed.

Through the ajar door I could see into a large room where my backpack was being disassembled item by item. Everything was spread out, including every single piece of paper from my clear plastic sleeve folder. Officers scoured through it all, at times trying to figure out what some of my gear actually was. With nearly a dozen officers rummaging through it I caught sight of one guy pick up the *Great Falls Tribune* front page. Vicki had given it to me as I left Great Falls, "Just in case you have any trouble crossing the border." The officer leaned back in his chair to read and his face dropped. Almost with a look of fear he peered over the paper and announced to the others, "Guys, he's on the front page of the *Tribune*." Gathering in to read the story the officer who'd brought me in pleaded his innocence, "He didn't tell me he was on the front page of the *Tribune*!" Another officer laughed, "We can't put him in jail. We'll have to find new jobs if we do!"

I sat in the interrogation room smiling, thankful for Vicki's foresight.

The officers' suspicions dissipated into nothing more than a desire to help. It had been determined that I was indeed a missionary. The visa-issuing company was only then found to be legitimate, tracked down and confirmation given that my passport was en-route to Great Falls.

After three hours of interrogation we'd become friends and one of the officers even wrote down my web address to check out the mission that night. I was embarrassed for the mix up, but they simply smiled, granted me a one-day extension on my visa at no charge and organised my accommodation in the nearby town of Sunburst with an Evangelical minister and his wife.

I rang Chris to find that he'd spent the day soaking in Wally's spa while Marlene practically waited on him. Not too surprisingly he was doing well. Greg and Karen had already contacted him so, after staying another night, he intended to grab a lift with them as they passed through with my passport.

Chris was enjoying his holiday.

No sooner had I hung up and three of the families I'd stayed with in the past week called the evangelical minister's home to make sure everything was okay. News travelled fast in Montana. It was embarrassing to explain what I'd written on the back of my passport photocopy, but it was worth a few laughs.

The minister held a bible study group that evening with three members of the congregation and he ran with the theme of unity. His knowledge of scripture was amazing and he took us through, verse by verse, the numerous sections imploring full Christian unity. To be honest, I wish I'd filmed his study group. It was profound and his deep radio voice just oozed authority, not that that counts for much. One of the women suggested they finish by praying over me for the mission ahead, so they gathered around while a lady ducked off to grab a bucket of warm water. To my delight, she washed my feet while the others prayed over me. I bet Marlene didn't do that for Chris.

I'd failed to mention in my introduction that I was Catholic and at the end of the night they launched into an attack on the Catholic Church, which got a bit personal. Realising that they had no idea I was a Catholic I just gently moved the conversation back to building up the body of Christ.

Greg and Karen arrived early the next morning with my passport and brother, who had a smug smile on his face. They kindly offered to drive us across the border and have lunch with us in Milk River. After eighty-nine days, consisting of fifteen rest days and seventy-four on the road, I'd made the Canadian border.

That's 3,119 kilometres on foot and twenty-seven kilometres in the back of a Patrol Car. So be it. The US experience drew to a close over yet another cheerful shared meal, before Greg and Karen set off to complete their 600 kilometre return-journey.

> *God is love, and those who abide in love abide in God, and God abides in them.*
>
> 1 John 4:16

Total walked: *9,206 kilometres*

# Tendinitis, Orthodox Candles & Passport Mayhem

*December 2007*

We set off from Milk River into an excruciating −27°C sunrise. We couldn't stop laughing, more out of shock than anything else. Pulling our balaclava mouth sections down momentarily we breathed out across our stubble beards, which immediately turned white. We walked briskly with heat pads stuffed into our boots and gloves, praying a rosary as we went ... not that we could hear each other.

Chris knocked off at lunchtime to rock back with a hot chocolate at the house of a rancher who stopped to say hello, so he waved me off as I stepped back into the frozen Canadian winter. The cloud cover thickened in the afternoon sending the temperature from −8°C to −24°C and the heat pads cooled slowly. By day's end I'd lost all sensation in my fingertips and they ached.

It was a similar story the next day with Chris staying for a ten-pin bowling Christmas party while I hiked and prayed out across sixty-one freezing kilometres, stopping only twice to rest. The top temperature of −14°C allowed me to push through with minimal fatigue. I made the mistake of pulling my balaclava down for too long while eating a muesli bar and the whole mouth section froze solid. It was a mass of heavy ice and as much as I tried to melt it with my breath, it stayed frozen, hanging low off my mouth like an open whale mouth.

I was to stay that evening in Lethbridge with an elderly couple named Stan and Kathy; not long after sunset they rendezvoused with me, with a smiling Chris sitting up in the back seat. I enjoyed having Chris with me … when I saw him.

Having crossed the border fifteen days ahead of schedule there was no reason to hurry. My flight to Russia left in a month and Edmonton was only two and half weeks away. We stayed in Lethbridge for two days, attended Sunday night Mass and, the next morning, spoke to the students at the local Catholic Central High about the journey. I recounted the stories of the Venezuelan puma and the encounter with Adolfo, showing them the Dino doll still swinging from my pack. I implored with them to pray for the complete unity of Christians. Some students were straight away setting their alarms for 4:01 while others were probably just looking at the clock wondering when lunch was. While speaking at the school, two Lethbridge news crews—a radio station and the newspaper—turned up for an interview and, after hearing of the hospitality we'd received so far, the newspaper reporter picked up his mobile and phoned his mum in the town we were headed to the next day. He had his story and we had yet another bed.

We capped off our Lethbridge stay by attending a fantastic youth group that night where the invitation to pray at 4:01 was again received openly.

We left Lethbridge at dawn. A warm Chinook wind had blown through the night and begun to melt the snow, but before dawn the temperature had dropped back below zero and had frozen the melted snow into solid slabs of ice. Within ten minutes of walking I slipped on an icy driveway and both feet shot forward in a flash, sending me airborne. I crashed to the cement flush on my backpack and my head jerked back savagely, giving me horrible whiplash. As I lay there like an upturned turtle I knew I'd escaped lightly. Twenty-five people were rushed to hospital that day after similar falls. The backpack had saved me. Chris helped me to my feet while residents peered out through lounge room windows and we walked on.

A freezing fog lingered over Lethbridge providing an amazing backdrop to Canada's longest railway-bridge; we walked under the eastern abutment of the steel structure that disappeared into the eerie blanketing mist.

The chilly fifty-three kilometres to Fort Macleod was filled with people hitting their horns. I hadn't seen any smiles so I said to Chris "Why are they tooting at us? We're not on the road!" Stan and Kathy pulled up with a bevy of warm food at lunchtime and the message that the local radio station was giving hourly updates of our progress, inviting people to encourage us by tooting their horn. I would have preferred they threw chocolate, but it was encouragement nonetheless.

Chris hitched a ride after thirty kilometres, so I prayed on alone and, with night setting in, it was a quiet haul under the guide of my flashing headlamp. The journalist's mum, Jean, welcomed us in and for the seventeenth day in a row I'd been invited into someone's home. At no other time did I experience such communal hospitality.

Jean invited us to speak at the Rotary Club the following day as well as the Pumpkin Club at the local A&W. We thought it was funny that I'd be speaking at a pumpkin club and assumed that the A&W stood for something like the Alberta Women's club, or something to that effect, but it turned out to be a women's prayer group meeting at a highway fast food restaurant. When we saw the A&W, Chris and I burst out laughing; he stopped for a moment and leant across saying, "You've really made the big time now." It was warm and cosy and we had hot breakfasts coming. I recounted the journey and extended the invitation to pray for Christian unity and they received the invitation openly … while I received the sausage and egg roll with French toast.

The Rotary Club welcomed me for lunch and I was given the floor for half an hour to share about the journey. It wasn't a straight out Christian audience, but the invitation was still received well. One old guy strolled up to me at the end and noted: "That's one heck of a story kid. I got no idea what you said half the time with that accent of yours, but it was one heck of a story!"

For dinner we were 'dobbed-in' by Jean to be waiters at the Fort Macleod annual Senior Citizens Christmas Dinner. How could we say no? We arrived early and actually worked hard, serving food and washing up. And we didn't break anything, although Chris did manage to drop a knife into the industrial dishwasher's drainage outlet causing a few blank looks between us. After some muffled giggles we managed to pluck it out before any damage was done.

After a huge day, Chris decided to wash a load of clothes back at Jean's, but managed to toss a full cup of bleach in instead of detergent. Much to his disgust his dark brown snow pants copped the brunt of it and he walked on the next day with bleached orange streaks across them.

"They look pretty, Chris."

"Shut up."

At day's end we checked into a hotel. When Chris removed his boots, complaining about foot soreness, he found the right sock blood soaked. His third toenail had sliced into the second toe. "It was the other foot that hurt! This was my good foot!"

Chris and I hitting the plains fully clad

With the jagged Rockies now only twenty kilometres to the west, running in the same north-south direction, we pushed on across the flat Alberta planes looking like Arctic explorers. Our water supply didn't remain liquid for long, and the freezing moisture from our breath caused the balaclavas to stick to our beards. We continued on to Nanton and then High River, but the walking continued to take its toll on Chris. His whole body was seizing up and we had to stop a number of times to let him rest. I'd been in that position before, particularly in Nicaragua, but it was now −20°C with a wind chill factor reducing it to −28°C, so stopping to rest was difficult. The juggling act between injury management and hypothermia aversion took a measured response.

The sun was setting when we called in for dinner at a Subway on the edge of High River. I left my bag with Chris and ran into town to find the Saturday night vigil Mass. Unlike the Latin American countries where the streets were filled with people to ask directions from, Canada and the USA were usually devoid of street life. Everyone drove past in cars. It took some time to find the church. There was only an hour to go, so, I hurried back to Chris, grabbed him and walked back the couple of kilometres for Mass.

We spent the evening singing Christmas carols with the parish youth group at a nursing home and hospital. We stood amongst them, acting like we knew what we were doing, miming through half the carol, but belted out the bits we knew. It slowly dawned on us that the youth group hadn't practised either. It was embarrassing, but brilliant. A few times we false-started with carols that only one person knew and there were plenty that dissipated into oblivion during the second verse, except for the senior citizens singing along. A few of the older youth group members even jazzed up one song by adding their own background rap, mainly to amuse themselves. As we finished the song the first comment offered by a pan-faced old lady was, "That was … interesting." One nurse, originally from Jamaica, couldn't contain her laughter; as Chris and I stopped to distance ourselves from the hall-wandering rapping carollers she laughed, "This is the funniest thing I've seen in here!"

Chris and I were offered accommodation on one family's farm and, as much as Chris wanted to walk on, he just couldn't. The dad offered to drive him to the following day's destination so I hit the road alone towards Okotoks, motoring along with the walking poles and praying in particular for my good friend Dave (not to be confused with puma-advice Dave), who was being ordained as a deacon back in Australia that day. Dave Callaghan was my man behind the scenes for the entire journey, providing endless spiritual and practical advice via email.

I met Chris in Okotoks and we walked the streets together, stopping at St Peter's Anglican Church, a Uniting church and then St James Catholic Church, where the invitation to pray for unity was received well at each. After Mass at St James, a husband and wife asked if they could take us out for dinner, and then a family asked if we'd like to stay at their house that night. We felt spoilt, again.

Frank, Louise, and their young daughter Kerry, were English immigrants and had a knack for creating a cheery home. We shared light-hearted stories over a cup of tea and then when they headed off to work and school in the morning, Chris and I were left to lock up the house once we'd finished breakfast. Their trust was inspiring.

A few days later I received an email from Louise. The night after we left, Louise, Frank and Kerry had chatted about the walk for unity and Kerry had sighed, "Mummy, I'm not excited about Christmas now."

Louise wasn't sure how to take the ten-year-old's statement and asked, "Why not?"

She pondered, "Well, because we're always being told that Christmas is about inviting Jesus into our home and last night we did that with Sam and Chris. We've already had the real Christmas." What an amazing ten-year-old.

Chris and I headed off through crunching snow to a coffee shop to meet with the parish priest—Fr Jack—and a few parishioners for a hot drink and conversation about unity. My metabolism was racing and I consumed four meals a day, with the fourth at around 2:30 am in between sleep, plus churned through around twenty muesli bars each day. Any offer of a 'hot drink' usually escalated into grabbing a bite to eat as well. Fr Jack had done extensive work with a Lutheran church in building a shared facility a few years earlier, and his assistant priest was originally ordained an Anglican priest. Our conversation went on to the international front, where there were encouraging works taking place between the Greek Orthodox, Russian Orthodox, Roman Catholic, Anglican and Lutheran churches at that moment. There were so many pieces to the puzzle of unification, but we agreed on two basic fronts: prayer and putting love into action.

Chris and I walked on towards Calgary under clear blue skies, but Chris's feet remained troublesome, to the point where something beyond general soreness had set in. We found a physiotherapist who checked him out and the diagnosis was worse than anticipated. Chris had pushed to the point of possible nerve damage and the muscle running along the shin had swollen within the sheath, making a cracking sensation as it tried to move in the constricted space. His foot was becoming limp and there was a possibility of him losing movement altogether. The basic prognosis was, "Stop walking."

So he did.

We talked about our options over lunch and he decided it was time to just enjoy his time overseas. "What have you been doing to this point?" I asked. He just stared back. We rang ahead to friends living in Edmonton and organised for him to catch the bus north to hang out for a while until I arrived. The bus departed the next morning, so we wandered out across the beautiful Bow River onto the northern bank as the setting sun burst rays of light through the higher floors of surrounding high-rise buildings and then danced across the frozen river. It was a beautiful sight.

Presiding over the dazzling river was a stunning Ukrainian Orthodox church. Wednesday night prayers (vespers) were commencing as we pushed into the stunning interior of art and craftsmanship. Taking a seat with the handful of attendees, we had no idea what evening vespers would be in an Orthodox church. The priest, adorned with golden garments fitting for a place of beauty, had a neat grey beard and a deep singing voice that drew us peaceably into the place of intimate prayer. Not understanding Ukrainian didn't seem to matter. It was prayerful and we entered into the vespers as best we could. The handful of people in there produced a collective singing voice of such clarity and volume that it almost defied logic.

We hadn't introduced ourselves, so it came as a surprise when an elderly lady leaned back and asked softly, "Can you hold the candles for the priest?" My eyes widened. I leaned forward, "But I'm not Ukrainian Orthodox. I'm a Catholic. I have no idea what to do." She didn't bat an eyelid. She just smiled and whispered back, "You'll be fine and you may just enjoy it!" We didn't have a say in the matter. I dug Chris in the ribs and whispered the deal to him, much to his horror. A distinct line appeared down the middle of his forehead,

"What are we supposed to do?"

I shrugged my shoulders, "No idea."

The priest paused for a moment and the elderly lady turned to us, nodding with a smile that our time had come. We shuffled out and approached the front hoping to not look like fools. Two candles sat to the left of the altar and two to the right. Two women also stepped forward and grabbed the ones on the left so, with a nervous grin to each other, we took the ones on the right and watched the women with an eagle eye, following their every move. We assumed our place directly opposite them and, with no objection from the priest as he stepped in between us to continue singing evening prayers, we stayed where we were.

We were still fully clad in thermals and jackets, so we quickly began to cook. Both hands clasped the huge candles firmly and there was no opportunity to remove a few layers. Fifteen minutes later, when we finally returned to our seats, the look of relief we gave each other while removing our outer layer was accompanied with a few quiet laughs. At the end of vespers the invitation to pray for unity was well received.

I received an email in Calgary from Padre Xiegdel in Panama saying that the new boots had finally arrived in the city of David! I requested for them to be posted north to Edmonton and looked forward to finally taking possession of them. I was also still trying to get to the bottom of the Russia/Belarus visa fiasco. When the passport was returned at the Canadian border it contained a Russian visa, but nothing for Belarus. I'd paid $200 for it so I was asking the company how I was to secure the visa I'd already paid for. They asked me to send the passport back, but I was no longer ignorant of international law, so decided to wait until I'd at least reached Edmonton.

I walked on alone the next morning in pre-dawn darkness for the final few hundred kilometres of the Americas. A gun-barrel straight road led me out across dead flat frozen plains to Airdrie and then further on to Carstairs, where the town's librarian, her assistant and assistant's husband invited me to dinner. They weren't Christians;

they were just offering good old hospitality to a stranger. The librarian drove me back to a motel and confessed that she didn't believe that the unity of Christians would make much difference to the world, that most of the world's problems were caused by religions and that the best thing that could happen would be the disintegration of the Church. She also felt it was sad that one of my good friends had just been ordained. For her it was a waste of a life, primarily because he'd remain celibate, but knowing what Fr Dave was taking up (rather than what he was putting down) I thought he'd chosen a life that would be far more rewarding and fruitful than most people's non-celibate lives. To my surprise though, she handed me an amount of money to cover the motel and next day's food, but made her point clear, "This isn't an investment in your mission. It's an investment in you. It's been a pleasure meeting you." I was somewhat speechless. Typically a person who rejects the message rejects the messenger. I was grateful, but couldn't help but invite her with a smile to say a prayer for me if she ever felt the inkling to.

She just smiled and said, "Enjoy your walk."

I was well out into the countryside before the sunrise broke through the chilled darkness with a splash of deep red across scattered clouds. It was an amazing contradiction. My eyes saw warmth, but my body froze. Long stretches of road leaned into beautiful crisp days north to the town of Olds and Bowden.

One basic motel I stayed in had dimly lit rooms and when I shuffled into the empty café for dinner the waitress offered to take my meal into the bar where everyone else was. I declined saying, "It's okay, I like the silence." She was fine with that, but she began flirting and I actually felt uncomfortable. Two pokies-machines beeped occasionally in the background and the waitress broke mid-sentence to apologise for them. I assured her it didn't bother me, but she pushed for justification saying, "We don't want them in here but the government won't let us have both the machines and the strippers in the same room." I nearly choked on my chicken. A long pause ensued before I eventually replied with something intelligent like, "Oh, okay." It now made sense why the room was so dirt-cheap. I walked on well before sunrise, passing a man passed out in his pick-up in the car park as I left.

North of a town called Penhold, which felt like a pre-1900s settlement tucked into the snow-covered wheat flats, the farmland gave way to swathes of pine forest for the first time since Texas. I'd missed trees. They were almost a novelty.

In the small city of Red Deer I spent the evening at a Lutheran church listening to Christmas carols with the locals, who took on the mission one by one. I was unable to find internet and so was unable to post my weekly blog. I didn't think much of it and presumed I'd find access the next day, but that opportunity didn't present itself and my friends and family would be left wondering if I was alive or lying lifeless in wilderness snow.

There was a lot on my mind, but I had to take a step back and look at the big picture. It was the 16th of December 2007, exactly one year since I started out in north-eastern Brazil. I'd stayed with a Pentecostal preacher that night and attended their Saturday night service on a dusty street with a truck used as a stage. A lot had changed and a lot of ground had been covered—that first month in Brazil felt like it was five years ago now.

It was satisfying that the media coverage from Wyoming's Shirley Basin had continued to roll on and, as I continued out of Red Deer in brisk −14°C conditions, a young lady from a Catholic publication found me wandering along Road 2A for an interview. During the interview she asked the sort of questions that made me comfortable that she understood why I was there.

I thought I had to cover thirty-five kilometres that day but, due to a basic map reading error, I'd missed that it was in fact fifty-four. That's a bad mistake. The two-hour interview over lunch now made it very difficult to even get close to my destination by sunset. The cold winter days were short, around seven hours in length, leaving me four hours short of Ponoka when darkness fell. I walked on into a frigid night along twisting roads through snow-covered pines lit softly by a high half-moon.

I rugged up, prayed a rosary and then began singing. The songs echoed off the dark forest that my little headlamp and the moon above illuminated gently in the calm, frozen landscape. When the hymns I was singing slid into U2's seemingly appropriate "Where the streets have no name", I realised I wasn't alone. Deep from within the pines a chorus of coyote howls and yelps chimed in. They were a little out of tune. Smiling, I sang louder while their song similarly grew in volume, howling for as long as I was within earshot.

Emerging out onto the open plains, the faint smell of smoke in the cool evening from the few farmhouses burning firewood reminded me of home. If it wasn't for the northern hemisphere stars overhead it very well could have been. I ambled down a gentle hill with a wide view and there was a gentle glow of orange above the northern horizon.

It was Edmonton.

I stayed in Panoka that night and continued on into the middle of an Indian Reservation the next day. An SUV driven by two young women pulled up alongside me and the tinted rear window rolled down. A young man in a hoodie, with a chipped smile and authoritative speech reminiscent of a New York gangster asked, "Hey man, what are you doing here?" I told him the deal, and he announced loudly, "He's from Australia and he's walking the world!" He gave a shuffle with his head, "You know, it could be dangerous walking through here. This isn't your land."

I wasn't in the mood for playing innocent and stared straight back, replying, "I'm dangerous too. So what's dangerous around here? Are you?"

He lifted his hand up over his mouth and forced out a laugh saying, "No man, I'm cool, but hey, you never know."

I raised my eyebrows and agreed, "No, you don't do you."

I wished him well and walked on, leaving him to wind his window up before being frostbitten.

From Wetaskiwin, the mission continued to be handed on one person at a time until I reached Leduc. I ducked into a supermarket to top up my supplies, but struggled to find muesli bars. I found a worker and asked him, "Excuse me sir, do you have granola bars?" I kid you not, the guy replied with something along the lines of, "Agh, da end u ul se." I had no idea what he'd said.

I leant forward and asked, "Sorry, what did you say?"

He repeated a little slower, "Agh, de end o iyl sek."

I apologised with a laugh, "Sorry, I'm Australian, I can't pick your accent. I have no idea what you just said."

He laughed and spoke even slower, "It's okay. Em frem New Foundland. Lots o people cen't understand mi. What I said was, I (meaning 'yes'), the end of aisle six."

Right, so that's what "agh, da end u ul se" means. It turns out that New Foundland, just like my island state of Tasmania, copped relentless jokes from mainlanders for being inbred. The guy was good for a laugh and kindly showed me to the end of aisle six.

It was also in Leduc that I was finally able to jump on the internet to let everyone back home know I was alive. There were a few emails enquiring anxiously of my whereabouts.

Sorry all.

The Catholic church secretary and her husband extended warm hospitality that evening, allowing me to head off into my final day for the Americas well fed and rested. Continuing north along the Queen Elizabeth II Highway, with the air hovering at −23°C, I felt semi-frozen all day. A global television news crew shot footage of me walking while conducting an interview, and then left me to continue on up to the large city. While walking through populated areas I almost always pulled my balaclava down, but the Edmonton air was too frigid. My beard quickly developed icicles and my lips numbed. I looked like Sir Douglas Mawson.

Chris and the Quist family, my friends in Edmonton, had organised to meet me at the Calgary Lutheran Church, five kilometres south of Edmonton central, with a plan to walk that final section with me. The dad, Paul, was once the minister at Calgary Lutheran, but a number of years before, after a long deliberation, he and a number of his congregation decided to become Catholic. For Paul, that meant unemployment. It was a huge decision and he approached the Archbishop of Edmonton with his plight, asking to somehow still be involved in ministry. As it was, Paul and his wife, Carol, had a strong interest in the beauty of Pope John Paul II's Theology of the Body and the archbishop was looking to establish a new Marriage and Family Planning Centre. He made an offer they couldn't refuse and the whole family arrived in Melbourne, Australia, in 2005 for Paul to study at the JPII Institute. When they moved to Melbourne they attended St Benedict's parish in Burwood—my parish. Their son, Jon, became a great mate and I gave maths tuition to their second eldest, Kari. They were all back in Edmonton now and I was looking forward to seeing them.

I was an hour late arriving at the church and sore from the lack of breaks. They'd waited patiently and we were ready to get underway right on 4:01 pm. Chris had settled into Edmonton with ease and was doing well. We all knelt at the church's communion rail to pray alongside the current minister and his assistant. We prayed for the unity of Christians, in truth and in love, and then set out for the final five kilometres.

Chris, Paul, Jon, Kari and the youngest daughter, Kirsten, walked and chatted with me towards downtown Edmonton while Carol drove ahead. It was a blast seeing them all again—even Chris!—and we approached the Saskatchewan River at sunset. I filmed Jon's humorous interpretive guide of his home city, "This is a shop where you can buy things and that is a bridge. It's a big bridge. Down the river there you'll see a Power Station. It's very pretty I think you'll find."

We marched our frozen bodies across the big bridge into Edmonton central and right on 5 pm, as we approached St Joséph's Basilica, snow drifted in through the city's high-rises. Amidst Edmonton's hustle and bustle there was a sense of peace, and I stepped up onto the basilica steps 370 days, and 9,856 kilometres on foot (plus a few thousand more by motorised transport), after setting out from Cabo Branco.

I knelt in St Joséph's Basilica, praying prayers of thanks for still being alive, for providence, for the people I'd met, especially Adolfo and those who struggled similarly, and for my aggressors, of whom a few I still wanted to thump. I needed to regularly forgive them. It was Christmas time, again.

Twelve rest days preluded my flight to Vladivostok, which included a few speaking engagements teed up by Paul and Carol. I was introduced as, "Sam Clear from Tanzania, Austria." I corrected the geography and shared the mission.

Global Television aired their interview throughout the following day and I copped the humorous humiliation of having the midday news co-host ask after my story, "What did he say? I couldn't understand a single word he said! Was he speaking English?" The woman co-hosting came to my aid offering, "Well I understand Australian perfectly," and interpreted for him, reiterating the mission.

Chris and I took the opportunity to teach a few willing Canadians the traditional Australian Christmas pastime of backyard cricket. Unfortunately, Paul swung so hard with the fence-paling-bat that he lost his grip and it flew through the air a good twenty metres … and cracked his brother-in-law fair across the head as he stepped out of the front door, splitting the plank in two. Game over. We retired to a more traditional Canadian Christmas of sitting around the piano belting out carols with great harmony, and tackling snow-covered hills with a large sled. I'd particularly like to thank Jon and his cousin's boyfriend for breaking my fall that one time when we became airborne. Sorry if I broke any ribs …

My body wasn't used to not walking and when I headed off to bed one night I was so wide-eyed that I rugged up and ducked outside for an 11 pm jog along the frozen country road. In the end Jon, Chris and I packed up and set off to Jasper National Park for two days of skiing. It was absolutely brilliant.

The thick leather of my walking boots had cracked and the sole had worn badly, exposing the inner cushioning, but new boots were not on the way. The difficulty of communicating with Padre Xiegdel led us in circles and the boots remained idle in Panama. After hours of internet searching I deduced that there was only one

pair of size sixteen Scarpas in the world: in Panama. With nothing in stock within a 40,000 kilometre radius, I was forced to move on to Russia with what I had. The Scarpa motto is, No destination is too far. It was about to be put it to the test.

While talking to Mum over the phone she mentioned the $1,000 she'd put in Chris's bank account for me. I put the phone down and yelled out, "Chris!

Where's my $1,000?"

He strolled out to the kitchen and screwed his face up, "What? Do you think I paid for all those hotels for you and bought all your meals out of the goodness of my heart? That was your $1,000. You've spent it." And walked back out.

"Mum, yeah, found it. You can have him back now."

On New Year's Eve we farewelled Chris; he returned to Australia having endured a frozen winter, serious leg pain and a few spas.

Upon arriving in Edmonton I'd sent my passport back to the visa-issuing company for the Belarus visa to be completed and I paid extra for it to be processed in twenty-four hours. It didn't return and the company closed for Christmas. I was not happy. I was scheduled to leave on the 2nd of January, which happened to be the day the company re-opened. I made contact with them on the 2nd as they opened up to find they'd forgotten to place the passport on the twenty-four hour turn-around list. To make matters worse my passport wasn't in their office; it was sitting in the Washington DC Belarus embassy. The absolute earliest I could receive the passport by was the 4th. I wasn't making my flight to Russia.

The company refused to cover any losses I incurred and after a long argument about their culpability, we'd gone nowhere. I forfeited a large portion of my airline ticket and purchased a new one, costing another $870. That flight would land me in Vladivostok after the trans-Siberian train had left for Moscow, meaning I'd have to wait for the following train. My good friend, Justin, was already on his way to Vladivostok to travel across Siberia with me and his return flight was booked for the afternoon of the day after the following train's arrival into Moscow. Our plans were shot to pieces. We'd have to make a near direct path to Moscow over seven days with time for only one stop.

On the 4th of January there were a lot of prayers being prayed. We discovered that the passport had accidentally been sent to the wrong town and wouldn't be retrievable for three more days. I needed to get out of the house and just pray my way out along the snowy country road. If I missed the second flight I wouldn't be able to afford to continue on. The journey would be over.

Paul and Carol helped me find out exactly where the passport was, piled us into the van, and raced across the frozen landscape to find it. Paul didn't stop singing Christmas carols the whole way. I was so thankful for their generosity, persistence and hospitality, particularly when I was able to jump aboard the 7 pm bus to Calgary Airport with my passport in hand.

I checked in for my flight right on 4:01 am, I kid you not. Nice. The mission was back on. Without having slept a wink, I boarded the plane to San Francisco and connecting flight to Vladivostok via Seoul, cramped into the ridiculous airline seats.

I was left to ponder what had arrived with my passport. It contained a Russian visa, but again nothing for Belarus. There were, however, a series of papers written in Belarusian with official stamps. I couldn't read Belarusian so had no idea what it was and had no way of telling if it was somehow a visa or not. I'd never heard of a visa being a series of papers outside the passport, but perhaps that was exactly what it was. One thing was for sure; it wouldn't be too long before I found out.

> *Truly I tell you, whoever does not receive the kingdom of God as a little child will never enter it.*
>
> Luke 18:17

**Total walked :** *9,863 kilometres*

# Part 3

*Russia and Europe*

*Beginning with 9,200 kilometres* of train-ploughed Siberian wilderness to Moscow, I planned to then set out on foot through western Russia's winter towards Spain, six months away. In the year of planning before the journey Dad made an astute observation, "Sam, both Hitler's and Napoleón's campaigns came to their demise while trying to walk across Russia in winter. What makes you think you're any different?" I understood his concern but answered, "I'm headed in the other direction." I knew the winter walk from Moscow would be perilous, but had to add, "Plus, they were being shot at." European politics had changed, but the weather hadn't. Any thoughts of Europe being easier than what I'd encountered so far would be greatly misguided.

## Trans-Siberian Railway, Seized Knees & a Drunken Punch-Up

*January 2008*

I couldn't fall asleep on the flight to Seoul. The seat finished at my shoulders and my knees were jammed into the seat in front. I had no choice but to sit bolt upright, head and shoulders above everyone else as Alaska, the Bering Strait and the fire and ice of the volcanic Kamchatka Peninsula passed by underneath.

Justin had planned his trans-Siberian Railway trip well in advance but was now affected by my passport fiasco, so had been forced to sit in Vladivostok for four days by himself, practising Russian with the hotel staff.

My flight touched down at Vladivostok airport and decrepit-looking decommissioned aircraft were parked all along the runway. There were soldiers standing guard in bushy black head attire and around half of them were women with long blonde hair. If I'd seen it in a Hollywood film I would have thought it was pathetic casting. They didn't smile much. I was ushered through security quickly with plenty of forceful instructions, but without much fuss. I was keen to move on into the country.

Justin was waiting in the lobby of Hotel Vladivostok and was immediately describing the exact same sequence of events from touchdown to the hotel.

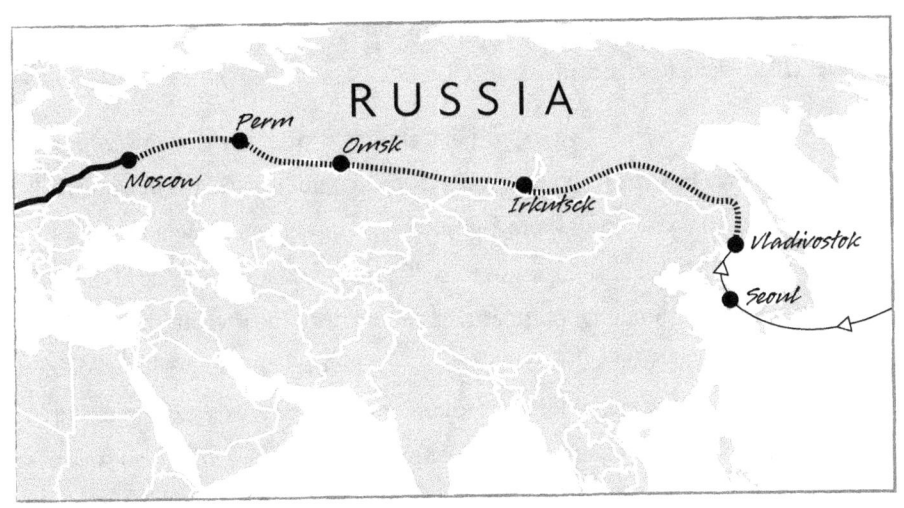

## LEGEND

By Plane →  On Foot*  
By Rail ·········  SC Projection

Russia and Europe

*On foot for the majority; but occasionally by motorised transport in impassable sections

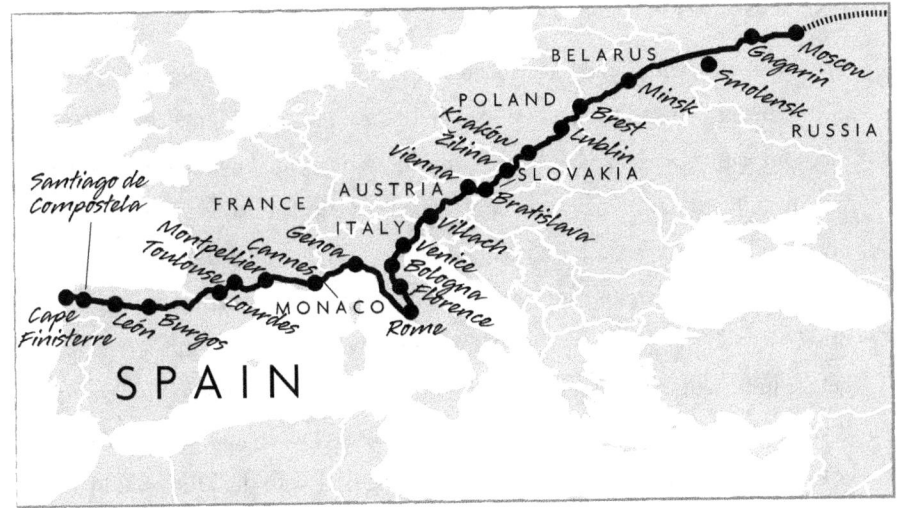

walk4one *Paving a Path to Unity*

We were pretty sure we had the exact same taxi driver too. It was great to see him and to again enjoy his observational humour in such a unique city. He'd familiarised himself with our surroundings and pointed out from our hotel on a hill the Bay of Vladivostok, the city centre and the famous naval base. More than ever, I felt like a foreigner in a strange land.

After some tentative tests we stepped out onto the frozen bay amidst a wonderful mixture of ice fishermen and kids being dragged in toboggans. I wanted to walk a few hundred metres from shore, but Justin was more than content to stay close to land. My original hope was to walk across Russia from a place called Magadan, further up in the north east, all the way to Moscow, but the perilous crossing would have added an extra year to the journey and numerous wilderness areas where towns were hundreds of kilometres apart with average temperatures hovering around −40°C, dropping regularly to −60°C. The agreed plan was to travel by train, stopping at nine of the major cities along the 9,200 kilometre trans-Siberian railway. That plan was now obsolete. With Justin's return flight from Moscow leaving the day after the next train arrived we could afford only one stop. We decided it would be Irkutsk, on the shores of the world's largest and deepest fresh water lake, Lake Baikal.

We set about learning the Russian alphabet plus a few phrases, beginning with please, thank you and our names—Samuel: 'Самуэль', and Justin: 'Джастин'. At the train station we had a hard time communicating with anyone. Our Russian was in its infancy and English was not spoken. Hours later we still hadn't found our train until a soldier came to our aid with a friendly smile and informed us that the Tuesday train had been cancelled. Our only option was to catch a slower second train the next day that would arrive in Moscow only a few hours before Justin's departing flight. There would be no opportunity to visit churches. It would be seven days of confined prayer, Russian lessons and Justin's wry commentary of the world around us. Checking back into the Hotel Vladivostok, he joked that we could checkout anytime we liked, but never leave.

We visited a few beautiful Russian Orthodox churches and received a cheerful response to the call to pray for unity, while Justin filled me in on his research regarding the train ride. Each carriage was looked after by a worker called the provinitser and it was their responsibility to maintain cleanliness, order and general operation of the carriage's toilet and hot water urn.

As we approached the next morning's train Justin commented that, "Because we're going to have a language barrier on this journey we should do what we can to get on the good side of the provinitser." The platform was empty apart from one woman who knocked on a carriage door and was let in by the provinitser, so we stepped up and did exactly the same. There was no answer. "I might try again," Justin suggested, and knocked a second time. The provinitser appeared at the door, but didn't open up … oh no … she thumped the door's glass window repeatedly and opened her mouth with possibly the most severe Russian tirade since Germany breached their borders. Unable to understand a single word we just backed away, letting her disappear back into the carriage.

I offered Justin my thoughts: "That wasn't the start to our relationship we were hoping for was it?"

Twenty minutes later a few patrons had gathered silently with us, and the five foot tall, petite provinitser opened the door to our home for the next week. She didn't crack a smile once. The carriage consisted of a narrow hallway along the side of nine cabins with two double bunks in each. Our ticket indicated which bunk was ours, but with no one else in our cabin Justin decided he didn't want his allotted top bunk and threw his gear on the bottom one opposite me as the train pulled out.

We wound our way along the surreal frozen shoreline which had tiny, wood-burning houses scattered along it. Hundreds of men sat out on the ice on boxes ice fishing as we click-clacked out into frozen wilderness. I approached the carriage's hot water urn when we drew to a stop at a secluded town and I spotted the provinitser struggling at the door with a new passenger's over-sized travel case. It was a bit of a divine appointment. I helped her haul the bag in and then carried it to the cabin. Although the provinitser didn't say thank you she did give me a smile three hours later.

Justin and I were impressed.

Our course continued north to the Russian city of Khabarovsk, where we came to a second stop well short of the platform. We sat there for ten hours as they swapped the engine and dining cart. They really weren't kidding about it being the slower train. Four young men were drawn into conversation in the hallway outside our cabin and it became apparent that they wanted a pack of playing cards. Justin had one. He retrieved them from his bag and the young man at our door yelled triumphantly to his three comrades. They each popped in, thanking us profusely before disappearing into the cabin next door to play poker for seven days straight.

At some time in the night we started moving again, collected a few new passengers at the platform and continued on into the darkness around the northern edge of China towards Ulan-Ude and Irkutsk. Justin was forced to quickly clean his gear up off the lower bunk when a father and daughter joined us for the majority of the way to Moscow on their hometown-bound journey. Alexi and Angela didn't speak English and we didn't speak Russian, but they were sociable and it made for animated conversation using mime and sketch. Alexi was in his late sixties and Angela probably in her late thirties. They were ideal cabin mates.

Angela was a passport officer on the Russia/China border, so I fumbled through my bag for the Belarusian documents and tried to think of a way to explain what I wanted. In the end I just handed them over and shrugged my shoulders, hopefully asking the question, "What is it?" She understood exactly what I wanted and read it through page-by-page, shaking her head and screwing her lips up as she went, as though it didn't make sense. Eventually she relaxed with a look of mild surprise and handed them back saying, "Is visa." They were the exact words I'd wanted to hear. "Da, is Belarus visa."

Alexi and Angela patiently took us through the phonetic sounds of the Cyrillic alphabet, teaching us numerous useful Russian words and simple phrases. I was intent on minimising my accent to maximise my chances of being understood. I always knew that I'd have to learn at least a little of eight different languages over the course of the walk, but my absolute favourite word, the one I loved hearing roll off the tongue, was the Russian word for 'please'. It is something like, "Pa-zhal-sta," and sound like it had been invented specifically for Sean Connery.

"Would you like to travel first class, Mr Bond?"

"Pazhalsta."

Justin taking shots of the sunset from the train

I loved it. I wanted people to ask me something so I could just say, "Da, pazhalsta." I was shaping up to be the most polite Australian to ever enter Russia.

When conversation became too difficult to maintain we simply resorted to sharing food, smiling and drawing each other's attention to sights out the train window. Isolated Russian towns settled by Europeans, Mongolians and Tatars provided the only interludes to the deep freeze. The architecture was usually simple, but some towns looked like fairy tale versions of the North Pole with small wooden houses camped side by side and thin columns of smoke rising from each chimney.

Somewhere out in the middle of eastern Siberia, the train screeched to a halt sending water bottles and books flying off our cabin table onto my head. Justin and I were thrown against the cabin wall while poor Alexi and Angela very nearly ended up across the divide to join us. Something was being spoken in Russian with great concern throughout the carriage. I went and found Vasili, the only English-speaking passenger and he simply said, "They are saying we just hit someone. Apparently there is someone lying in the snow. I don't know." Our entire carriage peered out the right-hand side windows and sure enough, directly outside was a man lying on his back in the snow.

The man pulled himself up out of the snow, yelling abuse at the train. He was heavily intoxicated and when he saw us staring out at him he picked up a rock and hurled it straight at a window, leaving a substantial spider web fracture across it. A train engineer appeared, walking down the side of our carriage. Justin piped up, "He's carrying a hammer!" A heavy hammer slung low in his right hand and it left us ... well ... concerned. The two men entered a heated verbal exchange until the engineer cut to the chase, karate-kicked the drunken man in the chest and sent him stumbling backwards into the snow. He picked himself up just in time to receive a royal boot up the backside and was forced to stagger back into the sparse forest towards a smouldering campfire. The engineer, with the hammer remaining idle at his side, stood like a shadowed comic hero between his train and the hunched drunkard staggering back into the frozen wilderness. We prayed for him as he disappeared.

On and on the journey went, hour after hour and day after day. Sunrise would kind of come, but was all too soon followed by sunset as we crossed one time zone into the next. We sat on our beds reading or walking slowly along the carriage hallway watching the frozen Siberian landscape pass by. Occasionally something bizarre would flash by, like the one little village hut ablaze in a consuming fire that lit up the previously darkened −39°C streets. The neighbouring identical huts continued to puff away neatly from their chimneystacks under a bright moon without a single person attending the blaze.

Alexi bought a slimy, smoked fish at one stop while Justin provided analytical commentary in the background during the bartering process. And as the fish was pulled apart carefully on our cabin table Justin proceeded to hum the theme song from Dr Zhivago. I think he was feeling cooped up.

In time pretty much everyone on the carriage knew each other and even the provinitser seemed to enjoy our company. She had an okay job, except for when we pulled into a station. It was so cold outside that the waste being dumped from the carriage toilet inevitably froze to the drop chute. That's where she came in with her heaviest winter clothing on and a miniature axe in hand. She'd crouch on the tracks underneath, along with all the other provinitsers at their respective carriages, and chip away at our … waste. She at times banged away with that axe for ten to fifteen minutes and never returned in a good mood.

Travelling on the train for seven days straight meant that at some point it was Sunday. Not able to attend Mass, we instead set time aside for a mini service up on Justin's top bunk. We chose a scripture passage each that was meaningful to us and shared about its impact on our lives, then entered a time of intercessory prayer. We both prayed each day, but in that simple way we came together in the only way we could to be part of the wider Church gathering around the world that day.

Justin and I decided to have a nice meal in the dining cart, but our carriage was the very last one and the dining cart was up the front, so we jumped off at Omsk station and walked forward along the platform for seven carriages. Upon finishing our meal we made our way back through the now moving train to the back carriage to be met with a bizarre mixture of smiles, confusion, laughter, arms in the air and a very stern word from the provinitser. They'd seen us step off at Omsk, but not reboard, and all mayhem had broken loose. They'd been quite upset that we'd been left behind and decided to turf our gear out at the next station to make it easier for us to get it back. We were thankful for having arrived back before the next stop! The provinitser stood with her hands on her hips before letting go with a grin. Old Alexi just shook his head and clicked his tongue at us.

Having crossed the Ural Mountains and only a few hours short of Moscow, we were sad to say goodbye to Alexi and Angela at their home city. Alexi offered a sturdy handshake while Angela gave us a big hug each, wishing us all the best in our travels. I think we'd become friends.

We'd travelled across seven time zones and when I looked at my watch as the sun rose at 2 pm, I decided it was time to change it. I'd enjoyed Justin's company and as the train click-clacked into the city of Moscow our journey was at an end. He had only a few hours to make his flight home to Perth so, after saying goodbye to the original passengers from carriage number eight, he jumped in a cab and without too much fuss was off.

Out front of St Basil's Cathedral

I was alone, staring down the barrel of a lot more walking across Europe to Rome and then around the Mediterranean to Cape Finisterre in Spain. Firstly, I had to figure out where I was. The city centre looked to be a few blocks away; under the gaze of a Soviet Union sickle and hammer stone carving I walked off down the bustling Moscow street into a settling snow shower.

Times had changed. History sang from the buildings surrounding the Red Square. The imposing Kremlin with Lenin's tomb in front, St Basil's Cathedral with its colourful onion domes, and the red bricks underfoot—that had seen communist military parades through to coronations, and produce markets come and go—was now offset by a modern ice skating rink. Locals and professionals carved out their winter passion opposite Lenin's tomb. It was a beautiful combination of kids struggling to stay upright and the Russian skate team pushing the sport's boundaries. One guy in a Russian tracksuit gathered speed around the outside and pulled his path in quickly, launching into a huge triple-axle. He nailed the landing to the applause of the crowd.

I found a tucked away hostel and let my body recover from the plane and train travel over the next two days. I pottered around Moscow, translating my introduction letter, learning as much of the language as possible and approaching a number of churches. I rarely found anyone to talk to, so I just spent a lot of time praying in them instead.

Well before dawn on the 18th of January 2008, I departed Moscow in mild conditions under the haunting gaze of the Soviet architecture. The city was quiet and the mix of history and modern life was like no other I'd ever seen. I hummed a feel-good tune and took aim at western Russia.

My effort to frighten my family back home (It wasn't moving, Mum...)

The road was lined with army tanks; no one was around so I took a few self-portraits with the retired armoury, but by mid-afternoon that bounce in my step had faded to a limp. Christmas and the Siberian crossing had sapped more fitness than I'd realised. My left Achilles tendon began to strain and my right knee ached, forcing my pace to drop. My face increasingly contorted under stress until I was a disjointed hobbling mess at the end of the forty-nine kilometres to the town of Golitsyno.

Unlike the beautiful sunsets of Canada, the sun in Russia set behind blanketing cloud and the day simply dimmed into darkness. I found a small, run-down communist era hostel called a gostinitsa, where I was more of a hindrance than a guest. They handed me my sheets and sent me off to find my room, slamming shut the counter window in my face. Welcome to Russia.

I could hardly move and I felt disgusting as my temperature fluctuated. All I wanted was to take a hot shower and sleep, but there was no hot water. I plucked up the courage to jump in for a freezing three-second shower before dressing fast. I threw my underwear into the sink for the nightly wash, but the foulest orange water spewed from the tap, staining everything it touched. Wouldn't you know it, I was wearing white undies that day. I just sighed and left them.

The short bed combined with writhing leg pain woke me repeatedly and I was still half asleep when I slowly walked on through sweet smelling pines the next morning. It was twenty-two kilometres to Kubinka—the small town where inclement weather halted the Germans in World War II. Their aspirations of kicking the Kremlin doors down were buried there. The Kubinka town's folk were enjoying a winter festival at a small Orthodox church and the bearded priest's reception was just as cold. Without even acknowledging that I'd introduced myself he turned and walked away, while a few locals gave me a quick look up and down before following suit. It was embarrassing.

My knee and Achilles ached as I limped off to find a motel. A gorgeous young woman by the name of Victoria came to my aid and travelled with me by bus to the gostinitsa on the edge of her husband's army base. She asked for a room for me, but the receptionist yelled at her in Russian through the small service window, "We're full!" and slammed it shut. I couldn't believe the rudeness. Victoria didn't bat an eyelid and continued to talk through the closed screen. The lady yelled something back and that was that. As we walked away Victoria noted that she and her husband recently holidayed in Spain and, "The hotels were a lot friendlier there."

Any country in the world was friendlier than that.

Victoria pointed me on my way to a second gostinitsa, but it was also full, so a soldier came to my aid and showed me on my map a third place a few kilometres inland. I put my head down and hobbled on painfully … so relieved to find a room there. My leg had deteriorated and the knee had almost seized completely. I could bend it no more than five degrees and no manual manipulation could bend it further. I used a walking pole just to get around the hostel with my old-man 'swing-of-the-stiff-leg' shuffle.

My circumstances were about to nose-dive further.

The weather, just as it had done for the Germans seventy years earlier, turned inclement. I left the infamous World War II town before dawn and a nasty storm drove snow in sideways. It consumed the roads. Kubinka's final orange street lamp ushered in the freezing darkness beyond, with the strained Achilles tendon and seized knee making it tortuous to push on.

I hoped to attend Sunday Mass in a Russian Orthodox church, but each town I passed through had already concluded their services. For the second week in a row I was left to simply put aside a more structured prayer time. I knew a lot of the Catholic Mass by heart, so I prayed a rosary and then began to pray the prayers the Church would be praying at that time. It was good, but incomplete.

The snowploughed highway had only enough room for cars to drive along, leaving me to trudge through a foot and half of snow for the majority of the day. My pace was painfully slow and, in a small town ten kilometres from Mozhaysk, a little old lady with a hunchback overtook me. I was that bad. I staggered down the highway and then up along a country road in darkness to Mozhaysk. My headlamp led the way and little by little the town lights drew near. After another forty-nine kilometre stretch, I was delighted to rest in a cheery family-run store; they gathered dinner for me and then called a taxi to drop me at the town's hotel.

As I hobbled towards the hotel I realised that I was missing one of my inner gloves, so I swung around, but the taxi was off. I'd dropped it on the floor and it was now gone. I crossed the street and jumped up off the bitumen into the mounded snow, but misjudged the depth and the toe of my boot caught in the snow. All my weight hit straight down in-line with my heel and the other Achilles tendon strained so badly that I was left grimacing in agony, struggling to breathe.

Every single step pierced with pain until I collapsed on the hotel bed and lay there for an hour trying to manipulate the locked right knee. It was a lost cause and the two Achilles tendons were beyond my capacity to help. My body was a sad mess.

I rolled out of bed onto the floor the next morning and commando-crawled to the bathroom, very aware of how far away Spain really was. Dressing was difficult and I had to stand still breathing deeply for a while before I could move any further. But, one proppy step after another, I moved towards my backpack, swung it up, said a prayer and took the first steps into the day. I hadn't come that far to stop now.

After fifteen minutes the knee and Achilles tendons had warmed up enough that the thirty-two kilometre day looked do-able. The snow banked up on the side of the road remained treacherous for ankles. But what I most feared began to happen … It started as a slight soreness, but then the other knee gave way. It locked dead straight. I struggled along at a snail's pace.

I had a strong sense that I needed to call home. Mum seemed to always know when I was in trouble so I just thought that maybe God wanted me to let her know I was okay. I couldn't find a phone though, so it had to wait.

After nearly a week on the road I still hadn't been invited to step inside a single home, but a Belarusian truck driver parked off the highway called me into the warm cab of his new Volvo as I hobbled past and offered me half his lunch. Vitali was a gem of a bloke. He didn't speak a word of English and my Russian was horrible, but he was patient and we communicated smoothly.

I later passed an old guy sitting in a tractor and noticed a portrait of Joseph Stalin pressed against the front windscreen. I was taken aback as to why on earth anyone would display his image. At an isolated service station with a hotel attached I met a young English-speaking Polish truck driver named Gabriel. I mentioned the portrait of Stalin and he shrugged his shoulders saying, "Many elderly Russians hail Stalin as the Father of Russia. They are desperate for communism to return."

I was shocked, "But he killed over ten million of his own people!"

He nodded and replied, "Yes, but some people think it was worth it for national security. They see that he made sacrifices to hold Russia together."

I was speechless.

The diner had a menu in both Russian and English so I learnt a few more words, such as fish. I ordered, "Ryba, pazhalsta." Gabriel joined me for the meal and brought some humanity to a cold week. I continued searching for a phone to call home, but still couldn't find one.

Staggering on along a wooded route to rural Sverchkovo, and nearby Gagarin, I was walked to a gostinitsa by a beautiful, chatty, English-speaking girl. She wasn't sure about 'organised' church, but said she'd at least remember unity when she did pray. The gostinitsa receptionist couldn't fill out the appropriate government forms because no allowance had been made for non-Russian customers. I was their first. Ever. The young lady stepped in and offered her details in my place and so, for one night in Gagarin, I was officially known as 'Julia'.

I called into a shop the next morning to pick up my day's food supply, but it was difficult to find healthy food for the road. Muesli bars and fresh fruit were non-existent and unless I wanted to buy everything in bulk to cook over a stove I was left with few options. I grabbed what I could and hit the road. A couple of hours of prayer later I reached for something to eat and was absolutely livid to discover that my food pouch was empty. I'd left all the food sitting on the shop counter! It was too much. I forget things every now and then, but with everything that had already happened that week, it really ticked me off. I was hungry, annoyed, painfully sore and tired. My stomach rumbled as I prayed on with a double-limp through crunching snow.

The day clouded over and the sun disappeared from view; I pushed on into uninviting frozen wilderness with few spots to rest. The road remained dead straight and dead flat for the body-numbing fifty-four kilometres to Vyazma. I only have a vague recollection of the place and have no idea where I stayed. I was numb.

When I thought it couldn't get any tougher, the following day presented a kind of worst-case scenario. Walking slower each day and finishing later, coupled with near exhaustion, meant I'd then sleep-in longer and it snowballed. The sun had risen when I left Vyazma and I was forced to regularly stop due to severe leg soreness. Electric shocks then began emanating from one knee causing me to just stand idle, staring down the road. I wanted out. I knelt in the snow and packed ice around the inflamed knees, hoping to reduce the swelling. It relieved some pain, but the constancy of walking ensured that the electric shocks soon returned.

Hour after hour on into the night I staggered towards my isolated destination. It was 10 pm when I arrived, but there was nothing more than a solitary wind-swept service station. With a foot of snow everywhere pitching my tent wasn't desirable. The service station workers had their photos taken with me, but no one offered assistance. They apologetically pointed out the two nearest hotels, roughly thirty-five kilometres in either direction. With nothing available I put my head down and fumbled on into the night for an in-total seventy-two kilometres to Safonovo.

I made a few more quiet snow pit stops, gingerly kneeling to apply ice, and while there asked God for some extra help. I staggered on down the darkened empty road, thankful that within a few minutes the worst seized knee freed up somewhat and I was able to increase my pace for a while.

Over the many hours that followed I gradually slowed again and my body ached. By 3 am I was a walking corpse. I didn't know if I was hungry, tired, in pain or … whatever. I was at a point I'd never been before, or since. I wanted the pain to stop any way possible and I needed sleep. My knees seized tight again and the pain around my Achilles tendons was energy-sapping. I couldn't bend any of the four joints and had to push harder through the poles to take the weight off my feet until my arms succumbed to the burning workload.

Snow whipped in from the west, sticking to me, and the side exposed to the blustery sleet numbed. On two occasions I simply couldn't go any further. I stopped and stared off to the side, fighting myself to not lie down in the thick soft snow to curl up and sleep. I knew that if I did I'd more than likely slip into an icy coma and not wake up. I couldn't walk on though. I just stood there for ten minutes on that abandoned road staring at the cotton-like snow, weighing up whether it was worth the pain to continue on or to just … lie … down. I didn't want either. I just stared at the snow and cried, pleading with God to grant me the strength to walk on.

I felt a sense of acceptance …

… that I could accept lying in the snow to die …

… but …

… with all the purpose I could muster … I turned and faced the road again.

With one feeble stiff-legged step after the other, I continued on into the sleet with electric shocks snapping at me. I was so exhausted that I began falling asleep while on my feet. Each sleepy head-nod was jolted back into reality with the next knee shock.

I wanted to lie down and let go.

I stopped a second time, staring at the soft snow with glazed eyes. I prayed: "God, I don't want to be here. Please." Surely it wasn't beyond Him to send a random Good Samaritan to pick me up. In my mind's eye though I glimpsed a bloodied Christ draw alongside, struggling under the weight of the cross. He looked over and, without a word spoken, the glance said, "Thank you for being here with me," and He continued on.

I was smashed.

The real question was whether I was with Him, not the other way around. He was likely already walking that journey and feeling more pain than I ever could. The pain of a broken Church; his body would be unescapable. His love for those who were isolated, abandoned or separated from him couldn't allow him to escape it. There was no lying down. I stumbled on.

Right on 4:01 am I caught the first glimpse of Safonovo. I didn't smile, or cry, or react much at all. I just staggered towards the light and at long last was able to escape the sleet at a roadside hotel. I lowered myself into bed in agony. The soles of my feet had lost all circulation and turned a ghostly white. They felt like there was no skin, just exposed flesh. My hips felt like they had nails driven into them and my knees and Achilles tendons burst with electric shocks. It was gut-wrenching.

By 10 am I still hadn't fallen asleep so I stood back up, grabbed hold of anything I could and limped into a hot shower. After breakfast, I still couldn't sleep so I methodically pulled those ratty boots back on and wandered out into the cold day searching for internet or a phone. Again I, found neither. I pushed on out to the other side of town and down the highway, not in first gear, nor overdrive. I have no idea what gear I was jammed in but it felt like somewhere between unconscious and dead. After seventy-two kilometres, and without sleep, I walked another horrible eighteen to a second motel in tiny Vyshegor. I fell asleep there for nearly twelve hours straight.

The need to sleep had outweighed the pain.

Yartsevo was only four hours' walk the next morning, so I took my time, but there were isolating moments out there, resting on the edge of the frozen forest trying to un-seize my knee. When I did arrive in Jarcevo there was little to see but tall pines shielding everything except for an Orthodox church spire well inland. I wandered through the forest along a snow-covered firebreak hoping to find it. With stiff legs I nearly upended on the slippery track before emerging in the open spaces surrounding the beautiful church.

I tentatively knocked and a solid man with a neat black beard opened up. I introduced myself in Russian and showed him my letters of recommendation, but he pushed them back and said (in English with a thick accent), "Hang on, my son speak English very well. Come in." His son, Alexi, translated everything and at last I was welcomed into a home to stay the night. Fr Vasil, his wife and the teenage son Alexi welcomed me with open arms. We attended the vigil service and it felt like I was finally at home and in comfort. The singing was heavenly and the architecture, portraits of the saints, and opportunity to pray with the small community life-giving.

Over the next day Fr Vasil and his wife fed me more food than I think I'd eaten for the entire week. He'd been a soldier in the Soviet army, but when communism collapsed he handed his rifle back and headed straight to the seminary. After the Sunday morning service we were drawn into a heavy conversation about the state of the world before he paused and commented, "Ausdralia, you have new government." To my surprise he knew about our Federal elections and Kevin Rudd's Labor Government being voted in.

"Yes, we have," I replied.

He lifted his chin, "They are communist!"

I laughed, "No, no, they're Labor."

He leant forward with a wry smile, "Da! Communist!"

I couldn't stop laughing. I had plenty of friends back home who couldn't have agreed more. Fr Vasil asked if I needed to check my email so I was at last able to log on. My smile was drained by a progression of emails detailing the ill health of my Nan, whom we called Mumma, then her deterioration, then one asking me to call home immediately because she'd passed away and another letting me know how beautiful the funeral was. The emails spanned four or five days and each ended with, "Please call home as soon as you can." I didn't even need to ask for the phone. Fr Vasil was watching and asked, "How is your family?" As soon as I explained what I'd just read he picked up the phone, placed it in front of me and said sternly, "Call your mother."

I spoke to Mum for some time. Mumma had passed away silently with most of the family at her side and there had been growing concern that they might bury a second family member after my no-replies to the succession of emails at a time when they knew the Russian winter had turned ugly. I chose not to tell Mum at that point that I was also developing a heart arrhythmia. The week and a half from Moscow to Yartsevo was for so many reasons the longest yard. Fr Vasil's hospitality was a refuge in a frozen country.

My knee's mobility increased slightly and I was able to walk and pray westwards to the outskirts of Smolensk city. There was no ATM and my zip-lock moneybag was running low. I chose not to disclose to anyone back home that I was running out of savings, not just money in the zip-lock bag. I had only A$108 left in the bank with the ability to cover roughly one more week before needing to make that final withdrawal. I was still 5,000 kilometres from the Atlantic Ocean. There were people in Australia who would have bailed me out if they knew I was broke, but the mission had never been about sponsoring, so I decided to walk on in prayer for as long as I could, extending the invitation to pray for unity to everyone I met and, if I ran out of money, so be it. Adolfo still nagged at me. How could I ask to access all that money when he had to fight so hard for his? If the mission was to reach Spain then God would have to provide either financially or through incredible hospitality. After all, it was His walk, not mine.

With the temperature hovering above freezing I removed my gloves and enjoyed some mild conditions through the snow-covered countryside while praying a rosary. I was meditating on the sorrowful mysteries, in particular Christ's docility before his aggressors, when I approached a quiet intersection. On the opposite side of the road, in the snow-covered section between the overpass and off ramp, two men were thumping each other senseless. The men, one dressed in black and the other in an orange jacket, traded blows, one head shot after the other. I was amazed that they remained standing. The man in the orange jacket pushed away and ran up the highway towards me while the man-in-black stumbled backwards, turned and sprinted up the highway exit slope.

Orange-jacket walked past briskly on the other side, trying to thumb a ride. I shouted out to him to see if he was okay, and he half-acknowledged it, but kept moving … fast. I walked on and looked up the side of the intersection to see the man-in-black hurtling back down the snow-covered hill with a friend in tow. My heart sank. I was wearing a reddish orange jacket. The two men locked in on me and sprinted through the snow. I had no way of explaining that I was the wrong man. Please, thank you, and fish weren't useful words to know at the moment. They ground to a halt at the highway due to some traffic and at that point noticed the other fellow half a kilometre away. They were visibly confused and stood there deep in discussion.

I walked on fast.

They must have decided that I was an easier target because the first guy just shrugged his shoulders and ran towards me, firing questions as they came. I kept walking. One walked up alongside and the other walked backwards in front of me. I couldn't understand a single word they said and explained that I didn't speak Russian. Even so, I could tell that, whatever they were asking, it wasn't after my health …

I held both walking poles in my left hand, with the straps firmly around my wrist, and prepared to protect myself with the right. They stopped me from walking and, after a quick discussion, it actually looked like they were going to leave me alone, until the fellow in front nodded to the other and they lunged at me.

It was on.

Front-man tried to reef the poles from me while Blind-side-Charlie grabbed my backpack straps and pulled hard with one hand, and punched me with the other. I had a firm grip on the poles with the straps around my wrist so I struggled with Front-man in a frantic tug-o-war until I managed to grab him around the throat. Blind-side-Charlie couldn't get a grip on the backpack and got too close at one point so I thrust my right hand out and grabbed him around the throat as well, pushing him out at arms-length. I had a Russian in both hands. He took a few solid swings as I choked him, but I'm 6' 5" and he wasn't so he couldn't land a punch because of my wingspan. Front-man slipped from my grip and yanked hard on the poles, while Charlie clawed at my hand trying to release my grip. His nails ripped skin off in chunks.

I yelled desperately for help to a few passing cars, but no one was about to stop to be a part of this. Charlie twisted in closer, exhaling his vodka-breath on me while grabbing the backpack chest strap in a desperate swipe. The chest strap ripped clean off and he fell back. I released his throat and grabbed him in a headlock, dropping him to my hip. Front-man changed tactics and moved further up the poles to my hands. He tried to simultaneously punch me with one hand and claw my hand away from the poles with the other. All I could do to keep him at bay was kick hard. His right hooks missed their mark, but his clawing thumbnail pierced straight through the webbing between my thumb and index finger.

Blind-side-Charlie swung a few wild punches so I rammed my right knee up into his chest a few of times: he became more defensive. It was my chance to go on the attack with Front-man, so I kicked out hard a couple of times, dropping him to his knees. He still wouldn't let go of the poles. I raised my heavy walking boot and stomped forward onto his shoulder, but Charlie went back on the offensive at that moment and knocked me off balance, causing my boot to crack down fair on his friend's head, making a sickening sound. He still didn't let go. I gave Charlie another sharp knee to the chest and yelled at Front-man to let go of the poles. He pulled again so I raised my foot once more: "Let go!" And stomped hard on his right shoulder. He crumpled backwards with such force that both poles snapped clean in half sending me staggering in the opposite direction. In one motion, I let go of Charlie and sprinted off down the road with partially seized knees and Achilles tendons. "Who cares? Run!"

Charlie snatched the broken poles from his downed friend and sprinted after me, lashing out with the broken poles trying to hit me. I was wearing a backpack and he was really unfit, so it was kind of an even race down the side of the road. After the initial scramble sprint I breathed in deeply, leant forward and ran hard. It turns out that a twelve kilogram backpack is less of a hindrance than vodka.

He fell further behind and eventually pulled up. He must have realised that his friend was still down so he jogged back to help.

I stopped to catch my breath and pulled the camera out to film. It was a struggle to say anything as I zoomed in on them. Front-man was helped to his feet and I have to say I was thankful to see him get up. I thought I'd broken his collarbone.

While I was explaining to my recording camera what had just happened, a third guy came barrelling down the hill, also dressed in black, but with a bottle of vodka in hand and whistling out to the other two guys because he wanted in on the fight. I turned and ran with the vodka-man (let's call him Smirnoff...) chasing me down the other side of the road.

As much as Smirnoff wanted to fight me, he obviously didn't want to do it alone. The other two had already turned around and headed home. Smirnoff stopped, cursed me across the busy road, and went back the way he'd come.

As painful as it was to run with the injuries I had, I put in a solid 400 metres before becoming asthmatic and needing to slow down. I was paranoid that they'd go home, grab a weapon, and jump in a car to come after me. I was on edge. I hastily made my way along the highway cutting through thick snow-covered forest. My plan was simple: stay on the opposite side of the road to cars approaching from their direction and, if they do come back, hit the forest. If all three had polished off some vodka they'd be next to useless in a snow-clad forest and if they had weapons the trees would provide some protection.

I was still firmly holding the walking pole handles. When I held them up to examine them, blood dripped off. The webbing between my thumb and index finger was torn open and blood ran across a Christmas Canadian smiley-face sticker the Quists had given me.

I passed a police car parked on the side of the road and tried to explain what had happened, but they just shrugged me off nonchalantly and drove away. I walked on for hours, nervously checking over my shoulder before finally spotting a petrol station up ahead. At that moment a bus drove past and in the front seat was Front-man staring straight out at me. Or was it Smirnoff? To my horror the bus indicator then flicked on. My heart thumped. "The petrol station or the forest?" It had to be a quick decision and I chose civilisation over vegetation.

I put my head down and ran harder than ever. The bus drew to a halt ahead of me. I didn't know if I'd make it before he disembarked and crossed over, but I was sure going to try. As I careered along I was panicked to realise that the stand-alone petrol station was still under construction! It was empty!

I frantically kept running down the road and looked over to see the man jump off the bus, look across at me and then walk off down a dirt track in the other direction. It wasn't him. It was a random guy dressed in black with the same shaved head. I slowed down while watching him wander off. But, just as my breathing calmed down, three men in black burst from the forest along the same track, fixated on me. "This time we're on for real!" The bus was taking off so I sprinted after it and, as I started to gain on it, I looked over my shoulder to see the three men pull up a seat on the other side of the road, laughing with each other and cracking open a drinking thermos.

It wasn't them either.

This was like being in a horror movie. Everyone looked the same. They all wore black clothes and had shaved heads. Everyone was a threat.

I limped down the road trying to recompose myself with prayer. What played on my mind was that at the very moment I was attacked I'd been praying about Christ's docility before his aggressors. There was a point during the fight where I had both men at arm's length and the thought went through my mind, "This is not what Jesus did!" I had the strength to fend off two drunk Russians, but I didn't have the strength to not fight back: to remain silent under persecution. "Lead us not into temptation" suddenly meant a whole lot more.

In the following weeks people commented that I had every right to defend myself. I agreed, but the point was that I realised that Christ did too. He had the right to defend himself and could've done so, but chose not to. I wasn't strong enough to do that. I'd caught a glimpse of how difficult it was to not fight back. Costa Rica was easier: the baddies had knives and other lives were on the line, and if I were honest in answering the question, "What would you do if the Russian fight happened again?" the answer would be, "Probably the same thing." I had a long way to go before I could be strong enough to surrender everything.

Many Christians were similar, fighting back against each other, launching their next defensive attack, but neglecting love while claiming they were loving because truth was on their side. The duty of standing in and for truth while loving with humility hasn't been a strong point for many Christians.

"Lord, please lead us not into temptation."

With blood-soaked hands, and without walking poles, I continued on to a truck stop hostel. I'd lost the ability to move my left hand, which ached from all the yanking on the poles while the straps were wrapped around. I couldn't even undo my bootlaces. If it weren't for a compassionate Lithuanian truck driver I would've sat on my bed for a long time. He removed my boots and fetched medical supplies for my ripped hands. I thanked God for him.

A powdering of fresh snow fell that evening, making the roads slippery; without poles, it was a cautious hobble past the ridiculous line up of traffic marking the Belarusian border. Through the snowy mist I spotted the compassionate Lithuanian driver pulling into one of the many queues. I hoped to walk past and say, "Good morning," but before I could a woman pulled in behind him just as he began reversing to move over a lane. She'd stopped too close and he couldn't see her. The reverse lights flashed on and even though there was nothing behind her she hit the horn rather than reversing and with truck drivers standing off to the side running to stop the impending accident he crushed the front of her car. I felt horrible for both of them. He jumped out to the abuse of other truckies and absolutely copped it from the woman. There was no fight in him. I watched from afar as he raised his hands to his head in anguish while apologising and disappeared to sort it all out.

The border wasn't as neatly set up as any other I'd crossed and I was at a loss as to where to go. While trying to figure it out a voice cried out, "You made it!" Standing off to the side was Gabriel, the Polish man I'd met the previous week. He was a welcome point of familiarity and pointed me in the right direction.

I approached a soldier standing in the middle of the road and he asked sternly, "Documents." This was the moment of truth. I reached for my passport, but he shooed it away and said, "No. Papers!" I pulled out the documentation I'd received and he flicked through it expressionlessly, then looked back up, handed them back and said, "Enjoy your walk." And that was that. I was in. No visa in my passport or a stamp.

I missed my poles as I limped on. Booking in for the night at an isolated motel also proved difficult. The woman at the counter waved off my passport, so I tentatively produced the documents. She smiled, "Da, pazhalsta," and flicked through them, writing as she went. She struggled to find some answers and had to search diligently, but in the end I was invited in to enjoy the clean and warm motel. It took some time to untie my laces one handed. It'd take even longer to undo the introduced psychological conditioning and physical ailments.

*If anyone strikes you on the cheek, offer the other also; and from anyone who takes away your coat do not withhold even your shirt.*

Luke 6:29

Total walked: *10,373 kilometres*

# Heart Arrhythmia, the KGB & a Twilight Pursuit
*February 2008*

Dull sleeting conditions enveloped the open, undulating countryside of the anti-western 'outpost of tyranny for the axis of evil' dictatorship. That's a mouthful. The old Russian secret police, the KGB, were still active in Belarus, and the government took an interest in more than just taxes. I was nervous about being in a country where the leader wanted to reunite with Russia to form another communist super power, but I was also intrigued by what had been described as one of the unhappiest nations on earth.

Four middle-aged men deep in conversation stood beside a parked car out in the countryside and they didn't see me approaching until I was close enough for them to hear my crunching boots. They swung around, looking me up and down, and three of them peeled backed against the car leaving one standing firm with a smile. The others remained pan-faced and watched the one smiling at me. It was an uncomfortable setting.

Like a politician on campaign the smiling man greeted me and tried to communicate, asking where I was headed. When I said, "To Minsk," he shook his finger and pointed back the way I'd come, saying, "No, no. Minsk." It was the first time I'd been in Belarus in my life, but I was sure I was headed west, and that Minsk was in the centre of the country. I disagreed and pointed westwards, "No, Minsk." The three men standing behind him all shook their heads and pointed back towards the border, "Minsk, Minsk." I was bemused. I wasn't carrying a map because I'd studied the country on the internet before crossing over and memorised the road systems and location of the cities I'd be travelling to, but I wasn't only sure that I was right, I was adamant. There was something no-good about them. I pointed to myself, then down the road, indicating that I was walking west and wished them all a good day. "Okay," said the main guy as I moved on, shaking his hand and nodding to the other three.

It was only then that I caught a split second glimpse between the three men into the car they shielded. It dragged on dauntingly slowly. Draped across the back seat was a man's body, propped up in an unusual fashion. At the very least he looked unconscious, but likely deceased. I didn't bring attention to what I'd seen as that head nod concluded and I walked on with eyes wide open. I regularly checked back over my shoulder.

When I'd started in Brazil, unity had seemed pretty straightforward; pray and work for truth. I'd encountered so many areas of fracture now that it was hard to know where to start. That likely place seemed to be the unity of the family. It's a bit rich to expect unity on a global scale while having massively disjointed family structures. I zeroed in on what looked like the darkest division on the dignity of the family—being abortion—and thought through each argument I've ever heard from both sides, trying to understand why that dark place was permitted, if not encouraged as a responsible option. In the end I just couldn't understand why society widely accepted the intervention of the process of life that had been set in motion in order to cut our selves off from the life developing in the womb. It was the silent, ugly side of disunity in all its fullness: "My life must continue as unaltered as possible, therefore your life must not develop at all."

Night came well before I'd finished and my feet, hips and knees deteriorated. I found accommodation in a lonely run-down two-storey building in a snow-covered field, which was unlocked for me by a cook at a nearby roadside kitchen. It was rickety and the warped wooden floor looked close to condemnation, but the room was mine ... as eerie as it was.

At the end of the next day's forty kilometre stretch, through sleeting rain, I detoured slightly to the south to a town called Talachyn and their evening Orthodox service. I was unable to grab the priest before he left but a nun, who was a little stand-offish, accepted the invitation to pray for unity and offered to pass it on to the priest.

I hobbled along the darkened icy street slipping a number of times. Pain rifled up through my knees and hips. I stopped in agony at one point and looked off to the side through the window of a small house where a family had gathered around the dinner table with beautiful food everywhere. It was difficult to walk on.

At the large gostinitsa, my documents were again scoured with suspicion before I was permitted to stay. The bed was tiny and had an enormous bed-end which meant there was no chance of hanging my legs off. After a hot shower and a cold supermarket dinner I curled up and tried to sleep but, after so much walking, I needed to stretch out and although I hadn't cramped during the entire journey I felt my legs begin to twitch.

Over the past week, my heart had skipped a few beats—almost like a spasm—and although it was a concern, it was relatively painless. I figured that for what I was putting my body through it was inevitable. That night in Talachyn my heart struggled. It spasmed, stopped for a fleeting second and then restarted time and time again. Sometimes there was hardly any time between spasms and for the first time I was seriously anxious. It worsened during the night to the point where I wondered if my last hour was near. I laid there helpless and scared as it continued to stop beating. I was so exhausted as it dragged on until at around 1 am I asked God to take care of me, ignored it as best as I could, and shut my eyes in an attempt to sleep.

My heartbeat was normal when I awoke, but I felt disgusting. It was a quiet and steady-paced day for the sombre thirty-nine kilometres to Krupki; I passed memorials and graves of those killed during World War II.

When I passed a tiny group of homes a solidly built young man with shaved blonde hair walked down his driveway to greet me. He smiled and in English asked, "Where are you from?" Pavel was a veterinarian who'd worked in England for a year and he invited me in to have lunch with his mum. He'd returned to Belarus for her when his father passed away.

Their home was small and each room looked like it had been extended onto the next using any material available. He apologised for their run-down house, which had something to do with the government's rules making it difficult to renovate. He spoke at length about the persecution of the Church and how only Russian Orthodoxy was encouraged, but even they were highly scrutinised. He laughed about a mural painted in a church nearby though. One of the faces leering out of hell was that of Lukashenko, the President. The artist swore that he didn't paint it and was ordered to paint over the face, which he did to the KGB's approval but, the next morning when the church re-opened, it was exactly as it had been before. This happened a few times over and there were a lot of little old women claiming it was a prophetic miracle. Whether the locals thought it was a miracle or not, they certainly didn't disagree with its sentiment. Lukashenko, the chicken farmer-cum-President, had sucked the happiness out of many lives.

I was thankful that the country's anti-western policies hadn't filtered through to its people. The Belarusians were actually one of the most patient and helpful people to date. I was stunned by their willingness to at least try and communicate. They were humble people in an oppressed country.

Spring was drawing near and my injuries were healing. My left hand was loosening up, so too my knees; a scar was forming neatly between the thumb and index finger, and the sun was out. I'd missed it. It revealed a hint of green through the melting snow.

I searched for churches and hotels along the Barysaw main road, but found neither, so I cut across a few side streets to the city centre. I stopped for a few minutes to help a mum and her two daughters pluck their kitten from a tree, and under mother's orders the girls led me on to the town's gostinitsa. Unlike at the other gostinitsas, the woman at the front desk couldn't find the information she needed, and kept asking for my visa. She was confused, which in turn confused me. She finally fudged the transaction and I was in.

It was time to make my final ATM withdrawal. I had roughly only another two weeks before I was bust. With young couples laughing and chatting their way along the main street in the twilight I stood at the ATM, took a deep breath, prayed, "I trust you Lord," and keyed in my pin. The transfer went through and the cash was dispensed. That was it. Two weeks to go. I looked down at the receipt and mumbled, "What? That can't be right?" I stared at the receipt. It read, 'Available Balance: $5,746.68'.

I was dumbfounded.

"Okay, God, so we're finishing this walk thing then?" I had no idea where the money had come from.

Arrangements had been made for me to stay that night with a Canadian couple living in Minsk by the names of Dan and Rose. I needed to cover a whopping seventy-five kilometres to reach their home. It was well into the night and I'd only covered fifty-six kilometres. Even though they had said they didn't mind waiting up for me all night, I didn't want to abuse their hospitality, so I caught a bus and hoped to return to complete the leg the next day. Dan and Rose had organised for me to meet a few people in Minsk and a rendezvous in the next town the coming day, so as frustrating as it was to not walk that lost nineteen kilometres, it had to take second place to the mission.

It was bliss to extend the mission from Dan and Rose's apartment without leaving the building. A beautiful young woman by the name of Olga translated for me when a large group arrived to meet me and she did a pretty good job. When I thanked everyone for coming and asked for their prayers in fluent Belarusian, Olga wasn't expecting it and without thinking twice turned to the group and translated everything back into English for them, much to her embarrassment.

She laughed it off and grabbed another drink.

I was eventually on my way to Dzyarzhynsk (which is easier said than spelt) to stay the night with Dan and Rose's friends who lived in a typical communist block of flats with little room or convenience. They had four children, with whom I shared the only bedroom, while the mum and dad slept out on a foldout couch. Their offer of hospitality was remarkable. The kids were classic, ranging from one to ten years of age. The one-year-old, Matthew, spent most of his time giving his food to the pet dog and then taking equal portions back from the dog's scraps. The second youngest ate half my dessert while my back was turned and the third had a tendency to smile and then punch me in the groin. It was chaos. I appreciated their generosity, though I was a little sore by the end.

I continued southeast. The temperature was hitting 7°C and green grass was breaking through, but the peace didn't last long. Along a heavily trafficked country road I caught a glimpse of two men dressed in black running through the forest off to the side. They were deep within the forest, flashing in and out of view as I walked on. A cleared field between two pockets of forest allowed me to clearly watch the distant shadowy figures dash across the gap. The country road suddenly felt very isolated.

A minute later the two young men burst from the forest twenty metres behind me and when I swung around they stopped running, acting as normal as they could. I picked up my walking pace with another quick shoulder check to see them running flat out, but again immediately slowed to a walk and pretend to be just 'out for a stroll'.

"Great," I thought, "I'm about to be rolled by two twits."

Catching up to me they flanked out on either side, much like the two Russians did. I didn't stop walking and didn't stop praying. They asked if I had a cigarette, for which the answer was no, but then asked if I was carrying any money. They were slightly ahead of me, so I stopped dead so they'd turn to face me. I said firmly, "Go home." They were in their mid-to-late teens, one was half my size and weight, while the other looked like he could pack a punch. What made him a scarier prospect was that when I told them to go home he reached for something tucked into the back of his trousers.

I backed away, walked off to the side and around them, keeping the smaller guy between us. They hounded and ridiculed me for the next kilometre. The bigger guy walked up to within a metre and his eyes lit up as his right hand slid back to grab what I presumed to be a knife. I put my head down and ran. It was tempting to stand and fight, but I wanted to avoid confrontation and have a better conclusion than the previous week. Running flat out down the edge of the road with the two guys excitedly giving chase was the order of the day. Unlike the Russians, they were sober and kept up without too much effort. After a good 400 metres I slowed down with them right on my tail. I hoped I'd have better endurance than them. Just as they caught up and slowed to a jog behind me, I launched straight back into another four-hundred. They yelled out and again started chasing. As they bore down on me I pulled to a sudden stop and fronted up as though to fight. They shot out to both sides, cowering away.

I turned and ran again.

The young men caught up fast, but this time came at me with extra pace. I dropped my body weight down, grinding to a sudden stop and doubled back between them. A line of traffic was just about to pass so I raced out across the road, cutting us off from one another as the cars raced past, and I ran on down the opposite side. The two men ran on ahead, laughing at me and mocking the situation by over-exaggerating their running styles while calling back over their shoulders.

A break in the traffic gave them the opportunity to cross over, but they were too busy watching the traffic in the other direction that they didn't notice me also cross back over. We ran across the centre line at the exact same time, thirty metres apart, and when they made the other side and looked up to see me walking back down the side they'd just come from they weren't quite as jovial. I gave them a big smile as the traffic split us again, but that only incensed them. We ran on.

At the next chance the two men split, but the big guy stayed where he was and the little guy ran back to my side ahead of me. They resumed their mocking jibes as they walked back towards me. I couldn't believe that the smaller weapon-less guy was the one on my side! They thought they'd checkmated me. I slowed to a jog, but a small line of traffic approached and I took the opportunity with both hands. The bigger guy was stranded on the other side as I tightened my backpack straps and launched into a sprint straight at the little fellow. His smile vanished. My premise was simple; "If you stay where you are it'll hurt you more than me." He frantically jumped aside and allowed me to run on down the road.

The big guy ran across at the next chance and the chase was back on in earnest. A rock whooshed past me at hip height, crashing down the road ahead of me. I shoulder-checked to see the little guy scoop down on the run to pick up another stone just as the big guy let fly without breaking stride. I flinched back around, ducking my head while running on and the stone bulleted into the middle of my backpack, splitting a huge hole in the waterproof cover. It thumped around for a while before dropping out at my ankles mid stride. The poor old backpack was really in the wars. Rocks whizzed past without finding their mark, plus a few solid sticks until, at last, the barrage ceased and they finally gave up. It had taken nearly three kilometres to break them. It was four kilometres before I stopped.

My injured legs had turned to jelly and my heart felt like a big lump of concrete as I walked on towards Stoubcy. Suddenly, another young man dressed in black shot out from behind a row of small trees directly in front of me. Everyone wore the same black clothes! We reacted sharply away from each other, having scared each other half to death. He ran on across the road apologising.

"Yeah, no worries."

Once again, a lady at a gostinitsa had trouble finding the necessary details in my documents. She wasn't happy that I didn't have a visa in my passport and didn't smile once. While showing me to my room she nervously kept her distance, keeping her eyes low. I made myself at home in the twin single-bed room, throwing my gear on one and sitting on the other with my dinner, but after only a few bites there was a knock at the door. It was the woman again, but accompanied by a man in a three-piece suit. I innocently presumed he was occupying the other bed, so I just let him in and apologised while clearing off my gear. He stepped into the room, closed the door and sat in the room's only chair directly opposite me as I picked my dinner back up. He fired questions at me. With my fork half raised to my mouth I looked up at him thinking, "Damn it, he's not here for the bed." The Suit continued firing questions, so I interjected with an apology, "Sorry, I don't speak Belarusian." He wasn't happy with that and after a short pause he showed his frustration with some sort of slander at me.

Suit sneered at me, "Passport." I placed my plastic fork down and grabbed the passport and documents. He pulled out a black book and wrote down all the possible information he could find before asking to see any other documentation I carried. I handed over my itinerary and insurance, and then sat patiently for ten minutes while he flicked through them. Looking back up at me he asked in English, "What is your purpose for being here?" I explained, but he just flicked on through my little notebook and copied over the addresses of people I'd met along the journey. He then asked how many people made up my family, their ages and occupations.

The guy was intimidating and looked official, but I hadn't seen any identification so I spoke over the top of him as he asked for more information saying, "Sorry, but I don't know who you are. Do you have identification?" He stopped writing, glanced up and said nonchalantly, "Yes," and proceeded to ask another question regarding my notebook. I reached forward and took it from him, asking again, "I want to see your I.D. first." That ticked him off to no end! With a look of total disdain he flicked open his identification. I gulped. He was a Belarusian soldier in a three-piece suit. That pointed pretty heavily to the KGB. At least I knew, so I handed the notebook back.

A nerve-racking thirty minutes passed before he handed my personal affects back, packed up his briefcase, smiled for a tenth of a second and thanked me.

"So, is everything okay?" I asked.

He replied with an expressionless, "Yes", and left me sitting on the end of my bed. I glanced over at the stone-cold dinner, but I'd lost my appetite.

It was a nervous sleep not knowing why he'd come or if he'd be back with other soldiers. Also … I didn't fit the bed—again. I started out at sunrise on a beautiful day. I visited the Orthodox church, where the invitation was received well, and got out of there as fast as I could.

After a knee-busting fifty-nine kilometres to Baranavichy, I thought I'd found refuge in a large hotel there, but I woke in the morning to an ominous view. From the sixth-storey window I looked down at a division of the Belarus army on display in the city centre, lined up in companies, parading just like I'd seen in documentaries about the old Soviet military displays. I again didn't hang around. I ate breakfast and headed out along a quiet country road, away from the military.

The next town was a whopping seventy-three kilometres away, so I'd stocked up on food supplies and walked on with the intention of thumbing a lift in either direction at sundown and then returning in the morning to continue on. The country road to Ivatsevichy was one phenomenally straight road cutting through a massive forest with no civilisation whatsoever. A solitary car drove past every twenty minutes or so; sometimes the emptiness of that road was all consuming. The likelihood of hitching a ride at day's end was minimal. The various possibilities of what to do at the end of the day ran through my mind, but I wasn't particularly keen on any of them.

I'd made it difficult for myself to cover the whole seventy-three kilometres in a day by leaving late, and camping in my tent wasn't appetising with wolves, wild boars and the last wild bison herds calling that forest home. I wasn't sure if I was out of brown bear territory yet, but I added that to the list too.

I kept my headlamp tucked into the backpack's belt pocket for easy access at day's end, but when I reached for a muesli bar I discovered I no longer had it. Both pocket's zips had broken and the lamp had escaped. I didn't like that.

At sunset I tried to thumb a ride but, after two hours and only five cars, I was left stranded in the darkness. The sky clouded over blocking out any moonlight. It was complete blackout. I couldn't see the edge of the road, the road signs or even my hand in front of my face. It made no difference if I walked with my eyes open or shut. I felt my way down the road keeping bitumen under foot as strange sounds emanated from the forest.

The one tool I eventually realised I did possess was the camera with its infrared night vision setting. It didn't allow me to see much, but its five-metre range was enough to correct my path, find signs at intersections and check strange forest sounds. Without poles, my hands were free to hold the camera the whole time, though I used it sparingly to conserve the battery. That little screen was my lifeline to sanity.

I couldn't remove myself from the darkness or make it safe by flicking a switch. It was one intense test of trust to just keep calm and put one foot in front of the other. I prayed and I sang praise songs, both as prayer and to ward off anything I couldn't see ... which was everything. My ears worked overtime.

After nearly four hours of blind walking I considered praying for it all to be over, but instead prayed for just a little comfort as I continued on. Two minutes later there was a big flash of light to my left and then another. I'd walked up alongside a huge clearing stretching a kilometre through the forest to the M1 Freeway. It was a beautiful sight. Still unable to see a single thing I flipped the LCD screen open and painstakingly guided my every step through the overgrown, tussock riddled clearing for the thousand-odd metres to the freeway.

Prayers of thanks and a big sigh of relief accompanied stepping up onto it as car headlights flashed past every few seconds. Without even contemplating hitching a ride I continued on. I had the comfort I'd requested. I wasn't sure where I'd end up, so I just kept praying for over twenty kilometres. It became the most painful walking since the icy seventy-two kilometres in Russia. The hours dragged on, the traffic thinned out and the lights of my destination still weren't in view. I checked my watch to see how I was doing. It was 12:20 am. I smiled. The passing of midnight had ushered in the 10th of February and I was now twenty-nine years old. "Happy birthday to me."

Pretty soon I was forced to stop every few hundred metres to rest my back and hip until the pain subsided. I missed my poles so much, and new ones were non-existent in Minsk. Every step became a forced action.

By 3 am I'd covered the full seventy-three kilometres—teeth-gritted—to Ivatsevichy. I couldn't find the town's hotel and just wanted the day to be over when, at 3:30 am, a man strolled casually down the street and came to my aid with a smile. He led the way to an unsigned hotel, thumped on the thick-glassed window of the modern complex and yelled for them to open up. I was shocked at first, but then so grateful, because I wouldn't have done it and pretty soon a sleepy young lady appeared at the door with half a smile and let me in. The gentleman shook my hand and walked off. Thank you sir, whoever you are. I booked in for two nights and celebrated my 29th birthday with a rest and an ice cream.

I was moderately okay after a rest day and plodded on down the country road across dead flat fenceless plains to Biaroza. I was the only customer at a small grocery there, so the three women serving happily chatted away in Belarusian trying to figure out who I was. They were excited to have an Australian in the store and even more so when they heard about the mission. They pointed to an icon of Jesus sitting above the counter, happy to share their common faith and to receive the invitation to pray for unity. I was also happy to receive a box of chocolates as a parting gift.

It was fifty-eight kilometres further down to Kobryn followed by another day's walk to Brest. Every time I stopped to rest all I wanted was a hot shower and bed. It was the first week of Lent though, so it gave me something to let go of. I walked on praying, "Lord, please unite all Christians in truth and in love, for the glory of your name and for the salvation of souls. And please bless Pope Benedict XVI, the Archbishop of Canterbury, the Patriarchs of the Eastern Churches, those serving on the World Council of Churches and all the world's Church leaders, with faith, hope, love and wisdom, so that they may better lead us to you, and into unity with one another."

I excitedly left Brest bright and early for the five kilometre walk to the Polish border where I presented myself to a guard. He asked to see my visa, so once again I handed over my documents. The guard flicked through them, then said in broken English, "No, I need visa. Passport!" I slipped my passport through and he opened it up, flicking through. He stared back out at me, "Where is your visa?" I was stumped and pushed my documents back through the window saying, "This is my visa."

He shook his head and said, "No, I translate for you. This is invitation from hotel in Minsk for you to stay with them if you get visa. This is no visa. Is hotel invitation."

I pulled out the receipt from the Belarus visa purchase and pushed it through the window, "But see, I've paid for a Belarus visa and that was what they sent me."

He shook his head, "Sorry, you cannot leave the country without a visa," and he wrote down an address for me saying, "You must return here in Brest to take matter further."

I turned and frustratingly headed back to the city. The address wasn't easy to find and when I did find the large, flat, three-storey building with no signage or doorbell I still wasn't confident I'd arrived at the right place. I knocked a few times without answer, so heaved the massive doors open and entered the cold, sterile, dark and unwelcoming place full of massive leather-padded doors. The posters on the wall indicated it was a police station, but it actually wasn't a police station, it was the police station. It was the southern Belarus' police headquarters.

A policeman strolled through the foyer and, surprised to see me, asked what I needed. I explained myself in broken Belarusian and he understood enough to point me up a tiered staircase. There were still no signs so once I'd arrived at the next floor I was faced with two more closed doors, one to the left and one to the right. It felt like a scene from *The Matrix*. I ran up the next two flights of stairs, but it was exactly the same, and the next set had me emerge on the roof. I wandered back down and figured I'd just walk through a door and take a punt.

An English-speaking passport officer greeted me and asked what the problem was. I described my journey, showed him my documents, receipts and passport, and explained why I was now sitting in front of him. He flicked through everything and then peered up without raising his head, "You are in very big trouble." I wasn't sure if that meant I was going to prison or being flown home, but I figured that at least I'd get a bed for the night. The four pages of documentation were indeed requests for a visa from a Minsk hotel.

I was left alone to ponder how exactly I'd been able to pass through the country without a visa. The officer returned and led me down the hallway to the Chief of Police. Our introduction was short and our conversation similar. He verified my story before asking one simple question, "You just want to leave the country now, yes?"

I nodded humbly: "Yes."

And that was that.

Still none the wiser I was led back to the first officer and asked to hand over my passport, with the added question, "Do you have money? So you can leave Belarus, I give you on-the-spot visa for R$400,000." (about A$200) I'd already forked out a few hundred dollars for a Belarus visa back in the USA, but I agreed.

As the Chief of Police had said, all I wanted to do was get out.

A plain-clothes KGB officer escorted me to the bank to make the withdrawal, which I handed over on the spot and we returned to the headquarters. The first officer set about writing my visa by hand and then pasted it into my passport with a glue stick, adding the finishing touches with a signature. He lightened up somewhat and asked a few personal questions and when I mentioned that my dad owned a Belarus tractor he thought it was brilliant, amazed that a Belarus tractor could make it so far from its birthplace.

With a shake of the hand he wished me well with the mission, but added, "I'm sorry, but you cannot cross the border on foot with this visa. You must take the train." I'd already walked to the border anyway. I was escorted to the train station by the KGB officers, who watched me buy my train ticket, gave me a simple nod and departed.

When I attempted to board the train officers came from everywhere to check my passport and visa, while looking me up and down. I just stood there smiling for half an hour telling myself, "Just act like a hand written visa is perfectly normal." The queue behind me was redirected to other booths as the officers debated something back and forth. It appeared that they became so frustrated in the end with whatever the problem was that they just stamped my passport and told me to get out of the country. I happily obliged with one last, "Da, Pazhalsta."

It was a tediously slow train ride across the border to Terespol and an even longer wait for Polish guards who boarded to process everyone. As an Australian citizen I didn't need a visa for Poland but when the guard finally got to me, he was puzzled. He'd never processed a non-Belarusian and so was looking for a visa. I had the, "Oh please, not again" feeling, but said matter-of-factly, "I'm not required to have a visa for Poland." He called down the carriage to another officer (which reaffirmed that I had a whole new language to learn) and the other officer thought for a moment before yelling back, "Ausdralia? Tuk, no visa." Lesson one; Tuk means yes. The guard relaxed with a grin, stamped my passport and invited me to enjoy my time in Poland.

Only once in Poland did I learn that the crossing of Belarus could've come under a lot more fire than it did. As the weather warmed up I'd removed my jacket revealing the red and white striped soccer shirt over my thermals. I'd inadvertently displayed the banned colours of revolution against the Lukashenko dictatorship. The outlawed red and white stripes normally resulted in arrest. In a country devoid of red and white stripes I hadn't been difficult to spot. "Thank you, Lord …"

I attended Mass at a Catholic church in Terespol and the difference in the people was immediately obvious. The Polish smiled a lot, laughed more and wore colours. I was filled with great anticipation as I walked on towards Biała Podlaska. Winter unexpectedly set in again for ten minutes, slamming me with ice and snow, before the sun broke back out and I walked on smiling.

The priest at a quiet town welcomed me in by marching me next door to the primary school to meet the young English teacher, Kasia, who translated for us. As I extended the invitation to pray for unity the priest nodded in agreement and then happily accepted the mission, offering to pass it on in Mass.

I entertained myself as I pushed on by trying to pronounce the town names. Polish was the most confusing language I'd attempt. I just raised an eyebrow at Piszczac and Ksiazecy Pierwszy. That's just mean.

I was in Biała Podlaska in time for the packed Friday night Mass and, when I grabbed the young parish priest at the end, I was delighted to find that he spoke fluent English. Fr Bogumil was energetic, focussed and straight away inviting me to stay as his guest so that I could meet the youth group.

I had a blast with the parish young adults. Fr Bogumil translated, along with the five or six others who spoke English, and we discussed unity and the need for prayer. They also took on the unenviable task of teaching me Polish and I genuinely tried to learn fast, but the persistent use of 'psh', 'ksh', 'fsh' and 'zsh' made it difficult, especially when used in combination. They laughed repeatedly at my sincere efforts. By the end of the night I'd learnt a number of words and phrases, but at lesson's end one of the girls tried to speak over another while explaining the intricacies of a certain word and drew laughing jeers. Embarrassing her, one of the guys asked me, "Do you know what 'Babar' means?" Everyone roared with laughter. I replied, "Yeah, Babar's the elephant," referring to the books and TV cartoon of the same name. From the extra roar of laughter from Fr Bogumil and the youth group, plus a few girls blushing, I knew I'd answered incorrectly. It turns out 'Babar' means, "An old Woman", not the elephant. It was bad enough that she'd been told she was a nagging old woman, but being referred to as an elephant by the visiting Australian was something she wasn't about to live down easily.

Hearing of the US and Canadian media coverage, Fr Bogumil assured me he'd do what he could to spread the mission. I took it as a nice gesture, but didn't think he'd pull through as significantly as he did ...

The next morning I woke well before sunrise. I did my routine peer out the window to check the weather and was met with a peaceful world of white. It had snowed overnight. Walking alongside the road through snow was tough enough, but the fifty-three kilometres to Radzyn Podlaski without walking poles to propel me and maintain balance made it hideous. It was a long day, but the Radzyn Podlaski priest, much like Fr Bogumil, welcomed me with open arms. This priest didn't speak English and our communication was stifled, but it didn't bother him one bit. As Sunday Mass grew near, he enthusiastically, and surprisingly, invited me to share the mission with the congregation and invite them to pray for unity. With my limited Polish we needed a plan and the priest had one. He spoke fluent Italian so with his "Don't worry about it, we'll get through" mentality we ended up in a bizarre position where I, an English speaker, would speak to the congregation in Spanish, which he'd interpret into Italian and then translate back to Polish. The people laughed when he announced what we were about to attempt. I couldn't believe we were even contemplating it.

It worked a treat. The congregation was with us the whole way, enjoying the show and receiving the invitation with a huge round of applause. Or perhaps they were just applauding because the priest's plan had worked? God bless him.

En route to Lubartów and neighbouring Lublin the thing under my right foot burnt horribly and my left shoulder began to ache. It felt like a knife was jammed up under the shoulder blade. I was constantly readjusting my backpack position. My worn boots had seriously deteriorated but, still, no size sixteen Scarpas could be found, and my waterproof clothes were no longer waterproof. They'd succumbed to the salt spray produced by passing cars sloshing along salted roads in Canada, Russia and Belarus. The bottom of my pants had been eaten away. My backpack was also falling apart: holes grew larger and zips broke.

Poland, however, seemed new: it felt like a country still celebrating its freedom from an oppressive past.

Well, mostly. I knocked on the door of a church beyond Lubartów and after my thirty-second introduction the priest threw the prayer invitation slip in my face and slammed the door. I paused, then finished the sentence I was halfway through and called out, "I take it that's a no?" and walked on.

Members of a Catholic charismatic group in Lublin, called the City on the Hill Covenant Community, had contacted me with an offer of accommodation. I entered the city and was picked up and escorted to a prayer meeting with a lot of energetic young adults before being whisked off to the Lukasik household to sleep. The family's twenty-something daughter, Ella, spoke fluent English. Even better than that was her concern for my ailments and injuries; Ella found everything I needed to rehabilitate. She was a saint.

I spent a rest day in Lublin with Ella and some of her male friends who showed me through the bustling little city to a boutique sports store. At last I was able to purchase new, sturdy walking poles and a new headlamp. I was so happy, and completely amazed when one of the guys stepped in and paid for them all. One of them just smiled and said, "This is our contribution to the invitation to pray for unity."

I walked on from Lublin using the new walking poles out into a cool misty day. Having poles again was like sticking nitrous oxide in a sports car. I motored into a gear I'd forgotten existed.

I'd covered twenty kilometres into the south before being set upon again by three men …

... this time, three smiling journalists. Fr Bogumil had pulled through with a few phone calls and the journalists from the national Catholic magazine had driven over 300 kilometres to find me, looking to spread the call to pray for unity a lot further than my legs could carry it. They were pretty pleased with themselves to have found me.

During our hour-long interview they took a particular interest in the call to pray at 4:01 every day, and in Dino, Adolfo's daughter's toy that still swung from my pack. I'd recounted Adolfo's story a number of times and the feeling of having left behind a guy in need never diminished. As much as they were interested in 'the story', I wondered when the opportunity would come to find 'the man'. At the very least, he was always in my prayers.

When I arrived in accommodation-less Annopol the next day, I was told I could find a hotel fifteen kilometres further on, so I crossed the wide mist-covered Wisła River and walked on into the twilight. The hotel they were referring to was full, so it would be an extra forty-one kilometres to the town of Sandomierz if I wanted a bed. I felt fine, so I walked on.

The narrow country road to Sandomierz was lit by a bright full moon allowing me to see for kilometres ahead. I prayed a rosary and, while contemplating Jesus carrying his cross up Calvary through the persecuting crowd, I was joined along a fence line by a few angry dogs. I thanked God for the help in visualising the ugly path up Calvary, but asked if we could skip the visuals for the crucifixion. Why did I have to joke? A man drove past slowly, pulled over, stepped out of his car and walked straight towards me jabbering in Polish. He stopped me in my tracks, putting his hand on my chest and despite me telling him to back off he just kept rambling.

Once I got a whiff of his toxic vodka breath I felt comfortable in my ability to manoeuvre away from him, but less so in his ability to be rational. In limited English he put his request across for me to drive back to his place for a drink. I declined, but he wouldn't take no for an answer and pleaded, "Please! Pleeease." I explained in Polish what I was doing, but that only made him excited. Now he really wanted me to go back to his house. He wanted to take a photo of me for his friend at the newspaper.

I asked what his name was and he replied, "Thomas".

I shook his hand, raised my eyebrows and said, "Goodnight, Thomas." I walked on. He drove after me. Three kilometres down the road, Thomas flashed past, but it took him a good 200 metres to pull over due to his alcohol-affected reactions. I was in a patient mood so I stepped off the road and sat behind a bush, waiting
for him to either move on or pass out. My shoulderblade ached, so I was happy to take the pack off for a few minutes.

Thomas staggered out of his car looking for me, confused. He hopped back in and turned the car around, driving off slowly. As his taillights disappeared, I walked on across the moonlit countryside stepping off the road out of sight for every random car that came from his direction. I felt like a fugitive on the run.

Thomas didn't come back, but an hour later a new white hatchback driving from the other direction pulled over. I've never seen gangsters driving new white hatchbacks so I felt pretty safe. The driver wound his window down and in perfect English asked, "Do you need help? My friend Thomas called and said you are walking around the world?" Michael was a journalist for the state's newspaper and had all his photography gear sitting on the back seat. I couldn't help but laugh. Thomas actually did want to help. Michael requested an interview the next day and offered me a lift to Sandomierz, but I assured him that it was a nice road to walk along and that the only problem I had was drunken Thomas. He looked at me sharply asking, "He's drunk?" At that very moment Thomas rang on Michael's mobile and Michael ripped into him, "You're drunk! You are. I can't believe you're drunk! You scared him, Thomas! You idiot."

Poor Thomas.

Michael left me to walk on, grimacing from shoulderblade pain and limping from the stinging foot and seizing knee. I arrived in Sandomierz at 1 am and the only car on the road was Michael's. He made sure I was okay and offered a quick tour around 'Poland's oldest town' before dropping me at a hotel. I struggled to stay awake, but it was great nonetheless. One Sandomierz church first opened its doors in the 700s and was still in full use! It was amazing. At 1:30 am Michael dropped

Raphael's photo-portrait of me using his antique camera

me at a hotel saying, "I'll catch you in the morning, sleep well." And I did.

Michael and Raphael, the newspaper's photographer, strolled with me through Sandomierz speaking at length about the mission. We visited the town's churches with a few receiving the invitation, but they were more or less just being polite. Michael was disgruntled by what he perceived as a lack of enthusiasm. I reassured him that it was the same the world over. "Some welcome the mission. Others couldn't care less. In the end, Michael, I'm thankful that you welcomed me. Cheers."

He went the step further of arranging for me to meet privately with the pastor of a Sandomierz church whom he knew was a generous man. In fact Adam was the only person for the week to actually sit down and pray with me.

With Michael's article and Raphael's photo in the paper the next day, I walked on with locals waving me on. The mission was passed on easily that sun-filled day.

In the middle of the following day a young man on a bicycle rode up to say hello and asked me: "Where are you from?"

"I'm Australian," I replied.

His eyes lit up and he smiled dreamingly, "Wow! Australia. You have so many bitches there."

I was wide-eyed. "Excuse me?"

Matter-of-factly he said again: "Bitches. You have so many beautiful bitches all around Australia. And you all live so close to the bitch!"

I burst out laughing and corrected him, "I think you mean beaches."

I explained the two meanings and he laughed, "Oh! I see. Yes, we have similar word in Polish, but I hear no difference in what I say. I should use another word perhaps? I like your ocean. You all live so close to the beautiful ocean!"

Indeed we do.

Late in the day I stepped over a number plate and for whatever reason, memorised it. Five kilometres later a brand new BMW roared past and the driver slammed on his brakes, ripped into reverse, lit up the tyres and swung around alongside me. I wasn't sure what to expect. The driver jumped out and announced, "I have a problem! I've lost my number plate, have you seen it?" He was dumbfounded when I reeled off his plate number. He nearly hugged me. He asked if I could show him where it was, so I jumped in the hotted-up BMW and we ripped back down the country road. Only then did it dawn on me that he was also drunk! I held on for dear life. As we rapidly drew near I told him to stop up ahead, and stop he did, as fast as anti-lock braking allows. He jumped out, grabbed the number plate, kissed it and held it aloft like the newly crowned heavyweight champion of the world, then jumped back in and swung the car into a U-turn without checking for on-coming traffic … which there was. He took off back down the road as fast as traction-control allows and twice in one minute he ran off the road only to swerve back on amidst a flurry of gravel.
I almost fell out of the car when he dropped me off. "I think I might walk."

After a few more days I was approaching Kraków at sunset. I pushed deeper into the city under the gaze of looming power station stacks before the more historic and elegant homes of the central district began to emerge. Bathed in sunset hues, the Kraków Cathedral—with its bells ringing—towered above antique buildings surrounding the massive central square abuzz with markets, cafés and exclusive stores. It was an impressive sight.

The City on the Hill Community in Lublin had organised a place for me to stay in Kraków and I rendezvoused with my contact—Marek—in the central square. I stayed for two nights with him, his wife and their four children; and the extent of their generosity became evident over dinner when Marek asked me where I was from and what I was doing in Poland. I was wide-eyed. They'd invited me into their home solely on the premise that they'd been told that a man passing through needed a bed. That was enough for him to open up to a complete stranger and for his daughter to give up her room. I explained my background and, to their surprise, why I was there.

I spent a good part of my rest day in the Basilica of the Sisters of Divine Mercy, before moving on into the west the next morning with Marek's aunt and uncle's address in hand. The priest at a modest little church halfway through the day served me up a wonderful lunch and prayed with me and, by day's end, I was wandering into Zebrzydowice. With wry smiles, the locals forced me to pronounce the town's name. I didn't fair too well.

Marek's uncle drove me to Mass in the morning at a nearby monastery where Pope John Paul II had visited often as a priest and then as Pope. A number of the priests and brothers accepted the mission gladly and sent me on my way with their prayers as I continued on towards Wadowice and Andrychów. I stopped for only a short time in Wadowice, the birthplace of Pope John Paul II, and after a good chat with the parish priest I continued on.

Late in the day a fellow named Michal, from the nearby city of Bielsko-Biała, met me in Andrychów. He was also a member of the City on the Hill Community and, by the prompting of the Lublin lot, had arranged a bed for me for the night. He was in his mid-twenties and about as sincere and down-to-earth as can be. I wasn't scheduled to pass through Bielsko-Biała, but was passing so close to their city that the community had invited me to stay. They offered to return me to Andrychów to continue walking after my stay. I thought I'd stay one night and walk on, but that wasn't the case. They'd organised a few engagements for the next day. I was annoyed at first, which was probably a bit stupid in hindsight, but I was glad I stayed.

I spoke at a youth meeting that first night and almost lost my bottom jaw when I walked into the jam-packed church filled with hundreds of youth from all over southern Poland. I was expecting a twenty-something youth group with pizza. It was an amazing evening filled with song, drama, film, adoration and a beautiful altar call where hundreds walked forward. Michal translated most of the night for me, including summarising with a smile one particular enthusiastic minute-long preaching as, "God is good. Amen."

A young priest preached before the adoration altar call about an archery school. He spoke about a wise teacher who tested his students by asking them what they saw as they lined up to fire their arrows at a target. Many listed off all the things around them, in front of or behind the target, but he wouldn't let them fire. Only when one student answered, "Master, I see a bullseye," did he allow him to fire. The priest concluded: "Over the course of tonight there has been so much happening. There have been inspirational talks, hilarious dramas and brilliant music provided by the band. You've been able to catch up with old friends, meet new ones and let's be honest, you may have even spotted someone in the crowd who you think you might like to get to know before you leave tonight, but that's not why we're here. It's easy to have such a great night, but to miss the bullseye. You can participate fully, but miss the point. Our bullseye is Christ Jesus. Everything tonight should draw us to focus on Jesus and its only in focussing on him that we truly come alive. We aren't here to be spectators to a spectacle. We are here to be participants in a relationship with the creator of Heaven and Earth."

> *Be on guard so that your hearts are not weighed down with dissipation and drunkenness and the worries of this life, and that day does not catch you unexpectedly.*
>
> Luke 21:34

Total walked: *11,453 kilometres*

# Trumpets, Troubled Gear & New Boots
*March 2008*

Michal and his two best friends, Anna and Wojtek, took great care of me on my unscheduled Bielsko-Biała rest day; despite heavy rain, they took me on a tour of the region. They did this while playing two traditional straight-line trumpets out the window: very random … but exceptionally fun. As we mucked around we heard over the radio that a ferocious storm was lashing the mountain pass I was supposed to be covering that day. If I had, I would have encountered a 100 km/h sub-zero blizzard. When they announced the deaths of a number of locals due to the excessive winds and snow, our trumpets fell silent. I was grateful, to say the least, to not be stuck on that mountain pass struggling to stay alive. To have chosen the walk over the people may have ended the mission.

We ventured off to a young adult prayer meeting to share the mission and invite them to set their alarms for 4:01. One man introduced himself as a Polish television station reporter. He made arrangements on the spot to meet me on the road for an interview but his crew wasn't available for a few days, so we just agreed to wing it and find each other somewhere near the Slovakian border.

The most dangerous part of the storm had blown over, but torrential rain still fell. Wojtek cited that: "It's too dangerous to travel that road you have planned to. I know a safer route through the mountains. If you're happy to trust me I'll lead the way." It was bliss to have someone join me in horrible conditions rather than trying to convince me not to walk. I was happy to have his company and to follow his lead through the Miedzybrodzkie Valley.

Michal drove us back out to Andrychów and sent us on our way with a trumpet strapped to Wojtek's pack for the thirty-three kilometres to Zywiec. It was a Sunday so, half an hour into the day, when we passed a farm-surrounded Catholic church we stopped to attend Mass. We sat up in the choir loft of the full church and halfway through Mass Wojtek leant over and asked, "How many men can you see?" I looked down over the roughly 150 parishioners and was genuinely shocked to see a sea of women, mainly middle-aged and up. We could count only five men.

Walking on along a fast flowing river into the valley, with the rain pouring down on us, we discussed the lack of roles being taken up by men in many churches, and the extra roles that could be established if only we were more willing! At a small village the local priest cut us off halfway through my introduction exclaiming, "I know you!" He had no idea who Wojtek was but, if he was with me, he was in too. The interview carried out a week earlier by the three journalists had been published as the central article in the national Catholic magazine; the priest ushered us in out of the rain, racing around gathering food while asking about the journey. It was great to have a translator.

Wojtek announces our arrival in Żywiec

Walking on through persistent rain we watched a gaggle of geese fly overhead with no formation. I jokingly said to Wojtek, "Look at these guys, no organisation," and yelled out in full voice, "Form a V, it's easier!" The geese suddenly changed position into a sort of flying 'T' across the sky. Wojtek cupped his hands around his mouth and yelled out, "No! He said a V, not a T!" The formation straight away slid into a flying 'V' and powered on out of site. With great cheer we high-fived each other. St Francis would've been proud.

Wojtek tipped out a good few inches of rain from his trumpet upon our arrival in Zywiec, an hour after sunset, and we announced our arrival in the empty town square with two trumpet blasts that echoed wonderfully.

Michal's relatives put me up for the night in Zywiec and saw me off in the morning for my last day in Poland. The rain eased into a cloudy and wet-underfoot day. I continued to enjoy the fruits of the magazine article, including morning tea with two elderly women who were hanging out of a second storey window in their village, yelling for me to come on up and join them for a cup of tea.

"Don't mind if I do."

Steep, mist-shrouded and tree-covered hills contained the deserted Slovakian border, which had been made obsolete by the European Union. I just walked straight on through to the small Slovakian town of Skalité. The next morning, a few hours down the road, I spotted a church and did the usual detour to extend the mission. The spritely priest greeted me and asked me to join him in the school which turned out to be an adjacent classroom. The students welcomed the mission eagerly and then helped me to learn a few Slovakian words and phrases. It was a great start to the country.

I made it to the town of Cadca by mid-morning, but then needed to head back to the border to rendezvous with the Bielsko-Biała television crew: they were ready to shoot their interview. I grabbed a bus and met them right on time.

The interview took a few hours and included driving up to a mountain village where I was asked to introduce myself to the parish priest. He had no idea we were coming, but he recognised me and was happy to oblige. It was incredibly staged, and we had to do a couple of takes of me walking up to his door, knocking and then explaining in Polish who I was, but it came together well.

The film crew generously drove me back to Cadca but, having taken such a large chunk out of the day with the interview, I was left to walk on into fading light well before my destination—Kysucké—came into sight through the darkness of thick isolating forest. At least I now had a headlamp again. It was still a little eerie out there though.

I arrived in one piece and, the next morning, four local parish youth workers were keen to help me in any way they could, which included another impromptu Slovakian language lesson and contacts in the next city of Zilina.

Those contacts in Zilina then promptly organised for me to attend an ecumenical meeting that afternoon. A Lutheran pastor named Rad drove me there and I was afforded the opportunity to extend the invitation to pray for unity to those gathered. Representatives from numerous churches attended and although their opposing theologies weren't tabled, they did spend a lot of time organising mutual prayer events and missions. It was great. The gathered group invited me to attend their prayer evening the following night at Pastor Rad's church, which I accepted, but with the intention of walking on from Zilina before returning in the evening. I didn't want to sit around all day.

Pushing on along a wide glassy river, I made it all the way to Ladce by late afternoon the next day ... but it wasn't all smooth sailing. I could only find carbonated water in the shops to refill my three-litre water bladder, so I filled up with the stuff and figured the carbonation would dissipate in time. I failed to factor in one very important fact though. Pouring carbonated water into a sealed bladder in a shaking, moving backpack, will build pressure.

A few kilometres on, praying as I went, I reached for my first sip. The water system had a tube running from the bladder, so all I had to do to drink was place the tube in my mouth, bite down on the mouthpiece to open a valve, and suck.

The water bladder was near bursting point: when I bit down ...

... water cannoned into the back of my throat and straight down into my lungs. Half drowning, I reefed the tube out, but the pressure was so great that the valve stayed open and water sprayed everywhere. Coughing up half a day's supply of water while trying to breathe left me reeling. With a few heaves on the side of the road the water fell from my mouth and nose and I was able resume breathing. "I'm okay folks. Nothing to see here ..."

I bussed back to Zilina and headed straight to Pastor Rad's house for a huge Slovakian dinner before we popped next door for the evening of prayer. The service was fantastic: music, readings, preaching and prayer contributions from many denominations. It was a beautiful step towards Christian unity. One of the women attending, Tracy, invited me to travel to the capital city of Bratislava for a major unity concert in two days' time so, after a careful look at the map, we agreed on a pick-up point 130 kilometres down the road.

The plan soon had a spanner thrown in the works. A journalist from the region's major newspaper asked for an interview the next morning. It was well worth staying for the few hours, but it added extra pressure to my schedule. Pastor Rad threw me in his car afterwards and sped me along the freeway back to Ladce, giving us a chance to chat as we went. To my surprise, he spoke fondly of the communist years, having missed the job security and peacefulness. It was the first time I'd heard of it in that light.

I was on my way from Ladce late in the morning and in desperate need of a haircut, so I found a hairdresser during my lunch break. I ended up with a cut-throat-blade wielding stylist who gave me a mullet. It took a few minutes of painful debate to convince her that a mullet was not on and that the back had to go. I ended up with a roughed-up just-got-out-bed look at the back and a Nike swoosh across the front, which was promptly covered up with a cap.

I walked on.

I met a middle-aged man on the edge of town who spoke fluent English, so we spoke and I reiterated Pastor Rad's comments about communism and asked him if that was the general consensus. He shook his head and his mouth contorted; he muttered, "They took my life and my dreams! Everything I hoped to be or do … they took. My dreams of travel, of adventure, of life; they took it away and forced me to work in a factory."

Obviously safety and security can't be forced on everyone.

I think I fall into that category.

Towards the end of the day, a Catholic priest invited me to stay the night at his parish, but I insisted that I had to push on to cover more ground to make my rendezvous for the concert, so, to my surprise, he opened up his wallet and gave me the money I'd need for a hotel, "In case no one else offers you a bed." I was amazed at his generosity and his assurance of prayers.

The quaint city of Trenčín sat astride the Váh River: a massive headland containing the third oldest castle in Slovakia overlooked it. The castle dated back to 1000 CE, with a stone inscription at its base dating back to 179 CE. It was all beautifully silhouetted against a sunset sky.

I walked along the cobblestone streets and medieval terraces to a dirt-cheap pub and hotel for a bed. I still wasn't in the habit of asking churches for a place to sleep so that the full emphasis was placed on the mission and not on the backpacker standing at the door wanting a pillow.

Slovakia was a gem of a place: wonderful people and superb scenery ... including huge rivers, big mountains, sprawling forests and clean crisp air. Chirping birds accompanied me through the fading darkness the next morning; I set off to cover forty-four kilometres in just eight and three quarter hours to meet Tracy. I still stopped at the churches along the way. In one of them I met three mischievous old women who were happy to take the prayer for unity to the rest of the congregation. The most elderly of the three—walking stick in hand—hobbled over with a partly toothless smile and slipped money into my hand for the journey ahead.

It hurt covering that distance in that time, but I arrived in Piešťany only five minutes late, and Tracy and her daughter whisked me off to Bratislava in the south-western corner of the country. The multi-denominational night of praise and worship began with another journalist meeting me for an interview before one of the young organisers, Vlad, invited me to step up and speak for a few minutes, with his translation. I was then free to enjoy the night while a beautiful young woman named Ivana sat beside me, translating everything.

At night's end, Ivana made a call back to Piešťany to her friend, Lucas, and organised a bed for me. Lucas didn't speak English, but when I was dropped back up the highway he welcomed me into his small apartment. We prayed together before breakfast and then attended his Evangelical church for their Sunday service. I enjoyed the congregation's company and was thankful for meeting them all but, having not been to Mass, I asked Lucas if there was a Catholic Mass in town. He was taken aback and asked, "Why do you want to go to church again? You've just been. There's no difference between church there and church here. Church is church." As much as I enjoyed worshipping with the Evangelicals, I couldn't turn my back on receiving Christ, body and blood, soul and divinity, in the Eucharist. It was always a difficult point to raise while staying with non-Eucharist believing Christians, because as much as I wasn't trying to force my own beliefs on others, I also wasn't about to back down from a belief that I fervently embraced and felt short-changed without. Lucas respectfully pointed me towards the town's Catholic church.

Mass had just finished, but the priest assured me there was one that evening in Trnava, thirty-five kilometres away. I was off again, pushing hard and praying. The sun had set by the time I made it there. When I approached the dimly lit church and saw it was empty, I just sighed. I really wanted to attend Mass. Tentatively pushing open the front door to the massive darkened church, I removed my backpack and slumped to my knees in a pew, exhausted. I prayed for only a few minutes when, all of a sudden, every light in the place flickered on.

"I'm not alone."

A man walked out near the altar and then a family walked in behind me and found a seat, and then another. For once in my life … I'd arrived early! Fifteen minutes later, when Mass did start, I felt very privileged to be there.

I extended the invitation to pray for unity after Mass and received an offer of accommodation from one of the young women who had rung her parents on the spot. They approved and I had a bed. I couldn't believe she'd opened up her home to a complete stranger but, then again, it wasn't exactly the first time that had happened.

The Slovakians encouraged me more than ever that there really was hope for a united Church, but what really made me smile was that I received word that the hunt for size sixteen walking boots was finally over. Puma-advice-Dave had found a pair in an Australian warehouse and thrown them in the mail. They were on the way.

I continued south from Trnava across quiet countryside towards Bratislava over a few days. On the first day, the sun set behind a solitary leafless tree out on a fenceless plain. It was wonderfully peaceful. By the end of the second day I was walking straight through Bratislava and out over a bridge crossing a large river full of activity. I had an innocent thought of, "Wow, this must be some sort of major river or something?" and checked my map.

It was the Danube.

A bed had been arranged at a seminary and I made it there after some tiresome searching. From there, amidst drizzling rain, I crossed out of Slovakia the next morning into Austria. I was exhausted from learning Russian, Polish and Slovakian and so—to be honest—I couldn't be bothered learning Deutsch. Most Austrians spoke English so I wasn't forced to learn more than the basics. It was a welcome mental siesta.

The gorgeous little village of Hainburg on the Danube was a stunning introduction to Austria with window flower boxes filled with new shoots, striking stone architecture and tight cobblestone streets designed for horse and cart. I passed on the invitation to pray for unity and headed to Vienna. For most of the journey a bicycle path followed the country road, so for the first time in a long time I was able to maintain a constant speed. The fifty-three kilometres were knocked off neatly before sunset and it was conducive to prayer, even if it didn't stop raining. Unfortunately, my old boots didn't cope well and my feet were saturated.

Green rolling hills surrounded Vienna. In the late afternoon I arrived outside Mozart's childhood church in Schwechat where my good Austrian friends, Alexander and Birgit, who'd lived in Australia for two years, picked me up. They now had two young boys, Raphael and Daniel, and the brothers were close to hyperactive. Despite the gap between their car seats they managed to push, poke and prod each other amidst a barrage of laughter, all the way home. The younger of the two, Daniel, had trouble pronouncing my name, so I was Yam for the duration of my stay. I once boarded with a family who had an eighteen-month-old boy who couldn't pronounce my name either. He referred to me as Dum, so Yam was an improvement.

That night, I removed my socks to a worrying sight. My right foot was covered in a red rash and badly swollen and a rash was developing on the left foot. Birgit drove me to their doctor the next day, where I also raised the heart problems from Belarus. The doctor didn't quite know what to say. He put it simply, "I don't know how the body should react to walking the distances you are. Perhaps this is normal!" We agreed it would be okay for me to continue so long as it didn't worsen.

Alexander and Birgit generously bought me gloves, trousers, sunglasses and a fantastic North Face winter jacket to replace my no-longer-waterproof one. I stayed with them for three days. When I walked on, Birgit would drive out and pick me up each evening, returning me for dinner and my own room. It kind of felt like I had a nine-to-five job.

Despite the horrible conditions, the swelling in my foot reduced, but the response from the churches was average. They received the invitation, just not with much enthusiasm. I walked on to Sollenau and then Wiener Neustadt where the Saturday market was in full swing amidst historic buildings surrounding the town square and the beautiful array of blossoming new-season flowers. A bank representative tossed me a free yellow stress ball with a smiley face on it and I cheerily walked on bouncing it off stone walls and tree trunks as I prayed my way to Neunkirchen. The sound of birds filled the soundscape and the smell of spring permeated everything. I struggled not to be distracted while praying and again became distracted while apologising for being distracted.

The clouds had blown through and the sun ushered in beautifully warm days. The Neunkirchen Catholic Church received me warmly, but the few Protestant churches I approached were empty, so I just left a calling card. Birgit picked me up from there for one last time, with the boys in the back yelling out the whole way home, "Hi Yam. Yam! Hi!" It was difficult to let go of the comfort of their home and move on into the middle of Austria.

The road from Neunkirchen squeezed up through a sheer cutting into a tree-lined valley and then wound sharply up the valley walls towards Mt Semmering. That sight induced a disgruntled moan. It didn't level out for as far as I could see. It then rained heavily. The new jacket gave me a new lease on life, but my tattered boots filled fast—particularly with the torrent running down the road splashing up over them.

I squelched my way into a small church at the quaint village of Maria Schutz where an order of Passionist priests ushered me into their abbey. They gathered up hot food for me while I changed into dry socks and introduced the mission. The exchange was done with a smile.

Continuing on with dry feet, I wound up along the taxing mountainous twenty-six kilometre road to Semmering. I arrived at night, but ski resorts threw light in all directions and everything was well signed; however … finding something reasonably priced took some time.

I stepped out of the hotel in Semmering into a misty morning and my jaw dropped. The cheap hotel surrounded by trees sat at the highest point on the road nestled between two towering peaks. Only thirty metres away was a chairlift up into the low lying clouds shielding Mt Semmering. On the other side of the road it was the same deal and, being a Monday morning at the end of the season, the slopes were empty. A couple about to board the lift were the only people around. I was in ski-heaven. I wanted to drop my pack and hit the slopes, so it took some real focus on the broken Church to turn and walk on through the mist. I watched a solitary shadowy figure ski down a massive slope to my side.

After another long day of prayer, I extended the mission to a priest and wrapped up by asking where the nearest accommodation was. He invited me to wait while he returned inside, so I was hopeful that he was organising something for me, but he never returned. I waited twenty minutes in the cold night, standing there in silence until all the house lights flicked off and I was left in darkness. "He's not coming back." I tightened my backpack straps and walked on in search of a bed.

By the time I arrived in Kapfenberg it had been fifty-three kilometres all up and I was tired. I'd picked up a little of the language, but the only sentence I knew fluently was provided by puma-Dave who sent through another 'helpful' email, being the German phrase, "I am a little fat pig." I could've hit delete, but I instead chose to learn it. Not surprisingly it didn't come in handy in general conversation, but it was a superb icebreaker. I was asked a few times if I knew any Deutsch and, without fail, if I pulled that line out, the person would burst out laughing and our relationship seemed to take a few steps forward. Not that I'm giving puma-Dave any credit for his 'help'.

From Kapfenberg a cool, overcast day made for a pleasant stroll to Leoben and its enormous Redemptorist Monastery, and then on to Knittelfeld. The weather was downright bizarre on approach to Knittlefeld. The temperature rose sharply. I applied sunscreen and slapped on sunglasses and t-shirt and walked on through a lush green valley surrounded by snow-capped mountains. Still bathed in sunshine … it then snowed. It was still warm and I was left looking skywards trying to figure out where it was coming from.

Barrier-rails separated the roads from forest-clad terrain that sloped away at near cliff-like angles. Some sections were impassable so I had to wait and listen until no cars were approaching, put my head down and run to the next safe spot. More than once I was caught out and forced to jump the barrier and just hold on.

My metabolism had shot through the roof but, with ample food available, incredibly I began to put weight back on! Walking an average forty kilometres a day and still putting weight on is no mean feat! Healthy food was devoured hourly as my body counteracted weight loss due to walking, sickness and my body's attempts to keep warm in the colder conditions. I began in Brazil at ninety-three kg, fell to as low as eighty-one kg and was now edging back towards eighty-seven kg.

From Knittelfeld to Scheifling and then on again at sunrise towards Friesach; I was running the gauntlet down narrow traffic-filled forested roads. I even resorted to zigzagging across the road like a tacking yacht to take advantage of any available space. I kind of enjoyed the challenge, waiting patiently for cars to pass by, listening intently and then running around corners where the road butted up against rock faces with nowhere to shelter. It was always nice to make it around before being run over.

In Friesach, with its 12th century double steeple Catholic church and chapel perched on a hilltop, I spoke with the secretary and then at last found a non-Catholic church 'open for business' nearby. A Lutheran congregation was meeting for their Good Friday service and, although I wasn't able to talk to the minister, who was already preaching, I chatted with a member who was happy to extend the invitation to the congregation.

Continuing on into a misty afternoon I was excited by the coming prospect of disposing of my ratty old boots. Puma-Dave had mailed my boots to his Austrian friend, Eva, who would be waiting for me at the St Veit an der Glan train station with the boots and a lift to her parents' place for the night.

Puma-Dave and our Austrian hosts

When I arrived in St Viet an der Glan I was exhausted and Eva was nowhere to be seen. The thought crossed my mind that it wasn't beyond Dave to have flown over to visit Eva and hand-deliver the boots, and ten minutes later when a car pulled into the train station with a young lady driving I didn't recognise her, but I did recognise the smiling mug in the passenger seat. Puma-Dave stepped out with a grin, "Hello Samuel." The remainder of Good Friday, Easter Saturday and Sunday was filled with a lot of storytelling and laughter.

We were treated to a true Austrian Easter at the Strombergers' farm in the village of Tauchendorf, from painted Easter eggs to a sensational selection of food, a Saturday night candle-lit vigil Mass back at Friesach, and the full orchestra and operatic choir at the Sunday morning Mass. It was an amazing couple of days. The two daughters living on the Strombergers' farm—Eva and Carol—had strong ties to the Franciscan order, which led to hours of conversation about areas of struggling unity and places-of-need for mission work. Easter was brilliant.

Dave brought with him a couple of presents from friends and of course those brand new Scarpa size sixteen SL-M3 walking boots. The old ones were now 8,500 kilometres old. Phenomenal. The new boots looked good, smelt great and felt amazing to slip on. I hadn't suffered a single blister since the USA, but I was conscious of not reliving the agony of Nicaragua. In an attempt to avoid a repeat of that horrid experience I wore my new boots at every possible moment: to

Mass, to dinner, everywhere ... except bed. I walked the twelve kilometres from St Veit an der Glan to the Strombergers' farm on Easter Sunday evening, which was just the thing to at least take the edge off them.

I was excited to push on towards Italy, France and Spain but, as I peered out from the Strombergers' farmhouse that night, I watched heavy snow drift in, and the Austrian/Italian Alps were looming imminent.

From old to new ... thanks to Puma-Dave

My worn-out backpack was the only original item I had left and every zip was broken, outer pocket torn and strap frayed. It was handled with due care. In keeping with the plan to not wreck my feet in new boots I walked only twenty-two kilometres to Steindorf through the heavy snow and then on around Lake Ossiacher the next day to the city of Villach. Three men working at a Lutheran church received the mission and offered their assistance for the journey ahead, pointing out a safer and more peaceful little-known historic route through the hills towards Tarvisio in Italy.

The track led me away from modern life, penetrating deep into the forest-covered hills. It was the original Roman road carved through solid rock, winding up through the rolling foothills. It was quiet amongst the trees as the odd snowflake drifted through. Emerging into an enormous valley I walked along the edge of tranquil roads for the final few hours before the Italian border. The Alps were monstrous and by late afternoon I'd crossed the unstaffed border high above the valley. I was in Italy.

The road climbed higher as night fell and I was left walking precariously along a cliff edge under lamplight. The town of Tarvisio was built into the bottom third of a steep valley and as I rounded the final corner I looked out across the glistening snow village from above. It really was beautiful.

A middle-aged man named Raphael pointed me towards an ATM and, after making the withdrawal, I walked back up the village street and ran straight back into him. His huge smile, olive skin, shaved head and fine goatee gave him a somewhat royal appearance, only he wore a fitted brown pullover, jeans and white street shoes. This time he asked me why I was in Tarvisio.

Raphael had trekked the 900 kilometres across northern Spain along the Camino de Santiago with his daughter a few years earlier and he smiled, "I understand what it's like being a pilgrim." He ordered what he believed was the best pizza for a walking missionary and he was right on the money. The slices of fresh vegetables on it were so chunky that it deserved to be eaten with a knife and fork, not by hand. He also stepped me through a few Italian phrases and the more I learnt the more I saw the similarities to Spanish. I was excited to tackle the language head on. Raphael then negotiated a half price room for me.

I met with the Tarvisio parish priest in the morning, who was sceptical at first, but quickly lightened up when he saw my itinerary and insisted that I share breakfast with him before undertaking the crossing of the Alps.

That crossing was extraordinary. I'd only ever seen mountains like that on postcards and every kilometre presented a new view of absurdly steep ragged mountains covered in snow. Much to my delight, the country road passed through long sweeping tunnels, allowing me to launch into a couple of reverberating big tunes.

Accommodation was organised for me in Dogna at a parish two-storey villa on a narrow cobblestone street with a wonderful view out over the empty road and mountains above. I slept well—even with my 2:30 am wake up for another meal—and I set off before sunrise continuing through the magnificent valley.

Low-lying clouds raced between the mountains and condensed into misty rain. I discovered that my waterproof backpack cover was no longer waterproof. It had no other redeemable features, so that was a shame. I walked on out of the shadow of the Alps across drenched plains and was again reaching for the yellow Costa Rican sticky tape when both of the shock absorbers in the middle of walking poles gave way within a few kilometres of each other. They were taped together solidly.

I met an old man in one village who pointed out that every single building there had been levelled in an earthquake, and so his 500-year-old village was in fact only thirty years old. The very stones that had crumbled were used to build every building back up. He smiled and in broken English replied, "It fall down, we build it up better!" Indeed we do.

Continuing south across farming plains to San Vito al Tagliamento, the suspected corn on my right foot caused a grimacing burning sensation: the new boots finally took a bite out of my feet and formed a blister. The narrow roads built up off the surrounding fields didn't help. As heavy traffic passed by I was constantly forced to walk with my left foot on the slope and it consequently suffered.

A band of Franciscan brothers welcomed me in with a bed and an encouraging atmosphere for the mission before sending me on my way to San Donà di Piave along more narrow roads sloping away into canals. I leapt across a small canal at one point, overbalanced and, in an act of desperation, I placed too much weight on one pole, trying to stop myself from falling. It bent at the base. The pole now matched the rest of my equipment.

The Mediterranean climate saw the temperature rise to nearly 20°C, but the warmth was offset by me accidentally snapping the mouthpiece clean off my water system. A number of times that day I was caught off guard after placing my pack down allowing valuable water to escape. Just to keep me on my toes, the backpack shoulder straps then began pulling apart at the seams. Once again, yellow sticky tape pulled it all back together.

As I approached San Donà di Piave in the fading twilight, an intoxicated man was struggling to walk his bike along the road eighty metres ahead of me. Without any thought he turned the bike to stagger across the road. I could hear a car coming from behind and without having turned I instinctively shouted out, "No!" In that split second I knew that the car approaching from behind was on his side and travelling much faster than his stagger. The car flashed past and I watched helplessly as the driver slammed on the brakes hard, locking up all four wheels under a rising plume of smoke. The squealing tyres frightened the man so much that he literally leapt backwards as the car crunched his bicycle from his grip, sending him twisting through the air, legs brushing the door, and landing with a thud.

I ran to help. The bicycle lay twisted in the car's grip, but he was unscathed. He was still drunk, but unscathed. I think the poor driver was the most shaken.

The limestone-induced aqua blue Piave River was beautiful at sunrise and lined with vine-covered trees; flower boxes filled with yellow and white blossoms cascaded over the bridge's handrail. Northern Italy was stunning. After punching out 257 kilometres in seven days across the Alps, my body really hurt. There was just no room on the edge of one bridge so, wedged between the crash barrier and railing, I was forced to crawl under the low road signs. The consistently difficult roads produced some of the worst back-to-back walking conditions I could remember, but the warm-hearted people left an indelible mark.

On approach to Venice I received an encouraging email from English Anglican Bishop, Tony Palmer. He began with:

> *Jesus prayed for it in John 17, "That we may be one, so that the world would believe!" Christian Unity is not an effort for "good Church politics," it is our Lord's dying prayer! Our Lord prayed for unity of the Church BEFORE He had even given birth to it!!!*

Christ longed for unity ... and so did my feet ... as I traversed the five kilometre long bridge connecting Venice to the mainland. I was at a complete loss when the footpath suddenly ended a few hundred metres from the island. For the entire five kilometres across the bridge a large crash barrier separated the footpath from the four lanes of traffic and there was absolutely no way of walking down the edge of the road if I jumped it. The traffic was thick. The only way into Venice was to walk an hour back to the start of the bridge, cross underneath and walk back down the southern footpath, which continued into Venice. I didn't want to walk another two hours to get back to the same spot so I resigned to turning on my heals and heading off towards Padua.

After only a few steps I noticed a substantial gap in the Venice-bound traffic and as it approached, with the heavy Padua-bound traffic flowing beside me I turned and saw a huge gap from that direction as well. I stopped dead and watched. The gaps were about to align right in front of me! You snooze, you lose. I placed one foot up on the crash barrier and waited. As the last car flew by the five-second gap lined up perfectly and I leapt over, hitting the road running. I sprinted hard, hurdled the centre barrier cleanly, snapped straight back into a sprint and with a couple of quick balancing steps leapt up over the southern barrier, landing hard against the bridge railing as the traffic swallowed up the gap.

"Thank you, Lord."

I would've had so much fun growing up in Venice. The gondolas looked great, but I was imagining paddling off to work each day in my kayak and the peacefulness of peak hour traffic. It was a tourist city, but I'd find a way to slot into the background somehow. It was indeed the romantic setting it's portrayed to be, only … I spent my hour there uploading my weekly blog at an internet café before visiting a few churches.

I was back out on the bridge quickly and pushing on into the countryside towards Padua when I had to take a few settling breaths. Two young men ducked in behind an abandoned farmhouse up ahead before one of them peered around the edge at me and then quickly disappeared. My grip tightened on the poles. I passed the run-down house and they ran out briskly telling me to stop. I took in my surroundings and weighed up my options, but the open fields offered little protection, and they looked fit, so running was a last resort. I turned to them and stood my ground. I must have looked shorter from afar because as I looked down on them they backed away a half step. One raised his chin while making the hand signal for a cigarette, exactly as the two men in Belarus had done. Maintaining eye contact and keeping a higher position on the edge of the road I shook my head, "No."

When I explained (in poor Italian) who I was and why I was there, their demeanour changed. "You are walking around the world?" they asked.

I nodded, "More or less." The two men smiled, but I kept my distance. They told me I should pitch my tent next to the abandoned house, but I thanked them for the advice and assured them I was continuing to Padua. Backing away from them I said goodbye and walked on with a close watch over my shoulder. They slowly returned to the building and stayed. At least once a day across Europe I thought that a person ahead of me might pose a threat. It was difficult to shake that instinctive defensive response, but winter had indeed passed, in more ways than one.

*And now I am no longer in the world, but they are in the world, and I am coming to you. Holy Father, protect them in your name that you have given me, so that they may be one, as we are one..*

John 17:11

Total walked : *12,479 kilometres*

# Hookers, Saints & Vatican City
*April 2008*

While passing through Padua's grassy city centre square—complete with a statue-guarded moat—I decided to detour to St Anthony's Basilica. I wasn't overly hopeful of talking to a priest there, considering five million people passed through its doors each year, but it was a church, so I popped in. One of the English-speaking Vatican Guards struck up a conversation with me and to my surprise he was genuinely interested in the mission. At that moment a man in civilian clothes walked past and the guard reached to stop him. He was the St Anthony's Basilica Franciscan Friars provincial. He was the boss. Pretty much like any other Franciscan I'd ever met he was also humble and generous, and without any fuss he invited me to join him for lunch.

Out through the basilica's guarded doors we went, through a beautiful courtyard and a few sets of private doors to a mess hall filled with sixty loud, jovial Franciscans. I'd never seen so many priests in one place. In complete contrast to the quiet reserved atmosphere of the basilica, the mess hall was filled with raucous conversation. A young seminarian walked past just as the eldest friar, in his late eighties, wrapped him around the back of the legs with his walking stick and waddled off with a cheeky grin as quick as his frail legs could carry him. Everything about the poor seminarian said he wanted to hit back, but couldn't justify cracking the old guy.

An English-speaking friar was soon translating my tale to a table full of friars and the invitation to pray for unity was received with added encouragement ... plus a room for the night. Despite my plans to keep walking that day I accepted without hesitation.

The room was a simple Franciscan cell with a window overlooking the inner courtyard with an enormous tree growing in the middle. After settling in I ducked down the road to the church of a personal hero, Saint Leopold Mandic, who Deacon Dave had introduced me to before I left Australia. It was an honour to be at the church he ministered from. St Mandic spent the majority of his life sharing the Gospel, living a life of poverty, prayer and sacrificing his time in the confessional for both the unity of the Church—particularly of the eastern and western traditions—and to offer the comforting words of God's forgiveness to all. His little words of wisdom were never far from my thoughts.

A young man with a broken leg was sitting outside the church, passing the day in quiet contemplation. I asked him how he was doing and John, a Sudanese refugee with fragile English, opened up slowly. His life was one of uncertainty, having arrived in Italy months earlier without family or friends. He'd found accommodation with locals for each night, but was left to fend for himself during the day. The Franciscans fixed him lunch daily and, with his family still back in Sudan, the Church was his one point of community. More than anything he just wanted his family. We chatted slowly for half an hour and prayed together. I left him with some money to help get by, but it was tough moving on from another 'Adolfo'.

When I returned to St Anthony's Basilica, the provincial taught me about the life of St Anthony. If Leopold Mandic was a hero, Anthony of Padua soon joined him! The guy was amazing; so straight down the line and forthright in his preaching that he made a mockery of unbelief and lukewarm Christianity. He converted and built up thousands of people in that region. It fascinated me to think that St Anthony and St Francis were, if you will, friends. I could only imagine how direct their conversations must have been. Perhaps they did talk about the weekend jousting games, but I doubt it.

Around the dinner table the consensus was that unity was a lifelong task where we draw each other into truth through love. They were adamant that neither truth nor love could exist in fullness without the other. I drifted off to sleep in my cell inspired beyond anything I'd expected from that day.

Leaving food with the sleeping homeless strewn across the town's grassed centre, I walked on humbled for what I had. I entered the rolling Italian hill country under a warm sun, but arrived in Rovigo at sunset to extend the invitation to pray for unity to a priest who just stared back at me before asking, "What do you want? Nothing? Good. Have a good walk." And closed the door.

I was tired, cold and wet. A thunderstorm opened up and every hotel in town was full due to a conference. To make matters worse all the cafés closed in a flurry of clanking security shutters before I'd eaten dinner. On the far edge of town I found a service station that hadn't quite finished closing up, but the food had been packed away. I took a deep breath and prayed, "Okay, Lord, where are we going?" Two young women and a man were waiting for their friend to close the station and one of them, Barbara, asked what I was looking for. I replied, "Food and a bed." She called in her three friends and brainstormed a solution in melodic Italian, before pulling out her phone and making a few calls. Within five minutes she'd found a B&B with a cheap late night restaurant next door. The four of them squeezed me into their car and whisked me off.

A parish priest and group of youths at Pontelagoscuro the next day jumped on the internet to check out the walk4one website and—to my delight—there was a new addition to the unity prayer list: Barbara from Rovigo, Italy.

I stayed in Ferrara that night and walked on past orchids in full blossom. Twelve kilometres down the road, two police officers stopped me and asked to see my passport. I'd left it sitting at the hotel reception in Ferrara. I was so embarrassed as I tried to explain why I didn't have it. They weren't happy with my explanation and reiterated, "You need your passport!"

I agreed, "I know. I'm sorry."

They lectured for five minutes, but I was relieved when all they did was tell me to go back on the train and get it. Much easier than the USA.

With my passport in hand I made it only as far as San Pietro in Casale by sunset, but there was no hotel. The parish priest knew of a place where I could stay and asked a random guy to drive me there. It was a homeless men's shelter. I had to concede that a homeless man was indeed what I was, so I accepted the rural hospitality with a smile and enjoyed the night communicating with the twelve men sleeping there that night.

I came to know one man well. He was a humble soul and had a job lined up in twenty days' time, but until then had no money or a home. What amazed me was how hard-faced everyone was when they arrived compared to how relaxed and jovial we were by breakfast. Two good meals, a bed and relative security make a world of difference.

With no shops open in the next town I stopped for lunch at an expensive restaurant and ordered the cheapest item on the menu; a beef salad. I didn't know that a beef salad in Italy means long slivers of thinly cut raw meat draped across artichokes. The sight alone made me feel sick. I was so hungry and embarrassed that I just put the smell out of my mind and tried to eat … but I couldn't stomach it.

I arrived in Bologna hungry and found no one to speak to at the churches. The history-saturated architecture was captivating, but merely provided a neat backdrop while I searched the narrow streets for a bed.

While so much of my journey had me feeling that little bit weaker, either physically or in regards to a loss of security, I was now on the mend and, in particular, revelling in my Padua experience. I was smiling from ear to ear when I received an invitation from the Vatican to 'pop in and say hello' when I arrived in Rome, thanks to a little 'head's up' from Deacon Dave to an archbishop in Rome.

On the outskirts of Bologna the next morning I met three locals at a church door. I attempted to stumble through Italian to explain the mission, but didn't get much further than, "Hi, I'm Sam," before the cultural norm of finishing each other's sentences kicked in. They turned, shutting me out of the conversation, and entered a heated debate about where I could sleep that night. I had no intention of staying a second night in Bologna, but as much as I tried to enter the argument they simply told me to wait until they'd sorted it out. The heated argument was getting out of hand so I gave a mighty farmer's whistle and shut them up.

They turned to me, surprised at the rude interruption, and I spelt out in Italian, "I-do-not-need-a-place-to-sleep." All three were confused and one asked, "Well, what do you want?" but before I could answer she quickly added, "Do you want food?" And they were off again, arguing about food options. It was crazy. I shook my head and yelled over the top of them, "No! I don't want food!" Only when they'd run out of possible endings to my introduction did they give me the chance to explain myself. Walking around the world praying for the unity of Christians and extending to them the invitation to join in that prayer wasn't on their radar. They didn't see that one coming. They accepted the invitation with wide eyes.

I walked up through a valley to a small village containing a beautiful little Catholic church run by a short, rotund elderly priest full of energy. Fr Luciano ushered me through to the kitchen for a mouth-watering home-cooked meal amidst a room with a library of books blanketing the walls. The church had been used as a starting point for many pilgrims heading to Rome in centuries past, but also by the German-Italian army in World War II as a last stand against the advancing allied forces. Scars from artillery fire were still evident and Fr Luciano had few positive words to say about either side. "One used a place of worship as a hideout and the other bombed it."

The hill country roads became increasingly curvy and undulating from there, presenting fantastic views across farmland at sunset. At Loiano, perched on the side of a large hill, Fr Luciano came bouncing into the hotel just as I was booking in. He paid for my room and dinner, over which he taught me a great deal more of the Italian language. After dinner, he blessed me and headed back to his home without any fanfare. He was an amazing guy.

Stepping over a huge dead snake the next morning brought the snake hunter back out in me. The temperatures continued to rise and the twisting country road descended into a valley lined with oaks and elms to a quaint mountainside village. I knocked at the three-storey Catholic church presbytery and the third floor window flung open. A lady stuck her head out, so I smiled and said, "Hi, I'm Samuel," but I didn't get any further than that before she'd pulled her head back in and left me talking to myself about this mission thing. I trailed off into silence and waited. She reappeared at the window and tossed something out wrapped in a tissue. I caught it cleanly and opened it up to find a few coins. I was confused. I looked back up and explained, "I'm not here for money," but she just smiled, pulled her head back in and closed the window, along with the conversation.

I reluctantly ambled back down an alleyway into the village with an angry dog barking its head off at me. "Shut up."

I chose from then on to open my introduction with, "Hi, I'm a missionary." Most pre-conceived ideas about me were associated with pilgrimage, but there were few about missionaries. I also dropped any use of the word pilgrim or my end point of Santiago de Compostela, which had pilgrim connotations plastered all over it. When asked where I was headed, I simply referred to the Atlantic Ocean in western Spain. Learning Italian was one thing, but learning to communicate was a whole different story.

Steep fields of blooming clustered yellow buttercups dominated the landscape under a crumbling misty mountain: I delved back into prayer. What simmered away was how multitudes of interpretations of 'truth' had wedged a vice between Christians. I'd been rocked by the love side of disunity in South and Central America, but since crossing into Italy my mind was set rolling on truth again. The primary question was how do Christians accept one another in love without encouraging heresies that may exist? How do we eradicate heresy while still fully loving each another? All week I went back and forth through various accusations from pretty much every Church to at least one other. The list steadily grew and as I thought through each one; the weight of the problem felt overwhelming.

I walked forty-one kilometres through the valley to Barberino. After securing a room above a little pub, I opened up a booklet I'd grabbed at the church of

St Leopold Mandic in Padua. It was the right time to open it up. A line from Leopold's diary placed my day's vexation into some perspective. It roughly read, "The most important factor in the reunification of Christians isn't our prayers, nor is it unity dialogue, but God's grace." It was the humble reality of being able to rest in God's love knowing that he is God, and with an adaptation of a St Francis' prayer, "Lord, save me from the desire to be heard," I headed to bed.

In the next city of Prato I was pointed to the nearby town of Iolo. An intense hayfever reaction had swelled my right eye nearly closing it completely and with my watery vision failing I struggled to complete the tight rope edge of narrow roads. I'd again been directed to a homeless men's shelter. Despite my unsavoury appearance, the Corpataux family welcomed me and allowed me in.

The Emmaus Community Workshop's mission was to provide work and a bed for those in need and Mr and Mrs Corpataux had set it up with a priest friend thirty years earlier. All three were still there, welcoming homeless men and training them up to rejoin the workforce. The big difference now was that the couple's eight children had joined them! I only learnt three names. I ate with the homeless guys and enjoyed hearing their stories of the day, but my swollen eye was the topic of conversation for most of the night.

To keep the facility operating, the Emmaus Community Workshop ran a second hand warehouse where all the profits went back into the project. I was carrying two books and good winter clothing I no longer needed, so I left them with the guys. It was a win–win situation. They received money for selling them and I walked on with a lighter pack.

The mission was received well in Florence, with its pastel multi-storeyed buildings forming a guard of honour along the mighty River Arno. I persisted in stopping at churches until I was out the other side of the city and walking up into the surrounding hill country.

The warm muggy day darkened overhead and, with a flash of lightning, I was sent scurrying for shelter under a gaping farm hedge. I looked like a drowned rat in five seconds flat. Dripping from head to toe I walked on into Solaia, on the edge of the famous Chianti wine making region, where everything looked like it was a country club owned by a plastic surgeon or inherited from a great uncle who'd defeated NapoLeón. My shuffling drowned-rat appearance devalued the place and I likely corrupted the expensive hotel room I snagged by hanging washed clothes all over it to dry alongside saturated boots.

I was back on the road by 6:30 am, powering on up a hill past a sea of vineyards emerging from the pre-dawn mist, when an unexpected visitor joined me. A low shadowy figure stared at me from a hundred metres down the road until it turned and scampered away at speed through a vineyard. Only then did I realise what it was and so reefed my camera out to snap a couple of seconds' worth of footage before the dimly lit rows of misty grapevines swallowed it up: a wolf! I shared the wolf sighting with a few locals, but one by one they disputed their existence in the area, until they watched the footage. Their eyes widened and they inevitably asked me to replay it as they called others in to watch. Truth, it would seem, is often accepted through experience, not trust.

For most of the day the only sound I could hear was that of tweeting bathing birds and persistent rain hitting my jacket's hood. I plodded on into Tuscany along serene winding roads past uncharacteristically quiet villages due to the inclement weather. I occasionally caught glimpses of my day's destination of Siena, perched high along the ridgeline of a distant hill. Very slowly, it drew nearer.

On the outskirts of Siena I stopped at a small Catholic church where the priest hardly allowed me to introduce myself before flicking me off to a group of young women meeting for a prayer group. Unlike the priest, they listened to me. Two of them spoke English so a conversation opened up and they took great delight in the journey. After scouring my itinerary, writing down the website address and asking a number of questions they pulled out cameras to take a few group shots just as the priest walked back in. He was genuinely taken aback and stood at the door with a look of concern. He grabbed the girl closest to him and asked something. She appeared to reel off the story of the mission and the expression on his face changed to something resembling both surprise and regret. He didn't say a single word from then on. He just drew closer to listen in as the invitation to pray for unity was taken on one by one.

Rain-soaked Siena sparkled in the afternoon sun as I rounded out a fifty-five kilometre day to the main cathedral. A similar length day back in Russia took five hours longer. I had to give thanks to God for the ability to roll on through Italy with nothing more than shoulderblade pain and that thing on the sole of my foot.

At dawn I set out onto the "Road to Rome" contemplating the sign off of an email that Dave Raba in Montana had sent me. He finished with, "May we always be inspired by the unity of the Father, the Son and the Holy Spirit." There's a thesis in unpacking that.

I passed through misty historic villages towards Radicofani, perched high on the point of a farm-covered mountain that could be seen for nearly half the day. At the very top sat a fortified castle and the quaint village under it seemed to look out over all of Italy. The winding road was so steep that the back of my right heel rubbed hard against the boot and split open a skin-crease around my Achilles tendon. Moving my foot up and down opened and closed it like a little mouth, allowing me to see through to the tendon sheath. I patched it up with a mixture of cream, bandaids and cushioning and limped on.

Radicofani was extraordinary. The village of only a few hundred warm-hearted residents—jam-packed into a sandstone labyrinth of tight alleyways— welcomed me in and invited me to sit in an old café amidst chatter and laughter. I loved it. After a time of question and answer I turned the tables and asked the man closest to me, "So, what do you do in this town?" He sipped his coffee to the laughter of everyone else, and then smiled, "I'm the Catholic priest. Give me a minute and I'll show you around." We toured the village, extending the mission to pray for unity to all we met.

From Radicofani, a secluded gravel road led me into the lakes district for five hours without passing a single vehicle, just sheep, cattle and friendly farmers. I wished the entire walk to Rome was like that. Eventually I met back up with the main road to be surrounded by noise and petrol fumes with no space to walk again.

I pushed on to Acquapendente, Montefiascone and then Ronciglione over three days with a fantastic response to the mission from those I met, particularly a Franciscan monastery halfway through the third day. And when I arrived in Ronciglione a wonderful priest welcomed me. Despite being in a hurry he was determined to take care of me and while having off-hand meetings with the locals as we walked, he rushed me through town to a tiny one room guesthouse in a compact alleyway. He noted that it wasn't much and smelt bad, but it was mine if I wanted it. I shook his hand and took it, grabbed dinner at a nearby restaurant and finished it all off with a gelato with the friendly locals.

After a freezing cold basin splash, I entered the next forty-three kilometre day filled with anticipation. I wasn't sure were I'd finish up exactly, but the lush rolling countryside and dew-covered forests were gradually passing into the madness of Rome. I was afforded a few final hours of peaceful country roads before being thrust onto the edge of a major highway, filled with cars doing everything from forty km/h to well in excess of one hundred and fifty km/h.

In an attempt to walk away from the busy highway I headed down a dead end back-road for three kilometres through thick bush and, over thirty minutes, I spotted two wolves slinking away, a herd of wild boar running away, two more wolves checking me out and then a young couple, shall I say 'making out' in their Volkswagen Beetle ... I guess that back-road wasn't as empty as they'd hoped. The march to Rome had become an unexpected wildlife safari ... wild in more ways than one.

I thought the safari experience was over when I made it back to the highway, but I was soon walking through knee-high grass and very nearly planted my foot right on top of a curled-up viper. I caught sight of the circular pile of snake right at the last second and thrust myself backwards with the walking poles. It shot off into the thick undergrowth. Wolves, boars, vipers and immoral relativists: welcome to Rome. "Where's the gelato?"

In an outer suburb I ate dinner over a great conversation with the English-speaking pizzeria owner and slept the night on the tiled floor of the church presbytery next door. I slept on my spare clothes and despite horrible tiredness I was up before dawn with a spring in my step. Rome beckoned!

Light rain fell right up until I finally caught sight of St Peter's Basilica and, as I walked across St Peter's Square, the sun came streaming through. While the historical architecture was phenomenal, what weighed on my mind was the invitation I'd received from the Pontifical Council for Christian Unity to meet with them first thing Monday morning. I had no idea how much time I'd have in there and I considered how to make the most of my time.

The weekend lines to enter the basilica were enormous so I instead struck up a light-hearted conversation with two Swiss Guards at the Vatican's vehicle entrance, which was interrupted only when the Vatican's gardener passed through on his little tractor. The two young men hardly drew breath as they asked about Australia, unity and the world.

I had a day and half at my disposal before the Monday morning meeting, so I wandered the streets looking for a place to stay, but everything was either full or too expensive. I ended up being directed deep into the heart of an industrial suburb devoid of life or working street lamps. It was again a homeless men's shelter, which was somewhat amusing at first, but when they rejected me at the door because they were already full it felt a little low.

I sat on the steps with a homeless African immigrant who'd also arrived too late, and we shared a makeshift meal together, chatting about our very different journeys to those steps. With cash in hand we wished each other well and headed in separate directions searching for a bed.

The old hotel I found at last was next to a parish, so I slept in, attended Mass the next morning and rested. An email from the Pontifical Council for Christian Unity confirmed that they were expecting me the next day at 8:30 am so I could "… meet everyone as they come in for work." It would only be a short visit before turning my sights to France, but it was a real a gift.

After a good sleep, I was off towards the Vatican. The horrendous traffic made me glad to be on foot.

A multitude of seminarians passed by, heading to their morning classes as I wandered through a large plaza with beautiful water fountains and what looked like an Egyptian obelisk propped up in the middle. I was ignorant of Rome.

Everything looked significant, but I walked on with no idea what I was passing by.

St Peter's Basilica emerged directly ahead of me. With a nervous smile I walked through the front door of the unity council offices, directly outside St Peter's Square. I was phoned through to the Pontifical Council for the Promotion of Christian Unity and invited into a lift to send me on my way. I'd failed to take into account that the men and women working there didn't simply work there. The unity of Christians was their passion, not their job. There would be no 'quick visit'. A secretary greeted me as the lift opened and introduced me to Monsignor Bollen, the Catholic representative for Anglican dialogue, who welcomed me with a firm handshake, "I've been following your blog all across Italy!" and after a lengthy chat he requested that I sign his copy of the International Week of Prayer for Christian Unity. With that tucked away back into his library he introduced the priests in their various offices with responsibilities ranging from the dialogue with the Greek Orthodox, Lutherans and Jews to the World Council of Churches.

I assumed the Vatican offices would be quiet and reverently silent, but they loved the privilege of working there so much that they were joyful to the point of being down right raucous. I asked one priest what he did there, but before he could answer, two priests called out from their offices down the hallway, "As little as possible!" and "Absolutely nothing!" Laughter erupted from the neighbouring offices as the poor priest in question defended his work. The mood was the same all day long. There was such an incredible admiration for all the Christians they worked alongside. The young Dominican in charge of the Greek Orthodox dialogue spoke of the Greek Orthodox Church with greater affection than I'd heard most Greek Orthodox speak about it! His office was decked out with everything Orthodox to the point that I became confused as to whether he was Catholic or Greek Orthodox. He loved them so much that he simply longed for the two churches to be united, side-by-side, worshipping God.

Bishop Brian Farrell, the Council Secretary, found me and invited me to follow quickly. Cardinal Walter Kasper, the man in charge, was in between meetings and wanted to say hello. We raced through the corridors to his office for a five-minute introduction and assurance of each other's prayers as he noted,

"Sam, unity is far from being a political gathering. It's a passionate desire to worship God alongside all Christians in truth and in love." Everyone in those offices spoke about the visible unity Christ spoke of in John 17 and St Paul's exhortations, and how the lack of it was in direct conflict with our calling to live as Christ's followers.

Monsignor Bollen called me aside after lunch and apologised, "Sorry Sam, I should have asked first and I hope it's okay, but I've organised media interviews for you." I couldn't believe he was apologising. I was halfway through thanking him when he cut me off and pointed to the door: "You only have twenty minutes to get to the first interview. Run."

I dashed off across the front of St Peter's Square to the Vatican Radio studios and then up the road to Catholic News Services to meet with one of their journalists. No sooner had that interview finished and I was sent off through the streets of Rome with directions scribbled on a piece of paper to the Franciscan run Centre for Unity. By the end of the day, I was stuffed: but the mission's call was about to head out across the globe … again.

Fr Vladimir, the young Dominican in charge of the Greek Orthodox dialogue, invited me to stay in their spare apartment just outside the Vatican walls. As I settled in, Fr Oliver, responsible for the Lutheran Church dialogue, showed up with a gift from Secretary Bishop Brian Farrell. It was a place on the following morning's tour of the excavations of the first Christian martyr's tombs underneath St Peter's Basilica. I was so excited.

There was confusion at the Vatican gates after I called the excavations by an incorrect name, which was actually the name of another similar sounding sight inside the basilica. The guards directed me that way and by the time my pronunciation had been ironed out the tour of the tomb excavations had departed. I was bitterly disappointed.

A final interview in St Peter's Square with the Zenit television station was my final appointment before aiming for the coast and hitting the road once more. It was a breath of fresh air to be out walking again in quiet prayer as Rome gave way to farming land.

I soon approached a few young women and my heart sank. They were in their mid-twenties, wearing ultra-short mini-skirts with skimpy singlet tops and standing on the roadside presenting themselves to passers-by for potential takers. I smiled and said hello. Two acted as though they hadn't heard me and fidgeted with their handbags, but one girl smiled slightly and, with sincerity, said hello. She asked where I was headed and when I responded, "Spain," her eyes lit up. She asked about all the countries I'd visited and spoke candidly of the places she'd love to see one day. She also said she understood the purpose for the mission, agreeing whole-heartedly. I asked her the crunch question, "Why this job? Why work like this?" She fell silent, breaking eye contact, before quietly admitting, "For the money. The money is good."

Inside the Pontifical Council, with Fr Vladimir and the Tanzanian representative

A man pulled off the road behind us to negotiate terms with one of the girls as I extended my hand to the young lady in friendship. She gave a small smile again, extended her hand and shook. I gestured towards the man in the car and said, "You're worth more than this. He can't buy you. You're beautiful." And she was. The young woman tucked her lips up, while looking down at her feet. I stepped back and asked one more thing before I left, "Please, will you pray for me as I walk?"

She looked back up, surprised. I added, "I'll pray for you." With a relaxed smile she murmured, "Grazie".

I was sad for her and angry with the men who used her. It was difficult to think of anything else for the rest of the day's walk, musing on the broken love and dignity relationships face day-in, day-out.

From a hotel near the west coast of Italy I continued towards the Mediterranean Sea the next morning before veering north along a less travelled route. My reception in each town worsened over time and, although there was almost always someone to offer a smile, there seemed to be more Italians with some sort of vendetta against me. At one seaside town there were no signs indicating the town's name, so I approached a lady walking past to ask her, but she tucked her handbag under her arm and ran like blazes all the way up the street. "Am I that ugly?" A young man then exited his front gate right beside me and looked up at me. I smiled and said hello, but he continued to stare at me, while shuffling along the hedge fence line and ducking back inside through a second gate. At a café down the road an elderly lady sat outside with her coffee and as I walked past she became fixated on me. Her stare did not waiver for a second. I felt so uncomfortable. I nodded and said good afternoon, but she didn't move a muscle. I walked on, checking my reflection in a window, trying to figure out if there was something wrong with me. It was one cold stare after another with countless pedestrians crossing the street to avoid me.

Thanks to some elderly nuns I was offered a quiet room for the night in a convent in Santo Severa before pushing on through increasing heat to Tarquinia and Pescia Romano. I shared my lunch with two playful white fluff-ball pups, but that was about the extent of my socialising there. The road was also difficult: there was no option but to squeeze along the edge of the heavily trafficked freeway; there was no grassed easement—just a half metre space between the white line and a crash barrier with humid air wafting out from the thick mass of trees overhanging it. It was a type of torture to walk within a metre of cars and trucks travelling past at between 100 and 130 km/h every few seconds. It was mentally exhausting. That corn-thing had been with me since Mexico and the chronic soreness in my right shoulderblade since Poland. Both were bearable, but on this day they sang loudly. My foot felt like it was on fire and my back like the knife was back … but jammed between shoulder blade and ribs.

One of the Vatican journalists had realised I would pass close to her mother's house and so had organised for me to stay there. I had instructions to wait at a particular town in the central square. I strolled in by mid-afternoon and waited until the parish priest invited me in for a cool drink and placed a call through to the mother. She said, "I'll pick him up soon," but it was nearly two hours before the English-speaking eighty-one-year-old turned up.

As we drove off she asked why I was so late arriving. I explained that there must have been a breakdown in communication because I'd finished earlier than normal, but the frail woman rebuked me, "I received the priest's phone call a few hours ago and I came down to pick you up and you weren't there." I was confused, but apologised, thinking the conversation would move on, but she smiled and asked me, "So, why were you so late arriving today?" I paused and then slowly re-entered the same conversation.

Living alone she fended for herself on a small farm. We regularly entered the same conversation three or four times over, and I had to restrain myself from laughing when she stopped suddenly and asked, "Do you murder cats?"

I held a straight face, "No, not at all."

"Good," she said, and the conversation moved on. What did concern me was what would happen the next morning when I walked downstairs for breakfast. Would she remember me or think I was a robber, or cat-murderer? She recycled through an endless list of three options for dinner, so I just offered to cook for her, which she gladly accepted and took a seat at the table. As I prepared dinner she recounted her amazing life spying for the British during the war. Her memory hadn't faded there.

I woke early on the Friday and sat in the kitchen waiting anxiously, hoping she'd recognise me. Appearing at the door she stopped with a look of confusion, before relaxing and commenting, "So you're off then! Where to today?" Thank you Lord. She served up home-made marmalade to go with the last few pieces of bread that sat on the table under a tea towel, but as I finished off the last piece she walked over to the table and announced, "Now! I have a couple of pieces of bread here. You can have them if you like," and flicked over the tea towel. Of course, it was now empty. Her eyes lit up, "Now where the Dickens has that bread gone!" Her hospitality was as good as gold, it just took a long time to say goodbye.

I headed off praying and humming between painful grimaces along the quiet country road to Orbetello meandering through fields of wild poppies. The only church I passed was on top of a large hill with the most spectacular view down along the rural coastline; but it was empty, so I was left to walk on past a mass of expensive homes hidden behind huge walls, hedges and security gates. It was about as far from Brazil as I could get. There were no kids playing soccer on the road and definitely no adults sitting back in armchairs having a chat with their neighbour. It was a kind of sanitised perfection.

It was pretty dull.

The walk from Orbetello to Grosetto was one of the most complicated of the entire journey. It was a brutal challenge both physically and mentally; there was no option but to hug the narrow shoulder of the main highway for most of the forty-four kilometres in sweltering heat. Intense holiday traffic made the less than thirty-centimetre gap between the white line and crash barrier a nightmare. A few times I was able to hop over and push through the knee high grass, but my arms inevitably ached from constantly dragging the walking poles through and my legs burnt from lifting my size sixteen boots up through it. When there was no option but to walk along the thirty centimetre gap, many drivers wanted to make a point of their disapproval of my presence by veering as close as possible, shunting me up into the chest-high barrier as the whoosh of rear-vision mirrors and speed-effected slurs raced by.

In the confined space, my left hand clipped a crash barrier join and it sliced the index finger open. Blood flowed, but there was nowhere to stop and grab supplies from my bag so it was left to run its course, dripping down across my hand. That day, the crops began to turn and a warm breeze started blowing; my hay fever allergies kicked in. My eyes watered so badly that I struggled to see anything and I regularly erupted into fits of sneezing. I had no choice but to hang onto the crash barrier for balance and let the energy draining sneezes take their course ... to the sounds of passing slurs. I could only wipe the water from my eyes, refocus and walk on, narrowly avoiding stepping on a metre-long Biacco snake. I was utterly exhausted when I caught site of Grosetto. I felt inebriated.

A youth group was setting up for their Sunday meeting and they eagerly listened to the mission to pray for unity. "Can I help you find accommodation?" a young lady asked. She'd recently walked from France to Santiago de Compostela in Spain, and said she knew how difficult it was when no one welcomed her. I completely agreed. She walked me to a second church to introduce me to the parish priest, who opened his arms with a smile and hugged me.

I needed it.

They apologised for there being little accommodation available, but suggested that if I wanted to sleep in the primary school's change rooms (with access to a shower, a wash basin, fresh water and benches to lay my sleeping gear on) I'd be most welcome. It wasn't comfortable—not by a long shot—but the shower was great, and I was so incredibly tired that it didn't make much difference. I slept remarkably well.

It was fifty kilometres on to Follonica along a maze of rural roads. An hour short of the town, I visited the local church and decided to call it a day. I walked into a small motel ... but before I'd said a word, the lady at the counter took a defensive step back and stared at me. I said hello and asked for a room, but she remained silent and shook her head with a scowl. My Italian was poor, so I politely asked again, but she'd understood the first time. She shook her head: "No!" and flicked her hand towards the door, gesturing for me to leave. I wasn't sure how to react. It looked pretty obvious that the hotel wasn't full. There were only two cars in the car park and no people to be seen anywhere. I pressed once more: "No rooms?"

She screwed her face up, stood tall with folded arms and said again, "No!" Again, she flicked her hand at me and stared me out of the building.

Ten minutes later four fire-trucks roared into view at full speed with their sirens wailing. They roared past and I turned to see a billowing plume of black smoke rising from what appeared to be the back of the motel! I turned slowly and walked on, as the plume of smoke grew larger by the minute.

From Follonica I headed on towards Donoratico, past olive groves and vineyards sweeping down to the Mediterranean Sea. While deep in prayer, I suddenly fresh-aired with one walking pole. It had fallen in half mid-stride. "You're not finished yet," I told it, and pulled out the trusty yellow sticky tape and set to work with tight precision taping until it was good to go.

I called into a small supermarket in Donoratico to buy supplies and every single person stopped to stare at me. There was no movement whatsoever. As awkward as it was the hilarity of the moment was mine to enjoy alone. Blaring out through the supermarket's sound system was a newly released song in English with a chorus line of, "stop and stare." It was as though I'd walked into my own mini-musical. I ignored the stares, grabbed what I needed while humming along to "stop and stare", jumped the motionless queue, paid my dues and left.

I walked on the next day humming "stop and stare", but battling the burning sensation of my foot and sharp shoulderblade pain. It was so intense at times that I had to just find a place to stop, remove my backpack and rest.

By sunset I'd covered fifty-one kilometres to Collesalvetti, but couldn't find the front door to the hotel. It was the most obscure postmodern building I've ever seen. After walking around it twice I was left baffled. A group of teenagers were mucking around outside a pizza restaurant in the adjacent shopping village when they caught sight of me. They whistled out and shouted taunts. I immediately tensed up. The mugging in Costa Rica and good ol' Smirnoff back in Russia had announced their presence with similar whistles. My reaction was instinctive and I had to force myself to relax as the twenty or so teenagers continued yelling. One of them, wearing a yellow hoodie, yelled out in English: "Hey, hillbilly!" They roared with laughter and mocked me with bizarre actions, swearing at me and pretending to call me over to fight. "Come here, hillbilly!"

I couldn't find the stupid hotel door and I'd had enough of their patronising rhetoric, so I turned and walked straight at them.

I had no intention of fighting them, but was intent on calling their bluff. Most of them scattered like seagulls, leaving the quiet few remaining to look up at me wide-eyed, wondering what they'd gotten themselves into. The ones running away persisted in yelling abuse, particularly the guy in the yellow hoodie. I towered over the small group remaining and simple said, "Hello," and they took a backward step. A few polite ones said hello back and one kid sincerely asked, "Where are you walking to?" So I told him. They were suddenly interested in asking questions. A few of them even said they'd take up the prayer.

The guy in the yellow hoodie strolled back out of the restaurant, as cool as could be, and joined the back of the group as though he'd played no part in the previous jibes. He looked around at the other guys with a smirk, looking for any sort of eye contact possible. He stopped smirking when he realised I was staring straight at him and the other teenagers turned and did likewise.

He now had his eye contact.

I walked towards him and the group stepped aside like the parting Red Sea. He looked around for help, but there was none forthcoming. I asked what he'd wanted to say, but he said nothing and shook his head. I told him that I wasn't going to touch him, at which point one of the younger kids piped up from behind with a ten second brief of the mission. We chatted quietly off to the side and he agreed that it wasn't a smart thing to yell abuse at complete strangers. He probably offered the resignation because I was twice his size, not so much out of goodwill, but there comes a point when resignation, repentance and forgiveness have to be completely independent of stature and be compelled by love, not fear.

> *And hope does not disappoint us, because God's love has been poured into our hearts through the Holy Spirit that has been given to us.*
>
> Romans 5:5

Total walked: *13,454 kilometres*

# Money, Monks & Cosmic Energy
## *May 2008*

Leaning into the north towards Pisa I arrived in the late morning at a centrally located Catholic church. A deadpan-faced nun greeted me and when I introduced myself in poor Italian while reaching for my official letters she cut to the chase and said, "No, we're not interested," and flicked her hand at me to get out. I was shocked, so cut to the chase myself and told her, "I'm a Catholic missionary from Australia. I have letters here from my archbishop and from the Vatican."

She didn't care.

Leaning forward with a scowl she repeated in English, "We are not interested," and again flicked her hand at me.

I asked her, "What are you not interested in? I haven't said anything."

She made it clear, "Whatever you have to say, we are not interested."

I took a deep breath, heaved the backpack back on and left her with, "You obviously speak English. It's sad that you aren't interested in the unity of Christians; that you aren't interested praying for love or truth. Are you even interested in Jesus?"

She flicked her hand again and I walked out into the street.

A young couple were chatting on the other side of the street and when the woman caught sight of me she burst out laughing—masking it poorly—and pointed. Her boyfriend turned and stared, laughing through a tight-lipped smirk. It ripped me. I had no idea why they had laughed at me and for the rest of the day I was left mulling over my appearance every time I caught sight of my reflection. I was clean-shaven, wearing normal clothes and, well, nothing out of the ordinary.

I walked on out of Pisa and crossed a large grassed area filled with people. I noticed they were all looking in one direction taking photos. I turned. Ah, the leaning tower of Pisa. "Well, there you go. I didn't expect that." I also didn't really give a stuff. It was standing there, albeit on a slight lean, next to an impressive cathedral, so I took a photo and walked on.

Within a few minutes a passing driver hit his horn and when I turned to him he thrust his middle finger up aggressively. None of them had any idea what I was doing and I was sick of being taunted just for being a non-Italian, or a backpacker, or a pilgrim, or whatever they despised in me. I was so angry, but the only non-violent protest I could think of was to toss my backpack in the ditch and somehow walk the rest of the way to Spain with nothing more than my passport and wallet. The backpack never made it off my back. I concluded that maybe I should just pray more.

I pitched my tent at a coastal campsite between two fully decked out campervans owned by Dutch couples. They'd only just met each other and the four of them welcomed me, generously changing all conversation to English so I could participate. We shared dinner and many travelling stories. Perhaps walking across Holland would have been a more pleasant experience.

I was scheduled for a rest day, but I didn't feel like sitting still; after breakfast with the Dutch couples, I walked on along the urbanised coastline. The twenty-six kilometre coastal footpath to Marina di Massa was a world of rollerblades, bicycles and pooch-walking. For most of the day my gaze was slightly to the left, out across the Mediterranean Sea.

A welcoming priest went out of his way to find accommodation for me, but, even after a solid sleep, I hit the road sporting a massive headache. I had to cut the day short in a village that was just beginning their Saturday vigil Mass when I arrived. My halt was rubber-stamped.

Afterwards, I ate dinner in the village pub that was decked out in motorcycle memorabilia. The owner's favourite rider happened to be Australia's Casey Stoner; being a resident of Stoner's country, and a motorbike rider myself, I was welcomed like a VIP. I was fed at minimal expense.

In the end, with the headache lingering, I craved nothing more than sleep.

Sixty-three kilometres of wild rivers, dense forest and massive hills lay ahead of me. I left in darkness, watching the twinkling lights of distant hillside villages fade into the dawn light. I followed a bitumen track along the rushing river with the heavily trafficked main road on the other side seeming a world away. The lush forest provided cool escapes and after bouncing along a thirty metre suspension footbridge across the river back onto the main road, I listened cautiously for oncoming traffic while walking on to the villages tucked into the hillsides.

The Sunday motorbike riders were out in force for the final twenty kilometre mountain pass to Lavagna and the riders took risks beyond what I perceived as reasonable. They took dangerous lines through blind corners at maximum speed and I twice watched riders flinch onto new lines when an oncoming vehicle suddenly rounded the corner in front of them. A third motorcyclist had to change his line and speed so drastically when a family van rounded the corner that he locked up the rear wheel, fish-tailed sideways and shaved past the van by centimetres.

I wound down the mountain onto the northern coastline of Lavagna tired and hungry. A young priest named Fr Stefano—with his Italian good looks—beckoned me inside to share a meal and take up the spare room, which was exactly what I needed.

The undulating forty-five kilometres to Genova—past cliff-clinging mansions—was my last alone for a while. Anne, an Irish wife and mother who'd been following my blogs, was going to walk a section with me. It took some time to find her in Genova but, with introductions over, and a few laughs at the height difference, we found accommodation and set about preparing for the week ahead. She was a veteran of pilgrimage and for one week she'd decided to wave goodbye to her husband and working sons.

Wow ... could she talk. I'd been starved of English conversation so between the two of us we hardly drew breath.

Ann was half my height and I was half her age, so we were an odd couple walking side by side around the Genova Gulf to Voltri and Savona, by which time her Irish storytelling skills were in overdrive. I was but a listener from then on.

Three Catholic churches received the invitation to pray for unity with enthusiasm and encouragement, but what really stood out was that each priest asked if they could pray for me before I walked on. It had been a long time since I'd been offered that. The first priest, after hearing the invitation, searched through his drawer and pulled out a tiny brick, about the size of my thumbprint. He signed and dated it before handing it to me with a smile saying, "We each must play our part in building the house of God: to build unity."

At the next church the young priest spoke a little English and was keen to catch up on some of the past blogs so promptly jumped on his computer. As the blog loaded he started laughing, "It's Fr Stefano from Lavagna!" I'd uploaded a photo in Genova and the young priest just shook his head, "You met Fr Stefano?" The two priests were good friends, with Stefano being a bit of a mentor to this young guy. It was a great conversation starter being able to tell him how Fr Stefano was and what was happening in his parish. The young priest just kept smiling and placed his hand on my shoulder, asking if he could pray for me.

Irish Anne ... and the height difference

The more headlands we rounded the more wealth we encountered. Yachts and powerboats filled the small ports, leaving little water to sail in. When we arrived in Savona, Ann bought food supplies while I searched for churches. I found two young Carmelite priests and they asked how my day had been and I commented on the flash watercraft and massive mansions. One of them said, "In this part of the world we have a real mission field. Ninety-eight per cent of the population say they are Catholic; the problem is that no one is Christian. There is a low level of faith."

The two young priests prayed with me before I headed off. I was left with a sense of hope in the prayerfulness of the Christians I did meet.

On the road to Finale Ligure, Ann and I watched the bizarre intricacies of the Genova Gulf lifestyle, which I didn't understand. I grew up on Flinders Island out in Bass Strait, so the coastal environment was familiar, but the hundreds of lifeless bronzed bodies beached on the shoreline weren't. Our family went to the beach to swim, but not one person touched the liquid stuff on this 30°C day. Everyone tanned. Ann suggested that the water might have been polluted, and sure enough, down the road we walked past an old man standing at the water's edge in his swimmers urinating into the sea. "Yep," I said to Ann with a smile, "it's polluted." Even buying sunscreen was an eye-opener. The chemist shelves were full of tanning lotions. After a few minutes of searching, I was sent on my way with 'SPF50 Babies Milk Lotion'.

No pride lost. I liked it. It wasn't greasy.

The beaches—one after the other—were a mass of lifeless bodies ... and clothing was optional. The car parks were filled with expensive vehicles reflecting the million dollar yachts anchored beyond the section of water reserved for urinating. I just didn't get it. Why did they live their lives like that? It was so plastic.

A landslide had closed the road up ahead so we were forced to follow a track up through the vineyards and market gardens to the country road on top. The view grew increasingly spectacular the higher we pushed, but we needed to wipe the sweat from our brows before being able to see it.

We were sore by the time we emerged onto the downward slope into a campsite at Finale Ligure. Ann's feet hurt so she rested the next day with a bus ride. I walked on to a Franciscan friary and then Cape Mele, where I found Ann perched up in a camping ground with dinner waiting. The week's scheduled distances were more than Ann had anticipated, so she decided a few half-day walks were in order.

The views over the Mediterranean Sea were beautiful as I moved on to San Remo, meeting up with Ann at the halfway mark. I lamented having only found Catholic churches that week and wondered if somehow I'd missed the others, but as we ambled into San Remo in the evening I at last spotted a Lutheran church and then, the next morning, six Evangelical Christians gathering for a meeting. They welcomed the mission and gladly prayed for me, before I walked on to a Russian Orthodox church. Three parishioners were standing at the door, but one of the men spoke only Russian, so I asked him in Russian, "Can I have fish please? Thankyou." That was all I remembered from Russia, but he laughed and shook my hand, enjoying the challenge of communicating with me. When his friend (who spoke fluent English) joined us the conversation about complete unity ... and Russia ... rolled on.

Ann walked for the first half of that day, leaving me to continue on foot along the rugged coastline to cross into France late in the afternoon. No borders, no stopping, nothing but a sign welcoming me to France.

Sadly, I was happy to have finished the tour of duty in Italy.

Ann and I found a camping ground with a spectacular spot for our tents overlooking Menton and the coast it sat along. My right toenail had grown back since the operation in Billings and was now pressing hard against the skin, enflaming it to within a whisker of splitting again. I was determined to avoid a three-peat and so used that evening to work on it slowly with small scissors, tweezers and a nail file. Over an hour, the nail was cut away and the inflammation reduced. I settled back with the bandaged foot and started learning my eighth language, French. "Je suis Samuel."

Italy yesterday, France for breakfast, opulent Monaco for lunch and back into France by dinner. I was a jetsetter ... on foot. With emails flooding in from Malta, of all places, as the Vatican interviews circulated through their media, we trekked along the famous Monaco Grand Prix racetrack and through that tunnel. Monaco overflowed with mansions, landscaped gardens, sports cars and the single biggest luxury watercraft I've ever seen. I counted four helicopters in the sky at one time. What really underscored the amount of money in that place was the footpath. It wasn't concrete—that'd be too Italian—and it wasn't bitumen—far too American—no—

it was synthetic rubber, like you'd find on an Olympic running track.

"I'm just popping out to grab milk! I'll be back in 24.2 seconds!"

Ann grabbed a lift from there as I trekked on towards Nice. The whole day left me with an overwhelming sense of sadness. Walking back across the border into France along a high, winding cliff past a mansion-clad nudist beach I prayed, "Why? How can so many of us live like this when so many fight to stay alive?" Adolfo kept entering my mind, but it was also on that day that a tragedy unfolded in Myanmar, where 5000 people lost their lives to severe monsoonal flooding. It all hit home pretty hard. Amongst that physical wealth it seemed clear that unity was a choice. To not choose it in its fullness was to not choose love in all its fullness. That coastline oozed self-love. It painfully reflected my own life in Australia: well … apart for the nudist beach.

Past one final headland, I walked out to an ocean view across the city of Nice. I was never a big fan of urban walking and again the stop/start nature of road crossings prolonged my arrival. It was there in Nice, once Ann and I had rendezvoused, that her week came to a close. I'd enjoyed her storytelling company, but also admired her for knowing her limits and not killing herself by trying to walk further than she could. I appreciated her no-fuss wisdom.

Believing that the end in Spain was now a real possibility, I booked myself an airline ticket home for two months' time. The farm felt closer than ever; but with my toe, foot and shoulder all in trouble, the last few thousand kilometres looked very real. My toe wept over the course of that day and I just hoped it would last the distance.

I walked on into the city of Cannes right on the eve of the internationally renowned Cannes Film Festival. The city was abuzz. My main issue was finding food. I couldn't find a single supermarket, just one casino after another. I stayed for a rest day at a camping ground and asked the caretakers for directions back to a supermarket. They sent me back the way I'd come the previous night, which confused me, but I was soon shaking my head. The supermarket chain was called Casino. Did I feel stupid or what? I went into the casino and came out a winner.

I met two young English directors at the campsite, one there to present his short film and the other to secure funds for his first feature film, but I also met two guys from South Korea. They were there to do nothing more than watch the films and enjoy the festival. They invited me to eat dinner with them and they set about cooking a Korean meal over their campfire, while I chipped in with a French dessert … from the 'Casino'. As soon as I shared about the mission for unity one of them piped up about North and South Korea saying, "We need to be united with those suffering across the border." He flicked through his rice and reflected. "They are our family. Some argue that we should cut all aid to force the government to change, but the people need help now. There is a lot of suffering on both sides because we cannot unite fully."

The mission was to invite people to at least pray that we'd be united in truth and in love. Perhaps some of us start with uniting ourselves in love and humbly work towards truth, while others begin with truth and are compelled towards love. "Lord, who is my neighbour?"

As if on queue, I then met an American Episcopalian preacher camping nearby. He was all for Christian unity and had no problem praying for it, but was more intent on highlighting his freedom in Christ as opposed to my guilt as a Catholic. He joked about how he was saved with nothing else to pay but that I, as a Catholic, was apparently lamenting my sin. His way of highlighting that can't be written here, but after a short conversation I realised I hadn't introduced myself by name, so offered, "Oh, by the way, I'm Sam." He responded with a laugh and said, "I'll call you mother f___ing ____ if I want to because I'm Episcopalian and free to do what I want!"

My dad sometimes used colourful language while yelling at the sheepdogs, but even they weren't degraded to the level of this guy's alternative name for me.

Apparently he was free to do what he likes. I guess I am too.

I walked on.

From Cannes to Le Muy it was a hot, tiring fifty kilometres over mountains. For the first time on the journey, I felt a longing for home. I hadn't felt that longing while at knifepoint, gunpoint or being beaten up but, while eating lunch on the side of a hairpin corner on a near-deserted mountainside, I longed for familiarity. I missed my own bed, a familiar view and a fridge. More than anything I think I just wanted to reach the end. After a long silent break under a small tree I stood back up (somewhat reluctantly) and walked on in prayer.

In Le Muy I passed a few campsites, but felt God say, "If you want to organise your own accommodation, you'll sleep well, but if you finish each day in its entirety, I can do better for you."

I ambled on into town towards the main church. A woman crossed the town square holding walking poles and yelling out to me in French. I quickly interrupted with an apology for not understanding her and she said, "Great! You speak English! I'm originally from England." Margaret and her now deceased husband had lived in Le Muy for thirty years. She'd been out walking with a club that morning in the same mountains I'd traversed and spotted me trekking along the road. She couldn't believe I'd made it all the way to her town.

The church was shut, so Margaret promptly offered me her spare apartment in the town centre. It was perfect. We ate dinner together and, despite being an atheist, she knew the bible well, so an in-depth discussion about all-manner of things pertaining to the Church ensued. She was a retired university English lecturer and was more than apt at constructing well thought out questions around unity and its place on the world stage. The evening was a pleasure and my little apartment for the night was so much more spacious than a one-man tent.

Twenty-five kilometres down the road I was welcomed by a Polish priest named Fr Andrew, but my French was still poor so we resorted to a humorous combination of Polish and English instead. He took on the mission and sent me on my way with extra food and a drink.

Similar to my arrival in Le Muy, I was looking at hotels and campsites as I walked into Le Luc, only this time through a saturating thunderstorm that seemed to travel in the same direction as me. The only dry patch left on me was a tiny area on my shirt until a large truck rushed by and found a huge puddle in front of me. I didn't even flinch. I just closed my eyes and kept walking. "Whoosh!" It was like being dumped by a wave at the beach.

I found the central Catholic church and rang the doorbell. Standing in the pouring rain I was pondering the discomfort of having to put my tent up in those conditions when a twenty-seven-year-old Argentinean missionary priest opened up and without any questions ushered me inside. I apologised for dripping water all over the tiled floor, but he said not to worry about it and called for his fellow priest to fetch towels. Fr Santiago and his counterpart, the Chilean Fr Jose, introduced themselves and within a few seconds French was put to the side and we rabbited on in Spanish. The invitation to pray for unity was well received and they in turn offered me a room, a shower and access to a washing machine.

Bliss.

The following day was a cracker. I woke at 8 am and didn't get back to bed until 9:30 am the following day.

Never let a monk give you a job.

When I arrived in the town of Brignoles I met an English-speaking monk who bounced down the stairs with youthful vigour. Fr Tarcisius received the mission and as quick as a flash gave me two options. I could sleep the night there or I could join him and a small group as they traversed the mountains southwards over the course of the night to La Castille to attend a special consecration Mass for the diocese the next morning. I was kind of hoping for a good night's sleep after a day of walking, but Fr Tarcisius made his opinion clear, slapping me on the shoulder and saying, "God has provided an international walker to come with us. You can lead us! The youth group will love this."

I really did want to sleep.

I remembered Fr Fox in Casper, Wyoming, reckoning that God only put people in his life at inopportune moments, so I swallowed my desire to be normal, and walked on with them. Fr Tarcisius was thrilled and slapped me on the shoulder again, "You can have a power nap before we walk and then I'll make sure dinner is waiting for you when you wake up."

The monk showed me to a small room with "Agape" written on the wall. It meant a great deal in the moment to have that word in front of me reminding me why I was there. Upon removing my boots I found that the big toe had succumbed to the workload and the skin had split open. It was bleeding badly. Fr Tarcisius fetched first aid supplies and offered all he could, except an option out. While I disinfected the wound he ran off to make dinner, reappearing with pasta and hot soup. It was a walker's version of a Grand Prix pit stop. I scoffed the meal down and the lights were flicked out for a ninety-minute nap.

That hour and a half felt like five minutes. I was so tired that I felt sick. I grabbed a clean pair of socks, cautiously slid the boots on, and we were away. Fr Tarcisius, the seven young locals and I set off into the night along a misty rocky mountain trail introducing ourselves as we went. There was just enough starlight to see our path without torches so we trekked the first half of the night unaided. I prayed a lot of quiet prayers that I'd simply stay conscious.

After midnight clouds rolled in and darkness descended until it rained heavily. No one complained. There was just a lot of annoyed laughter. For half an hour it poured and we sloshed across the mountain towards La Castille. The rain eased to light drizzle and at 6 am, with the final pass into La Castille in view, it stopped altogether. Despite feeling drunk I was content to complete the journey.

A rising sun through scattered mist uncovered a magnificent rural seminary set on tens of acres of gardens. A few residents welcomed us enthusiastically, ushering us into a 7:30 am Mass followed by a hearty breakfast. After a few formalities, I slunk off to a quiet room to sleep for three hours. I hadn't even understood why we'd walked there, so was completely unaware that the La Castille adventure was only just beginning.

Fr Tarcisius woke me for lunch and I was groggily introduced to a number of seminarians, including a fellow by the name of Michael of Jesus. He was also a monk, a 6' 5", basketball-playing, Chicago-come-Texas monk studying in the south of France. The guy was awesome. His passion for Christ and the Church jerked me out of the "I want to be at home" mindset so hard that I nearly got whiplash. We spent most of the next two days together, rarely shutting up, sharing our respective journeys and the troubles in the world we'd witnessed that cried out for God's love.

Br Michael explained why that afternoon was so important and why the Brignoles group had traipsed across the mountains to be there. The entire diocese was gathering to consecrate themselves to Mary: to commit to serving Christ alongside Mary. The bishop was a missionary at heart and led from the front, encouraging the diocese to surrender to God and serve one another.

Thousands of people were arriving through the front gate for the outdoor Mass and, as Br Michael and I wandered through the swelling crowd, a voice shouted out: "Samuel! You made it!" Fr Jose and Fr Santiago were standing in the crowd with their arms outstretched triumphantly. "You made it!" Quickly moving through the throng of people they hugged me and then began sharing the invitation to pray for unity to all the priests passing by. A figure walked through the surrounding group with a broad smile and said, "Samuel! Dzie dobry!" (Polish for "Good day"). Fr Andrew shook my hand and joined in spreading the mission to everyone passing by.

The Mass was engrossing and emotional … for one that stretched over three hours! The day was a consecration like I'd never seen before and at the end of it Br Michael led me through the dispersing crowd to the bishop, but warned me, "He is such a missionary that he'll give you a job to do in the Diocese. Be careful what you say yes to." Sure enough, after an animated introduction, the bishop paused and posed the question, "Are you staying here at the seminary tonight?" I had no idea and responded accordingly. He smiled and thrust his pointed finger at me, "Yes, in fact you should stay two nights!" He looked across at Michael, "The two of you need to spend time together. Catch up and learn from each other. Two nights." And with that the conversation was over. It wasn't the worst request he could've made. I stayed an extra day at the seminary for what was a perfect God-given antidote to lethargy.

Br Michael arranged for a young seminarian doctor to tend to my feet, but he made it clear that he was not a practising doctor at that point, but a seminarian. I didn't care. I trusted he'd do a better job than my feeble attempts. He patched up the bleeding toe, found the necessary medical supplies for me to carry and then tended to the burning right foot. I told him it was a corn, but he shook his head and said, "That isn't a corn. It is not like anything I've ever seen before." He hacked at it with a scalpel without anaesthetic, but the pain was manageable, despite blood being drawn. Once he'd finished he cleaned the scalpel and handed it to me asking, "Did you see what I just did then?"

I nodded, "I think so."

"Good. Just scrape it back everyday. Just try not to make it bleed like I did."

I wasn't too keen, but would at least give it a go. Anything to stop that burning sensation.

I was ferried back to Brignoles where Fr Tarcisius welcomed me into the Community of St John Monastery and offered me the Agape room once again.

"Are you sure? You don't have any other jobs for me?" It was a pleasure to be there.

I headed west from Brignoles through fields of poppies, towering forests and centuries-old stone villages, while narrowly avoiding a massive charging Rottweiler that copped my slamming walking pole across its snout for its troubles.

It seemed to be the day for it. Just a little later I passed a small warehouse with a huge security fence around it and on the other side was a massive black German Shepherd that wasn't happy to see me. He charged the fence with aggressive snarls and barks, smashing into the wire sending saliva flying. He was wild, but with a huge fence between us I couldn't help but backchat while walking as close to the fence as possible. I tapped him on the nose with my walking pole and calmly said, "Behave yourself."

As I taunted it with, "What are you going to do? Hey big fella?" the fence stopped at a wide-open gate and we walked out in front of each other. My life flashed before my eyes. A glob of saliva dripped from his mouth. The black German Shepherd then turned and trotted on across the gateway to the other fence where he waited patiently for me to resume walking. First I had to start breathing. I walked on across the driveway and as soon as I was alongside the fence again he resumed his aggressive snarling and fence-smashing. Humility was the lesson.

After fifty-eight kilometres I was left hotel-less in Aix-en-Provence. At 11 pm I was pointed to the dimly lit riverside park. With no other choice, I pitched my tent down there, while a homeless man rolled his sleeping gear out fifty metres away under a lamp pole. We were all alone with the constant sound of the trickling creek nearby and the echoes of drunken university students partying in a house somewhere up the gully.

Packing up to move on early I noticed that the homeless guy was awake so I said good morning. He lifted up a bottle of wine and asked in English, "Do you drink?"

I declined and extended some of my breakfast to him, "Do you eat?" With a broken tooth smile he said, "Yes," and accepted his share.

The long, hot forty-four kilometres to Miramas was filled with snakes ducking off into surrounding fields. At day's end I was again left without a bed. As all moments of decision require … I grabbed a souvlaki. I asked the souvlaki maker about accommodation options and a young kid piped up behind me in broken English, "I know hotel." Zaheer was a ten-year-old Iraqi boy who'd been listening to our conversation.

"You know a hotel?"

He nodded and ushered me to follow.

Zaheer chatted away as he led me across the railway tracks and, when he learnt what I was doing, he opened up about his faith. For a brief moment, there we were, a Christian and a young Muslim, chatting away about prayer. He was a humble little kid full of confidence and he led me to a run-down bar with a few rooms available upstairs. Apart from the girl behind the bar, I was the only non-French, non-Muslim guy in there. I had a great time. Zaheer shook my hand, proud of having solved the problem, and set off for home. A fellow at the bar named Mohammed offered to shout me a glass of Coke. A deep conversation opened up with the Muslim guys sitting there and, to my surprise, they not only understood why I was walking for Christian unity, but why the unity of Christians was important from an Evangelical perspective. One of them said, "How are you ever going to pass on your faith to others if all your Churches keep fighting against one other and teaching different truths?" They even opened up about their experience of intolerance within their own community.

At the end of the night one fellow wrote down the blog address saying he'd like to keep following the journey, to pray for unity. "… and if the Christians can unite, and the Muslims can unite, then we need to look at each other and unite in truth and love."

After a good night's sleep I headed out for a hot and sticky fifty-five kilometres across the Rhine floodplains to Saint-Gilles. I visited the churches along the way and apart from my feet killing me (and the snakes trying to) it was a beautiful sight: the patchwork of rice paddies, fully grown barley crops, hay cutting in progress and flourishing vineyards amidst the tangle of swamps.

I pushed on to arrive in Saint-Gilles right on sunset at 9 pm, but I couldn't see any churches as I approached the village. I wasn't in the mood for wandering the streets aimlessly so I stopped to ask for assistance from an elderly beret-wearing man sitting at a bus stop. I asked in my poor French if there were any churches in town and he nodded, "Oui, oui," and tried to explain the complicated route, but in the end said, "It's too difficult to explain. Come on, I'll walk you there."

Rohan was eighty-something years old. He stood up with his walking stick in hand and was only just taller than my hip. We pottered along the road at a snail's pace, one tiny walking stick step after the other, and I felt like telling him I was in a hurry and walking on alone. I knew I should trust in God's perfect timing though, so I slowed my focus and accepted this old guy's generosity. We chatted slowly in French until a steep alleyway caused him to start breathing heavily. He stopped for a few minutes to catch his breath and gave a genuine smile that read something like, "It wasn't always this tough." He then motioned with his walking stick for us to push on up through the quiet town.

Rohan directed me the full kilometre and a half to the Basilica of Saint-Gilles and when it came into view he nodded at it saying, "There it is. Good luck with the mission. Enjoy your journey." He shook my hand and ambled back down the alleyway to his bus stop. I was floored by his selflessness.

The church square was empty, but a gentleman walked out of his house off to the side and saw me wandering through. He piped up with, "Do you need a bed?" Jean-Claude happily showed me around the corner and up a flight of stairs to an old stone building. I had no idea what was going on, but another man, Regis, opened up and greeted me into his home as Jean-Claude waved goodbye. Regis' home was decked out for passing pilgrims and he'd even cooked too much pasta for dinner that night so there was a huge bowl of spaghetti sitting on the table waiting for me. I was dumbstruck. Regis showed me my bed for the night and then said goodnight with, "I'm leaving at 5:30 am so I won't see you

Rohan stops to catch his breath

in the morning. Just make sure you pull the door closed behind you when you leave." And he was gone.

God's perfect timing indeed.

There was a tense moment on the journey from there to Lunel. I passed three dodgy looking late-twenties men gathered outside a cluster of countryside homes and they followed me down the road in a beat-up car. When they pulled off a few hundred metres ahead of me I started praying for God's help, but maintained my forward direction. The three men stepped out and leant against the car, while occasionally glancing back up at me. There was nothing around except overgrown fields and tall woodlands. There was no easy escape if it turned ugly. The threat of that happening grew when one man crossed the road and walked back in my direction. I crossed to the other side just to see what he'd do. He maintained his course and walked up until we drew level.

I fastened the grip on my poles as he continued on a little further behind me. I now had two threats: one behind and the two in front. The guys at the car stood firm, occasionally glancing up. I shoulder checked the first guy just as he double backed and walked back down the road behind me. It was getting cramped. I swapped sides again, and the two guys ahead stepped forward. As I walked by I nodded hello and one returned it ... just. I walked on praying and periodically doing innocuous shoulder checks as an animated conversation opened up between them. Their glance was thrown my way a number of times, but they never returned.

It was about time one of those encounters ended that way.

An Evangelical Baptist church in Lunel received the mission joyfully, as did the priest at the Catholic church, who showed me to a safe tent pitching spot out the back. It was a quiet night for tent sleeping in a populated area with the only noise waking me during the night being that of light rain on my tent.

The tedious twenty-five kilometres from there to spectacular Montpellier saw me arriving late in the afternoon along the main city arterial and I somehow landed in a conversation with two hippies, for want of a better word. Alternative lifestyle'ers? Standing idly beside their kombi van, the middle-aged man and young woman were adorned with coloured clothes, bare feet and a plethora of dangling ornaments, but the conversation was what was truly alternative. He was all for unity and loved what I was doing, but we weren't exactly on the same … shall we say … wavelength. He agreed with the mission, saying, "Yes, we need to pray to the sky for the cosmic energies of all religions to unite as one so we can all come together."

I'm still contemplating what that actually means.

I looked for an opportunity to make a stand against the absolute mish-mash of relativism with little understanding of what each religion consisted of. He spoke of his favourite religion, a tribal belief system of South America, and I prayed for an opportunity to say something that could introduce Christ into the conversation. I noticed that one of his many 'dangly things' was a Franciscan tau. I also wore one, so I pulled it out and drew the conversation towards St Francis. The man knew of St Francis as a man who talked to animals and plants and so he carried the tau as a reminder to do the same. I smiled and said, "Well, Francis wasn't exactly Dr Doolittle …" though he did scold a wolf and had a particular love and appreciation for God's creation. "He was most passionate about the Church and following Jesus." I shared for a quick moment about how it was Francis' way of following Christ that was most attractive to me.

As I shared about how awesome Francis' faith was the young woman presented a bouquet of colourful flowers and said, "These are for you to carry." I wasn't keen to carry a bouquet through Montpellier, but with two walking poles, one in each hand, I was able to decline politely, "Sorry, I can't carry them." Unfortunately, that didn't faze her and she shouldered up alongside and jammed the stems between my backpack and neck such that the flowers poked up over the back of my head like a floral halo. I looked like a peacock with a backpack. I offered for them to instead be placed on the side of my backpack where they'd be 'better protected'.

I walked on, leaving the flowers as decoration at the first church I passed. On the large flight of steps leading up to the church, a loud gathering of theatre-sport-playing university students flooded down into the small plaza beneath. They were full of life, but it hit hard when I walked past the raucous crowd into a very empty church. For the size of the throng of people around the church, there was a notable absence within it. I was the only one in the old sandstone building, surrounded by the echoes of the festivities outside. I flinched as a cat caught me off guard, rubbing against my leg. It strolled to the front of the aisle and then jumped up onto the front row of seats, stood up on its back legs and reached out with its front paws to the railing. It then just stayed there, feet on the seat, paws on the railing, facing the altar and tabernacle.

I had a St Francis moment. I followed suit … only kneeling.

Montpellier to coastal Mèze was wet and wild as a storm whipped up off northern Africa. I set up my tent at a campsite with rugged coastal views and did my best to dry off, but the wind-driven rain put a dampener on everything. The storm buffeted my tent all night, to the point where I was concerned about it being ripped apart. It flapped and strained under the pressure of the howling winds. It was a rough night's sleep.

Although the rain eased off the next day, the wind didn't stop howling for the forty-three kilometres to Béziers. Béziers was stunning with its rich, crammed architectural history sprawling along a peninsula-like hill overlooking the flooded plains below.

A young kid playing in an alleyway with his friend led me all the way to a cheap hotel's front door and shook my hand while smiling broadly as we arrived. The French were proving to be extraordinarily generous. Every act of kindness made a significant impact.

My foot bled badly and showed signs of infection, so I cleaned it as best as I could and taped it neatly the following morning for the testing fifty-one kilometre haul to Saint-Pons-de-Thomières. My shoulder played up again and I had to remove the backpack a number of times to let the pain subside.

While praying the joyful mysteries of the rosary, a frighteningly close lightning bolt pierced the morning air into a field nearby. I flinched backwards, but being out in the middle of the countryside there weren't many places to hide. A torrential downpour ensued and engulfed me as I ran for cover under a hawthorn bush. It was too little too late. Half an hour later the storm faded and I reappeared from the dripping bush to continue on away from the Mediterranean, up into the forest-clad Pyrenees foothills.

Rain set in solidly at midday and the murky rivers burst their banks. I stopped at a village Catholic church to extend the mission, but the priest was cautious and dismissive, so I thanked him for his time and turned to leave. He had a sudden change of heart and somewhat reluctantly asked if I needed anything. I was saturated, so I asked if I could at least change my socks. He obliged and let me in, leading me to a room with a small fan-forced heater.

The priest left momentarily while I whipped my socks off and draped them in front of the heater. When he returned he glanced down and saw my wet, bleeding feet with soggy bandages clinging to the toe. He was shocked. His gaze rose slowly and he asked, "You actually walked all the way?" For the second time I explained the journey, only this time he believed me and received it with great encouragement. The bleeding feet came in handy after all. He ran through the house gathering food, medical supplies, a towel and two new pairs of thick walking socks.

Seasonal waterfalls burst over cliff faces as I headed higher along a winding mountain road past low-lying sprawling forest and dripping wet spring flowers. The higher I pushed the thinner the rain became until it was just a refreshing mist on the wind all the way into Saint-Pons-de-Thomières, where I was again led to accommodation.

The thirty-six kilometres on to Mazamet were awesome. The old railway line connecting the towns was gravelled over creating a seamless contour-following pathway passing uninterrupted through lush forests, small farms and long, well-lit tunnels to each village. It turned into a type of silent retreat. My French improved daily so the few passing salutations from locals out for a stroll stretched into passing conversations.

There was no accommodation to be found in the town centre, so I asked for directions from a passing teenage girl. To my surprise—in the same way as a number of her countrymen—she smiled and asked me to follow. Dorean was quiet and modest, but didn't lack any confidence. She uncovered the mission piece by piece and, by the time we arrived at a Catholic church hostel, she took it upon herself to do the talking. The hostel was a boarding house for students, but I didn't qualify to stay and the woman at the front desk was adamant of that. Dorean wasn't swayed. With what seemed like perfect innocence she pleaded my case and the woman relented. I was welcomed in for one night. I was so grateful for having Dorean fight for me and thanked her accordingly. She just smiled, hugged me and said, "You're welcome."

I loved France.

Summer was fast approaching and abundant supplies of mulberries and three species of cherry grew wild along the roads. I regularly stopped to top up my vitamin C intake en route to Puylaurens and then Toulouse.

In Puylaurens I was given the town's 3 x 3 metre worker's cabin sitting between the concrete poles under a car park. It contained a bed, a shower and a toilet. Perfect. As I dressed for bed I dropped an item of clothing on the wounded toe and it nearly brought me to tears. I was left reeling and clutching my foot. If that clothing had been a knight's iron chest plate it would have been understandable, but it was my cotton undies. The toe was in bad shape and the infection had set in.

A permanent line down the middle of my forehead was present during the forty-nine kilometres to Toulouse, but it wasn't the bleeding toe that caused the grief, it was the other foot! That thing I was scraping away at with a scalpel flared up and the cigarette-on-the-bottom-of-the-foot sensation was relentless. Audible grunts slipped out all day long. I didn't pray much other than repeating the words, "Lord, please unite us." I didn't have the mental capacity for much else.

I was exhausted when I arrived in Toulouse; in fact, I was a lethargic wreck. I visited a few churches and was offered a bed at a pilgrimage house, where I attempted to write my blog. I was so tired and in so much pain that I did nothing for ten minutes but stare at the screen. Thinking back over that week took more energy than I'd anticipated. I lifted my hands to the keyboard and asked myself: "Where am I?" The longer I sat there the worse I felt. I didn't write that blog and I don't even remember going to bed that night. I was so close to the end, but so agonisingly far.

*My child, when you come to serve the Lord, prepare yourself for testing.*

Ecclesiasticus 2:1

Total walked: *14,441 kilometres*

# Shower Screams, Spilt Blood & Crushing the Serpent's Head
## June 2008

I struggled from Toulouse to L'Isle-Jourdain and further west to Auch, but was looking forward to dinner after receiving an invitation from the leader of the Toulouse World Youth Day pilgrimage group to meet him in the centre of Auch that night. Charles was driving 100 kilometres to meet me and he arrived with his friend, a local named Jean. They were superb hosts and keen for me to try the local produce at a restaurant. They ordered my food, but gave me the choice of entrée. I could either have duck's liver or garlic snails. Jean laughed and in his thick French accent pointed out that, "We French don't eat snails. We just feed them to the English as a joke."

I chose the snails and to my surprise they tasted pretty good.

That night Jean drove me out to his family estate set on hundreds of acres of lush rolling pasture with vineyards etched into the fields and forests of oaks and elms bordering it. He drove me back the next morning past an old ruined castle dripping in the morning mist which, in centuries past, had served as his family's home. They'd been there longer than my family's transient heritage from Ireland and Germany could be traced.

It rained heavily that day and at lunchtime I passed through the village of Mirande, where the wet narrow streets were named after Jean's forefathers. Jean had organised for me to meet the mayor and local media attention was given to the walk because of the meeting. The invitation to pray for unity at 4:01 went out that little bit further.

I still had some distance to travel that day, but the rain had set in hard, so Jean encouraged me to call it a day and just put in a big forty-eight kilometres tomorrow. My saturated, bleeding toe wasn't going well so I agreed and headed back to the estate to tee a few golf balls off through the rain to his par three hole. It's a wonder I didn't just stay there permanently.

A couple from the local church were invited over for dinner and they jumped on the phone to organise a bed for me in Tarbes, while Charles rang through with the news that he'd organised a bed for two nights for me in Lourdes. He knew I planned to take a rest day there so he'd organised my stay accordingly. I was so grateful.

Jean sent me on my way with a sturdy handshake for the long and painful walk to Tarbes. My bleeding foot was raw and the sole of my right foot taunted me, like I was stepping on a nail every step. I wanted to cut it off. The knife-in-the-back sensation also flared, exhausting me.

The Colonel family continued the French hospitality in Tarbes, opening their home up with dinner simmering away. We ate outside in the warm summer evening and shared a few stories while washing up, but I was slow moving and the last to head to bed. When I pulled the boots off the toe looked sickly and it took every ounce of energy to stand back up and limp into the shower.

I had to be careful not to let water drop onto the toe. Even that was excruciating. Then, in a moment of un-coordination, I lost my grip on the soap and, as if in slow motion, it fell in a direct line for the enflamed, fleshy toe. With a sudden reflex response, I snatched my foot away from its path, only to smash it straight into the shower wall, splitting it wide open. I couldn't breathe. My face contorted and I convulsed with pain. I didn't want to wake the now sleeping

Colonels, so I didn't make a sound. For at least a minute I shook uncontrollably and my eyes remained squeezed tight. It was a long time before I started breathing again and even then I couldn't seem to breathe in enough. Amid short, sharp breaths I opened my eyes to see blood interspersed with the water, flooding across the shower floor.

When I did make it bed I practically passed out and didn't stir until my 6 am alarm chimed. I was so tired that I just prayed, "God, please help me get up."

Halfway between Tarbes and Lourdes I was desperate for a toilet break. With a steep embankment on both sides of the road and thick forest surrounding it, I opted for the one path out of sight that I could find: down a steep, ten metre high concrete culvert for a small forest river. I left my backpack and poles resting behind the crash barrier and began my descent. After about half a metre I had that sinking feeling that I'd misjudged the steepness and with an innocent, "Oh-oh" my feet shot out from under me and I slid down the concrete slope on my back. The culvert's five metre wide semi-circle tunnel under the road had only a one-metre section of concrete actually touching down on the ground on either side. I was accelerating towards the culvert drop off. I was forced to manoeuvre away from a fall into the shallow, rocky river, so without a second thought I slammed my hands onto the concrete and, along with my boots, steered myself to the embankment side, launching off the edge with less than a metre to fall on to dry land.

Concrete: 1. Skin on my hands: 0.

The rips and tears on my bloodied hands stung intensely. I had to put it into perspective though. To fall off the culvert edge that now towered above me could have easily resulted in a broken leg. I shook the pain out while lamenting my decision to descend to a place that now looked near impossible get out of. Thick blackberries surrounded the ten metre embankment and I had to use them to help pull myself back up. It hurt a lot.

I settled into Lourdes for a rest day at a youth hostel overlooking the town. Lourdes was fascinating. Famous for a series of apparitions 150 years earlier, followed by thousands of miracles since, it drew people from around the world on Christian pilgrimage. The basic gist was that Mary, the mother of Jesus, had appeared to a young girl in a series of apparitions and on one occasion asked the girl to do penance for the return of sinners to her son. That act of penance was to drink from a muddy pool. The young girl did so and a spring of natural fresh water burst up. It continues to flow to this day and like a modern day 'Serpent on the Staff' in the book of Exodus, there had been thousands of healings attributed to the pouring on or submersion in the water. The young, the old, the walking, limping, wheelchair-bound or on crutches were everywhere.

In my state, I fitted right in …

After Mass at the shrine I made my way down to the flowing spring, but once standing on the edge of it I didn't want to dip my toe in. Was my faith wavering? I had to pray, "Jesus, I trust you," before deciding I'd better dip it in if I wanted to finish the journey. I slipped the left foot under the flowing water and prayed. I'm not sure what I expected, but nothing happened that I could see. I prayed that whatever happened I would accept, but that I would like it to finally be healed, please.

From Lourdes I followed a stunning fast flowing river with farms and chateaus lining its banks and, for the first time, I caught a glimpse of the true Pyrenees. Snow-covered peaks rose skywards well above the foothills for the forty-two kilometres to a centuries-old town of stone and mortar named Louvie-Juzon.

Due to confirmations at the Diocese cathedral in a nearby city, the local church was empty, but a worker at the bakery suggested I attend Sunday Mass at a village I was to pass through the next day twenty kilometres away. She thought it was at 10 am, so I woke early and hit the road for a brisk four-hour walk to Mass. The pre-dawn air was crisp under the shadow of the Pyrenees, and the rising sun revealed a stunning quiet narrow road. It was a beautiful setting of green fields and towering forest with white Charolais cows inquisitively following me down fence lines. For most of that day it was just the company of the wet, dripping forest.

I arrived at the tiny village for Mass with literally one minute to spare, but was saddened to find that the village was on a rotation system and I'd dipped out. The Sunday morning Mass was being held elsewhere. I prayed outside the church and then walked on to miss Mass in Arette that afternoon as well. I'd also gone without internet access in both Louvie-Juzon and Arette, so my weekly blog and contact with home was missed. The Pyrenees Mountains staring down at me were unlikely to yield internet access for at least a few days while crossing them, so I just hoped everyone back home wouldn't fret too much about my absence.

From a room in a small hotel in Arette I planned my attack on the Pyrenees into northern Spain. My destination on top of the mountains, a ski village, closed that very day for the rest of the season, I could either sleep in my tent at nearly 2,000 metres above sea level or walk fifty-three kilometres across the Pyrenees Mountains in one hit to the first Spanish town. It was a tantalising choice. Either way, I wouldn't be bored. As darkness fell in Arette rain set back in and the decision of how to tackle the Pyrenees loomed closer. It could wait for a few hours of sleep first though. I loved France and I'm indebted to its people for their warmth, hospitality and friendship.

After an average night's sleep I rose at 4:30 am to the sound of steady rain and decided to walk it in one hit. I began the wet ascent in darkness, following a narrow road that swept out of the countryside along a gushing creek that pierced a steep valley. The sound of rain hitting my jacket hood accompanied me through the sunrise behind dense clouds. The occasional farmhouse emerged slightly from the dim gloom and no more than four cars idled past that morning.

Breathtaking mountains, lush forest-swamped valleys home to deer and raging rivers filled every view. At nearly 1,400 metres above sea level I entered thick clouds and semi-whiteout. Alpine scree sprawled across the slopes and, every now and then, I heard distant clanking cowbells in the mist … but absolutely nothing else. It was sublime.

The wet weather and cool conditions enabled me to continue without a break until I was twenty-seven kilometres from Arette and 1,804 metres above sea level. Not a bad first leg.

It grew colder by the minute and without my true winter gear I was forced to improvise, pulling my spare socks on as gloves. I pushed on fast, trying to maintain body heat, but the cold winds cut through my spring clothing. I sought shelter behind a bolder at one point, but soon moved on just to get off the mountain and passed by an unassuming marker indicating that I was crossing the border.

Spain: the final frontier.

When my descent from the clouds began I was met with a remarkable view of dry, tree-filled valleys with rocky escarpments and five eagles circling it all. Within a matter of minutes, the clouds swept down the mountain and I was again plunged into whiteout. It took a few hours for it to clear again but when it did it cleared into warm sunshine, revealing the Spanish peninsula.

Looking down a steep section of road winding back and forth for three kilometres, I decided to hurdle the safety barrier and take off downhill in a direct line. After a number of road crossings I hopped and skipped into a thick section of pines and only then wondered if it might happen to be bear territory. I continued weaving at pace through the trees, but there are few things that can drag you out of a happy mountain-descending frame of mind quicker than discovering enormous foot-prints thirty centimetres deep in soft ground. My boots left a depression no more than five deep. I didn't hang around.

The next road cutting was a sheer cliff, so I had to lean out and grab hold of a pine tree growing up from the roadside and climb down it before moving on.

Spain was an immediate contrast to France with dry thorn bush covered slopes and ripened wheat fields. Cattle wandered freely across fenceless properties and old World War II gunner's stone hideouts sat crumbling on the valley walls.

In the first town of Isaba, only the elderly women were at Mass. They welcomed me with quiet smiles and, like music to my ears, the Mass in Spanish filled me with warmth. I could at last understand what was being said again. The Spanish language came flooding back and I passed the invitation to pray for unity on to the women before finding a bed and breakfast for the night.

I followed the Río Belagua down to the next village at dawn, but it wasn't so welcoming. A woman in full conversation with a mother and her children at the church office stopped and stared at me as I introduced myself, but before I'd even finished my thirty-second introduction she flicked her hand at me and told me to go away. She muttered a quick word to the mother, who struggled to hold back laughter. The woman made it obvious what her sentiment was as she scowled at me, "Shoo! Shoo!" The mother burst out laughing and turned away, trying to mask her insincerity. I backed away and asked if the priest was in town, but that made her aggressive and she turned me away as though I were a mangy dog.

I walked on for no more than half a kilometre before looking back over my shoulder at the village right at the moment when a massive lightning bolt struck into the heart of it, hitting the church, followed by an ear-piercing crack of thunder that echoed off the surrounding mountains. The dark cloud directly above opened up in a torrential downpour and I was left very wide-eyed, continuing on in sunshine. It was like something straight from the Old Testament.

The owner of a tiny bar at the next village down refused payment for my lunch when he learnt of the mission. He even sent me on my way with a free drink, while drawing my attention to a picture of Jesus sitting above the bar. "Lunch is my contribution to the mission," he said. Thank you sir.

The Pyrenees foothills gave way to open rolling fields of golden wheat dotted with ancient ruined castles. I skirted the edge of a massive lake and, below the ghostly remnants of a long abandoned fortified village atop a steep prominence, I found a campsite. I sat on the lake's edge at sunset tending to my injured toe and burning right foot, but both looked worse each day. Healing at Lourdes didn't seem to have been mine … but at least I was still moving.

I still hadn't found internet access since Lourdes so at the next large town I broke as many notes as I could and found a payphone. I rang home and Chris picked up, "Hey! We were wondering if you were dead somewhere up on the Pyrenees."

I told him my position plus the blog's username and password with a request for him to post a short blog on my behalf but, "Chris, remember there's a lot of people reading this. Don't write anything stupid."

He just laughed, "Why? How are you going to stop me?" And our conversation dropped out.

The priest and parishioners of Monreal were wonderfully receptive to the mission and I headed on from there towards Puenta la Reina and the beginning of the final route. After a number of solid hours of prayer along a heavily trafficked main road, I turned off along a country road. It was then that I caught sight of the others. One, then three, then countless pilgrims stretched back across the landscape along a narrow gravel track intersecting the road ahead. They were kitted out with brand new backpacks and walking poles and all headed in the same direction like cows to the dairy. It was the Camino de Santiago; an 800 kilometre pilgrimage route across northern Spain and over 100 000 people stepped out its length that year alone.

What I hadn't expected was the feeling of fear that set in. After so long alone, that stream of pilgrims scared me. Most of the time when people had walked down the road ahead of or behind me it escalated into something hostile; I just couldn't shake that. Coupled with that was a sense of confusion. They looked like me, but I felt that we had nothing in common. Their path was laid out neatly, their accommodation mapped out accurately and their journey mostly only a few days old at that point. I didn't know how—or even if I wanted—to relate to them.

At a tiny secluded circular church with a stunning surrounding columned courtyard, I joined the Camino de Santiago. I stayed at the church for a while, but didn't say a word to anyone. I just watched them. When I went to pick up my backpack and poles I noticed how incredibly different our gear was. Theirs was pristine, sparkling clean and all in order. My backpack had hardly any colour left, the stitching was frayed, there were segments of dirtied yellow masking tape everywhere and my walking poles were worn well past the metal tip with only a short stub of plastic remaining.

I bypassed the Camino track and continued down the edge of the road to Puenta le Reina. In Puenta le Reina I blended in for once: it was a town full of pilgrims wandering the streets, but when I booked a bed at the pilgrim's hostel the man asked to see my passport. I pulled it out and handed it to him only to have it pushed back at me. He reiterated, "No, no. Passport!" He reached across to a pilgrim signing in next to me and picked up their cardboard pilgrim's passport. I had no idea what it was. He asked me, "Credentials? Your credentials." I pulled my itinerary out and flicked open to my official letters of commendation, but he turned his hands up saying, "What is this?" Whatever it was he wanted I didn't have it. He didn't take it any further and took my real passport and commendations to fill out his sheet.

A tad confused, I wandered through the town to evening Mass feeling oddly out of place and angry that my credentials weren't sufficient. I refused to consider even trying to find one of those cardboard passports everyone else had that somehow proved they were 'real pilgrims'.

The parish priest's house sat in a narrow cobblestone street and I was afraid to knock on the door, thinking that I'd be seen as just another pilgrim, but he took the time to hear me out and welcomed me inside with a big smile for afternoon tea. He encouraged me that he'd pray for unity and kindly offered me the use of his internet facilities. Chris had written a good enough blog for me, but finished by saying, "Sam will be back soon, but for now, goodbye from Christopher—the more handsome and younger Clear boy."

Well, he is younger ...

I made it to Mass and as the opening hymn started I stood up and in one motion slid my flip-flop clad feet forward under the kneeler. The stand underneath the kneeler was right in front of my left foot and the big toe cracked fair into it, sending pain writhing through my body. I was as tense as is humanly possible and likely turning bright red clenching my jaw tight, desperately trying to not make a sound. The hymn progressed. I trembled with every vein in my body protruding. It must have looked like I was having a seizure. A small pool of blood seeped out across the church floor. I didn't sing a single word; in fact the only movement I made in the whole service was an ambitious walk forward for Communion as blood continued to trickle, sticking my foot to the flip-flop. I stopped frequently on the way back to the hostel to take photos, masking my inability to walk.

I bandaged it heavily in the morning, pulled my boots on slowly and headed off along the country roads, avoiding the pilgrim's trail. I passed through a number of churches along the forty-one kilometres to Los Arcos, but was again faced with the cardboard passport issue. This guy didn't give in like the last one and refused my letters of commendation. With fifty pilgrims looking on he made his stand, "No passport, no bed!"

I said in my defence, "I don't even know what you are asking for? I've walked for a year and a half and have never needed one of those passports."

He threw his finger at me, "Nine hundred people have passed through here in the last two weeks and you are the first—the first!—to not have a passport. How can you not know what a passport is?" In all my planning for visas, inoculations, survival gear and paperwork I just hadn't come across this cardboard Camino passport. I wasn't accepted as a real pilgrim, which was okay: I was a missionary.

Pilgrims flowed into the hostel's courtyard with bandanas around their heads and iPods in their ears. I felt so isolated and just said to the man, "Okay," and left. Both feet and the shoulder blade ached so I stopped at the hostel entrance to sit on a rock and remove my boots. A voice came from the registrations desk, "Hey! Australiano!" The man gestured for me to come back. I slipped my flip-flops on and ambled over as he put his hand out, "Give me your passport. You can stay tonight, but tomorrow you must find for yourself a pilgrim's passport."

I ate dinner at an outdoor table alongside an Episcopalian from Texas and a Free Evangelical from Norway. We discussed life and eventually unity. The Norwegian admitted that he didn't know what other churches believed and asked what the theological differences really were so piece-by-piece we listed and discussed a few areas of tension with an air of lightness and respect. We even managed to overcome a few prejudices based on half-truths we had heard about each other's Church's beliefs. The Norwegian commented at the end, "Wow, we actually have a lot more in common than not." That was a good place for us to wrap up.

Most of the pilgrims headed to the evening Mass, which I later discovered was a special Mass where the priest welcomed each nationality and blessed them for their journey, but I was fast asleep by then and well before anyone was awake, my watch alarm chimed and I was out the door, back on the road praying through the pre-dawn silence.

The road wound down through hill country to the plains below and it wasn't the safest place to walk with no space on the side of the road. The moment came. On a tight corner I watched a pilgrim walk up along the gravel Camino and cross the road. I paused at the intersection. It was nonsense to avoid the crowds by not walking on the gravel track. I stepped off the road and continued on along el Camino de Santiago.

I caught up to the man ahead of me and was dreading having to walk past. Would he attack me or even worse, try and talk to me? He had earphones in, but as I went to pass by he turned with a smile, pulled them out and said, "Hi." Despite my intention to walk straight past I found myself entering a lengthy conversation. For the past few days I'd seen the pilgrims as nameless, faceless— 'you have no idea how easy you have it'—partial pilgrims, but as I met that young Korean university student I realised that, just maybe, every single one of them was there for a unique reason. He'd set out on the 800 kilometre journey across northern Spain because it was a dream he'd held ever since reading the published diary of a Korean woman who walked the Camino many years earlier. He was anxious to make it to the end, but excited with his once in a lifetime opportunity to meet people, push himself physically and grow spiritually. I don't think I even told him where I'd started. The question didn't come up. I just shared with him my hopes for the journey ahead as well.

Truth dismissed fear.

I walked on ahead, but for a number of hours I was aware of my propensity to do shoulder checks on the pilgrims behind me while keeping a close eye on those out in front. I just felt awkward. I slowly relaxed and found space on the heavily trafficked path. The more people I met, the more comfortable I felt. I still wanted to make a stand against those stupid cardboard passports, but as I entered the small city of Logroño, I remembered a certain teaching from Pope John Paul II about Christianity not being about self-assertion, but surrender, so I sucked in my pride and found a priest. He happily issued me a pilgrim's passport, with my first stamp included.

Walking on down the streets of Logroño I walked up alongside two young men from the USA. They asked me, "Where did you start walking from?" I bit my bottom lip for a moment and wondered how to say it. In the end I just said, "I started in Brazil."

"No, I meant, where did you start walking from."

I paused for a moment before saying again, "Brazil. I started walking from Brazil a year and a half ago. Not that I walked the entire distance."

The other guy piped up with widened eyes, "You walked through my town! I'm from Laramie in Wyoming!" I couldn't believe it. He explained my journey to his friend and how there was a big write up in the paper after I'd passed through Shirley Basin. Fr Fox's media work was still making an impact.

Receiving my 'stupid little cardboard passport'

By day's end I'd made it to the small village of Navarette, and had no problem securing a bed at the pilgrim's hostel (known as an albergue). The man filling out the registrations asked why I only had one stamp, so I pulled out my other documents and explained why I'd only just picked up the cardboard passport. He stood up, shook my hand and yelled for a family member to grab the camera. I'd just broken the record for the longest journey to his albergue.

Under warm sunshine the gravel track from there draped from horizon to horizon across rolling hills of wheat and wild poppies. I passed a physical education teacher from Ireland named Oisin (O-sheen). He was struggling to maintain his pace because his knee had given way, but he wasn't about to give up. He was going to make the end even if it was one limp at a time.

I ran into Oisin again at Mass at the end of the day in Santo Domingo, along with another Irishmen named Pat and a Scotsman named Nelson. They were in their late thirties through to early fifties and family men who'd taken the opportunity to commence the Camino while their wives agreed. We gathered together for dinner in a grassy courtyard opposite the Church-run albergue, sharing our life stories and slowly growing in friendship.

Sitting in that courtyard eating cheese and crackers with a bottle of wine, I was hardly expecting the single most confusing, yet uplifting surprise of the entire walk to be literally just around the corner. I went to bed oblivious … simply happy that the two days from Los Arcos to Santo Domingo had been the first pain free days since Italy. The toe was somehow healing over despite covering around forty kilometres a day. I fell asleep content.

Oisin, Pat and I headed off together along the misty cobblestone streets and we were about to cross the village's main intersection when I glanced across at two pilgrims, a man and a woman, standing in matching walking gear and sipping coffee. I thought to myself, "Ha! That woman kind of looks like my mum." As we continued in conversation talking about Pat's family I became aware that the man and woman were staring at me. "That's so rude," I thought. I looked away and then glanced back over to see that they were still staring. I stared back, as if to say, "I know you're staring at me, now stop it," but they motioned towards me with a smile.

It was Mum and Dad.

"Bloody hell. What are you doing here?" The last time I'd seen them was early November in 2006. It was now June of 2008. It had been a long time. Fumbling for words I explained to Oisin and Pat who they were and they celebrated with handshakes and slaps on my back.

Mum gave me a big hug while Dad shook my hand with a casual, "G'day." I could only laugh at Mum's first question though, "So are you going to continue these adventures or have you been cured?"

Having a laugh with my Irish 'Camino' mates, Oisin and Pat

I reassured her, "Yes Mum, I'm ready to come home. I'm just not sure where home is."

And without thinking twice the second most important question flew out, "And who are you going to marry when you get home?" Dad stood silently, smiling. He wasn't having anything to do with this. I ignored that question.

For the first time since the early 1970s they'd taken a holiday, flown to Europe for a cruise to Malta and then followed my itinerary to Santo Domingo, and waited. Between leaving Tasmania and arriving in Santo Domingo I'd been a good son and phoned home twice. In relation to Mum and Dad's whereabouts Chris, and my older sister Sophie, had successfully lied to me and so it came as one almighty confusing shock to see them standing there. It was all part of one big conspiracy that appeared to have grown larger every time I talked to someone. Even my old cricket coach had spun some tales via email to help set up the reunion.

Mum and Dad intended to walk with me, but Dad had been hit by gastro, so after an hour-long reunion we parted company and they headed to the next town via bus while I continued on. I couldn't stop smiling.

I walked hard for the rest of the day, making up for lost time and racing an impending thunderstorm. It won. Mum and Dad were hanging out of the second storey window of a boutique hotel waving me in to Villafranca. The albergues were cheap, but it was so much nicer to have a pre-paid hotel. We continued to catch up throughout the night and it was a relief to have our reunion on 'my soil'. It meant a lot that they'd come all that way to join me.

They caught the bus again in the morning while I ploughed on into a misty, rainy day across steep muddy tracks cutting through scrub and forest. On top of a grassy hill at a small secluded church (the baptismal place of St Dominic) I bumped back into Oisin, Pat and Nelson. Nelson was on his way out, but Oisin and Pat were hanging around a little longer, so we ate morning tea and walked on together, chatting about my mum and dad's arrival.

It was great to chat, but I wasn't doing what I normally did: pray. I propositioned them, "Guys, would you like to join me in some time of prayer?" They eagerly accepted. For Pat it was the first time in prayer for a long time. We prayed for fifteen minutes, each taking the opportunity to pray for loved ones and for our respective journeys, plus a few traditional prayers. A discussion took off afterwards about prayer itself and, while we chatted, Oisin stepped right on top of a poisonous adder basking in the sun. He spotted it just as his full weight landed on it and with a hop and a skip he snapped his foot away mightily fast. Its side was split open and the foot-long snake was left writhing on the ground. Oisin backed further away. It was a fatal wound so I told the guys I'd put it out of its misery and lowered my boot down carefully, crushing its head. An animated Pat piped up, "Guys! This is really significant! Here we are having just prayed together and then talking about prayer and now you've crushed the serpents' head!"

"I just really hate snakes," Oisin said, deadpan-faced.

Unperturbed, Pat pushed on, "We have to crush its head too!"

"Hey, I've done my bit," Oisin laughed. "I'm not going anywhere near it."

"Well I have to then," said Pat. "I'm the only one who hasn't." The poor snake was already dead, but Pat was so enthusiastic to participate in what he saw as a significant moment that he practically jumped on it, vigorously twisting his foot back and forth to make sure the job was done. When he lifted his foot triumphantly it was with a certain confusion that we were left staring at an empty gravel road.

"Umm, Pat, I think it's stuck to the bottom of your boot." I've never seen a guy shake his leg so frantically and yes, it did peel back off, flopping to the ground.

The moment did stand as a very symbolic one, particularly for Pat who was rediscovering prayer. My apologies to the poor old snake, but the three of us walked on with a spring in our step all the way to the Burgos Cathedral.

I stayed in Burgos for a late breakfast with Mum and Dad before farewelling them and heading off to Homilos del Camino. It was beautiful praying my way alongside a large, slow-moving river and across undulating farmland. The Camino's white gravel track meandered from hilltop to valley floor and back over distant hills through golden sun-bathed crops.

At the secluded village I met a confident young man from Finland who was interested in why I was praying for unity. He introduced himself as an atheist, noting straight off the cuff that he thought that praying for Christian unity was intolerant of other people's beliefs. He was very philosophical, but after chatting for some time I concluded that he didn't actually believe in anything specifically. He believed that Jesus was a wise man, but that Christians had twisted his message, "The most important thing," he told me, "is that we do good in the world." I told him I thought his view was relativistic and asked him, "By whose standards are you going to do good?" He conceded that point, but that was the only one. Overall he thought I was just intolerant of other beliefs by actually believing that Christianity was true. He believed that every religion was good for the person so long as it helped them be good and that we needed to accept one another. I told him straight down the line, "You're ignoring the core beliefs of each religion and looking for spirituality without the need for faith or responsibility." The long discussion ended with him saying, "Let us breathe deeply and be at one," and me replying, "God bless."

I grabbed dinner and sat on the church steps in the fading sun when an attractive girl walked up and sat down beside me asking, "Are you the guy walking around the world?" She was relaxed, funny and eager to chat, asking about a lot of the places I'd passed through. She eventually asked me, "Why did you decide to walk the world?"

I answered by saying, "I'm a Catholic missionary. I'm walking around the world praying for the unity of Christians." She sat bolt upright, shuffled a half metre away from me, crossed her legs in the other direction and with concern asked, "Why are you praying for Christian unity if you're a Catholic. What does it have to do with you?" I was nearly beside myself that she'd actually felt the need to physically move away from me. Until that point I felt rather attractive! Containing my smile I answered, "There is one Church, and all those who believe in Jesus are called to be one. All the fragments of Christianity include Catholic, Orthodox, Evangelical, Protestant, Pentecostal, etc."

She didn't buy it, "I'm a Christian. If you're a Catholic then you aren't Christian. You're Catholic. I think it's arrogant of you to pray for the unity of Christians when you aren't even one yourself. It's a bit hypocritical." And with that she removed herself from the steps and walked off. I guess if I wasn't Christian then it would seem very odd and arrogant to be praying for Christian unity.

I ran back into Oisin and Pat and walked the next day with them to Castrojeriz. We had an in-depth discussion about the urgent need for unity of the family. Incredibly, Pat decided to head back to Ireland from there. He didn't have enough time to complete the whole journey in one hit, but after our conversation he decided his time would be better spent with his wife and kids, not on the Camino. He booked himself onto a bus to head to the nearest airport the next day.

Oisin did have the time, so he grabbed extra supplies, farewelled us and powered on across the hills. Mum and Dad arrived in the early evening by bus and after sharing dinner with Pat we bunkered down for a 7 am start.

Dad was now well enough to walk so we set out. The huge hill we rounded at sunrise provided superb views back across Castrojeriz and the undulating countryside. We could see Pat's bus leaving town, heading out along the country road. I prayed for him and his family, and thanked God for the energetic blessing he'd been. We walked on at an easy pace and Mum and Dad fought through the twenty-six kilometres in 32°C heat. Not bad considering Dad had spent the past week locked in the bathroom. Mum complained of shoulder pain and when I picked her pack up to feel its weight I was nearly bowled over, "Mum! What have you got in here?" I insisted that some of the weight be transferred to my pack, so she prised from her pack a solid toiletries and cosmetics bag, complete with moisturisers, perfumes and a hair dryer. Dad and I had a few choice words of advice, but it was all stuffed into my pack and Mum walked on telling us to shut up.

Mum had one pace: fast. She often had to sit down, smell the flowers and wait for us to catch up. Dad nicked my walking poles for some extra help and loved them. The problem was that I loved them too. It was slow going, but the conversation was great and, by day's end, we'd made it to an air-conditioned hotel in Fromista. What meant so much to me was that Mum and Dad weren't at any stage massively supportive of the walk for unity. Dad wasn't even a regular churchgoer. While preparing to commence the journey, Mum had commented that, "I always suspected you'd end up doing something as stupid as this." But, despite their concerns, they never tried to stop me. In fact, every time my life had been threatened during the journey they'd just put money in my account so I could rest at a hotel.

Mum and Dad needed a rest, so I was off on my own again the next day striding out across some of the driest, hottest, wide-open countryside the Camino had to offer. At a small church I ran back into Nelson, the Scotsman. We were both surprised to see each other and greeted one another with a big handshake while exchanging our experiences to that point. Nelson was enjoying the historical Camino with no interest in a spiritual pilgrimage, but it didn't seem to matter, there was still enough to chat about: whether we liked it or not … we were all a part of each other's journey.

I extended the invitation to pray for unity to a few churches that day, covering a stifling forty-five kilometres to the dusty forgotten outpost of Ledigos. Lemonade tasted exceptionally good at day's end.

I pushed on to El Burgo Ranero in stifling heat and then further afield to the city of León, where Mum and Dad rendezvoused with me once more. I spent some time praying in the León Cathedral before heading back to our hotel. They'd decided to make the most of Dad's lingering ill-health by jumping on a tour bus for the coming week and then meeting me in Santiago de Compostela. From there they'd attempt to walk the final three days with me.

Spain won the European Soccer Championship that night and when I headed off, the pre-dawn streets were filled with beer cans and the occasional passed-out reveller. Other than city employees hosing down the footpaths, it was very quiet.

Relaxing with Mum and Dad in León

By mid-morning I'd walked in amongst a train of pilgrims as they began their day from each little village. We rounded out a solid day to the classic Spanish town of Hospital de Órbigo, with its enormous stone footbridge spanning a river with jousting yards beside it. It didn't appear to have changed much in the past 500 years. I was a little disappointed that there was no jousting to be had.

I ducked off to Mass and then an internet cafe, where I was pleased to see the number of people signed up to pray for unity at 4:01 had jumped by over fifty signatures that week. I was so thankful that the invitation was spreading. I felt good, so as the pilgrims settled in for the night I packed up and just kept on walking into some more solitude, praying and humming all the way to Astorga. I regretted walking on as my right foot ached chronically. I was properly exhausted from the pain when I rounded out a total of forty-seven kilometres by early evening.

In a small village the next day I met two practising Anglicans from England, Philip and Pat, who had just completed a year of full monastic life with the Franciscans. The Camino was their re-entry into the outside world, which is what it was turning out to be for me. We discussed the re-entry process, prayer, theology and the Camino itself, but the resounding comment that stayed with me was Philip's observation of Spanish churches. He'd also entered the León Cathedral to pray within a building he described as, "Having been built to draw us into intimate prayer," but found it difficult being the only one praying. "The cathedral was packed with pilgrims taking photos, buying souvenirs and in general, talking very loudly. I felt like I was back in the Jewish temple just before Jesus came in and over-turned the trader's tables." Being young and idealistic we of course threw around ideas of how to enhance the Camino for pilgrims. There appeared to be plenty of pilgrims "searching," but unless what they were searching for was historical information for their next architectural project they were pretty much left to their own devices. There was little we could do to help pilgrims focus on the spiritual side of the journey, but after enduring the last eighteen months … well … I figured there was always hope and reason to give it a bit more thought.

I called it a day in the mountainside village of Foncebadón and the Englishmen walked on. My gear was failing fast and the race was on to finish before it did. Four out of five zips had broken, two rips had opened up in the hip belt pockets, the backpack shoulder straps where close to pulling apart completely, I'd worn three holes in my only shirt and the walking poles had now worn all the way back to the plastic protective guard. Everything was handled with care. Even my plastic spoon broke. Good thing I carried a spare. I pulled out a needle, grabbed some fishing line and, with a combination of running and blanket stitches, managed to patch the pack up.

And—of course—the yellow masking tape made yet another victorious appearance.

I set off before sunrise, making the mountain ascent in time to watch the sun peep over the horizon directly behind a massive pole, ten metres tall, with a small cross on top and a massive pile of rocks at its base. For years pilgrims had carried rocks from their homes or the bottom of the mountain to symbolise a burden they carried. They then dropped it at the foot of the cross and walked on lighter. That pile of rocks was three metres high and ten metres wide in a perfect circle. It was awesome. Who'd dropped that first rock off and how many years ago? The silhouette of the pole and cross cast against the rising sun as two pilgrims placed their rocks at its base was a beautiful sight.

Down the mountain I went along the edge of a massive valley to Ponferrada. Philip and Pat, the Englishmen, appeared at the albergue with a large group of energetic eighteen to thirty-year-olds from all around the world. They'd become friends on the Camino and stuck together, so we cooked our meals and sat around the table enjoying a diverse set of personalities. Two of the girls from England loved to sing while they walked, two of the guys from New York loved to rap, sing harmonies and talk about future plans, while others enjoyed the quiet of contemplation. Over dinner they declared themselves the 'Fellowship' and proceeded to hand out names to each person according to JRR Tolkien's *The Lord of the Rings*.

I was more than happy to snare the title of Strider.

Our room slept up to forty people and come 4:55 am one of the fellowship slinked off silently to the toilet, not realising that his alarm was about to sound. For fifteen minutes it grew louder and one by one we woke up. A sense of annoyance grew, until Philip woke up. It was pitch black so it was only the sound that we heard, … but we sure heard it. He woke in a panic, threw his blankets back and stepped out of bed, forgetting he was on the top bunk. The sound of rushing blankets and a faint English accent saying, "Oh crap," was followed by his head hitting the opposite top bunk and a horrible thud on the ground. Spurts of laughter filled the room.

"Are you okay?" someone asked.

"I hate bunks," came the whispered reply.

A couple of older pilgrims also decided to rise before dawn, but hadn't packed their gear the night before and they used plastic bags for added waterproofing. The noise of rustling plastic woke everyone a second time and after a few minutes of continuous noise one young pilgrim cracked, shouting, "Shut the hell up! We're trying to sleep!"

If anyone wasn't awake, they were now. The rustling faded. That room was a mini version of the Church.

I walked that day with Philip and Elizabeth, a young lady from the USA, and we decided to teach her how to play cricket. I still carried that small yellow foam ball from Austria, so Phil adjusted his walking pole into a comfortable length and I bowled down a village sidewalk to him. Phil swung through, connecting so well that the little foam ball disappeared skywards with a, "Thwock!" It was about then that we realised that playing cricket in front of the village's historic castle-like town hall wasn't a great spot. Location, location, location. The ball cannoned into the stonework centimetres above the top window of the three-storey building and lobbed back out into the main street, bouncing in front of the only car travelling down the road, bringing it to a stop. Phil, laughing uncontrollably, slinked away down the street leaving me to retrieve his handy-work.

"Sorry, he's English."

The three of us played a mixture of soccer and hockey with the ball on the secluded country road for the remaining ten kilometres to Trabadelo village, where witches-hats sat on the side of the road. We pulled one out, set it up as a wicket, and entered a more suitably placed game of cricket. Elizabeth was happy to just film the Australia vs England match and I'm happy to say that the Pom lost.

I intended to finish twenty kilometres beyond the fellowship's next day's destination so once they'd all arrived that night I said goodbye and headed to bed early. I was on the road by 5 am for the final cool mountain ascent in complete darkness with my headlamp guiding the way. The sun rose just before I reached the top, but the hardest part of the day was done. The view was extraordinary. The other side of the mountain disappeared sharply into a deep valley of mist extending to the horizon. I stood on an island mountain.

A dozen friendly cows shared the road with me for a short time before the descent down the mountain's western face. When I arrived at my destination I was excited to bump into Oisin. He was doing well, having pushed hard into some long days and after a quick chat we looked around for Saturday evening Mass. With nothing on offer he made a suggestion, "Ten kilometres further down the road is the town of Samos. It's got a huge Benedictine Monastery. They'd have Mass." We threw our packs back on and walked off through forested hills and over numerous rivers, picking up two other pilgrims along the way who were also headed to Samos for Mass. There was a great sense of being like the pilgrims of old, journeying together towards the church.

We arrived in plenty of time, but being in Spanish, Oisin and I didn't participate fully with the responses, but one of the pilgrims we'd met did. He responded in full and even said quietly the parts reserved for the priest. After Mass, Oisin and I were on to him. "How did you know all the priest's parts so well in Spanish?"

He smiled reluctantly, "Don't tell anyone. I'm a priest. I'm here for a holiday and it's difficult to have a holiday on the Camino if everyone knows you're a priest."

We laughed and Oisin asked, "What do you say if people ask what you do?"

"Well I can't lie!" he explained, "I just tell them I work in human resources."

While jibbing him about his hidden identity he turned the tables on me asking, "Have you avoided telling people where you started walking from?"

I had to admit, "Yes, there have been times lately when if someone asks, 'Where did you start the Camino?' I've replied, 'At the Pyrenees,' because it was where I started the Camino de Santiago." There was a lot of pride held by pilgrims as to who'd walked the furthest. It was easier just to avoid the competition and move on. The priest flicked his identification onto the table, so I followed suit, only they refused to believe that the photo was of me. They held it up alongside me to find any resemblance, but couldn't see it. Eighteen months of walking changes a man.

The *walk4one* prayer list had again grown significantly, but most notable were a number of additions from the Mediterranean island of Malta. An article about the walk had been published in the Maltese media and the invitation had been well received.

I walked on alone through the green countryside to Portomarin, passing a concrete post every now and then indicating how far it was to Santiago de Compostela. As I passed through a quiet stretch of oaks I passed the 100 kilometre marker at exactly 4:01 pm. I prayed, "Lord, please unite all Christians as one, in truth and in love, for the glory of your name and for the salvation of souls. May your holy Church, the body of our Lord Jesus Christ, be united as one and may your divine assistance remain always with us. Amen."

Pilgrim numbers swelled and the trundle out of the picturesque lakeside village over heavily forested hills was alongside hundreds of pilgrims from all over the world. For as far as I could see in either direction fresh pilgrims laden with backpacks marched to the same beat. The few pilgrims I ran into that I knew were having the same reaction to seeing all these new pilgrims that I'd had when I joined the Camino. They were suspicious, scoffing at them and felt crowded in. I laughed, "That's what I thought about you when I first saw you in your brand new gear. Look at all those toffs, I thought." Welcoming hands were soon extended to the newcomers and the age-old tradition of sharing stories began. A few new pilgrims asked me, "Where'd you start the Camino?"

I'd respond, "Near the Pyrenees," and the older pilgrims would just smile and walk on with their heads low. When the new pilgrims asked them where they'd started they'd answer, "A few weeks back," or, "A while ago." It was a subtle recognition that being caught up in where we'd come from wasn't nearly as important as who we'd become and where we were going.

I could barely stop smiling. Cape Finisterre was only 182 kilometres away. I had a million and one reminiscences of how long it had taken to get here. There was also a certain numbness associated with allowing myself to unreservedly turn my thoughts to home, or perhaps it was every possible emotion jammed into one.

> *Better is the end of a thing than its beginning;*
> *the patient in spirit are better than the proud in spirit.*
>
> Ecclesiastes 7:8

Total walked : *15,454 kilometres*

# Santiago de Compostela, A Health Scare & Cape Finisterre
*July 2008*

I was led from village to village by country lanes with sweeping views of hills that grew increasingly lush with thick leafy trees filled with chirping birds and scurrying squirrels. Even a farmer herding a handful of dairy cows down a shaded dirt laneway gave me a friendly wave. It was very peaceful.

I entered a large town to be greeted by a woman trying to strike up a conversation with anyone she could. The few pilgrims strewn along the route kept a wide berth. As I approached she asked, "Have you been saved? Have you accepted Jesus Christ as your Lord and Saviour?" I smiled, nodding my head, and gave the very Catholic answer of, "Yes, I have been saved, I am being saved and I will be saved, by the grace of God." The answer didn't suffice one bit and she asked why I was taking part in such an idolatrous and meaningless religious pilgrimage, "All you need to do is accept Jesus Christ! Are you Catholic?" and with my, "Yes," she 'enlightened' me on the errors of my ways and why I was going to hell. I attempted to converse a few times on each point she raised, but she kept yelling at me, not in the least bit interested in a discussion. I think the only reaction she wanted was for me to break down in tears and hit the road on my knees asking for repentance for twenty-nine years of tyranny and devil worship.

When she started yelling bible passages at me as if I didn't believe in Holy Scripture I'd finally had enough. With no pilgrims in sight I stepped in closer and gave her a one minute rebuke on the harm rather than good she was doing and on how she wasn't loving the people passing by, but passing judgement on them in a horrendous stream of puffed up pride. She shut up with a confused look. I listed off everything she'd thrown at me and ended each by saying, "I believe in that." I continued, "If you aren't interested in my answer, why ask the question? And yes, even though you haven't asked, I do believe in the real presence of Jesus in the Eucharist and I do believe that you can ask Mary to pray for you." I asked her, "Will you at least pray for the complete unity of all Christians, in truth and in love? Will you pray that God would unite us in truth and love?"

She screwed her lips up and burst out into another tirade about the Whore of Babylon Catholic Church and that, "You're going to hell!"

"No, madam," I replied, "I'm going to Cape Finisterre."

I ran into Oisin again at a café and I asked how his day was going. He raised his eyebrows, "Did you meet the Evangelical in the last town?"

I nodded, "Yeah, we had a chat."

He shook his head, "What's all that about? I wasn't getting near her!"

We grabbed a drink and walked on together to the next albergue, sharing more stories and prayer. We didn't plan to, but come morning we headed out at the same time into a damp, rainy day, passing through an extraordinary section of tightly woven forest growing up and over the metre wide walking track to form a brilliant tunnel. We had a spring in our step as we excitedly approached Santiago de Compostela. For Oisin the traditional end point of the Camino would be just that, but my aim wasn't to walk to Santiago de Compostela. I was travelling from one side of the Atlantic to the other, and that was another ninety kilometres further on.

From a hilltop we caught sight of the towering triple spire of Saint James'

Cathedral; with broad smiles we paced out towards the historic city and its narrow cobblestone streets lined with huge sandstone buildings. We soaked in the sounds of the street music, stalls and scores of pilgrims cheering for having made the end.

Mum and Dad stood in the main square outside the cathedral, so Oisin and I shook hands with great purpose, thanking each other for sharing the journey and wished each other all the best in life. I was so thankful for his friendship and ability to walk in silence at times and just enjoy the journey.

I'd filled my 'stupid little' Camino de Santiago passport with stamps and it had become horribly tatty but was good enough to earn me a certificate of recognition for having completed the Camino. I'd grown fond of it. Mum and Dad accompanied me as I met with one of the cathedral priests and extended the mission, which he received with a smile and a, "Yes, of course."

A huge Mass in the cathedral was celebrated for the pilgrims that evening, but I didn't go. I wasn't finished. I went to a regular local Mass instead and after a sound sleep the three of us set off under cool overcast conditions for the ninety kilometre walk to Cape Finisterre.

The hills of Galicia rolled on, sheltering quaint villages filled with friendly locals and—to our surprise—Tasmanian Blue Gum plantations! The white gravel track crunching underfoot winding through these iconic Australian trees reminded us of home. Everything looked and smelt like Tasmania.

We arrived at Negreira by mid-afternoon and I shot off to visit a church while Mum and Dad booked into a hotel. We met at the supermarket and grabbed a couple of frozen pizzas to cook in our hotel room oven. We'd all seen the four hotplates, but none of us had noticed that there was no oven underneath. When we arrived back I saw the cupboards under the hot plates and muttered, "Um, about that oven we thought we had …" And so it was that, on the second last night of the journey, Dad and I attempted to cook three frozen pizzas on hot plates using a flimsy aluminium dish. Mum was no help. She was using the bench to prop herself up while giggling and wiping tears from her eyes. Every time she went to give us advice she simply laughed even more.

Half an hour into the next day, a cold shower swept through and stayed put. The howling wind sent frigid horizontal rain at us. We weren't prepared for the icy temperatures and our saturated fingers soon lost sensation. Traversing the more exposed sections of the track was close to unbearable. My hands stung, but Dad's were particularly painful.

The area overflowed with Blue Gums, but this time with a noxious weed at its base called gorse, which also thrives in Tasmania. Walking in the cold driving rain it really felt like the farm! Dad yelled out through the roaring wind, "I could have stayed at home for this!" Our feet squelched and water whisked off our noses. We were so cold and uncomfortable that we didn't even stop for lunch. We kept our heads down and soldiered on for the entire thirty-four kilometres.

When we made it to a small village hotel with an open fire we took long hot showers, made makeshift clotheslines in the rooms and ventured to the bar for an overdue meal. Dad was shivering badly when we entered the hotel, but he was now finding it uncomfortably hot. He stopped eating and lethargically removed his jumper, but continued heating up. When he excused himself to the open doorway and sat in the cold breeze, Mum fell silent. She just watched, wondering if he was about to pass out or have a heart attack. I told Mum that the same thing had happened to me in Mexico, but that wasn't much comfort, "Sam, you're twenty-nine years old. He isn't." After a few minutes in the cold he regained his colour, took some deep breaths and resumed his place at the table.

I woke the next morning smiling. The final day had arrived. I packed fast, pushing Mum and Dad to, "Hurry up … please," as though I was five years old and it was Christmas morning. I'd waited a long time for that day and I didn't care to enjoy a long breakfast. The sun shone and we were off for the thirty-five kilometres to Cape Finisterre, the "Cape at earth's end". I drifted through so many memories of the past nineteen months and while some moments had faded from memory, as I pondered certain situations, I kept remembering more and more. Some made me smile ... even laugh ... while others caused me to breathe deeply and shake my head in disbelief.

Mum and Dad set their own ambling pace, so I had plenty of time by myself waiting for them on hilltops. Mind you, Mum would have made it a lot quicker if she didn't stop to pick flowers. Dad just smiled each time and shook his head.

They made it through the day with ease, aided by two Tasmanian Blue Gum walking sticks and at midday I caught the first glimpse of the Atlantic Ocean. I pointed it out to Dad, but after scrutinising it for a moment he corrected me, "You're looking at a hill on the horizon."

A few minutes later I made my own correction, "Dad, there's a yacht crossing your hill."

It was the Atlantic.

Three kilometres shy of Cape Finisterre we entered the fishing village of Fisterra and whether it was to let me finish alone or because they were simply tired, Mum and Dad called it a day, leaving me to continue on alone. I stopped at a supermarket to buy my celebratory dinner of Coco Pops and milk and headed on.

I walked up along the edge of the steep rocky cape and from a decent height the view opened up over the Atlantic Ocean. A number of Camino pilgrims had gathered at the lookout, but I wanted space, so I climbed down along the rocky face of the sloping cliff to a quiet ledge halfway down and sat there in silence. I watched the waves crash into rocks fifty metres below, while the ocean wind blew against my bearded face.

With a few hours before sunset, I sat back and enjoyed my bowl of Coco Pops.

At first, the end felt hollow. It was difficult to come to terms with what it even meant. The life I'd known intimately for the past year and half was over. However, as time passed I began to appreciate more than anything the journey that had brought me to that point, in particular: providence. All the way back in Brazil I'd threaded rosary beads onto a fence at Cape Branco, so I grabbed

568 days older, standing on the edge of Cape Finisterre

my slightly bent walking pole and jammed it into a crack between two huge rocks, then tied my rosary beads to it. They swayed in the sea breeze. I prayed one last time, "Holy Father, please unite all Christians in truth and in love, for the glory of your name and for the salvation of souls. Please bless Pope Benedict XVI, the Archbishop of Canterbury, the Patriarchs of the Eastern Churches, those serving on the World Council of Churches and all the world's Christian leaders with faith, hope, love and wisdom, so that they may better lead us to you and into unity with one another."

The rosary was opposed heavily by protestant Christians and so it hung there on the edge of Cape Finisterre as a strong symbol of both the prayer that unites us and the theology that divides us. The great lesson from the entire journey was that it's the lack of love that divides us most. I stood in silence on the ledge praying for all those I'd met and those I'd never meet, thanking God for all that had happened, whether I liked it or not. I re-committed myself for whatever lay ahead.

It was only then that I felt that the journey of 568 days, 9,350 kilometres by train, 9,824 kilometres by aircraft and 15,636 kilometres by foot—from the tip of Cape Branco to Cape Finisterre—was over.

I recognised a few pilgrims making their way down the cape's edge and Vin, from Brazil, was quick to whip clothes out of his backpack, bundle them up and throw a match on them as a way of saying, "I'm going home a changed man!" The two other pilgrims with him followed suit and I wasn't far behind, clambering over the rocks to greet them. I ripped my battered shirt off and tossed it in with theirs to be consumed quickly amidst a lot of cheer. I was fit when I started in Brazil, but I'd still managed to lose a lot of weight. I covered up from the sea breeze under my jacket.

Vin came back with me to my little spot to share the view and we sat silently for half an hour before he shook my hand and made his way back to the others, but just as he turned his back I saw a dolphin break the water out off the cape so I called to him, "Vin, a dolphin!" He scrambled back quickly, but as he did I couldn't help but think that the glimpse I'd caught was further out than I'd realised. With both of us watching intently, the dolphin broke the water once more and our eyes lit up. "It's a humpback whale!" One solitary humpback was heading north along the coastline, past the end of the world.

Vin found his own vantage point further along the jagged cliff face and we sat in silence on our separate ledges, looking out over the rolling sea, gazing back across the Atlantic towards Brazil. The sun kissed the horizon an hour later and the only thing I could fathom in the moment was that the sunset was beautifully simple. It slid behind low-lying clouds on the horizon, but just before setting at 10:20 pm, a gap appeared in the clouds and the glowing red sun reappeared for the setting. Muted cheers and clapping trickled across the Cape. To each came the congratulatory thumbs-up.

I smiled, "It's done. Thank you Lord. Thank you so much." And in the twilight shadow I climbed back up, said goodbye to the few pilgrims and we headed our separate ways. The Cape emptied and the sound of the sea rushing against rocks grew dim. I prayed as I went.

Thank you, Lord

*And now faith, hope, and love abide, these three; and the greatest of these is love.*

1 Corinthians 13:13

**Total walked :**

*15,636 kilometres*

Russia and Europe

walk4one *Paving a Path to Unity*

# Epilogue

## 2008–2012

*In the early hours* of Sunday, the 13th of July 2008, with my forehead pressed against the airline window, the southern hemisphere stars faded from view as a rainbow of predawn colours beckoned in my first sunrise over Australian soil since 2006. It was a beautiful sight from 20,000 feet above the red centre.

Brazil was so far away and my friends and family were so close.

Fifty friends welcomed me at Sydney airport and as we stepped out of the terminal the first car to drive past startled me. It was on the wrong side of the road with the driver on the wrong side of the car. I was home, but it felt foreign. It would be a long road to feeling comfortable in my own country again.

I jumped in a van with friends and we headed for Mass at a little church in the centre of Sydney. Throughout the walk two couples—John and Margaret, Charles and Beth—had emailed me weekly with words of inspiration and encouragement. I'd never met them. They'd just heard of the mission and decided to become active participants. Charles and Beth lived in Melbourne and John and Margaret south of Sydney where, as far as I understood, they attended an Anglican church. Before Mass began in the small Sydney church I sat down behind an old couple sitting at the front who I'd never met before. They turned with a smile and introduced themselves as John and Margaret, and said they were visiting Sydney, had been looking for a church service to attend and decided to attend that one. They asked if I was local.

I thought to myself, "Surely not. It couldn't be them." John realised I was staring at him and for a short period stared back. He then asked slowly, "Sam?" We greeted each other with heartfelt hugs and a few tears. We'd been on the journey together for so long without meeting face-to-face, but now entered the Mass side by side with incredible thanks to God.

The World Youth Day week was ramping up in Sydney and it turned into a huge reunion. I ran into Damien and Tatiana, the couple I was mugged with in

Costa Rica; a few members of Fr Fox's parish in Casper, Wyoming; Nikki and her new boyfriend; my brother Chris; and then, Deacon Dave Callaghan, my man behind the scenes. Dave was a good friend and had taken on the responsibility of being a sort of spiritual guide and all-round logistics guy for me. We grabbed a big bucket of ice cream, two spoons and sat in Hyde Park scoffing it down.

Fifteen thousand people turned out on Bondi Beach for a unity concert on the Wednesday night and most of them wore 4:01 wristbands. The World Youth Day week culminated for me personally on the Friday night with a huge concert called Receive the Power Live. I was the emcee for the joint Catholic Church and Sydney-based Pentecostal Church, Hillsong, collaboration in front of 70,000 people with Bishop Joe Grech and singer Matt Maher and his band leading us in a massive celebration. It was an incredible night for unity and for the Church in general. Speaking in front of 70,000 people sure was a long way from knocking on church doors and waiting patiently.

It was a struggle slotting into normal life. The injuries alone made resuming past pursuits difficult and forced me to take it slow for a few years. The left big toe didn't stop seeping blood for seven months and the right foot was found to be causing so much pain because of two problems: a Morton's Neuroma (a benign tumour), which had wrapped around a nerve, and a papilloma (plantar wart) growing right beside it. They took five years to remove ... piece by piece. The locking knee from Russia was found to be torn cartilage, which worsened until being operated on in 2011; while the rotated pelvis, torn hamstring from the Amazon, and heart arrhythmia caused continuing problems.

My body hurt.

The injuries were seen to medically, but the thing that caught me unaware was post-traumatic stress. I'd stopped walking, but I couldn't stop the instinctive reactions that had helped keep me alive while overseas. Without even being aware of it, I'd clench my fists while passing people on suburban streets, "Just in case."

I'd wake three to ten times every night and straightaway feel the need to check that the house was secure. There was no instinctive grading system for threats. Everything was either a threat or not a threat. It was as simple as that.

Slowly, I became more aware that my reactions weren't like everyone else's since I could see that they were able to trust so much easier than I could. It was hard to hide it from people. My reactions to certain situations were grossly out of place and I figured everyone would think I was just plain angry. What had been the difference between life and death was now just some sort of disorder.

I could re-train myself to rationally think through each situation, but stopping the nightmares was more difficult. The guys in Russia, the Costa Rican muggers, the puma, the snakes, the blackness of a shotgun barrel … they all reappeared time and time again. In a few dreams I even went as far as to bludgeon the aggressors to death before waking in fright in the silence of my room.

I often had to re-forgive the perpetrators.

It was so difficult to share my journey with anyone. Even those I knew well didn't understand what I'd done … let alone what I'd been through. Some thought I'd been overseas backpacking while others thought it was a personal pilgrimage. After all I'd seen and been through it was difficult to answer the question, "What was your favourite country? Where would you suggest for a holiday?"

The most common question was, "How was the walk?"

The only answer to that was: "Complicated, but blessed."

I was asked to consider writing a book about the journey, but every time I looked at my notes, emails, blogs, photos, video footage or newspaper clippings … it just felt too much. I didn't want to relive it. But, over time, the call to pray for unity was relit and, from where I stood, a year from Cape Finisterre, it seemed like little had changed as a result of the walk. Yes, some things had and murmurs of potentially big shifts taking place in the Church looked apparent, but I was almost brought back to the point of wanting to walk and pray again, frustratingly surrounded by Christians slandering one another and being apathetic regarding their disunity. As much as I needed to trust that my prayers had been heard I was gradually infused with the desire to again fight for 4:01, by sitting down to re-enter the mission through the written word.

The more I wrote the more comfortable I felt about the year and a half from Brazil to Spain. It didn't hurt as much to look back on it; the deeper I looked … the more I smiled, gave thanks and wanted to track down the people who'd helped me.

There was one guy I couldn't find: Adolfo. I had contact details for people in nearby towns and they offered to search for him, but always came up empty. He'd moved on. His daughter's pink dinosaur made it to Spain, swinging from my backpack, and has accompanied me ever since. I keep praying for him, hoping that perhaps we'll meet again, one day.

I finished in Spain with $164.40 in the bank, but I finish here with a heart full of thanks to the thousands of people who assisted me along the way. I think I lost that for the first year I was back home. More than anything I've become increasingly thankful to God for the absolute gift of the most amazing journey I could have hoped for.

When I touched down in Tasmania and travelled to Launceston for Mass at my old parish, the reading was from Matthew's Gospel. It told of the kingdom of heaven being like a treasure hidden in a field, which a man sells everything to acquire. It was three years to the day that I'd last heard that passage and God very neatly, I thought, sewed up the walk for unity. Or was He perhaps reminding me of the continued mission?

"Do you agape me?"

After a few quiet kayak laps of the irrigation dam I packed up and was off again. I worked in youth ministry, but also began to present the 4:01 mission across Australian, New Zealand and United States high schools and churches, as well as becoming heavily involved in the development of a pilgrimage route across

Tasmania. In 2011, I accepted the position of Managing Director of Harvest Inroads, a pilgrimage, immersion and adventure company for youth and young adults.

But, the most substantial step taken for unity since returning home happened two years later.

Fr Fox was right. I would, in time, lean towards marriage a few years after the walk … only it wasn't a fairytale ending. In fact it was devastating and left me far more broken than the walk. Forget bleeding toes. The disunity of the family, that's where it hurts most. It will be a long, humble road from here.

And those boots that never arrived in Panama, well they randomly landed on my doorstep one day, and unwrapping them drew from me the strangest smile. The leather smelt so good and it felt even better to slip them on. They were made for walking and in 2012 I bought myself a ticket and headed back to Panama to search for Adolfo. That's a whole new story in itself though.

By the grace of God, walk on and pray on.

*The kingdom of heaven is like treasure hidden in a field, which someone found and hid; then in his joy he goes and sells all that he has and buys that field.*

Matthew 13:44

*Please pray for the complete unity of Christians. May we be one…*

4:01

www.ingramcontent.com/pod-product-compliance
Lightning Source LLC
Chambersburg PA
CBHW070746230426
43665CB00017B/2273